Donald Andreas Cameron

An Arabic-English Vocabulary for the Use of English Students of Modern Egyptian Arabic

Donald Andreas Cameron

An Arabic-English Vocabulary for the Use of English Students of Modern Egyptian Arabic

ISBN/EAN: 9783337244521

Printed in Europe, USA, Canada, Australia, Japan

Cover: Foto ©Paul-Georg Meister /pixelio.de

More available books at **www.hansebooks.com**

AN
ARABIC-ENGLISH VOCABULARY.

AN

ARABIC-ENGLISH VOCABULARY

FOR THE USE OF ENGLISH STUDENTS OF

MODERN EGYPTIAN ARABIC

COMPILED BY

D. A. CAMERON

ONE OF THE ENGLISH JUDGES OF THE NATIVE EGYPTIAN COURT OF APPEAL, CAIRO;
FORMERLY STUDENT INTERPRETER, AND ONE OF HER MAJESTY'S CONSULS
IN EGYPT AND IN TRIPOLI.

LONDON
BERNARD QUARITCH, 15 PICCADILLY
1892

PREFACE.

THIS Vocabulary was originally compiled for my private use in order to retain a grasp on what, after ten years' practical experience, I considered to be the most necessary words of the Arabic language. It is now published, after two years' careful revision.

The following plan has been adopted in its compilation :—

1st. Taking Freytag's "Arabic-Latin Lexicon" as a guide, I went through the volume, selected what I wanted, and drew up a skeleton list of the most important verbal roots and their derivatives.

2nd. I then read carefully through the Arabic text of the Egyptian codes of law, line by line, adding words with their modern meanings to the skeleton list. This task supplied me with hundreds of terms relating not merely to law, but also to public and social life, government, commerce, crime, &c. ; moreover, it showed how the best Egyptian authorities translate good French into good modern Arabic. The phraseology of a code forms a high standard of the common language of educated natives; it is unpedantic, simple, accurate and concise.

3rd. I collected numerous words by a systematic course of reading of official MSS., decrees, circulars, annual budgets, reports and journals. I also added some colloquialisms, and a few military and scientific terms.

The entire draft was then revised with the aid of native clerks. I would read out an Arabic word, and ask them to explain it ; I would then translate my own explanation, and thus verify or correct it. The MS. was then submitted to the scrutiny of my native colleagues of the Court of Appeal, and it is to their never-failing kindness and assistance that I am most deeply indebted for all that is of value in this book. While, therefore, I alone am responsible for any defects or shortcomings, the student may feel confident that this is a serious professional attempt to furnish him with a concise abridgment, a coherent synopsis, of the vocabulary which is daily used by native officials of the Egyptian Government.

I would advise him to master this book almost in its entirety; to read carefully two or more pages up to ten or twenty a day, according to the time at his disposal; to select and note down in a blank book two or three words from every page; *and to try to be accurate in his Arabic spelling.* If he will take the trouble to go through this Vocabulary in the manner suggested, I am confident that in the course of a few months he will have gained a sound knowledge of modern Egyptian Arabic. His notes will have formed a short vocabulary of his own selection, and in addition to what he may remember, he will be better able to guess the root of a derived form, and to find it in this or any larger dictionary.

The cross-references should also be examined for synonyms, or for contrasts in meaning or in spelling. For example, تلف *talifa*, "it perished," [see هلك]. Reference to هلك *halaka*, gives us one or two more useful words for "ruin," "danger;" and *halaka* and *talifa* should be connoted in the student's memory. Again, تمر *tamr*, means "a dry date," but تمر *tamar*, means "fruit."

As a specimen lesson in the use of this book, let the student take the three roots عرف *'arafa* "he knew," علم *'alima*, "he knew," and خبر *khabar* "news." They unite in the main idea of "knowledge," but each differs from the others in its derived forms. This connotation of allied roots, by contrast and comparison, is the best way to attain accuracy in Arabic. If he will then look for *'arafa* and *'alima* in a large dictionary such as Kazimirski or Steingass, he will see how this vocabulary has been abridged for practical purposes.

One great obstacle to our progress in good colloquial Arabic is undoubtedly our helplessness in the hands of Berberine servants.

These Berberines are foreigners, whose native Nubian dialect (*rotn*, or non-Arab) is very limited and barbarous. Yet for our daily purposes we are obliged not only to learn their pronunciation, but also their grossly inaccurate *patois*, which some of us innocently suppose is good modern Arabic. The Berberine despises every word which he does not know as "*nahwiy*," or pedantic; and if we submit to his *dictum* we shall never make much progress beyond the familiar *bata'a* and *shoof*.

Those among us who speak the best Arabic are invariably men who have had to deal with *fellaheen* (soldiers, policemen, or peasants), and with junior native officials. Not only is the pronunciation of these Englishmen good, but they can speak Arabic intelligibly, and in connected sentences, upon matters which require a little thought to explain or to understand, even in English.

In conclusion, this book contains the result of twelve years' study and experience of Arabic in Syria, Egypt, the Soudan, and Tripoli; and I sincerely hope that it may not only encourage English residents and officials in the study of that language, but also prove useful to the numerous Egyptians who are learning English.

D. A. C.

CAIRO,
November, 1891.

INTRODUCTION.

The ARABIC ALPHABET consists of 28 letters:— Numerical value ("abjad," ابجد).

Álif	ا	á, as in *fáther*.	1
Bé	ب	b.	2
Té	ت	t.	400
Thá	ث	th, as in *think*; or *s*; or *t*.	500
Jeem	ج	j, but commonly g, as in *go*.	3
Há	ح	h, a strong h, as in *hurl*.	8
Khá	خ	kh, a harsh aspirate, as in *loch*.	600
Dál	د	d.	4
Zál	ذ	d; or z; or th as in *that*.	700
Ré	ر	r.	200
Zain	ز	z.	7
Seen	س	s.	60
Sheen	ش	sh.	300
Sád	ص	s, a double s, as in *hissing*.	90
Dhád	ض	dh, or strong double d, or z.	800
Tá	ط	t, a hard emphatic t.	9
Dhá	ظ	dh; or strong double d, or z.	900
'Ain	ع	'a, 'e, 'i, 'o or 'u, a guttural hiatus.	70
Ghain	غ	gh, like the French r *grasséyé*.	1000
Fé	ف	f.	80
Qáf	ق	q, a guttural k.	100
Kéf	ك	k.	20
Lám	ل	l.	30
Meem	م	m.	40
Noon	ن	n.	50
Waw	و	w, or ō; or oo.	6
Hé	ه or ة	h, a soft h, as in *head*.	5
Yé	ي	y, or ee.	10

Thus there are three letters for *t* :—

ت - توبة *tōba*, penitence.
ث - ثوب *tōb*, garment.
ط - طوبة *tōba*, brick.

Three letters for *s* :—

ث - ثبوت *sobóot*, proof.
س - سبع *saba'*, seven.
ص - صباع *sobáa'*, finger.

Two letters for *h* :—

ح - حبّ *habba*, he loved.
ه - هبّ *habba*, the wind blew.

Two letters for *k* :—

ق - قلب *qalb*, heart.
ك - كلب *kelb*, dog.

Four letters for *d* :—

د - دبّ *dubb*, a bear.
ذ - ذبّان *dibbán*, flies.
ض - ضرر *darar*, damage.
ظ - ظهر *dohr*, midday.

Four letters for *z* :—

ذ - ذكيّ *zakiy*, sagacious.
ز - زكيّ *zakiy*, pious.
ض - ضبط *zabt*, seizure.
ظ - ظاهر *záhir*, apparent.

The Vowel Sounds are as follows :—

I. Long.			II. Short.		
1. *á*	as in	*father*.	1. *a*, or *ŭ*, as in *cap*, or *cup*.		
2. *ō*	,,	*pole*.	2. *o*, or *u*, ,, *pull*.		
3. *oo*	,,	*fool*.			
4. *ee*, or *iy* ,,		*feel*.	3. *i*	,,	*pin*.
5. *ai*	,,	*pain*.			

INTRODUCTION.

I. *Long.* (1) ا *á*, as in *father*; e. g., باب *báb*, door. آ *aá*, double *á*, as in *baa*; e. g., آل *aál*, dynasty.

(2) وَ *ō*, which in *Arabic* words is pronounced usually as *ō* in *pole*, although the *ow* of *fowl* is more correct; e. g., قول *qōl* or *qowl*, speech; but in foreign words invariably as *ō* in *pole*.

(3) وُ *oo*, as in *fool*; e. g., فول *fool*, beans.

(4) ي or يّ *ee* or *iy*, as in *feel*; e. g., فيل *feel*, elephant; مصري *masriy*, or *masree*, Egyptian. يّة *iya*, or *eeya* (feminine termination of adjectives derived from nouns), e. g., مصريّة *masriya*, *masreeya*, Egyptian.

(5) يْ *ai*, indifferently pronounced as *ai* in *pain*, or as *i* in *pine*; e. g., عين *'ain*, or *'ine*, eye; but usually as *ai* in *pain*; e. g., بين *bain*, between, اثنين *etnain*, two.

II. *Short.* (1) *Fat-ha*, فَتحة َ, *a* or *ŭ*, as in *cap* or *cup*; e.g., جَرَس *jaras*, or *jŭrŭs*, bell.

(2) *Damma*, ضَمّة ُ, *o* or *u*, as in *pull*, *book*; e. g., أذُن *odon*, or *udun*, ear.

(3) *Kasra*, كسرة ِ, *i*, as in *pin*; e.g., صُرِفَ *sorifa*, it was spent. This *kasra*, or short *i*, is very common in the spoken dialect, and often usurps the place of *a*; e.g., بكي *baka*, is usually pronounced *biki*, he wept; مشى *masha* becomes *mishi*, he walked; كتب *kataba* becomes *kitib*, he wrote.

There are five letters—ج, ع, غ, ق and ك—which must be contrasted together.

1. ج *Jeem*, *j*, *g* as in *gin*, but colloquially as *g* in *go*.

2. ع *'Ain*, a hiatus, or peculiar guttural.

3. غ *Ghain*, *gh*, a guttural usually transliterated by the French *r grasséyé*.

4. ق *Qáf*, a guttural *k* or *q*; or hiatus; or, *very vulgarly*, as *g* in *go*.

5. ك *kéf*, *k*.

    a. Compare حج *hajj*, pilgrimage, with حقيقة *haqeeqa*, truth, and عقيق *'aqeeq*, cornelian. ح is colloquially pronounced *hagg*. حقيقة *haqeeqa*, may become *ha-ee-a*, and also, *very vulgarly*, *hagheega*. عقيق *'aqeeq*, may become *'a-ee*, and *very vulgarly*, *'agheeg*.

    b. So also حلّاق *halláq*, barber, may be confused with حلّاج *halláj*, carder of cotton. And زقازيق *Zaqázeeq* is *Zagazig*, or *Za-á-zee*.

    c. Again: فراغ *farágh*, emptiness; فراق *firáq*, separation; فرك *faraka*, he rubbed, require to be distinguished.

The student is therefore advised to retain the simple transliteration adopted in this book, and to consider: ج *Jeem* as *j*, or *g* in *gin*; ع *'Ain* as a hiatus, apostrophe *'a*, *'e*, *'i*, *'o* or *'u*; غ *Ghain* as *gh*; ق *Qáf* as *q*; ك *Kef* as *k*.

I have carefully avoided any *elaborate system* of transliteration with dots or strokes under certain letters. Experience has shown me that everyone likes his own ideas on this subject, and spells words (*e.g.*, *kurbash*, *dahabia*, *Ismailia*, *bawab*, &c.) according to his fancy.

The New Egyptian Weights and Measures, 1892.

By Khedivial Decree the metric system is officially recognised in Egypt according to the following Egyptian and English equivalents.

I. MEASURES OF LENGTH.—مقاييس الاطوال *Maqáyees el-Atwál.*

1 *Diráa' Baladiy,* ذراع بـلـدىّ ... 0·58 mètre ... 22·835 inches.
1 *Diráa' Mi'amáriy,* ذراع معمارىّ ... 0·75 „   ... 29·528 „
1 *Qasaba,* قصبة ... 3·55 „   ... 11 ft., 7·76 in.

1 *Feddán,* فدّان ... 4200·833 sq. mètres ... 1 acre, 6 rods.

II. WEIGHTS.—موازين *Mawázeen.*

1 *Dirhem,* ... درهم ... ·003 kilo. ... 1·76 drms. Avdp.
1 *Oqqiya* (12 dirhems), اوقية ... ·037 „   ... 1·32 ounces „
1 *Rotl* (144 dirhems), رطل ... ·449 „   ... ·99 pounds „
1 *Oqqa* (400 dirhems), اوقّة .. 1·248 „   ... 2·75 „   „
1 *Qintár* (100 rotls), قنطار ..44·928 „   .. 99·05 „   „
1 *Qintár* of Alexandria } (112 oqqas), .139·776 „   . 308·15 „   „
1 *Hamla* (60 oqqas), حملة ..74·880 „   . 165·08 „   „
1 *Himl* (200 oqqas), جمل .249·600 „   . 550·27 „   „
1 *Tonaláta (Tonneau),* طونلاتة 1000·000 „   .2204·62 „   „
1 English *Tonaláta* (Ton), 1016·047 „   .2240·00 „   „

Weights for precious metals :—

1 *Mithqál* (1½ dirhems), مثقال 4·680 gram., 72·22 grains Troy.
1 *Dirhem* (16 qeeráts), درهم 3·120 „   48·15 „   „
1 *Qeerát* (4 qamhas), قيراط 0·195 „   3·00 „   „
1 *Qamha,* or grain of wheat, قمحة 0·048 „   0·75 „   „

III. Measures of Capacity.—مكاييل Makáyeel.

1 *Ardab* (12 kailas), اردب	... 198·000 litres	... 5·44 bushels.
1 *Waiba* (2 kailas), ويـبـة	... 33·000 ,,	... 3·63 pecks.
1 *Kaila* (8 qadhs), كيلة	... 16·500 ,,	... 3·63 gallons.
1 *Rub'* (4 qadhs), ربع الويبة	... 8·250 ,,	... 1·81 ,,
1 *Malwa* (2 qadhs), ملوة	... 4·125 ,,	... 3·63 quarts.
1 *Qadh* (32 qeeráts), قدح	... 2·062 ,,	... 1·81 ,,
1 *Nusf qadh* ... نصف قدح	... 1·031 ,,	... 1·81 pints.
1 *Rub' qadh* ... ربع قدح	... 0·515 ,,	... 3·63 gills.
1 *Kharrooba* ... خروبة	... 0·128 ,,	... 0·90 ,,
1 *Qeerát* ... قيراط	... 0·064 ,,	... 0·45 ,,

1 *Dareeba* (8 ardabs), ضريبة	1584.000 litres	... 43·58 bushels.
1 *Fard* (large), ... فرد كبير	115·500 ,,	... 3·17 ,,
1 *Fard* (small), ... فرد صغير	57·750 ,,	... 1·58 ,,

1 Litre = 0·005 *ardabs*.
1 Hectolitre = 0·505 *ardabs*.
1 Kilolitre = 5·050 ,,
1 Décilitre = 1·551 *qeeráts*.

1 Mètre = 1·724 *dirá'a baladiy*.

1 Centimètre = 0·172 *dirá'a baladiy*.
1 Kilomètre = 281·69 *qasabas*.

1 Gramme = 0·320 *dirhem*.
1 Kilogramme = 320·5 ,,

320 Rotls = 1 Ardab, beans.
300 ,, = 1 ,, wheat.
270 ,, = 1 ,, cotton-seed.

The Moslem Calendar.

1. Moharram	30 days	مُحَرَّم
2. Safar	30 ,,	صفر
3. Rabee'a el-Awwal	29 ,,	ربيع الأوّل
4. Rabee'a et-Táni	30 ,,	ربيع الثاني
5. Jamádi el-Awwal	30 ,,	جمادي الأوّل
6. Jamádi et-Táni	29 ,,	جمادي الثاني
7. Rajab	29 ,,	رجب
8. Sha'bán	30 ,,	شعبان
9. Ramadán	29 ,,	رمضان
10. Shawwál	29 ,,	شوّال
11. Zu l-Ka'ada	29 ,,	ذو القعدة
12. Zu l-Hijja	29 ,,	ذو الحجّة

The Moslem year consists of 12 lunar months, or 354 days. It is thus shorter by about 11 days than the Gregorian year; or 34 Moslem years are about equal to 33 ordinary years, or 100 Moslem years to only 97 ordinary years. The Moslems reckon from A.D. 622, the date of the Flight (*Hijra*, هجرة) of Mahomed from Mecca to Medina, and therefore 1892 A.D. is 1309–10 A.H. (Anno Hijræ).

The Coptic Calendar is used by Moslems and Copts for agricultural purposes. The names of the months appear to be taken from ancient Egyptian mythology:—

1.	Toot	توت	begins about	September 11.
2.	Bába	بابة	,,	October 11.
3.	Hátoor	هاتور	,,	November 10.
4.	Kiahk	كيهك	,,	December 10.
5.	Tooba	طوبة	,,	January 9.
6.	Amsheer	امشير	,,	February 8.
7.	Barmahát	برمهات	,,	March 10.
8.	Baramooda	برمودة	,,	April 9.
9.	Bashans	بشنس	,,	May 9.
10.	Ba-oona	بؤونة	,,	June 8.
11.	Abeeb	ابيب	,,	July 8.
12.	Misra	مسرى	,,	August 7.
13.	Nisi	نسىء	intercalary days	September 6–11.

The year consists of 12 months of 30 days each, = 360 days, and 5 intercalary days at the end of the year, with 6 in Leap-Year. The reckoning is from 284 A.D., the era of Diocletian, so that 1892 A.D. is the Coptic Year 1608–9.

ARABIC-ENGLISH VOCABULARY.

A.

ا *Alif.* Value = 1.

آ *á,* interrogative particle placed at the beginning of a sentence. [هل]

آب *Ab,* Syrian month of August.

آب *ába,* he returned.

اوب or اياب *ōb,* or *iyáb,* a return.

ذهاب و اياب *daháb wa iyáb,* a going and coming; there and back.

مآب *máb,* source, origin, focus.

اب ـ ابو *áb,* father (see *aboo*).

ابّادىّ ـ ابابدة *Abbádiy,* pl. *Abábda,* Soudanese Arabs of the Kena-Assouan-Kosair district.

ابد *abad,* future eternity. [cf. ازل]

ابدًا *abadán,* never.

ابّد *abbada,* be perpetuated.

مؤبّدًا *mo-abbadan,* perpetually; for life.

ابجد *abjad,* the series of the numerical values of the letters of the alphabet (see Introduction).

ابراهيم *Ibráheem,* Abraham.

ابرة *ibra,* needle.

ابريل *Abreel,* (European) April.

ابزيم *abzeem,* buckle.

ابط ـ آباط *ibt,* pl. *aábát,* armpit (see *bát,* باط).

ابق *aábiq,* fugitive slave.

ابل *ibl,* camel. [جمل]

ابليس *Iblees,* Devil, Diabolos.

ابلق *ablaq,* piebald.

ابن or بنى *ibn,* or *bin,* son. [بنى ـ بن]

بنى or بنون or ابناء *ebná,* or *banoon,* or (in construction) *beni,* sons, children.

بنى آدم *beni Ádam,* the human race.

بنى سويف *Beni Soo-ef,* a town and province in Upper Egypt.

ابنة or بنت *ibna,* or (commonly) *bint,* girl, daughter.

بنات *banát,* girls, daughters.

ابنة عمّه or ابن عمّه *ibn 'ammoh* (femin.), *ibnat 'ammoh,* his cousin.

ابنوس *abanos,* ebony.

ابهام *ibhám,* thumb.

ابهة *ubha,* pomp, magnificence.

ابهر *abhar,* artery, aorta.

اب or ابو *aboo,* or *ab,* father; possessor.

آباء *aábá,* fathers.

ابونا *aboona*, our father, title of the Coptic priesthood.

ابوّة *ubowa*, paternity.

ابو قردان *aboo qirdán*, white "paddy-bird."

ابو النظّارة *aboo n-naddára*, the man who wears spectacles.

ابو النّوم *aboo n-nōm*, father of sleep, poppy. [خشخاش]

ابو الهول *Aboo l-hōl*, father of terror, the Sphinx.

ابو قير *Aboo qeer*, Aboukir.

ابى – اباء *aba*, he refused; *ibá*, refusal.

ابيب *Abeeb*, Coptic month of July.

اتباي *Atbái*, mountain desert near Kosair.

اتش *atesh* (Persian), fire. "Fire"! as a military word of command.

اتشجي – اتشجية *uteshji*, pl. *ateshjiya* (Turco-Persian), stoker, fireman.

(اتم) مآتم *atem*), *máitam*, mourning, funeral.

اتمور *Atmoor* (Soudanese), desert.

اتى – ياتي *ata*, he came, reached; *yáti*, he comes.

اتيان *ityán*, arrival, consummation.

آت or آتٍ *áti*, a comer, coming, as follows.

كما هو آت *Kamá hoa áát*, as follows, viz.

ت – تعال *ti*, come thou! (unused). See *t'aála*.

تأتّى *táatta*, it resulted, became possible.

اتى ب *ata bi*, he came with, brought. [جاب]

اثاث *asás*, furniture.

اثر – آثار *asar*, pl. *aúsar*, trace, scar, monument.

اقتفى اثره *iqtafa asaraho*, he pursued, followed up its track.

اثريّة *atariya*, inheritance; succession to an undivided inheritance.

اثّر *assara*, he influenced, left a trace upon.

تأثير *tá-seer*, influence, effect.

مؤثر *mo-assar*, affected by, influenced, touched.

تأثّر *tá-assara*, he felt himself influenced.

مأثرة – مآثر *másara*, pl. *maásir*, trace, event, monument.

اثل – عبل *atl*, tamarisk articulata; also called *'abl*.

اثم *ithm*, sin, crime.

اجر – اجرة *ujra*, pl. *ujar*, hire, pay, fare, salary.

اجريّ *ujariy*, workman, hired labourer.

اجارة *ijára*, rent, rental.

اجّر or آجر *ajjara*, or *aájara*, he let on hire.

استأجر *istájara*, he took on hire, rented.

تأجير or إيجار *tá-jeer* or *eejár*, a letting on hire.

للإيجار *lil-eejár*, for hire, "to let."

استئجار‎ *isteejar*, a taking on hire.
مؤجر‎ *mo-ajjar*, let, hired; *mo-ajjir*, landlord.
مستأجر‎ *mostájir*, tenant, hirer, "*fermier.*"
اجرومية‎ *Ajirroomiya*. Grammar, an Arabic grammar by Daood es-Sanháji.
اجل‎ *ajal*, fixed time or date.
اجل‎ *ajjala*, he deferred to a fixed date.
مؤجل‎ *mo-ajjal*, deferred to a fixed date; a form of dowry.
اجل‎ *ajl*, cause, reason.
لاجل‎ *li-ajl*, because of.
اجواز - زوج‎ *ajwáz*, pl. of *jōz*, couples (see *zōj*).
احد - احدى‎ *ahad*, (femin.) *ihda*, one.
احد عشر - احدى عشرة‎ } *ahad'ashara*, (femin.) *ihda ashrata*, eleven.
حادي عشر‎ *hádi 'ashar*, eleventh in order.
آحاد - احد‎ *ahad*, pl. *aáhád*, unit, individual, some one.
ما جاءش حد‎ *má ja-sh had*, (colloquial) no one came.
يوم الاحد‎ *yōm el-ahad* (*yōm el-hád*), Sunday.
احدية‎ *ahadiya*, Divine unity.
احد, وحد‎ or *ahhada*, or *wahhada*, he unified.
اتحد‎ *ittahada*, he united himself to, agreed.

اتحاد‎ *ittihád*, unity, unanimity, concord.
متحد‎ *muttahid*, ally, allied, accomplice.
احليل‎ *ihleel*, urethra, duct, passage.
[مجرى]
اخ‎ *akh*, alas!
اخ or اخو‎ *akh*, or *akhoo*, brother, fellow of a pair.
اخوة‎ *ikhwat*, brothers of a family.
اخوان‎ *ikhwán*, brethren of a community or confraternity, colleagues.
اخوات - اخت‎ *ukht*, pl. *akhwát*, sister, fellow of a pair.
اخوة‎ *ukhowa*, brotherhood.
اخوه - اخيه‎ *akhooh*, (oblique cases) *akheeh*, his brother.
اخذ - ياخذ‎ *akhaza*, he took, began; *yákhoz*, he takes.
اخذ‎ *akhz*, a taking, commencement.
اخذ واعطاء‎ *akhz wa i'atá*, a taking and giving; trade.
آخذ - مؤاخذة‎ *aákhaza*, he blamed, *mo-ákhaza*, blame.
ما تؤاخذني‎ *má towákhiz-ni*, do not blame me!
اتخذ‎ *ittakhaza*, he undertook.
اتخاذ‎ *ittikház*, an undertaking.
مأخوذ‎ *mákhooz*, taken.
مأخذ‎ *mákhaz*, place of taking, source, manner.
آخر - اخرى‎ *aákhar*, (femin.) *ukhra*, other.

آخر (4) ارث

اَخِر ـ اواخر aákhir, pl. awákhir, end, last days.

اَخِرة aákhira (femin.), end; life to come.

اَخِير akheer, the last.

اَخَّر akhkhara, he adjourned.

تَاخِير tá-kheer, adjournment.

تَاَخَّر tá-akhkhara, he was late, in arrears, adjourned.

مؤخَّر mo-akhkhar, delayed, adjourned.

اَخُور akhōr (Persian), stable. [اصطبل

ادب ـ آداب adab, pl. aúdáb, good manners, culture, morals, education.

اديب adeeb, courteous.

ادبيَّة adubiya, education, culture.

ادَّب addaba, he educated, corrected, punished.

تَاديب tá-deeb, education, punishment.

تَاديبي tá-deebiy, correctional, disciplinary.

اَدُرَّة or دُرَّة or اِدُرَّة idurra, or durra, or izurra, maize.

ادمان ـ دمن idmán, perseverance (see damana).

آدم ـ آدمي Ádam, the first man; ádamiy, human.

بني آدم beni Ádam, human race.

آدميَّات ádamiyát, women.

اداة ـ ادوات adát, pl. adawát, tool, instrument. [عدَّة]

اداء adá, payment, fulfilment.

ادَّى adda, he paid, fulfilled.

تَاديَة tá-diya, fulfilment.

اودِّي وظيفتي owaddi wazeefti, I shall do my duty.

اذ iz, lo! and then.

اذا or اذا كان izá, or izá kán, if.

آذار Aázar, Syrian month of March.

دُرَّة or اِدُرَّة izurra, or durra, maize.

اذن له بعمل azina laho bi-'amal, he permitted him to do.

اذن izn, permission, licence. [رخصة]

كمبيالة تحت اذن kambiála taht izn, bill of exchange payable to order.

ادفع لاذنه idfa' li-iznihi, pay to his order!

مأذون mázoon, licenced, delegate.

استأذن istázana, he asked leave.

اذن ـ آذان odon, pl. aádán, (femin.) ear. The singular is usually pronounced widn.

اذان edán, cry to prayer (from a minaret).

مؤذِّن mo-addin, crier to prayer.

مئذنة ـ مآذن maidna, pl. maádin, minaret.

اذى or اذيَّة aza or aziya, torture. [عذاب]

آذى ـ ايذاء aúza, he tortured, cezá, a torturing.

اربيَّة arbiya, groin, root of thigh.

ارب irb, limb; desire, cunningness,

ارث ـ ورث irs, inheritage, succession (see warisa).

حقّ الارث haqq el-irs, right of succession.

ارجوان orjowán, purple.

ارّخ arrakha, he dated, chronicled,

تاريخ - تواريخ táreekh, pl. tawáreekh, date, chronicle, history.

يوم تاريخهُ yōm táreekhoh, of the same day's date.

تاريخيّ táreekhiy, historic, ancient.

مورَّخ mo-arrakh, dated.

مورِّخ mo-arrikh, historian.

اردب - ارادب ardab, pl. arádib, a measure of capacity, 44 gallons, 200 litres, 5½ bushels; 7½-8 ardabs to one ton of boat-tonnage.

اردو or اردي oordi (for Turkish ordoo), army-corps.

ارزّ or ارز aruzz (pronounced ruzz), rice.

ارز arz, cedar, fir, conifer.

ارض - اراضي ard, pl. arádi (femin.), earth, land.

اراضي arádi, landed estate, lands. [اطيان]

ارضيّ ardiy, earthly.

ارضيّة ardiya, floor; tax for warehousing.

اريكة areeka, throne.

ارمنيّ Armaniy, Armenian.

ارنب - ارانب arnab, pl. aránib (femin.), hare, rabbit.

ازب or وزب azaba, or wazaba, it flowed.

مزاب or ميزاب maizab, or meezáb, gutter, drain.

ازدياد - زيد izdiyád, increase (see zaid.)

ازار - آزرة izár, pl. aázira, white cloak worn by girls and negresses.

تأزّرت táazzaret, she put on the izár.

ازل or ازليّة azal, or azaliya, past eternity. [cf. ابد]

ازمير Izmeer, Smyrna; small crowbar, chisel.

آزى or وازى aáza, or wáza, it was opposite, parallel.

ازاء izá, in front of, parallel.

آس aás, myrtle.

اسّ uss, basis (unused in singular).

اساس or اسس isás, or usus, bases, foundations.

اسس - آساس asas, pl. aásás, foundation, basis, depôt of regiment.

اساسيّ asásiy, fundamental. [اصلي]

قانون اساسيّ qánoon asásiy, the law of the constitution of a country, "règlement organique."

اسّس assasa, he founded, based.

تأسيس tásees, a founding, basing.

مؤسَّس mo-assas, based upon.

اسبتاليّة isbitáliya, (European) hospital.

اِست ‎ *ist*, anus.

اُسْتاذ ـ أَساتيذ ‎ *ustád* or *ustá*, pl. *asáteez*, professor, master of a craft, teacher, "boss."

اُسطى ‎ *usta*, vulgar spelling of the above word.

اِسكونت ‎ *iskont*, (European) "*escompte*," discount.

اِستمارة ‎ *istimára*, specimen, official form, schedule.

اِستانبول ‎ *Istánbool*, Stambool, Constantinople, from the Greek εἰς τὴν πόλιν.

اِستانبولي ‎ *Istanbooliy*, Stambooline, of Constantinople.

اَسِتانة ‎ *asitána* (Persian), threshold; court.

اَسِتانة علِيّة ‎ *asitána 'aliya*, Imperial threshold or court; Constantinople.

أسد ـ آساد ‎ *asad*, pl. *aásád*, lion; Leo in the Zodiac.

أسر ‎ *asara*, be bound captive.

أسر ‎ *asr*, a binding captive.

أسير ـ أسراء ‎ *aseer*, pl. *usará*, captive.

بأسرِهم ‎ *bi-asrihim*, the whole, or all of them.

ماسورة ـ مواسير ‎ *má-soora*, pl. *mawáseer*, tube, drain; gun-barrel.

اِسرائيل ‎ *Isráyeel*, Israel.

اُسطول ـ أساطيل ‎ *ostool*, pl. *asáteel* (Greek), fleet, navy.

أسف ‎ *asaf*, regret, sorrow.

تأسّف ‎ *tá-assafa*, he regretted.

اسفكسيا ‎ *asfiksiyá*, (European) asphyxia. [خنق]

اِسفنج ‎ or اِسفنج *isfinj*, sponge.

اُسقُف ـ سقف ‎ *usquf* (Greek, *episcopos*), bishop (see under *saqf*).

اِسكلة ‎ *iskelé* (European, Turkish), *scala*, small seaport, "*échelle du Levant*."

اِسكملة ‎ *iskemlé* (Turkish), footstool, low chair.

اِسكندريّة ‎ *Iskandariya*, Alexandria.

اِسكندرانيّ ‎ *Iskandaraniy*, Alexandrian.

اِسلامبول ـ اِسلامبولي ـ سلم ‎ *Islámbol* and *Islámboliy*, corruption of *Istánbool* (see also *silm*).

أسلوب ـ سلب ‎ *usloob*, path, method (see *salaba*).

اِسم ـ أسماء ‎ or أسامي ‎ *ism*, pl. *asmá*, or *asámi*, name.

مجهول الاسم ‎ *maj-hool el-ism*, of name unknown, anonymous; passive voice.

اِسماعيل ‎ *Ismáyeel*, Ismail, Ishmael.

اِسماعيليّة ‎ *Ismáyeeliya*, a port in Suez Canal; a suburb of Cairo.

اِسنا ‎ *Isná* or *Esná*, a town and province of Upper Egypt.

أسيوط ‎ *Asioot*, a town and province of Upper Egypt.

أسى ـ آساء ‎ *asu*, grief; *isáá*, remedy.

أشّر ‎ *ashshara*, he put a *visa* upon, annotated.

تأشير ‎ *tá-sheer*, annotation, *visa*, mention.

يُؤَشِّر yowashshir, he annotates, mentions.

اشكين eshkeen (Turkish), amble.

اشنان oshnán, alcali.

اصبع asbo'a (femin.), finger, toe.

اصطبل istabl (Latin), stable.

اصل ـ اصول asl, pl. osool, origin, principle.

اصول osool, principles, manner, style.

اصول وخصوم osool wa khosoom, debit and credit.

اصله كذا asloh kida, (it was) originally thus.

اصلي asliy, fundamental, cardinal, radical.

اصلًا aslán, never.

اصالة asála, permanency, firmness.

اصيل aseel, firm, strong, noble.

اصوان Aswán, Assouan, Syene; a fort and village near the first Nile cataract.

اطلس atlas, smooth; satin; atlas; the empyrean.

اطار or اطارة itára or tára, circle, round piece.

اغا ـ اغاوات aghá, pl. agháwát (Turkish), squire, subaltern, captain; eunuch.

اغسطس Agostos, (European) August.

آفة aáfa, calamity.

افرنك or افرنج afranj or afrank, Franks, Europeans.

افرنجي or افرنكي afranjiy or afrankiy, European.

افسون afsoon (Persian), exorcism. [دعوة]

افعى ـ افاعي af'aa, pl. afá'iy (fem.), viper.

افق ـ افقي ofq, horizon; ofqiy, horizontal.

افك ـ افاك ifk, lie, affák, liar. [كذب]

افول ofool, sunset, decline.

افندي ـ افندية efendi, pl. efendiya (Greek αὐθέντης, through Turkish), a respectable person, Mr., Sir, Lord.

افندينا efendeená, Our Lord, the Khedive.

افنديمز efendimiz (Turkish), Our Lord, the Sultan, or Khedive.

افيون afiyoon, opium.

اوقة or وقة or اقة oqqa, weight of 2¾ lbs. avdp.; 400 dirhems; 1·25 kilog.

اوقية or وقية or اقية oqqiya, ounce, 1⅓ oz. advp.; 37½ grammes.; 12 dirhems.

اقحوان oq-hooán, pyrethrum parthenium.

اقليم ـ اقاليم iqleem, pl. aqáleem (Greek), climate, province.

اقاليم مصرية aqáleem masriya, provinces of Egypt.

اقنوم oqnoom (Greek), principle of nature.

اكتوبر *Oktober*, (European) October.

اَكَّدَ or وَكَّدَ *akkada*, or *wakkada*, he strengthened, assured, intensified.

تأكيد *tá-keed*, a strengthening, assuring.

اكيد *akeed*, certain, firm.

مؤكد *mo-akkad*, confirmed, certain.

اكل - يأكل *akala*, he ate; *yákul*, he eats.

تأكّل *táakkala*, it was eaten, eatable.

اكل *akl*, or *ukl*, food, eating.

مأكولات *mákoolát*, eatables.

آكلة *áakila*, itch.

اَكَّل or وَكَّل *akkala* (or vulgarly, *wakkala*), he fed, gave to eat.

اكليل - كلّ *ikleel*, diadem (see *kull*).

اكم - اكم يوم *akam*, some, a few; *akam yōm*, a few days. [كم]

آل - اول *aal*, dynasty, possessor (see *awl*).

آل عثمان *aal 'osmán*, Ottoman dynasty.

آل الخبرة *aal el-khibra*, professional expert. [اهل]

آلة - آلات *aala*, pl. *aálát*, weapon, tool, musical instrument. [اداة]

آلات مطربة *aálát motriba*, musical instruments.

آلاتيّ *aálátiy*, musician.

آل - اولو *ooloo*, possessors; pl. of *aal*.

الا - يألو *alá*, he failed in; *yáloo*, he fails in.

آلى - يولي *aála*, he swore off from his wife; *yooli*, he swears off.

ايلاء *eelá*, a swearing off, a form of divorce.

ال *al*, or *el*, the, of the; this.

الا *á lá*, is it not?

اَلَّا - والَّا *illá*, except; *wa illa*, or else.

ليس الّا *laisa illá*, nothing but that, merely that.

اللي *illi*, (colloquial) he, she, or they who.

الّذى - الّتى *ellazi*, (femin.) *ellati*, he who, she who.

الّذين - اللواتى *ellazeen*, (femin.) *ellawáti*, they who.

الديوان - الدواناتِ *aldiwán*, pl. *aldiwánát* (Turkish, *eldiven*), glove.

الف *alif*, the letter A.

الف - آلاف *alf*, pl. *aáláf*, thousand.

الف or الفة *ilf*, or *ulfa*, intimacy.

اليف or الوف *aleef*, or *aloof*, intimate, friend.

الّف *allafa*, he composed a book. [صنّف]

تأليف - تآليف *tá-leef*, pl. *taáleef*, authorship; composition of a book; book.

مؤلّف *mo-allif*, author.

تألّف or ايتلف *ta-allafa*, or *eetalafa*, he became intimate, fell in love with.

مؤالفة or ايتلاف *eetiláf*, or *mo-álafa*, intimacy, love.

مألوف *máloof*, intimate, conversant with.

الم يكن *á lam yakon*, was it not?

الم ـ آلام *alam*, pl. *aálam*, pain. [وجع]

الْأَلِيم *aleem*, in pain, painful.

تألم *táallama*, he felt pain.

الماس *almás*, diamond.

الْمانية *Alamániya*, German Empire, Allemagne.

اله ـ آلهة *iláh*, pl. *aáliha*, a deity, false god.

الله *Allah*, The God, Allah.

لا إلٰهَ إلا اللهُ *lá ilaha illá Allahu*, there is no God but The God. [هلس]

الاهة *iláha*, goddess, female idol.

الوحدية *oloohiya*, divinity.

الهيّ ـ الهيّات *ilahíy*, pl. *ilahiyát*, divine, theology.

اللّهمّ *Allahomma*, Oh, my God!

الية ـ الْيَتان *ilia*, pl. *iliatán*, buttocks. [ليّة]

الاي *alái* (Persian), regiment, procession.

مير الاي *meeri alái* (Persian), Colonel.

ميدان الاي *maidán alái*, military review.

الى ـ الىّ *ila*, to, for; *ilaya*, to me.

الى و على *ila wa 'ala*, for and against; *pro* and *con*; credit and debit.

الى ان *ila an*, until that.

ام ـ ام لا *am*, or; *am lá*, or not.

امّ ـ امّهات *umm*, pl. *ummahát*, mother.

امّيّ ـ امومة *ummiy*, maternal; *omooma*, maternity.

امّ الولد *umm el-walad*, a slave who bears a child to her master.

امام *amám*, in front of. [قدّام]

امام ـ ائمّة *imám*, pl. *ayimma*, leader, king, priest.

امامي *imámiy*, follower of the Imám 'Ali, dissenter.

امّة ـ امم *umma*, pl. *umam*, nation, people, sect.

امة ـ اموات *ama*, pl. *amawát*, female slave. [جارية]

اميّة *Omaya*, the dynasty of the Omiade Caliphs of Damascus, 661-750.

امّا *ammá*, but.

امّا ـ ان ما *immá* (for *in-má*), if, when, or.

امّا ـ او *immá-aw*, either, or.

امتياز ـ ميّز *imtiyáz*, privilege, concession (see *mayyaza*.)

امد *amad*, eternity, space of time. [صمد]

امر ب *amara bi*, he ordered, commanded.

امر ـ اوامر *amr*, pl. *awámir*, order, command.

امر ـ امور *amr*, pl. *omoor*, affair, business.

امارة *imára*, principality, post of command.

اِمَارَة amára, sign, trace. [اِشَارَة]

اَمَّارَات ammárát, the carnal passions.

اَمِير - اُمَرَاء ameer, pl. umará, Emir, prince, chief, lord.

مِير meer (Persian for ameer), lord.

اَمِيرِي or مِيرِي ameeriy, or meeriy, of the government, relating to government property.

المِيرِي el-meeriy, government property.

اَمِير البَحر Ameer el-bahr, Admiral.

اَمِير الاُمَرَاء ameer el-umará, chief of chiefs, a civil rank of Bey or Colonel equal to Meeri Alái.

مِير الاي meeri alái, Colonel, a military Bey of the highest rank.

مَأمُور mámoor, an official with and under authority; prefect, director.

مَأمُورِيَّة mámooriya, office or place of a mámoor.

اِئتَمَر iatamara, he met in congress.

مُؤتَمَر mo-atamar, congress, conference.

اَمس - مَسَاء ams, yesterday (see masá).

اَمشِير Amsheer, Coptic month of February.

اَمَل - آمَال amal, pl. aámál, hope, desire.

اَمَل amala, he hoped.

يَأمَل - يُومَل yámol, he hopes; yoomal, it is hoped.

مَأمُول mámool, thing hoped for, desire. [مَرجُو]

تَأَمَّلَ tá-ammala, he thought over, gave his mind to; hoped.

اَمن or اَمنِيَّة amn, or amniya, security, safety.

اَمَان amán, mercy! quarter! alas!

اَمَانَة amána, fidelity; hence a pledge, deposit, cash department.

اَمِين ameen, trustworthy; cashier.

صَندُوق اَمِينِي sandooq ameeni, treasurer, in charge of the safe.

آمِين aámeen, amen!

اَمِينَة ameena, lime-kiln. [كُوشَة]

اَمِن or اِئتَمَن amina, or iatamana, he trusted in.

اُؤتُمِنَ فَخَانَ o-otomina fa-khána, he was trusted and he betrayed; legal phrase for "breach of trust," "abus de confiance".

اَمَّنَ ammana, he assured, gave confidence.

تَأمِين tá-meen, assurance, guarantee.

آمَنَ aámana, he believed in God.

اِستَأمَنَ istámana, he asked for mercy, "amán".

اِيمَان eemán, faith in God.

اَيمَان - يَمِين aimán, pl. of yameen, oaths.

اَيمَن - يَمِين aiman, right hand side, happiness (see yameen).

مُؤمِن moo-min, believer in God, Moslem.

اَمِير المُؤمِنِين Ameer el-moo-mineen, Commander of the Faithful, the Caliph.

مأمون *mámoon*, safe (place or person), trusted.

مؤتمن *mo-ataman*, trustworthy. [cf. معتمد]

اموي - اميّة *Umawiy*, Omiade (see *omaya*).

ان or انّ *an*, or *anna*, that; *in*, or *inna*, if.

ان كان - انّما *in kán*, if; *innamá*, however, but.

ان لم يكن *in lam yakon*, unless.

انين *aneen*, groan.

انا - نحن *aná*, I; *nahno* (vulgarly, *ahna*), we.

انبار or عنبر *anbár*, barn, magazine.

الانبيق - انبيق *anbeeq* (*al-ambeeq*), "alambic," chemical retort.

انت - انتما *enta* (femin.), *enti*, thou; *entomá*, ye two.

انتم - انتنّ *entom* (femin.), *entonna*, ye.

انثى - اناث *unsa*, pl. *inás*, female. [cf. اناس

ذكور و اناث *zokoor wa inás*, males and females.

نتاية *nitáya* (colloquial for *unsa*), female.

انيث *anees*, effeminate, soft.

انّث *annasa*, he made feminine in gender.

تأنيث *tá-nees*, a putting into the feminine.

مؤنّث *mo-annas*, feminine gender.

انثيان *unsiyán*, the two testicles.

انكلترا or انجلترا *Inghilterra*, England.

انجليز *Ingleez*, the English (in general).

انجليزي *Ingleezy*, English, an Englishman.

انجيل *Injeel*, gospel, évangile.

انس *ins*, mankind.

انس و جن *ins wa jinn*, men and genii.

انسان - اناس - ناس *insán*, pl. *unás* (or colloquially *nás*), man, homo; pl., men, people.

انسان العين *insán el-'ain*, pupil of eye.

انسانيّة *insániya*, humanity, humaneness, culture.

نساء or نسوة or نسوان *nisá* or *niswa* (or commonly *niswán*), women.

انس or انسيّة *uns*, or *unsiya*, social life, domesticity, cordiality in society.

انيس *anees*, tame, docile.

انّس *annasa*, he tamed.

مؤانسة *mo-ánasa*, mutual intimacy or cordiality.

انسيّ *unsiy*, a medical term for inner, internal.

انف - آناف *anf*, pl. *aánáf*, nose, point, anterior part. مناخير

آنف *aánif*, anterior, aforesaid.

استأنف *istánafa*, he made a nose at; he appealed to a higher tribunal.

استئناف *isteenáf*, appeal (in law).

مُسْتَأْنِف *mustánif*, appellant; *mustánaf*, appealed against, respondent.

انفلوينزاء *inflooenzá* (European), influenza.

انوريزماء *anoorismá* (European), aneurism.

اناقة *anáqa*, beauty.

آنام *aánám*, creatures, men.

انموذج *onmoozaj* (Persian), sample, pattern. [نموذج]

اذ *aná*, moment, delay. [cf. آن]

استأنى or تأنى *tá-anna*, or (more commonly) *istána*, he delayed, acted with deliberation, waited.

استأنى *istáni* (*stáni*) (imperative), wait!

آوانى - اناء *iná*, pl. *awáni*, vase, vessel.

آونة - آن *aán*, pl. *aáwina*, moment, season.

الآن *el-aán*, now, this moment. [cf. حالاً]

اهبة *ahba*, preparations.

اهّب *ahhaba*, he prepared, equipped [جهّز]

تأهيب *ta-heeb*, preparation, fitting out.

تأهّب *tá-ahhaba*, he prepared himself.

اهلى - اهل *ahl*, pl. *aháli*, a person, possessor; capable of; wife; family (as a unit); pl., population. [عائلة]

اهل البيت *ahl el-bait*, household.

اهل الخبرة *ahl el-khibra*, a professional expert.

اهلى *ahliy*, domestic, native, "*indigène.*"

اهليّة *ahliya*, capacity, aptitude; relevancy, relationship; femin. of *ahliy*.

اهالى البلد *aháli el-balad*, population of the town.

اهّل *ahhala*, he gave (a girl) in marriage, married (her) to.

تأهّل *tá-ahhala*, he took a wife, set up house.

اهلاً و سهلاً *ahlán wa sahlán*. Welcome! [مرحبا]

استاهل *istáhala*, he deserved. [cf. استحال]

مستاهل *mostáhil*, deserving, meritorious.

اهليلج *ihleelij*, ellipse.

او *aw*, or.

اوباش - بوش *awbásh*, mob, ruffians (see *bōsh*).

اواسى *awási*, large landed estates.

اوج *ōj*, peak, apex, apogee.

اوجاق *ojáq* (Turkish), stove, hearth.

اوده - اود *oda*, pl. *owad* (Turkish), chamber, room.

اوروبا - اورپاوى *Awroba*, Europe; *Awrobáwiy*, European.

اوردى - اردو *oordi* (for Turkish *ordoo*), army-corps.

اورطة *orta* (for Turkish اوته *orta*, centre), battalion of Egyptian army.

اورغول *oorghool*, flute.

اورنك *oornak* (Turkish), sample, specimen.

وِزَّة or اوِزَّ *iwazza* (pronounced *wizza*), goose.

اواسي ـ اوسِيَّة *oosia*, pl. *awási*, large landed estate.

اوطه *oda* (Turkish), chamber, room.

اوطهلق *odaliq* (Turkish), chambermaid, "odalisque."

اوقِيَّة ـ اوقَّة *oqqa, oqqiya* (see اقَّة and اقِيَّة).

اكرة *okra*, handle, bell-pull.

آل ـ يؤل or اول *awl*, attainment, becoming, arrival; *aála*, he arrived; *yaool*, he arrives.

ايلولة *ailoola*, a becoming; title-deed from the Cádi, giving probate or inheritance.

آل ـ اولو *aál*, possessor, pl. *ooloo*.

آيل *aáyil*, arriving, resulting from.

اوَّل ـ تأويل *awwala*, he interpreted; *táweel*, interpretation.

اوَّل ـ اولى *awwal*, (femin.) *oola*, first, previous, before.

اوَّل البارح *awwal ambáriḥ*, day before yesterday.

الاوَّل فالاوَّل *al-awwal fal-awwal*, one by one in their order.

اوَّلاً *awwalán*, firstly.

اوَّلي or اوَّلاني *awwaliy*, or *awwalániy*, first, preliminary.

اوائل *awáyil* (pl.), first, early part.

اولئك or اولاء or اولا *oolá*, or *ooluyik*, those. [هؤلاء]

اولو *ooloo*, possessors [cf. اولياء ـ ولِيّ]

اولوِيَّة *oolooiya*, possessorship, right.

ولاية or ايالة *iyála*, or *wilaya*, government, province; guardianship.

مآل *maál*, meaning, signification, result.

اوى *awa*, he took shelter.

آوى *aáwa*, he gave shelter, received into his house.

اوِيّ or مأواة *oowiy*, or *máwát*, hospitality.

مآوي ـ مأوى *máwa*, pl. *maáwi*, place of shelter, fixed abode, domicile.

رجل بدون مأوى *rajil bidoon máwa*, a man without fixed abode; vagabond.

ابن آوى *ibn aáwa*, jackal.

اي *ai*, that is to say; i.e.

اي نعم or ايوا *ai n'am*, or *aiwá*, yes, certainly.

اَيّ *aiy*, what? which? what, which.

اَيّ من ـ اَيّ ما *aiy man*, whoever; *aiy má*, whatever.

لاَيّ *laiy*, why?

ايا *ayá*, come along!

اِيًّا كانت *aiyá kánet*, whatever it may be.

آية ـ آيات *aáya*, pl. *aáyát*, verse of Koran, a sign from heaven.

اِيًّا *iyyá*, particle prefixed to personal pronouns.

اِيَّاي - اِيَّاهُ iyyái, me; iyyáh, him.

اِيَّاكَ نعبدُ iyyák n'abodo, Thee do we worship.

اِيد aid, force, power.

اَيَّدَ ayyada, be strengthened, confirmed. [اكّد]

تأييد tá-yeed, a strengthening, confirmation.

تأييد الحكم المستأنف tá-yeed el-hukm el-mustánaf, confirmation of the sentence appealed against.

مُوَيَّد mo-ayyad, confirmed.

اَيَّار Ayyár, Syrian month of May.

اير air, penis.

ليس - اِيس aisa, there is (used only in the negative form, laisa, there is not).

اَيس ayasa, he despaired. [يأس - ييأس]

اِياس iyás, despair.

آيِس aáyis, forlorn, in despair.

مأيوس máyoos, despaired of.

اِيش شي for اَيّ aish (for aiy shay), what? what thing?

لَيش laish, for what? why? [لأيّ]

اَيضًا aidán, also, likewise. [كمان]

اِيَّل iyyal, stag.

اِيلجي elji (for Turkish elchi), ambassador.

اَيلول Ailool, Syrian month of September.

اِيلولة - اول ailoola, title-deed (see awl).

اَيّام - يوم ayyám, pl of yóm, days.

اين - من اين ain, where? min ain, whence?

في اين fi ain (fain), where?

اينما ainamá, wherever.

اِيوان eewán, saloon, hall. [ليوان]

اَيوب Ayoob, Job.

B.

ب Bé. Value = 2.

The letter p is wanting in Arabic; it was added by the Persians, thus پ, and the p sound in words derived from Persian, Turkish or European languages, is written and pronounced as b in Arabic.

ب - بدي bi (colloquial), sign of the present tense (see *biddi*).

ب bi, by, with, in, at.

بالله billahi, By God! [والله - تالله]

بمصر bi-masr, at Cairo; in Egypt.

بحقّه bi-haqqihi, with regard to him.

بموجب bi-mójib, because.

بالعكس bil-'aks, on the contrary.

ملزوم ب malzoom bi, responsible for, bound to.

امر ب amara bi, he ordered, commanded.

بسم الله bism-illahi, in the name of God.

باسم الخديوي bi-ism el-Khed'wiy, in the Khedive's name.

باب ـ أبواب *báb*, pl. *awwáb*, door, gate, chapter.

بيبان *beebán*, gates, tunnels, shafts.

بوّابة *bawwába*, large door, gate.

بوّاب *bawwáb*, doorkeeper.

بابا *Bábá* (Turkish), father, old man.

بابة *Bába*, Coptic month of October.

بابوش *báboosh* (Turkish, *pápoosh*), slippers.

بات ـ بيات *báta*, he passed the night (see *biyát*).

بادنجان *bádinján*, aubergine, eggplant.

بئر ـ آبار *beer*, pl. *abiár* (femin.), well.

بيّار *bayyár*, a professional clearer of wells.

بارود *bárood* (Turkish), gunpowder.

بارودة *bárooda*, musket. [بندقيّة]

بارة *bára* (Persian, *pára*), bit, piece, 40 paras equal one piastre, 2½d. [نصّة]

باز *báz*, drum, tom-tom.

بازار *bázár* (Persian, also *pázár*), market, bazaar. [سوق]

بأس *báas*, harm, calamity.

لا بأس *lá báas*, never mind! no matter.

باش *básh* (Turkish), head, chief.

باشي *báshi* (Turkish), its head, chief of it.

باش كاتب *básh-kátib*, chief clerk.

حكيم باشي *hakeem-báshi*, chief doctor, surgeon-major.

اون باشي *on-bashi* (Turkish), chief of ten, corporal.

يوز باشي *yooz-báshi* (Turkish), chief of a hundred, army captain.

بنك باشي *bing-báshi*, or *bin-bashi* (Turkish), chief of a thousand, major.

باش تخته *básh-takhta*, desk, chest of drawers.

باشا ـ باشاوات *báshá*, pl. *básháwát* (Pers. *páshá*), pasha, "bashaw."

باط ـ ابط *bát* (vulgarism for *ibt*), armpit, a big armful, embrace.

تحت باطك *taht bátak*, under your arm.

باع ـ بيع *bá'aa*, he sold (see *bea'*).

باع or بوع *bá'a*, or *bo'a*, fathom, stretch with both arms wide apart.

بال *bál*, heart, mind, memory.

خلّي بالك *khallee balák*, take care! keep in mind!

بالا افندي *bálá efendi*, (Persian, *bálá*, high), a civilian official corresponding in rank to our Right Hon., inferior to a *Musheer* or *Vizier*, but superior to a *Fareeq* or *Roumeli Beylerbey*.

بلاش *bálásh* (colloquial), never mind!

بالطة *bálta* (Turkish), axe, hatchet. [فأس]

بالو *bálo* (European), bale; dance, ball.

بالوظة *báloza*, pudding of sugar and starch. [فالوذق]

بامية‎ *bámia*, a small vegetable, hibiscus, or *abelmoschus esculentus*.

بان - بيان‎ *bána*, it appeared (see *beyán*).

بان‎ *bán*, weeping-willow; nut tree; *moringa*.

بتّة‎ or البتّة‎ *betta*, or *elbetta*, of course; not at all.

بتّا‎ *buttán*, for certain, decidedly. [قطعاً‎]

بتر‎ *batara*, he cut, amputated. [بطر‎]

بتع‎ or بتاع - متع‎ *bata'* (colloquialism), of (see *mata'*).

بتول‎ *batool*, Virgin Mary.

بثّ‎ *bassa*, he prompted to evil, told a secret.

بثرة‎ *basra*, pustule, carbuncle.

بحت‎ *baht*, pure in lineage.

بحث‎ *bahs*, inquiry, search for.

بحث‎ *bahasa*, he inquired after, searched for.

باحث‎ *báhasa*, he discussed.

مباحثة‎ *mobáhasa*, discussion.

مبحث‎ *mabhas*, subject of inquiry, topic.

بحر - ابحار‎ *bahr*, pl. *abhár*, ocean, sea, great river, canal; space of time.

بحر النيل‎ *bahr en-Neel*, River Nile.

بحر الأعظم‎ *bahr el-a'azam*, Nile, or greatest canal.

بحر يوسف‎ *bahr Yusuf*, canal of Joseph in Upper Egypt.

بحر الشيطان‎ *bahr esh-shaitán*, Devil's sea, mirage.

بحر الأحمر‎ *bahr el-ahmar*, Red Sea.

بحر المتوسّط‎ *bahr el-motawassit*, Mediterranean Sea.

بحر محيط‎ *bahr moheet*, surrounding ocean.

فى بحر المدّة‎ *fi bahr el-modda*, in the course of the interval.

بحرىّ‎ *bahriy*, maritime; a sailor.

الوجه البحرىّ‎ *el-wajh el-bahriy*, Lower Egypt, the part near the sea. [قبلىّ‎]

بحرية‎ *bahriya*, naval affairs; sailors.

برّىّ بحرىّ‎ *barriy-bahriy*, amphibious.

بحيرة‎ *bohaira*, lake.

بحراية‎ *bahráya*, depression, hollow place, sink.

بحيرة‎ or بحيرا‎ *bahaira* or *bohaira*, Delta of Nile as a whole; especially the N.W. province, of which Damanhoor is the capital.

بحراً و برّاً‎ *bahrán wa barrán*, by sea and land.

باحور‎ *báhoor*, dog-days; Sirius.

بحران‎ *buhrán*, crisis, delirium.

بخت‎ *bakht*, good luck.

بخيت‎ *bakheet*, lucky.

بخر‎ *bakhara*, it gave out smoke, exhaled.

بخار - أبخرة‎ *bukhár*, pl. *abkhira*, exhalation, odour, vapour.

بخور (17) بدلاً

بخور bakhoor, incense.

باخرة - بواخر bákhira, pl. bawákhir, steam-engine. [وابور]

تبخّر tabakhkhara, he perfumed or fumigated himself.

بخس bakhs, very low price, minimum price.

بخشيش bakhsheesh (Persian), gift, "tip," reward, bribe.

بخل - بخيل bokhl, avarice; bakheel, avaricious.

بدّ badda, he dispersed.

لا بدّ lá bodd, no escape, inevitably.

بدّد baddada, he squandered, made away with.

تبديد tabdeed, extravagance, misuse or misappropriation of money.

استبدّ istabadda, he became absolute, behaved like a tyrant. [استقلّ]

استبداد istibdád, absolutism, tyranny, autocracy.

استبدادي istibdádiy, tyrannical, autocratic.

مستبدّ mostabidd, tyrant, autocrat.

بدأ or ابتدأ badá, or ibtadá, he began.

بدء or بدء beda, or bedáya, a beginning.

بادي bádi, a beginning, beginner.

بادي الامر bádi el-amr, the beginning of the affair.

ابتداء ibtidá, a beginning.

ابتدائي ibtidáiy, preliminary; first instance.

محكمة ابتدائيّة mahkama ibtidáiya, court of first instance.

مبتدى mubtadi, novice, a beginner.

مبدأ - مبادئ mabda, pl. mabádi, origin, first principles.

ابدأ abdá, he created, put forth, spoke.

بدر - بدور badr, pl. bodoor, full moon. [قمر - هلال]

بدر badara, he came upon, surprised.

بادر bádara, he undertook, hastened, set about.

مبادرة mubádara, undertaking, energy.

بدارة badára, basket, market-basket.

بداري badári, chickens; i.e. early hatched. [فروج]

بيدر baidar (Syrian), threshing-floor. [جرن]

بدري badri, early.

ابدع or بدع bada'a or abda'a, he invented, started a novelty or heresy.

بدعة bida'a, innovation, heresy.

ابداع ibdá'a, invention, imagination.

بديع badee'a, strange, eccentric; rhetoric.

بدل badal, a change, exchange. [غير - عوض]

بدلاً عن or من badalán 'an or min, instead of.

بدليّة‎ badaliya, substitution; fee for exemption, e.g., from conscription.

بدلة‎ badla, change of linen, suit of clothes.

بدّل‎ baddala, he changed, exchanged, substituted. [غيّر‎]

تبديل‎ tabdeel, a causing of change or substitution; disguise.

بادل‎ or تبادل‎ bádala, or tabádala, he exchanged, interchanged.

بدال‎ or مبادلة‎ bidál, or mubádala, mutual exchange.

استبدال‎ istibdál, rotation or roster of officials on duty, change or relief of garrison or of time-expired men.

بدن - ابدان‎ badan, pl. abdán, trunk of human body, bulk.

بدانة‎ badána, corpulence.

بدني‎ badaniy, physical, corporal, corporeal.

بادنجان‎ bádinján, aubergine, egg-plant. [حدق‎]

بداهة‎ (بده‎ badah), badáha, suddenness.

بديهيّ‎ badeehiy, obvious, evident; sudden.

بدو‎ or باديه‎ badoo, or bádiya, desert, waste place.

بدوي‎ badawiy, Bedouin, desert Arab.

بدا - بجا‎ Bedá, or Bejá (Soudanese), The "To-Bedawiyet" language of the native non-arab tribes of the Eastern Soudan—Assouan, Berber, Kassala, Suakin.

ب - بدّي‎ biddi (Syrian), a colloquial unwritten expletive marking the future or present tense. This, in Egypt, is shortened into a simple b prefixed to the present tense. [see ود‎

انا بدّي اكتب‎ aná biddi aktib, I am going to write, I wish to write.

انا باكتب‎ aná biktib, I am going to write, I am writing.

بتشوف‎ bi-tashoof, you will see, you see.

بيعمل‎ bi-ya'mil, he is doing, making.

بذر‎ bazara, or badara, he sowed seed, threw down.

بذر - بذور‎ bazr, pl. bozoor, seed for sowing. [بزر‎]

بذّر‎ bazzara, he squandered, was lavish.

بذل‎ bazala, he was profuse, lavish, generous.

بذل جهده‎ bazala jahdoh, he strained every effort.

بذيّ‎ baziy, obscene.

برّ‎ birr, innocence, virtue. [برأ‎]

برّ - ابرار‎ or بارّ‎ barr, or bárr, pl. abrár, pious, virtuous.

تبرّر‎ tabarrara, he was or became pious.

برّ - برور‎ barr, pl. boroor, mainland, land.

برّا و بحرا‎ barrán wa bahrán, by land and sea.

بَرَّأ (19) بَرَاح

بَرَّا barrá, or burrá, outside, out of doors.

بَرَّانِي barrániy, foreign, an outsider, extraneous; false (money); external.

بَرِّي barriy, wild (birds, animals); of land.

بَرِّيَّة - بَرَارِي barriya, pl. barári, desert, waste land.

البَرَارِي el-barári, the waste lands near the mouth of the Delta.

بَرَأ - يَبْرُو bará, he created; yabro, he creates.

بَارِي bári (God), the Creator.

بَرِيَّة - بَرَايَا bariya, pl. baráya, creature.

بَرِئَ baria, he was innocent.

بَرَّأ barrá, he acquitted, absolved.

تَبَرَّأ tabarrá, he showed his innocence.

اِسْتَبْرَأ istabrá, he asked for exemption; abstained.

بَرَأَة baráa, innocence (see berát).

بَرَأَة سَاحَة baráa sáha, innocence of status; legal term for acquittal of a crime.

تَبرِيَة tabriya, an acquitting.

مُبَرَّأ mobarrá, acquitted.

بَرِيّ - أَبْرِيَاء bariy, pl. abriyá, innocent.

بَرَّ

بَرَأَة or بَرَاة berát (innocence). Used in Turkish for a brevet, diploma, or royal commission from the Sultan, declaring that the holder is of high character, rank, &c.

اِسْتَبْرَأ istibrá, the purification of women.

مُبَارَأَة mobárát, mutual release; divorce.

بَرْبَخ barbakh, small culvert for drainage or irrigation; aqueduct.

بَرْبَرِي - بَرَابِرَة berberiy, pl. barábra, Berberines from the Wadi Halfa district.

بَرْبَر Berber, a town on the Nile near its junction with the Atbara River.

بَرْبَرَة Berbera, a British protectorate on the Somali coast.

بِرْبَة birba (Coptic), ancient Egyptian temple.

بُرْتُقَان bortuqán, Portugal; a Seville orange.

بَرْتَمَان - مَرْطَبَان bortamán, or ma'tabán, jar, ewer.

بَرِيتُون bariton (European), peritonæum.

بُرْج - بُرُوج borj, pl. borooj, tower, "burg;" a sign or constellation of the zodiac.

مِنْطَقَة البُرُوج mintaqat el-borooj, the whole zodiac.

بُرُوج الأَفْلَاك borooj el-aflak, the signs of the zodiac.

بَرْجَل bergel (Persian pergár), compasses.

بَرَح baraha, it passed away.

البَارِح el-bárih (embárih), the day that has gone, yesterday. [أَمْسِ]

بَرَاح baráh, land not yet built upon.

برد *barada*, he felt cold; he filed.

برد *bard*, coldness, cold.

برودة *borooda*, coldness, freshness of weather.

بردة *barda*, a thick cloak.

برّادية *barrádiya*, a cooler, porous water-bottle.

بردان *bardán*, feeling cold in body.

بارد *bárid*, cold to the touch.

بريد *bareed*, official name for the postal service; express, courier; four leagues.

مبرد *mibrad*, a file.

بردعة *bard'aa*, humped donkey-saddle.

بردُهْ *bardoh* (colloquialism), also, likewise.

بردي *bardi*, cyperus papyrus.

برز *baraza*, it came in sight.

ابرز *abraza*, he showed, displayed.

بروز *borooz*, appearance, conspicuousness.

بارز *báriz*, apparent, conspicuous.

ابراز *ibráz*, a displaying.

براز ـ برازي *biráz*, sewage; *biráziy*, of sewage.

برزخ *barzakh*, isthmus; space between.

برسام *birsám*, pleurisy. [بلورة]

برسيم *barseem*, clover, green fodder.

براسيمي *baráseemiy*, seller of clover.

برش *barsh*, opium-paste for smoking; aphrodisiac.

برش *borsh*, mat of palm-leaves or fibre.

برشيد *barsheed*, clods of earth.

برشم *bursham*, wafer; soldering.

برص *baras*, leprosy, skin-disease. [جذام]

ابرص ـ برصاء *abras*, femin. *barsá*, leper.

برص *bors*, house-lizard. [سحليّة]

برطل ـ برطيل *bartala*, he bribed; *barteel*, bribe. [رشوة]

برطال *birtál* (vulgar), carrier, porter.

براعة *bará'aa*, perfection, excellence; gift.

تبرّع *tabarro'a*, free gift, generosity.

برغوث ـ براغيث *barghoot*, pl. *barágheet*, flea.

برق *baraqa*, it lightened; *barq*, lightning.

برقات *barqát*, fringe ornament of necklace.

برقع ـ براقع *borqo'a*, pl. *baráqi'a*, Egyptian woman's veil.

برقوق *barqooq*, apricot. [مشمش ـ خوخ]

برقاء مصراء *barqá misrá*, anethum graveolens.

برك *baraka*, he knelt.

برّك *barraka*, he blessed, congratulated.

بارك *báraka*, he asked God's blessing.

بروك *barook,* herd of kneeling camels.

بركة *baraka,* or (in Turkish) *bereket,* prosperity, blessing, abundance.

بركة *birka,* pool.

مبروك or مبارك *mabrook,* or *mobárak,* blessed; a euphemism for syphilis.

بركار *bergár* (Persian *pergár*), compasses.

برم *barama,* he twisted.

ابرم *abrama,* he twisted, strengthened.

نقض و ابرام *naqd wa ibrám,* "cassation."

مبرم *mubram,* strengthened; inevitable.

برام *brám,* earthen pot.

برمة *barma* (Turkish *parmaq*), spoke of wheel.

بريمة *bareema,* a twist, corkscrew, screw, gimlet.

برميل *barmeel,* barrel, cask.

برمودة *Baramooda,* Coptic month of April.

برمهات *Barmahát,* Coptic month of March.

برنس *burnus,* burnouse, cloak.

برنيطة *bornaita,* hat.

برنوف *barnoof, conyza dioscordis.*

برهة *borha,* moment, a unit of time.

برهن *barhana,* he demonstrated.

برهان - براهين *burhán,* pl. *baráheen,* argument, demonstration. [دليل]

برواز *barwáz* (Persian *perwáz*), cornice, frame.

برى *bara,* he cut a pen, whittled.

مبراء *mibrá,* pen-knife. [مطوة]

بروتستو *brotesto* (European), a legal protest.

بزّ - ابزاز or بزاز *bizz,* pl. *abzáz* or *bizáz,* teat, breast.

بزّ - بزوز *bezz,* pl. *bozooz,* cloth.

بزر *bazara,* the seed sprouted.

بزر - بزور *bizr,* pl. *bozoor,* seed for sowing.

مبزور *mabzoor,* sprouted, a growing crop.

بزق or بصق *bazaqa* or *basaqa,* he spat. [تفل]

بزلية or بسيلة *bezeliya,* green peas.

بزيم or ابزيم *bizeem* or *abzeem,* buckle, hasp.

بس *bes,* enough; that will do; that is all.

بستان - بساتين *bostán,* pl. *basátern,* park, orchard. [جنينة]

بستنجي *bostánji* (Turkish), gardener.

بستيناج *bastináj, ammi visnago; tribulus terrestris.*

باسور - بواسير *básoor,* pl. *bawáseer,* piles, hæmorrhoids.

بسط *basata,* he spread out.

انبسط *inbasata,* it was spread out, he was glad, amused himself.

مبسوط *mabsoot,* glad, spread out.

انبساط *inbisát,* gladness.

بساط ـ بسط *bisát*, pl. *bosot*, carpet, rug.

بسطة *basta*, a landing on the stairs.

بسيط ـ بساطة *baseet*, simple, easy; *basáta*, simplicity.

باسل *básil*, good, pretty good, indifferent.

بسالة *basála*, courage.

بزلية or بسيلة *bascela*, green peas.

بسم الله *bism-illahi*, in the name of God.

البسملة *el-bismila*, the phrase "*bism-illahi*."

بسم or تبسّم *basama*, or *tabassama*, he smiled.

بشاشة *basháshα*, cordiality.

بشر *bashara*, he skinned, peeled.

بشرة *bashara*, epidermis.

بشريّ *bashariy*, epidermic.

بشر *bashar*, the human race.

بشريّ *bashariy*, human.

بشارة *bishára*, good news; the Gospel.

بشر *bashara*, he rejoiced.

بشّر *bashshara*, he announced good news; he announced the rising of the Nile.

تبشير *tabsheer*, preaching the Gospel; announcement of good news.

تبشير النيل *tabsheer en-Neel*, announcement of the rising of the Nile.

بشير *basheer*, evangelist.

باشر *báshara*, he undertook, set about.

مباشرة *mobáshara*, an undertaking.

مباشرةً *mobásharatán*, direct, without intermediary.

تباشير *tabásheer*, good news; (Turkish) chalk.

بشقة *bashqa* (Turkish), other, different.

بشين *basheen* (Persian, *pesheen*), ready-money, cash.

بشنس *Bashans*, Coptic month of May.

بشنين *bashneen*, *nymphæa lotus* or *cærulea*.

بصّ *bassa*, it shone, glowed.

بصّة *bassa*, a live coal.

بصّاص *bassás*, eye; spy.

بصبص *basbasa*, he courted, flirted; looked for, searched.

بصر *basara*, he saw, perceived.

بصر ـ ابصار *basar*, pl. *absár*, eye, sight.

كفيف البصر *Kafeef el-basar*, blind, almost blind.

ابصارای *absár ai* (colloquial), "and what not," "etcetera," "and so on."

باصرة *básira*, the eye.

بصيرة *baseera*, intelligence, perceptive faculty.

بصرة *Basra*, the town of Basra or Bussörah.

بصق or بزق *basaqa*, or *bazaqa*, he spat.

بصاق *busáq*, spittle.

بصل ‒ بصلة *basal*, onions, bulbs; *basala*, an onion, bulb.

بصم ‒ باصمق *basama* (Turkish *basmaq*, to stamp), he stamped his seal on, imprinted.

بصمة *basma*, imprint of a seal.

مبصوم *mabsoom*, stamped, imprinted.

بضع *bada'a*, he cut into pieces.

بضعة *bida'a*, some, a few pieces, a share.

بضاعة ‒ بضائع *bidáa'a*, pl. *badáy'a*, goods, merchandise. [امتعة]

ظروف البضائع و اوعية *zoroof el-bidáya' wa awa'ya*, "tare" of weight, i.e. the cases and vessels containing goods.

بط *batta*, he flattened; flat.

مبطط *mobattat*, made flat, flattened, flat.

بطة *batta*, wild duck.

بطيء ‒ بطاء *bati*, slow; *bitá*, slowness.

بطح *bataha*, he threw (a man) face downwards.

انبطح *inbataha*, he lay prostrate on his face. [see سلقى]

بطيخ or بطيّخ *bateekh*, water-melon.

بطر *batara*, he lanced an abscess, &c.

بيطار ‒ بياطرة *baitár*, pl. *bayátara*, veterinary surgeon.

حكيم بيطري *hakeem baitariy*, veterinary surgeon.

بطرخ *batrakh*, dry roes of fish.

بطريرك *batriark* (Greek), Patriarch, Archbishop.

بطش به *batasha bihi*, he persecuted him.

بطش *batsh*, courage, strength; attack, violence.

بطاطس *batátas*, (English) potatoes.

بطل *batala*, it was in vain, futile, null.

بطل *botila*, it was spoiled, annulled.

بطلان *butlán*, nullity, voidness.

بطّل or ابطل *battala*, or *abtala*, he annulled.

تبطيل or ابطال *tabteel*, or *ibtál*, an annulling, nullification.

باطل *bátil*, null, void.

بطّال *battál*, bad, useless, altogether void.

بطل *batala*, he was out of work.

بطالة *batála*, idleness, vacation.

بطل *batola*, he was brave.

بطولة *botoola*, heroism.

بطل or بطّال *battál*, hero.

من الابطال *min el-abtála*, one of heroes, a hero.

بطن ‒ بطون *batn*, pl. *botoon*, belly, womb, hold or hull of a ship; interior; section of an Arab tribe.

باطن *bátin*, internal.

بطيني *bateeniy*, glutton.

بطين *buteen*, corpulent.

بطانة *batána*, lining of clothes.

بطانية ‒ بطانيات or بطاطين *batániya*, pl. *batániyát*, or *batáteen*, blanket.

بظر or بيظر *bazar*, or *baizar*, clitoris.

بعبص *ba'basa*, he tickled, used his finger.

بقل (21) بعبع

بعبع boa'bou', bugbear, "bogey."
بعث ب ba'ta bi, he sent, caused.
باعث bá'yis, sender, cause. [سبب - حامل]
مبعوث maba'oos, person or thing sent, envoy.
بعد ba'd, after.
بعداً ba'dan, or ba'dain, afterwards.
بعد bo'od, distance.
بعيد ba'yeed, far, distant.
باعد or تباعد bá'ada, or tabá'ada, he kept himself apart, separated from.
ابعد aba'da, he kept it apart, distant.
ابعاد ibá'ad, a keeping (something) apart.
ابعادية ibá'ádiya, or aba'ádiya, a parcel of land "kept apart" from the land-survey, i.e. unregistered (originally) and free from taxation (1829); *now it means a country-house or estate, large farm.*
استبعاد istiba'ád, a being far from; distance from; a rejecting.
بعير - بعران ba'yeer, pl. bo'rán, camel. [قاعود - جمل]
بعض ba'd, a portion, some; a certain one.
بعض الأيام ba'd el-ayyám, a certain day.
مع بعض ma' ba'd, with one another, mutually.
بعضنا بعضاً ba'dná ba'dán, one another (of us).

بعضهم بعضاً ba'dhom ba'dán, one another (of them).
بعضهم على بعض ba'dhom 'ala ba'din, one over the other (of them).
بعل ba'l, husband, spouse.
بغتةً baghtatán, suddenly. [فجاةً]
بغجوانجي bagjawánji (Persian bágchawán), gardener.
بغداد Baghdád, town of Baghdád.
بوغاز bóghaz (Turkish), throat, strait, channel.
بغض baghada, he hated; boghd, hatred.
بغل - بغال baghl, pl. bighál, mule.
بغغال baghghál, muleteer.
بغى bagha, he desired, oppressed.
ينبغي yanbaghi, it is necessary, essential.
بغي baghi, iniquity.
بغية baghiya, aim, desire.
باغي - بغاة bághi, pl. boghát, wicked, tyrant.
بفتة - بافتة bafta (Persian báfta), woven; cloth, white cloth.
بق baqq, lice.
بوقجة or بغجة boqja (Turkish boqcha), bundle.
بقدونس baqdonos, parsley.
بقر baqar, cattle, kine.
بقرة - ثور baqara, cow; tór, bull.
لحم بقري lahm baqariy, beef.
بقعة boqa'a, stain, patch, piece of land; a district in Syria.
بقل - بقول baql, pl. boqool, germ, sprout, vegetation.

rocer.
(Turkish), a sort of
 lette."
ad-beans.
large boat, barge,
 ngalow."
d dye from wood;
 wood.
 ia, it remained, re-
r; yabqa, it remains.
tion, survival; how-

'-baqá, Heaven, land

emaining, balance,
 e Eternal God.
 aqiya, pl. baqáyá,
 rplus.
made endure, per-

remained, remained

Bey (Persian Beg;
en in Arabic as
Colonel; a civilian
 e rank as Colonel.
 hree ranks of Beys:
ayiz, " selected;"
a second rank, or
 olonel; (3) Sálisa,
or Qáyim-maqám,
Colonel.
rose early.
ukra, or bákir, to-
 wn of to-morrow.
 rly in the morning.

بكرة باكراً bukra bákirán, early to-morrow.

باكورة bákoora, first-fruits.

بكر ـ ابكار bikr, pl. abkár, virgin; first-born.

بكارة bakára, virginity; hymen.

بكريّة bikriya, primogeniture.

بكرة bakra, pulley.

بكرج bakraj (Turkish), pail; coffee-pot; especially a pot with a lid.

بكم bakam, dumbness.

ابكم ـ بكماء abkam, fem. bakmá, dumb.

بكى ـ يبكي baka, or biki, he wept; yibki, he weeps.

بكاء buká, a weeping, tears.

باكي ـ بكاة báki, pl. bokát, a weeper, mourner.

بل bel, but, on the contrary.

بلي beli, yes, certainly.

بلّ balla, he wetted, moistened.

مبلول mablool, wetted, wet, soaked.

بلّانة balllána, a bath-woman, masseuse.

بلابل balábil, anxiety.

بلبل ـ بلابل bulbul, pl. balábil (Persian), nightingale. [عندليب

بلح balah, fresh dates. [رطب

بليخاء bolaikha, luteola tinctoria.

بلد ـ بلاد or بلدان balad, pl. bilád, or buldán, village, town, country.

بلدة balda, a village.

بلدي baladiy, native, rustic; municipal.

E

دائرة بلديّة *dáyira baladiya*, municipality.

بلديّاتك *baladiyátak*, thy compatriots, fellow-townsmen or villagers.

بليد *baleed*, clown, rustic, stupid.

بلادة *baláda*, stupidity, rusticity.

بلّور *balloor* (*bannoor*), crystal, glass.

بلسم *balsam*, balsam, balm.

بلسان *balasán*, balsamodendron, opobalsamum.

بلّاصي *bullásiy*, a species of earthenware jars made at *Ballás* in Upper Egypt.

بلّاص - بلاليص *ballás*, pl. *balálees*, same as *ballásiy*.

بلاط or بلطة *balta*, or *balát*, piece of rock; paving-stone.

بالطة or بلطة *balta* (Turkish), axe, hatchet. [فأس

بلّط *ballata*, he paved; (vulgarism) he stopped work, cheated; (the boat) ran aground.

بلّط عليك *ballata 'aleik*, he has cheated you, kept back a deposit from you.

تبليط *tableet*, a paving; pavement; cessation from work.

بلّوط *balloot*, oak-tree; acorn.

or ابتلع بلع *bala'a*, or *ibtala'a*, he swallowed.

بالوع - بواليع *búlooa'*, pl. *bawáleea'*, sewer, sink, drain.

بلعوم *bola'oom*, œsophagus, pharynx.

بلغ *balagha*, it reached, became adult, ripened.

بلغني *balaghani*, it reached me, I heard of.

بلّغ *ballagha*, he made reach, informed.

بالغ *bálagha*, he exaggerated.

بلوغ *boloogh*, a reaching, arrival at; puberty, a becoming adult or ripe.

بالغ *báligh*, adult. [minor = قاصر]

بلاغ *balágh*, information, letter, news; petition.

تبليغات *tableeghát*, information, news.

مبلّغ *moballigh*, informant.

مبالغة *mobálagha*, exaggeration.

مبلغ - مبالغ *mablagh*, pl. *mabáligh*, amount, sum of money.

بلاغة *balágha*, eloquence, rhetoric.

بليغ *baleegh*, eloquent; severe; effective.

جرح بليغ *jorh baleegh*, a severe wound.

بلغة *balgha*, or *bolgha*, native yellow shoes.

بلغم *balgham*, phlegm.

بلق - ابلق *balaq*, piebaldness; *ablaq*, piebald.

بلكي or بلكِ *belki* (Persian), perhaps. [ربما]

بلاهة *baláha*, stupidity; *naïveté*.

ابله *ablah*, stupid, *naïf*.

بلوراوي - بلورة *bloora* and *blooráwiy* (European), pleura, pleurisy.

[برسام]

بلي *balia*, it became worn out, used up.

بالى *bála*, he was anxious, took thought.

ابتلى *ibtala*, he afflicted.

بلوى or بلاء *belá*, or *balwa*, affliction, calamity.

بلايا - بليّة *baliya*, pl. *baláyá*, calamity, disaster.

بلية *baliya* (colloquial), lazy.

رجل بلية *rajil baliya*, a lazy man, good for nothing.

مبالاة *mobálát*, anxiety.

مبتلى *mubtala*, afflicted, insane, a prey to.

بالي *báli*, worn out (dress, tool, &c.).

بنّ *bunn*, coffee-berry.

بنج *binj*, "bang," a soporific, *jusquiame*.

بنجر *banjar* (Turkish), beet-root.

بنود - بند *band*, pl. *bonood* (Persian), paragraph, article, section; aqueduct, reservoir.

بندر *bandar* (Persian), town, seaport, wharf.

شهبندر *shahbandar* (Persian), a Turkish Consul. [قنصل]

بنديرة *bandiera* (Italian), flag. [راية - علم]

فندق or بندق *bunduq*, or *funduq* (Turkish), nuts.

بندق *bunduq*, Venedig, Venice.

بنادق - بندقيّة *bunduqiya*, pl. *banádiq*, Venetian; gun, rifle, which came to the East, perhaps originally, from Venice.

بنش *binish* (Turkish), robe, loose gown.

بنصر *bansar*, third or ring-finger. [خنصر]

بنفسج *banafsaj*, violet flower or colour.

بنوكة - بنك *bank*, pl. *bonooka* (European), money bank, banking establishment.

بنك *bing*, or *bin* (Turkish), thousand.

بنكباشي *bing-báshi*, or *bin-báshi* (Turkish), major, chief of a thousand.

بنى - يبنى *bana*, he built; *yabni*, he builds.

بناء - ابنية *biná*, pl. *abniya*, edifice, a building.

بناءً عليه *bináán 'aleih*, founded on that, for that reason, therefore.

بناية or بنيان *bináya*, or *bonyán*, construction; a building.

بنية *binya*, build of human body.

قوي البنية *qawiy el-binya*, a man of strong build.

مبنيّ *mabniy*, built, founded upon; an indeclinable noun.

بنية *bonia* (French *poing, poignet*), fist, wrist; a blow.

انبنى على *inbana 'ala*, it was founded upon.

بنّاء *banná*, builder, mason.

بَنَّاء حُر bunná horr, freemason.

بَنِيان banián, Hindoo trader.

تَبَنَّى tabanna, he adopted a son.

اِبن or بِن bin, or ibn, son.

بَنِي or بَنُون or اَبناء abná, or banoon, or beni, sons.

بَنات ـ بِنت or اِبنة ibna, or bint, pl. banát, daughter, girl.

بَنَوِيّ banawiy, filial.

بَنِي سُوِيف Beni Suoef (for Beni Yusuf), children of Joseph; a province and town in upper Egypt.

اِبن آوى ibn áwa, jackal.

اِبن عِرس ibn 'irs, weasel. [عِرسَة]

بَنات نَعش banát n'ash, the constellations of the Great and Little Bear; a star in the Great Bear.

عِنب بَناتِي 'anab banátiy, pipless grapes.

بَنَّانِي bannáni, pigeon-house. [برج حمام]

بَنها ـ قَلِيوبِيَّة Benha, a town in Lower Egypt, capital of the Calioubiya province.

بُهت or بُهتان baht, or bohtán, lie, slander.

بَاهِت báhit, pale, wan.

بَهاتة baháta, pallor, anæmia.

بَهجة bahja, gaiety, jollity, buxomness.

اِبتَهَجَ ibtahaja, he was gay, jolly.

بَهدَل bahdala, he shook, ill-treated, used violence.

بَهار bahár, spice, condiment.

اَبهَر abhar, artery; aorta. [شِريان]

بَاهِر báhir, evident, bright, beautiful.

بُهظ bahz, heaviness, seriousness.

بَاهِظ báhiz, a serious or important matter; improper (conduct).

بَهَق or بَياق bihaq, dartre; vitiligo, leprosy.

بَهلول bahlool, idiotic, foolish, silly.

بَهلَوان bahlawán (Persian pehleván), athlete, gymnast, acrobat.

بَهامة baháma, stupor.

اَبهَمَ abhama, he hid, left vague or dubious.

اِبهام ibhám, doubt, incertitude.

مُبهَم mubham, left vague, doubtful, hidden.

اِبهام or باهِم ibhám, or báhim, thumb, great toe.

اَبهَم abham, inarticulate beast, dumb animal.

بَهِيمة ـ بَهَائِم baheema, pl. baháyim, beast, cattle, "behemoth." [مَواشِي]

بَها bahá, beauty, brilliancy.

بَهِيّ bahee, beautiful, bright.

بَوَّاب ـ بَوَّابِين bawwáb, door-keeper (see báb).

بَوح bóh, an appearing.

اَباحَ abáha, he permitted, made lawful.

اباحة *ibáha*, permission, licence. [اجازة]

مباح *mobáh*, lawful, allowed; free (land).

باحة *báha*, a courtyard. [ساحة]

بوخ - بائخ *bōkh*, rottenness; *báyikh*, vile, stinking.

تزوير بائخ *tazweer báyikh*, foul perjury or forgery.

بور *bōr*, waste land, ruin.

بور صالح *bōr sálih*, waste, but fit for cultivation.

بائر *báyir*, waste, uncultivated, worthless.

بوار *bawár*, loss, ruin.

باورة or بَوْرَة *bawara* (English), bower anchor.

بورت سعيد *Bort Sa'eed*, Port Said.

بوري *boori* (Turkish), trumpet.

بوروزن *boroozan* (Turkish), trumpeter.

بوزة or بوظة *booza*, native beer, beer-shop; reeds.

بوز *booz* (Turkish), ice.

بوز *bōz*, muzzle, or jowl of animal.

بَوَّز - بوزمق *bawwaza* (Turkish *bozmaq*), he spoilt.

بوسة or بوس *boos*, or *boosa*, a kiss.

باس - يبوس *bása*, he kissed; *yaboos*, he kisses.

بوصة or بوسة *boosa* (French, "pouce"), inch.

بوسطه or بوسته *bosta* (European), post-office, post.

بوش *bosh* (Turkish), empty, nonsense, "bosh."

بوش - اوباش *bōsh*, pl. *owbásh*, mob, ruffians.

بوص *boos*, reeds, thatch.

بوزة or بوظة *booza*, native beer, beer-shop; reeds for seating chairs.

بوع or باع *bou'*, or *báa'*, fathom, a stretch with both arms wide apart.

بوق - ابواق *booq*, pl. *abwáq*, trumpet, horn.

بواكي *bawáki*, colonnade, arches.

بول *bōl*, urine.

بال or تبول *bála*, or *tabawwala*, he pissed.

مبولة *mibwala*, urinal.

بول سكّريّ *bōl sukkariy*, diabetes.

بولاد *boolád*, steel. [صلب]

بوليس *bolees* (European), the police.

عسكريّ البوليس *'askariy el-bolees*, a policeman.

بوليصة *boleesa* (European), a policy, bill of lading.

بولوك *bolook* (Turkish), company, squadron.

بولوك اميني *bolook ameeni* (Turkish), quarter-master. [صرل]

بومة - بوم *booma*, pl. *boom*, owl.

بؤونة *Ba-ona*, or *Ba-oona*, Coptic month of June.

بوه or باه *booh*, or *báh*, copulation.

بویة or بویا *boya* (Turkish *boyá*), paint, varnish, blacking.

بوياجي boyáji, shoe-black.
بيات biyát, a passing the night.
مبيت mabeet, night's lodging.
بات ـ يبيت báta, he passed the night; yabeet, he passes the night.
بيت ـ بيوت bait, pl. boyoot, house; recess, pigeon-hole; couplet of verses.
ابيات abyát, couplets of verses.
بيت العنكبوت bait el-'ankaboot, spider's web.
بيت الما bait el-má, water-closet.
بيت المال ـ مالية bait el-mál, sacred Moslem treasury for religious legal matters, such as inheritance; as distinct from the Máliya, or Finance.
بيد or بيت beet, or beed, or baid, ruin, dilapidation.
بد بيد bád beed, a bad part of the bank of the Nile or a canal; the danger of scouring; whirlpool.
روست بيد rost beed, a reserve bank, behind the threatened bank of a river; a reserve, extra, a substitute. [تحويلة]
بيادة biyáda (Persian piyáda), infantry.
بيراق bairáq (Turkish), banner, flag.
بيرة beera (European), beer.
بيش beesh, aconite; a hole dug.
بياض bayád, whiteness, white of eye, or of egg.

ابيض ـ بيضاً abyad, femin. baidá, white.
بيض baid, or beed, pl., white people or things.
بيّض bayyada, he whitened, whitewashed; wrote out a clean copy. [سوّد]
مبيّض mobayyid, copying clerk.
باضت bádet, (the hen) laid an egg.
بيضة ـ بيض baida, pl. baid, egg.
بيضيّ ـ مبيض baidiy, oval; mabeed, ovary.
بيطار ـ بطر baitár, veterinary surgeon (see batara).
بيع beea', or baia', sale.
بيع منعقد beea' mona'qid, complete or perfect sale.
بيع صحيح or جائز beea' saheeh, or jáyiz, valid or lawful sale.
بيع فاسد or باطل beea' fasid, or bátil, defective or invalid sale.
بيع بات beea' bátt, definite sale.
بيع قهريّ beea' qahriy, forced sale, distraint.
بيع الوفاء beea' el-wafá, "vente à réméré," "pacte de rachat," sale with option of re-purchase within five years; a species of mortgage or pledge.
بيع بالاستغلال beea' bil-istighlál, a "vente à réméré," in which the seller (pledger) retains the enjoyment of the thing sold (pledged).
باع ـ يبيع báa'a, he sold; yabeea' he sells.

انباع *inbáa'a*, it was sold.

بائع ـ بيّاع *báya'*, seller; *bayyáa'*, professional seller, tradesman.

بيعة *beea'a*, ancient name for a synagogue or church.

مباع *mobáa'*, sold.

مبيع *mabeea'*, sale; place of sale.

لمبيع *li-mabeea'*, for sale.

مبايعة *mobáya'a*, sale; contract of sale.

بيك ـ بك *baik*, a Bey, Colonel (see *Bey*).

بيمارستان or مارستان *beemáristán*, and *máristán* (Persian), hospital, asylum.

بيان *beyán*, declaration, a showing; eloquence.

بان ـ يبين *bána*, it was separated; was clear; *yabeen*, it is separated, is clear.

بيّن *bayyana*, he showed, proved, made clear.

تبيّن *tabayyana*, it was evident, was proved.

استبان *istabána*, it became clear.

ابان *abána*, he showed; it was clear.

باين or تباين *báyana*, or *tabáyana*, it was different, distinct from, it differed.

بين *bain*, separation, space between; between.

مابين *má-bain*, that which is between.

بينما *bainamá*, while that, during.

بيّن or بائن *báyin*, or *bayyin*, clear, evident.

بيّن *bayyin*, a witness. [شاهد]

بيّنة ـ بيّنات *bayyina*, pl. *bayyinát*, clear proof. [اثبات]

باين *báyin*, irrevocable divorce, a divorced woman.

تبييـن *tabyeen*, demonstration, a proving.

مبيـن *mobeen*, showing; clear, evident.

مبيّن *mobayyin*, showing, proving.

مباين *mobáyin*, distinct, separate.

T.

ت *Té*. Value = 400.

ت ـ تعال *ti*, come thou! (see *ta'ála*.)

ت ـ تاللّٰهِ *tillahi*. By God! [واللّٰهِ ـ باللّٰهِ]

تاب ـ توبة *tába*, he repented (see *tōba*).

تابوت *táboot*, wooden trough; a kind of *sáqiya*, or water-wheel; coffin, tomb.

تتار *tátár* (Turkish), Tartar, courier.

تاج ـ توّج *taj*, crown (see *tawwaja*).

تار *tár*, small drum, tambourine.

تارة ـ تارة *tára*, once, a time; *táratán*, at times.

تاريخ ـ ارّخ *táreekh*, date, time when (see *arrakha*).

تازة *táza* (Persian), fresh, new.

تاية *táya*, reeds, rushes. [خص]

تَيِه - تَاهَ *táyih*, gone astray (see *tih*).

تَأْم *táma*, he was born a twin.

تَوْأَم - تَوْأَمَان *tawám*, twin; *tawámán*, twins.

تِبْت *tibet*, a kind of cloth.

تَبَار *tabár*, ruin.

تَبَاشِير *tabásheer* (Turkish), chalk.

تَبَع or تَابِع or اتَّبَع *taba'a*, or *tába'a*, or *ittaba'a*, he followed; was subject to, dependent, conformable.

اتْبَع *atba'a*, he made follow, sent in pursuit.

تَتَابَع *tatába'a*, it was consecutive. [تَتَالَى]

تَبَع - اتْبَاع *taba'*, pl. *atbá'a*, result, belongings.

تَابِع or تَبَّاع - تَبَعَة *tábia'*, pl. *tubbá'a*, or *taba'a*, follower, servant, dependent, subject, annexe.

تَابِعَة - تَوَابِع *tábia'a*, pl. *tawábia'*, result, dependent.

تَبَعِيَّة *taba'iya*, allegiance, nationality.

مَتْبُوع *matbooa'*, king, master, he who is obeyed.

مُتَتَابِع *mutatábia'*, consecutive.

تِبْن *tibn*, chopped or threshed straw.

تَبَّانَة *tabbána*, straw-market; sellers of straw.

تَجَرَ - يَتْجُر *tajara*, he traded; *yatjor*, he trades.

تِجَارَة *tijára*, trade, commerce.

تِجَارِي *tijáriy*, commercial.

تَاجِر - تُجَّار *tájir*, pl. *tujjár*, trader, merchant.

سِرْتُجَّار *sir tujjár*, President of guild of merchants.

مَتْجَر *matjar*, trade; merchandise, subject of trade.

اصْطِلَاح تِجَارِي *istiláh tijáriy*, usage of trade, a trade custom.

تُجَاه - وَجْه *tujáh*, in front of (see *wajh*).

اتِّجَاه - وَجْه *ittijáh*, a turning toward (see *wajh*).

تَحْت *taht*, under, underneath, downstairs.

تَحْتَانِي *tahtániy*, lower, inferior, underside.

تُحْفَة - تُحَف *tohfa*, pl. *tohaf*, a gift, rarity.

تَحَف *tohaf*, (in Turkish) funny, strange.

اتْحَف *at-hafa*, he bestowed.

تَخْت *takht* (Persian), throne, sofa.

تَخْتَة *takhta* (Persian), plank. [لَوْح]

تَخْتَه بوش *takhta-bosh* (Turkish), hollow planking, scaffolding, shop-counter.

تَخْتَه روان *takhta-rawán* (Persian), a palanquin for women carried by two camels one in front of the other.

تَخْم - تُخُوم *tokhm*, pl. *tokhoom*, limit, frontier, boundary. [حَدّ]

تُخْمَة *tokhma*, indigestion. [هَضْم]

تراب ـ اتربة‎ *toráb*, pl. *atriba*, mould, soil, earth, dust.

ترابيّة‎ *torábiya*, grave-diggers; navvies.

ترب ـ تربة‎ *torba*, pl. *torab*, grave, tomb. [قبر]

ترباس‎ *terbás*, bolt of a door. [ضبّة]

ترجم‎ *tarjama*, he translated, interpreted.

ترجمة‎ *tarjama*, translation; biography.

ترجمان‎ *tarjumán*, dragoman.

مترجم‎ *mutarjim*, translator, interpreter.

مترجم‎ *mutarjam*, translated.

ترازي‎ *tarázi* (Persian), scales, balance. [ميزان]

ترس ـ اتراس‎ *turs*, pl. *atrás*, round buckler; *tirs*, a wooden cogged wheel of *sáqiya*.

مترس ـ متارس‎ *mitras*, pl. *matáris*, rampart, trenches.

تراس‎ *tarrás*, one who lets donkeys on hire as beasts of burden.

عرس و ترس‎ *'aras wa taras*, a term of abuse. [معرّس]

ترسانه ـ دار الصناعة‎ *tersána* [originally the Arabic phrase *dár es-sanáa'a*, which passed into Europe and became *tersana* and *darse*, and has returned as an apparently Italian word], dockyard, arsenal.

ترع ـ ترعة‎ *tira'a*, pl. *tora'*, canal. [رَيَّة]

تارع ـ توارع‎ *tária'*, pl. *tawária'*, cadastre; the ordnance survey.

ترفة‎ *tirfa*, a delicacy, early fruit or vegetables.

ترقوة‎ *tarqoa*, clavicle, collar-bone.

ترك ـ اتراك‎ *turk*, pl. *atrák*, used in *Arabic* to signify Turk; but the *Turks* only apply the word to Turkish peasants or Turcoman Nomads, and call themselves Ottomans, *'Osmánli*. [عثمانلي]

تركيّ‎ *turkiy*, Turkish.

ترك‎ *taraka*, he abandoned, let go.

ترك‎ *tark*, abandonment.

تارك‎ *táraka*, he left alone (mutually); made a truce.

متاركة‎ *mutáraka*, truce, mutual concession.

متروك‎ *matrook*, abandoned.

تركة‎ *tarika*, legacy, inheritance. [ميراث]

ترمس‎ *tirmis*, lupin, *lupinus termis*.

ترنج‎ *turunj*, large lemon. [ليمون]

ترياق‎ *tiryáq*, (Greek), antidote, electuary; ancient elixir.

تسع‎ *tosa'*, one-ninth part.

تسع ـ تسعة‎ *tisa'a*, femin. *tisa'*, nine.

تسعون‎ or تسعين‎ *tisa'oon*, or *tisa'een*, ninety.

تاسع‎ *tásia'*, the ninth in order.

F

يوم تاسوعاً *yom tásooa'á*, ninth day of Moharram.

تشرين *Teshreen*, Teshreen I. and II., Syrian months of October and November.

تشري *Tishri*, Jewish month of September.

تعب *ta'iba*, he was tired.

اتعب *ata'ba*, he made tired, wearied, bored.

تعب ـ اتعاب *ta'ab*, pl. *ata'áb*, fatigue.

اتعاب *ata'áb*, a polite word for the fees of a professional man, lawyer, doctor, &c.

تعبان *ta'bán*, tired. [snake = ثعبان

متعب ـ متاعب *mata'b*, pl. *mata'yib*, annoyance.

تعس or تعاسة *ta's*, or *ta'ása*, ruin, upset, muddle.

تعالى ـ الله تعالى ـ علا *ta'ála*, in the phrase *Allah ta'ála*, God ! how great He is ! (see *a'lá*).

تعال ـ تَ ـ اتى *ta'ála*, come thou ! for the imperative *ti* of *ata*, he came.

تف *taffa*, he spat.

تفل *tafala*, he spat.

تفاح *toffáh*, apple, apple-tree.

تقن *tiqn*, nature ; intelligent.

اتقن *atqana*, he perfected, made solid.

اتقان *itqán*, perfection, solidity.

متقن *mutqan*, perfected, perfect, solid.

تقى or تقوى ـ وقى *toqa*, or *taqwa*, piety, fear of God (see *waqa*).

تقيّ *taqiy*, pious, God-fearing.

تقاوى *taqáwi* (Coptic ?) seed corn.

تقى *taqqa* (provincial), he sowed seed.

طقية or تقية *taqiya*, small cotton cap worn under the turban.

تكة or تكيّة *teké*, or *tekiyé* (Turkish), dervish monastery or asylum.

تكة or دكّة *tikka*, or *dikka*, waistband ; string for fastening skirt or drawers.

تكرورىّ ـ تكارنة *takrooriy*, pl. *takárna*, Black or negro pilgrims from Central Soudan.

تكملة ـ كمال *takmila*, complement (see *kamál*).

تكوين ـ كون *takween*, Genesis (see *kōn*).

تل تلال *tell*, pl. *tilál*, hill, mound. [كوم]

التلّ الكبير *et-tell el-kabeer*, the Great Hill, on the edge of the desert, E. of Zagazig ; battlefield of 13th September, 1882.

تلد ـ تليد or تلد ـ ولد *teled*, or *teleed*, birthright (see *waluda*).

تلد ـ ولد *talid*, she bears a child (see *waluda*).

تلف *talifa*, it perished. [هلك]

تلف   (85)   تنّور

تلف *talaf*, ruin, waste, destruction.

تلفيّات *talafiyát*, losses in battle, or from fire, &c.

اتلف *atlafa*, he ruined, destroyed.

تالفة ـ توالف *tálifa*, pl. *tawálif*, waste lands. [بور]

تلقاء ـ لقي *tilqá*, in front of (see *laqia*).

من تلقاء نفسه *min tilqá nafsihi*, of his own accord or right.

تلك ـ ذلك *tilk*, femin. of *zalik*, that.

تلميذ ـ تلاميذة *talmeez*, pl. *talámiza*, pupil, disciple.

تلا ـ يتلو *talá*, he read aloud; *yatloo*, he reads aloud.

تلاوة *tiláwa*, a reading aloud.

تلي *tolia*, it was read aloud.

تلا *talá*, it followed, came next.

تالي *táli*, the next, the following.

اليوم التالي *el-yōm et-táli*, the next day.

تتالى *tatála*, it was consecutive. [تتابع]

متتالي *mutatáli*, consecutive. [متوالي]

تمّ *tamma*, it was complete, came to an end.

تمّم or اتمّ *tammama*, or *atamma*, he completed.

تتميم or اتمام *tatmeem*, or *itmám*, a making complete.

تتميمة *tatmeema*, amulet; complement.

تمام *tamám*, all right! complete, completeness; geometrical complement.

بالتمام *bit-tamám*, completely.

تامّ *támm*, complete, entire.

تمثال ـ مثل *timsál*, image, statue (see *misl*).

تمر ـ تمور *tamr*, pl. *tomoor*, dry date. [cf. ثمر]

تمر هندي *tamr hindiy*, tamarind.

تمّوز *tammooz*, Syrian month of July.

تمساح *timsáh*, crocodile, hypocrite; name of a lake in Suez Canal.

تماشى ـ مشى *tamáshá*, promenade, sight-seeing (see *masha*).

تمغة or دمغة *tamgha* (Turkish), often written and usually pronounced *damgha*; official stamp; bill stamp.

ورق تمغة *waraq damgha*, stamped paper for petitions and official documents.

تمل *tamal* (Turkish ?), basis, permanence.

تمللي *tamalli* (Turkish), always, constantly.

تنبورة *tanboora*, lute, guitar.

تنبك or تنبك *tunbak* (Persian), tobacco; Persian leaf tobacco for narghilehs.

تنبل *tanbal* (Turkish), idle, lazy.

تنّور *tannoor* (sometimes pronounced *tandur*), brazier, oven; mutton cooked in the oven.

تَنَكَة *tanaka* (Turkish), tin-ware; metal pot.

تَنْوِين - نون *tanween*, the final sound of *n* (see *noon*).

تَهْلِكَة - هلك *tahlika*, danger, ruin (see *halaka*).

تَهَامَة *Tahāma*, lowland coast of Arabia.

تُهْمَة - وهم *tuhma*, accusation (see *wahama*).

اتَّهَم or اتْهَم *at-hama*, or *ittahama*, he prosecuted or accused before a criminal court.

اتِّهَام *ittihám*, indictment, an accusing.

مُتَّهَم or مُتْهَم *muttaham* or *mut-ham*, the accused man, prisoner at the bar.

تَوًّا *tawwá*, now, simply, merely; directly.

تَوْبَة *tōba*, penitence to God [ندم -

تَاب - يتوب *tāba*, he repented; *yatoob*, he repents.

تَائِب *táyib*, penitent.

توت *toot*, mulberry, mulberry-tree.

توت *Toot*, Coptic month of September, beginning the Coptic year, Sept. 11th.

توتيا *tootyá*, zinc, zinc ore.

توج or تونج *tooj*, or *tunj*, bronze.

توّج *tawwaja*, he crowned.

تَتْوِيج *tatweej*, coronation.

تَاج - تيجان *táj*, pl. *teeján*, crown, diadem; large turban.

تَوْرَاة *tōra*, Pentateuch, Mosaic law.

توم or ثوم *tōm*, or *thōm*, garlic.

تونس *toonus*, Tunis; coarse rope of palm-fibre.

تَيَّار *tayyár*, strong current of river.

تيس - تيوس *tais*, pl. *toyoos*, he-goat, buck.

تيل - تيلة *teel*, or *teela*, jute, hemp; whip; flogging.

تيمار *teemár* (Persian), care of sick.

تيمارجي *teemárji* (Turkish), hospital attendant.

تين *teen*, figs, fig-tree.

تين شوكي *teen shōkiy*, prickly pear, cactus fruit. [صبّيرة]

تيه *teeh*, error, going astray.

تَاه - يتيه *táha*, he strayed; *yateeh*, he strays.

تائه *táyih*, gone astray (animal).

TH

ث *Thá*. Value = 500.

Th, as in "*think*," but usually pronounced *s* or *t*, without any fixed rule.

ثأب or تَثَاوب *thába*, or *tatháwaba*, he yawned.

ثأر *thár*, vengeance. [نقم

ثبت *sabata*, it was firm, proven.

ثبّت or أثبت *sabbata*, or *asbata*, he proved.

ثبوت or اثبات *soboot*, or *isbát*, proof, proof positive.

اثباتات *isbátát*, good proofs.

ثابت *sábit*, proved, firm, enduring; *real* property.

مثبوت مثبّت *masboot*, or *mosabbat*, proved.

محو و اثبات *maho wa isbát*, erasure and substitution.

تخونة or تخن *tikhan*, or *tokhoona*, thickness. [ضخم]

تخين *takheen*, thick, gross, coarse.

تخانة *takhána* (for *tokhoona*), thickness, calibre.

ثدا *thadá*, it bedewed.

ثدي - اثداء *thady*, pl. *athdá*, woman's breast. [نهد]

ثديّ *thadiy*, mammal.

ثروة *sarwa*, wealth.

ثريّا *Turayyá*, the Pleiades; chandelier.

ثعبان - ثعابين *tho'bán*, pl. *tha'ábeen*, snake. [حيّة]

ثعلب - ثعالب *tha'lab*, pl. *tha'álib*, fox.

ثغر - ثغور *thaghr*, pl. *thoghoor*, front teeth; sea-port or frontier town.

ثقب *thaqaba*, he pierced. [نقب]

ثقب - ثقوب *thaqb*, pl. *thoqoob*, hole.

ثقل *thaqola*, it weighed heavy.

ثقل - اثقال *tiql*, pl. *atqál*, weight, gravity.

ثقيل *taqeel*, heavy, unsympathetic.

مثقال - مثاقيل *mitqál*, pl. *matáqeel*, standard weight; also 1½ dirhems, 72 grs. Troy.

استثقل *istasqala*, he found it heavy, wearisome.

ثقة - وثق *tiqa*, worthy of confidence (see *wasuqa*).

ثلث *tult*, or *suls*, one-third part.

ثلاث - ثلاثة *talátu*, femin. *talát*, three.

ثلاثين or ثلاثون *talátoon*, or *talátéen*, thirty.

ثالث *tálit*, the third in order.

يوم الثلاثاء *yōm et-talátá*, Tuesday.

ثلّث *tallata*, he tripled, cubed.

مثلّث *mutallat*, tripled, cubed, cube.

ثلاثيّ *tolátiy*, a triliteral root.

ثالوث *táloot*, the Holy Trinity.

ثلثيّ *sulsiy*, an ornamental style of handwriting for official documents.

تثليث *tathleeth*, a tripling, cubing, Trinity.

ثلج *talaja*, it snowed, froze.

ثلج *talj*, snow, ice or frozen snow; an ice for eating.

ثلم *tilim* (*talm*), furrow in ploughing.

ثمّ *thumma*, and then.

ثمر - اثمار *tamar*, pl. *atmár*, fruit.

اَثمر *atmara*, it was fertile, bore fruit.

مثمِر *mutmir*, fruitful, productive. [منبت]

ثمن *tumn*, one-eighth part; a parish or district in a town.

ثمانية ـ ثماني *tamániya*, femin. *tamáni*, eight.

ثمانين or ثمانون *tamánoon*, or *tamáneen*, eighty.

ثامن *támin*, the eighth in order.

ثمن ـ اثمان *tuman*, pl. *atmán*, price. [قيمة]

ثمّن *tammana*, he estimated, fixed a price.

تثمين *tathmeen*, valuation, appraising.

ثمين or مثمن *tameen*, or *mutmin*, valuable.

ثني ـ اثناء *thiny*, pl. *athná*, a fold, bend.

ثنى يثني *thana*, he bent; *yathni*, he bends.

انثنى *inthana*, it was or became bent, swayed.

استثنى *istasna*, it formed an exception.

استثناء *istisná*, exception.

استثنائي or مستثنى *istisnáiy*, or *mustasná*, exceptional; excepted.

ثناء ـ اثنية *saná*, pl. *asniya*, praise. [مدح]

ثنّى *sanna*, he praised; used the dual form.

اثناء *esná*, during, midst.

في اثناء ذلك *fi esná zalik*, in the meantime.

اثنان or اثنين *etnán*, or *etnain* (masc.), two.

اثنتان or اثنتين or ثنتين *etnatán*, or *etnatain*, or *tintain* (femin.), two.

يوم الاثنين *yōm el-etnain*, Monday.

ثاني *táni*, the second in order; another, other, next.

ثاني يوم *táni yōm*, next day.

الثانيين *et-tányeen*, the others.

ثانوي *tánawiy*, secondary.

مثنى *motanna*, dual; the dual form.

ثانو مشي *tánoo masha* (colloquial), he turned and walked away, he walked back.

تثنية *tathniya*, Deuteronomy.

ثوب *tōb*, a robe, toga, garment.

ثياب or اثواب *aswáb*, or *tiyáb*, clothes.

ثواب *thawáb*, reward of merit. [صواب]

ثورة *sōra*, uproar, revolt, agitation.

ثورة عرابية *sōra 'arábiya*, Arábi's rebellion.

ثار ـ يثور *sára*, it was excited; *yasoor*, it is in a state of excitement.

اثار *asára*, he stirred up a revolt, excited.

ثائرة *sáyira*, a state of excitement, revolt.

تثوير *tatweer*, a driving mad, exciting.

ثور - ثيران *tōr*, pl. *teerán*, bull; Taurus in the zodiac.

ثوم *tōm*, garlic.

ثيب *sayyib*, legal term for a woman who is not a virgin.

J

(Or colloquially G hard, as in *get*.)

ج *Jeem*. Value = 3.

جا - يجي *já* (*ghé*) he came; *yiji*, he comes.

جم *jum* (*ghum*), they came (vulgarism for *jaoo*).

جائي *jáiy*, a comer, coming, future, next. [آت]

الشهر اللي جائي *esh-shahr illi jáiy*, the month which is coming.

مجي *maji*, arrival, act of coming.

جاب *jáb*, he came with, brought.

يجيب *yajeeb*, he brings.

جار - جوار *jár*, neighbour (see *jiwár*).

جارية - جواري *járiya*, pl. *jawári*, female slave.

جار - جر *jarr*, he who pulls (see *jarra*).

جازية - ساقية *jáziya*, horizontal upper beam of *sáqiya*.

جاموس - جواميس *jámoos*, pl. *jawámees*, buffalo.

جاوب - جاوب *jáwaba*, he answered (see *jawáb*).

جائز - جواز *jáyiz*, lawful, licit (see *jawáz*).

جاه *jáh* (Persian), honour, majesty.

جب *jabba*, he lopped off, castrated entirely.

جب *jubb*, well, pit.

جبة *jubba*, loose outer robe.

مجبوب *majboob*, complete eunuch.

جبر *jabara*, he forced; cut; set a bone, put the pieces together.

جبر *jabr*, violence, pride; cutting of a dyke.

اجبر *ajbara*, he forced.

جبري *jabriy*, forcible, violent.

قوّة جبرية *qowwa jabriya*, main force, arm of the law, "*force majeure*."

علم الجبر *'ilm el-jabr*, Algebra, science of putting fractions together.

جبّار *jabbár*, violent, proud, tyrant, giant; constellation of Orion.

مجبور *majboor*, forced; a set bone.

مجبّر *mojabbir*, bone setter, quack surgeon.

جبرائيل *Jabráyeel*, Angel Gabriel.

جبران *Jabrán*, man's name, Gabriel.

جبس (40) جدي

جبس jibs, cement, gypsum.

جبل jabala, he created, moulded.

جبلّة jibilla, natural constitution.

جبلّي jibilliy, natural, innate.

جبل - جبال jabal, pl. jibál, mountain, desert.

جبلي jabaliy, mountainous; of the desert.

جبنة or جبن jibn, or jibna, cheese.

جبين jibeen, forehead.

جبان jabán, coward.

جبّانة jabbána, cemetery.

جبهة jabha, forehead.

جباية jibáya, tax, rent, collection of rent or taxes.

جابي jábi, rent collector.

جثث - جثّة jussa, pl. jusas, corpse. [رمّة]

جثمان jusmán, bulk, body. [جسمان]

جحد - جحود jahada, he denied; johood, denial.

جحش jahsh, foal of an ass, young ass.

اجحف - [جحف] [jahafa] - ajhafa, he slandered, injured.

جحيم jaheem, hell-fire. [جهنّم]

جدّ jidd, seriousness, earnestness, energy.

جدّاً jiddán, in earnest; very, exceedingly.

جادّ jádd, serious, earnest.

جدّة jidda, newness, Jeddah, the port of Mecca; a shore.

جدّ - اجداد jadd, pl. ajdád, grandfather, ancestor.

جدّة jadda, grandmother. [ستّ]

جادّة jádda, high road.

جدّد jaddada, he renewed.

تجديد tajdeed, renovation.

استجدّ istajadda, he came out new, suddenly became, was newly appointed.

مستجدّ mustajidd, recruit, newly appointed.

جدر jadar, jider, pustule, boil.

جدري jidiriy, small-pox.

جدر jadr, root, square-root, base.

جدار - جدر jidár, pl. jodor, wall, garden wall.

تسوّر الجدار tasawwur el-jidár, escalade; a French legal term for a form of burglary.

جدير jadeer, walled, firm, capable; small canal or rivulet.

جدع jada', mutilation.

جدل jadala, he twisted, plaited.

جديلة jadeela, plait, tress, fringe of hair. [ضفيرة]

جادل jádala, he quarrelled.

جدال or مجادلة jidál, or mojádala, quarrel, dispute.

جدول - جداول jadwal, pl. jadáwil, groove, channel, schedule, register.

جدا jada, gift, utility.

جدي jadi, goat, Capricorn in the Zodiac.

جذب jazaba, he attracted, charmed.

جذب jazb, attraction.

جاذبة ـ جواذب jáziba, pl. jawázib, attraction, attractiveness, charms of beauty.

مجذوب ـ مجاذيب majzoob, pl. majázeeb, insane, demented.

جذر or جذّر jazara, or jazzara, he got at the root, extracted the root.

جذر ـ جذور jizr, or jidr, pl. jozoor, root, root of a number; trunk of a tree.

جذع jada', a fine fellow; sapling.

جذع jida', trunk of tree.

جذام jozám, elephantiasis, leprosy. [برص]

جرّ jarra, he pulled, dragged, drew.

جرجر jarjara, colloquial for jarra.

جرّ or جرجر jarr, or jarjar, a pull, tension.

جرّة jarra, "kesra," or i vowel-sound.

جرجرة jarjara, agony of death, last gasp.

جرّة ـ جرار jarra, pl. jirár, jar, pitcher.

جار or جرّار jarr, or jarrár, he who pulls, pulling.

جرّارة jarrára, traces of carriage-harness.

انجرّ injarra, it was dragged, towed.

انجرار injirár, a towing, towage.

مجرور majroor, drain, water-course.

جرأة ـ جرى juráa, bravery; jari, brave.

اجترأ ـ مجترى ijtará, he dared; mujtari, daring.

تجارى على tajára 'ala, he ventured, had the impudence.

تجارى على سرقة tajári 'ala sariqa, a venturing on theft, a committing (the crime of) theft.

جرابندية jarábandiya, knapsack.

جرب ـ جربان jarab, mange; jarbán, mangy.

جراب jiráb, leather sack or case; sheath.

جرّب jarraba, he attempted, experimented.

مجرّب mojarrab, enured, tried, expert.

تجربة ـ تجارب tajriba, pl. tajárib, attempt, experiment, experience.

جرثومة jorthooma, root, origin, "blastème."

جرجا Girgá, a province and town in Upper Egypt.

جرجير jarjeer, cress, eruca sativa.

جرجس ـ مار جرجس Girgis, George; Már Girgis, St. George.

جرح jaraha, he wounded; he accused. [طعن]

جرح ـ جروح jorh, pl. jorooh, wound.

جريح or مجروح jareeh, or majrooh, wounded.

جرَّاح - جِراحة *jarráh*, surgeon; *jiráha*, surgery.

جارِحة - جوارح *járiha*, pl. *jawárih*, hands, feet, limbs; bird of prey.

جِراحة - جِراح *jiráha*, pl. *jiráh*, wound.

جرد or جرَّد *jarada*, or *jarrada*, he stripped bare, deprived; audited, made an inventory.

جرد *jard*, nudity, a stripping bare; audit, inventory.

حصرهُ بِالجرد *hasaraho bil-jard*, he entered it in the inventory.

جريد *jareed*, rib of palm branch, lance.

جريدة - جرائد *jareeda*, pl. *jaráyid*, rib of palm branch, lance, newspaper, schedule.

جراد *jarád*, locusts.

أجرد - أجرود *ajrad*, bare, stripped; *ajrood*, beardless.

تجريد *tajreed*, deprivation.

تجريدة *tajreeda*, military expedition.

تجرَّد *tajarrada*, he was stripped; quit of.

مجرَّد *mojarrad*, bare, simple, sole, alone.

مجرَّد حق *mojarrad haqq*, "droit incorporel."

جرس *jaras*, bell.

جرَّس *jarrasa*, he revealed another's vices, faults.

جرش *jarasha*, he crushed grain.

جاروش *jároosh*, hand-mill. [رحى]

جريش *jareesh*, crushed or pounded grain.

جراويش *jaráweesh*, sweetmeats sweetmeat paste of opium.

جرعة *jora'a*, potion, medicine.

جرف *jorf*, bank of river or canal embankment.

جرَّف *jarrafa*, he embanked shovelled earth.

جرَّافة *jorráfa*, spade, hoe. [لوح - ورك]

جرم *jarama*, he cut.

أجرم or أجترم *ajrama*, or *ijtarama* he sinned, was guilty.

جرم - جروم *jorm*, pl. *joroom*, sin crime, harm; *jirm*, bulk.

لا جرم *lá jorm*, without fail.

جرَّم *jarrama*, he imposed a fine. [رَّم]

جرامة *jaráma*, fine, penalty.

جريمة - جرائم *jareema*, pl. *jaráyim* sin, crime; fine, penalty.

مجرم or مجترم *mujrim*, or *mujtarim* sinner, guilty.

مجرم *mujrim* (colloquial), barefoot beggar.

أجرومية *Ajirroomiya* (*Agroomiya*) grammar.

جرن *jarana*, he threshed corn.

جرن *jorn*, threshing-floor, heap o corn for threshing; wooden pestle.

جرنال - جرنالات *jornál*, pl. *jornálá* (European), journal, newspaper

جرى ‎- يجري‎ *jara*, he ran, it flowed; *yijri*, he runs.

جريان‎ or جري‎ *jari* or *jarayán*, course, flow; a running.

اسرع بالجري‎ *asra'a bil-jari*, he hastened (with running), he ran away.

مسرع بالجري‎ *mosria' bil-jari*, running hastily.

جاري‎ *jári*, current, running, flowing; being in the act of; present (month, year, &c.).

جارية ‎- جواري‎ *járiya*, pl. *jawári*, female slave.

جراية‎ *jaráya*, ration of bread, wages.

اجرى‎ *ajra*, he made take its course; set about, carried out, put into execution.

اجراء‎ *ijrá*, execution of work.

اجرائي‎ *ijráiy*, executive.

مجرى ‎- مجاري‎ *majra*, pl. *majári*, course, means; duct, urethra.

جزّ‎ *jazza*, he cut, cropped.

جزأ‎ *jazá*, he took a share, divided.

جزء ‎- اجزاء‎ *juz*, pl. *ajzá*, part, particle, atom; in pl., drugs.

جزئي‎ *juziy*, relating to small matters; petty.

اجزاجي‎ *ajzáji* (Turkish), chemist.

اجزاخانة‎ *ajzákhána* (Persian), chemist's shop.

جزى‎ *jaza*, he rewarded (good or evil).

جزاء‎ *jazá*, reward, retribution.

جازى‎ *jáza*, he rewarded, punished. [قاس‎]

جوزي‎ *joozia*, he was rewarded, punished.

يجازى‎ *yojázi*, he punishes; *yojáza*, he is punishable, is liable to punishment.

جزاء‎ or مجازاة‎ *jizá*, or *mojázát*, punishment.

جزية‎ *jiziya*, tax, imposition.

جزر‎ *jazara*, he slaughtered. [ذبح‎]

جزّار‎ *jazzár*, butcher.

جزر ‎- مدّ‎ *jazr*, ebb-tide; *madd*, flood-tide.

جزر‎ *jazar*, carrot.

جزيرة ‎- جزائر‎ *jazeera*, pl. *jazáyir*, island; Ghezireh, the island opposite Kasr en-Nil, Cairo.

الجزيرة‎ *El-jazeera*, Mesopotamia.

الجزائر‎ *El-jazáyir*, Algiers.

جزع‎ *jaza'a*, he cut, broke up. [جدع‎]

جزاف‎ *jozáf*, in the lump, as a sale of goods in the lump, roughly; "*achat en bloc.*"

جزالة‎ *jazála*, energy, superabundance.

جزيل‎ *jazeel*, abundant, generous.

جزلان ‎- جزدان‎ *juzlán* (for Persian *jizdán*), pocket-book.

جزم‎ *jazama*, he cut, shaped. [صرم‎]

جزم‎ *jazm*, a cutting; the mark over a letter, also called *sokoon*. [سكون‎]

جزمة ‎- جزم‎ *juzma*, pl. *jizam*, boot.

جزمجي‎ or جزماتي‎ *jazmaji* (Turkish), or *jizamátiy*, bootmaker.

جَسَّ *jassa*, he touched, felt. [حَسَّ - مَسَّ]

تَجَسَّسَ *tajassasa*, he felt his way, investigated.

جاسوس - جواسيس *jásoos*, pl. *jawáseex* spy. [بصّاص]

جسد - اجساد *jasad*, pl. *ajsád*, human body. [جسم]

جسديّ *jasadiy*, corporeal, bodily.

تَجَسَّد *tajassada*, it became incarnate.

جسر *jasara*, he dared.

جسارة *jasára*, daring, courage.

جسور *jasoor*, daring, courageous.

تَجاسر *tajásara*, he had the impudence to.

متجاسر *mutajásir*, impudent, audacious.

جسر - جسور *jisr*, pl. *josoor*, bank of river or canal; dyke; causeway, bridge.

جسم - اجسام *jism*, pl. *ajsám*, body, substance; the human body. [جسد]

جسم صلب *jism salib*, solid substance.

جسم مرن *jism marin*, yielding, elastic substance.

سليم الجسم *suleem el-jism*, able-bodied, sound in body.

جسيم - جسامة *jaseem*, bulky; *jasáma*, bulkiness.

جسمان *jusmán*, bulk. [جثمان]

جصّ *jiss*, gypsum. [جبس]

جعد *ja'd*, crisp, curly hair.

جعران *j'arán*, beetle, scarab. [خنفس]

جعفر *j'afar*, canal, rivulet.

جعل *j'ala*, he did, made; began, set about.

جعل يكتب *j'ala yiktib*, he began to write.

جعل نفسه *j'ala nafsaho*, he made himself out to be, pretended to be.

جعل *j'ol*, wages, pension.

جغرافية *jaghráfiya* (European), geography.

جفّ - جفاف *jaffa*, it was dry; *jafáf*, dryness.

جافّ *jáff*, dry (as a dead body, flower, &c.).

جفّف *jaffafa*, he dessicated.

جفت *jift* (Persian *chift*, pair), tweezers.

جفير *jafeer*, sheath, leather case.

جفن - جفون *jifn*, pl. *jofoon*, eyelid.

جفاء *jifá*, cruelty.

جلّ *julla*, it was grand, illustrious.

جلّل *jallala*, he revered, extolled.

جليل *jaleel*, royal, majestic; the Turkish epithet for a Ministry of State.

جلال or جلالة *jalál* or *jalála*, majesty.

جلّ *jill*, grand, illustrious

جلّ *jull*, horse-cloth.

جلّة *jilla*, flat round cakes made of dung, and used as fuel.

مَجَلَّة *majalla*, book of Moslem Jurisprudence, or legal axioms.

جَلَّى *julla*, a serious matter.

جَلَب *jalaba*, he drew, attracted, made come.

جَلْب *jalb*, a making come, attraction.

جَلَّاب *jallāb*, slave-hunter, or slave-trader.

جُلَّاب *jollāb*, julep, molasses.

جِلْبَة *jilba*, clamp, iron-fastening.

جَلَابِيب - جُلْبَاب *julbāb*, pl. *jalābeeb*, smock worn by fellaheen men and women, and generally called "galábiya."

جَلَابِيَة *jalábiya*, vulgar form of *julbāb*.

جِلْبَان *jilbán*, pease, pulse.

اِسْتَجْلَب *istajlaba*, he procured, drew to himself.

جَلْجِل *jiljil*, small bell (worn by animals).

جَلَد - جُلُود *jild*, pl. *jolood*, skin, hide; leather; leather bound book; volume of book.

اِبْن جِلْدَتَك *ibn jildatak* (colloquial), your compatriot, fellow villager, one of your own flesh.

جِلْدِيّ *jildiy*, of the skin, leathery.

جَلَد *jalada*, he flogged.

جَلَّد - تَجْلِيد *jallada*, he bound a book; *tajleed*, book-binding.

مُجَلِّد *mojallid*, bookbinder.

جَلَّاد *jallād*, executioner; flogger; skinner or seller of hides.

جَلِيد *jaleed*, sleet, hail; strong, thick skinned.

جَلَس *jalasa*, he sat up, mounted to a seat. [cf. قعد

جُلُوس *joloos*, act of sitting; accession to throne.

جَالِس *jális*, sitter, seated.

جَلْسَة - جَلَسَات *jalsa*, pl. *jalsát*, a single sitting; *séance* or audience by a Court or Assembly.

مَجْلِس - مَجَالِس *majlis*, pl. *majális*, council, assembly, tribunal.

مَجْلِس أَحْكَام *majlis ahkám*, Final Court of Appeal. (This title is rarely used.)

جَلَم *jalam*, shears, large scissors.

جُلَّنَار *jollnár*, *punica granatum*.

جَلَا *jalá*, he polished.

جَلَاء or جَلْو *jalá*, or *jalo*, a polish, clearness.

جَلْوَة *jalwa*, fête, marriage feast. [فرح

جَلَاجِي *jaláji* (Turkish), polisher.

جَلَّى *jalla*, he made clear, showed.

جَلِيّ *jaliy*, clear, obvious, bright.

مَجْلُو *majloo*, polished.

اِنْجَلَى *injala*, he was glad, his heart was brightened.

جَمَّ *jamma*, it was abundant.

جَمّ غَفِير *jamm ghafeer*, a vast crowd.

جَمْجَمَة *jomjoma*, cranium, skull.

تجَمَّدَ or جمد jamada, or tajammada, it became solid; froze.

جمود jomood, solidity; torpor, numbness.

جامد jámid, solid, hard, firm. [صلب]

جوامد و سوائل jawámid wa sawáyil, solids and fluids.

جمادى jomáda (jomádi), Jamádi I. and II., the fifth and sixth Moslem months.

فوائد متجمدة fawáyid mutajammida, compound interest.

جمرة jamra, live coal, carbuncle (disease).

جميّز jommaiza, sycamore, wild fig; ficus sycamorus.

جاموس - جاموسة - جواميس jámoos, femin. jámoosa, pl. jawámees, buffalo.

فحل جاموس fahl jámoos, a fine (male) buffalo.

جمع jama'a, he added up, collected; formed the plural.

اجمع ajma'a, he collected, agreed upon.

تجمَّع or اجتمع ijtama'a, or tajamma'a, they assembled; the assembly or crowd formed.

جامع jáma'a, he copulated with.

جمع - جموع jama', pl. jomooa', plural; addition; crowd.

اجمع or جمع joma', or ajma', all, the whole.

اجماع ijmá'a, a collection or agreement of opinions on Moslem doctrines.

اجتماع ijtimá'a, an assembling.

جماع jimá'a, copulation.

جامع - جوامع jámia', pl. jawámia', mosque, as a place of assembly for prayer. [مسجد]

جميع jumcea', all.

جمعة joma'a, reunion; a week. [اسبوع]

يوم الجمعة yōm el-joma'a, day of reunion in the Mosque, Friday.

جمعية or جماعة jamáa'a, or jama'iya, assembly, society; crowd; troop, squad.

مجمع or مجموع majma', or majmooa', the united whole, total, collection; collected.

جمكية jamakiya, monthly wages, pay. [ماهية]

جمل - جمال jamal, pl. jimál, camel, male camel. [ناقة]

جمّال jammál, camel-driver.

جمال jamál, beauty, kindness, good conduct.

جميل jameel, handsome; kind; a favour.

حفظ جميل hifz jameel, gratitude, memory of a favour.

تجامل or جامل jámala, or tujámala, he repaid favours, was kind in return.

جملة - جمل jomla, pl. jomal, the whole; a phrase; several.

جملة مرار jomla mirár, several times.

بالجملة lil-jomla, in short; collectively; wholesale.

اجمل ajmala, he added up, summarized.

اجمال ijmál, summary, addition.

اجمالي ijmáliy, addition or total of accounts.

مجمل mojmal, added up; the total.

جمّل jommal, the numerical value of the letters of the alphabet when added up.

جمهور ـ جماهير jomhoor, pl. jamáheer, the public, republic.

ليكون معلوما للجمهور li-yakoon ma'loomán lil-jomhoor, Be it known to the public! Notice!

جمهورية jomhooriya, republic; republicanism, democracy.

جن janna, it was obscure; he hid, covered.

جنّ jonna, he was mad, silly, cracked.

جنّن jannana, he bewitched, maddened.

جنّي jinniy, a genie, spirit (good or evil).

جن or جان jinn, or jánn, genii, spirits.

جنون jonoon, madness.

مجنون ـ مجانين majnoon, pl. majáneen, mad, possessed of an evil spirit, cracked.

جنين janeen, a hidden thing, fœtus, embryo.

جنّة ـ جنّات janna, pl. jannát, Paradise.

جنينة jonaina, pl. janáyin, garden.

جنائني janáyiniy, gardener.

جنب ـ جنوب janb, pl. jonoob, side, flank.

اجتنب or تجنّب ijtanaba, or tajannaba, he avoided, kept himself aloof.

جانب ـ جوانب jánib, pl. jawánib, side, flank; also (colloquially) a piece, some.

جانب قمح jánib qamh, some wheat.

جناب janáb, vicinity; Excellency, Highness, Mr.

الجناب الخديوي el-Janábel-Khedewiy, H.H. the Khedive.

جناب مستر جونس janáb Mister Jones, Mr. Jones, Jones Esq.

جنابية janábiya, vicinity, alongside; sides of the embankment of a railway-line.

جنوب jonoob, south. [قبلي]

اجنبي ـ اجانب ajnabiy, pl. ajánib, foreigner, foreign, stranger.

جنب junub, impure, unclean.

جنابة janába, physical pollution (a gross term of abuse in Turkish).

جانباز jánbáz (Persian), acrobat; military extension-motions.

جناح ـ اجنحة janáh, pl. ajniha, wing; minion.

جناح ـ كناه jonáh (Persian, gyoonáh), sin.

جِنْحَة ـ جِنَح *jonha*, pl. *jonah*, the French "*délit*" or misdemeanour, as distinct from the French "*crime*," or felony.

جِنَح و جِنَايَات *jonah wa jináyát*, "*délits*" and "*crimes*."

مَحْكَمَة الجِنَح *mahkamat el-jonah*, "*tribunal correctionnel*."

جِنْد ـ جُنُود *jind*, pl. *jonood*, troops. [جَيْش]

جُنْدِيّ *jindiy*, a soldier, horseman.

جَنَازَة *janáza*, funeral-procession. [مَشْهَد]

جِنْزِير *jinzeer* (for Persian *zinjeer*), chain.

جِنْس ـ اَجْنَاس *jins*, pl. *ajnás*, species, kind, sex. [نَوْع]

جِنْسِيَّة *jinsiya*, sex, specification, origin.

جَنَّسَ *jannasa*, he specified, divided into species.

تَجْنِيس *tajnees*, specification; (in Turkish) pun.

جَانَسَ *jánasa*, it resembled in species.

جِنَاس *jinás*, similarity in species; alliteration.

جَنَى ـ يَجْنِي *jana*, he plucked, gathered; *yijni*, he plucks.

جَنَى ـ يَجْنِي *jana*, he committed a crime; *yijni*, he commits a crime.

تَجَنَّى عَلَى *tajanna 'ala*, he accused falsely.

جَنَى *jana*, the fruit or crop which is gathered.

جَانِي ـ جُنَاة *jáni*, pl. *jonát*, committer of a crime; guilty.

جِنَايَة ـ جِنَايَات *jináya*, pl. *jináyát*, "*crime*," felony; crime.

جِنَح و جِنَايَات *jonah wa jináyát*, "*délits*" and "*crimes*."

مَجْنَى *majna*, the crime committed.

المَجْنَى عَلَيْه *el-majna 'alaih*, the victim of the crime.

مُتَلَبِّسًا بِالجِنَايَة *mutalabbisán bil-jináya*, caught in the act, "*en flagrant délit*."

قَانُون تَحْقِيق الجِنَايَات *qánoon tahqeeq el-jináyát*, Law of Criminal Procedure, "*instruction criminelle*."

مَحْكَمَة الجِنَايَات *mahkamat el-jináyát*, "*tribunal criminel*."

جَهَدَ or اِجْتَهَدَ *jahada*, or *ijtahada*, he exerted himself.

جَهْد or اِجْتِهَاد *jahd*, or *ijtihád*, exertion, effort, zeal.

اِجْتِهَاد شَرْعِيّ *ijtihád shar'aiy*, legal opinion or deduction in Moslem law; "*responsa prudentium*."

جَاهَدَ *jáhada*, he exerted himself for Islam, fought the infidel.

جِهَاد *jihád*, exertion or holy war on behalf of Islam.

جِهَادِيّ *jihádiy*, soldier, military.

جِهَادِيَّة *jihádiya*, military (affairs), war office.

مَجْهُود *majhood*, result of effort, effort.

جهر or جهار *jahr*, or *jihár*, publicity. [شهر]

جهرًا *jahrán*, publicly, in public. [علنًا]

جهّز *jahhaza*, he equipped, fitted up, fitted out.

تجهيزات *tajheezát*, preparations, equipments for war, &c.

جاهز *jáhiz*, ready, equipped, fitted out.

جهاز *jiház*, equipment, outfit, apparatus; trousseau of bride.

جهض *jahada*, he thwarted, used violence.

اجهض *ajhada*, he caused abortion. [اسقط]

اجهاض *ij-hád*, a causing abortion.

جهيض *jaheed*, embryo, or abortion.

جهل or جهالة *jahl*, or *jahála*, ignorance, stupidity.

جهل *jahila*, he was ignorant.

تجاهل *tajáhala*, he shammed ignorance.

جاهل - جهّال *jáhil*, pl. *johhál*, ignorant, stupid.

جاهليّة *jáhiliya*, ante-Islam, Arab ignorance of the true faith prior to Mahomet's revelation.

مجهول - مجاهيل *maj-hool*, pl. *majáheel*, unknown.

المجهول و المعلم *el-máj-hool wa el-m'aloom*, passive and active voices of a verb.

مجهول الاسم *maj-hool el-ism*, anonymous.

جهنّم *jahannam* (femin.), hell, Gehenna.

جواب - اجوبة *jawáb*, pl. *ajwiba*, answer, reply; letter.

سؤال و جواب *sooúl wa jawáb*, question and answer.

جوابات *jawábát*, letters, postal correspondence.

جوائب *jawáyib*, current news, chronicle.

جاوب *jáwaba*, he replied.

استجوب *istajwaba*, he interrogated, asked for an answer.

استجواب *istijwáb*, interrogatory.

اجاب *ajába*, he answered, complied with.

اجاب بالايجاب *ajába bil-eejáb*, he replied in the affirmative, consented. [وجب]

اجاب بالسلب *ajába bis-salb*, he replied in the negative.

اجابة *ijába*, compliance, consent.

مجيب *mojeeb*, compliant, consenting. [cf. موجب]

جوخ *jókh* (Persian *choha*), cloth.

جودة *jóda*, excellence, goodness, kindness.

جود *jood*, generosity.

جواد - اجود *jawád*, generous; *ajwad*, more generous.

جيّد - جياد *jayyid*, pl. *jiyád*, good, excellent.

اجود *ajwad*, better, more excellent.

جوّد *jawwada*, he made good, improved

جور *jör*, tyranny, injustice; unjust.

جوار or مجاورة *jiwár*, or *mojáwara*, vicinity, nearness, a being a neighbour.

جاور *jáwara*, he was neighbour, near.

جار - جيران *jár*, pl. *jeerán*, neighbour.

مجاور *mojáwir*, near, adjacent; student of Moslem law.

جوراب *joráb* (Persian *choráb*), stockings.

جوز - جوزة - زوج *jöz*, femin. *jöza*, vulgar Arabic for *zöj*, femin. *zöja*, spouse, pair, couple.

جوّز - زوّج *jawwaza*, vulgarism for *zawwaja*, he gave in marriage.

تجوّز - تزوّج *tajawwaza*, vulgarism for *tazawwaja*, he married, took a wife.

جوز *jöz*, middle, kernel; walnuts.

جوزة *jöza*, a walnut; a cocoa-nut; hence, a "*hookah*," or cocoanut-bowled pipe, for smoking hasheesh, tumbak, &c.

جوزاء *jözá*, Gemini of the Zodiac.

جواز *jawáz*, lawfulness, permission, right of way.

جاز - يجوز *jáza*, it was lawful; *yajooz*, it is lawful.

جوّز or اجاز *jawwaza* or *ajáza*, he permitted.

جائز *jáyiz*, lawful, licit, permissible.

جائزة - جوائز *jáyiza*, pl. *jawáyiz*, prize, gift, reward.

اجازة *ijáza*, permission, leave of absence. [رخصة]

تجاوز *tajáwaza*, he gave himself leave, dared, overstepped a right or limit; it exceeded, was more than.

استجوز *istajwaza*, he asked leave. [استأذن]

مجاز *majáz*, passage, metaphor.

مجازيّ *majáziy*, metaphoric, unreal.

مجوز *mijwiz* (vulgar), doubled, double.

متجاوز *motajáwiz*, transgressor, overstepper; more than, excessive.

جيزة *jeeza*, shore; river bank opposite Cairo; town and province of Ghizeh.

هرم الجيزة *haram el-jeeza*, pyramids of Ghizeh.

جوع - جاع *jooa'* hunger; *jáu'a*, he hungered.

جائع or جوعان or جيعان *jáya'* or *jaw'án*, or (vulgar) *jeea'án*, hungry.

مجاعة *majáa'a* hunger.

جوف - اجواف *jöf*, pl. *ajwáf*, a hollow; belly, cavity.

جوّف *jawwafa*, he hollowed out.

اجوف or مجوّف *ajwaf*, or *mojawwaf*, concave, hollow, hollowed out.

جوقة *jöqa*, crowd. [سرقة]

جول or جولان *jōl*, or *jawalán*, a turning round. [دوران

تجوّل *tajawwala*, he made a tour (of inspection).

مجال *majál*, circus, arena, place of turning.

جون *joon*, gulf, inlet.

جوهر - جواهر *jōhar*, pl. *jawákir*, jewel; atom, molecule.

جوهريّ *jōhariy*, jeweller; atomic, molecular, substantial.

جوهرجي *jōharji* (Turkish), jeweller.

جوّ *jaw* (*jow*), atmosphere, air; the inside.

جوّا *jooá*, inside, at home, indoors.

جوّانيّ *jooániy*, internal, inner.

جي *ji*, (Turkish) suffix signifying the doer, actor, seller, like the English, -*er*, -*ster*, &c.

اجزاجي *ajzáji*, chemist, seller of drugs.

قهوجي or قهوه‌جي *qahwaji*, seller of coffee.

عربجي or عربه‌جي *'arabaji*, cabman.

جيب - جيوب *jaib*, pl. *joyoob*, pocket; sine (geometry).

تمام جيب *tamám jaib*, cosine.

نسبة جيبية *nisba jaibiya*, log : sine.

جير *jeer*, lime, mortar.

جيّارة *jayyára*, lime-kiln. [امينة

جيران - جار *jeerán*, pl. of *jár*, neighbours.

جيزة - جوز *jeeza*, shore, Ghizeh (see under *jōz*).

جيوس *jioos*, pistaccia vera.

جيش - جيوش *jaish*, pl. *joyoosh*, army.

جيش مصريّ *jaish masriy*, Egyptian army.

جيش الاحتلال *jaish el-ihtilál*, Army of Occupation.

جيشان *jayashán*, violent agitation, commotion.

جاش - يجيش *jásha*, it was in commotion; *yajeesh*, it is in commotion.

جوّش - جيّش *jawwasha* (colloquial for *jayyasha*), he stirred up strife, disputed.

جيفة - جيف *jeefa*, pl. *jiaf*, carrion, carcase.

جيم *jeem*, the letter ج j.

جيل - اجيال *jeel*, pl. *ajiál*, age, epoch.

جينه - جينهات *jeenaih*, pl. *jeenahát* (European), guinea, pound sterling.

H

(a strong aspirate).

ح *Há*. Value = 8.

حاجة - حاجات *hája*, pl. *háját*, necessity, thing needed, thing; affairs, baggage, clothes. [حوج

ما فيش حاجة *má feesh hája*, there is, or it is, nothing.

حوائج *hawáyij* (another pl. of *hája*), baggage, effects.

احتاج ل *ihtája li*, he had need for, it was needful to.

احتياج *ihtiyáj*, need, indigence, necessity.

احتياج ضروري *ihtiyáj daroory*, urgent necessity.

محتاج ل *muhtáj li*, in need of.

حاج *háj*, a thorny plant; *alhagi mannifcrum*.

حارة - حيرة *haira*, lane, narrow street (see *haira*).

حاط - حوطة *háta*, he guarded (see *hata*).

احاط *aháta*, he surrounded; warned, informed.

احاطة *iháta*, a surrounding, informing.

حوّط *hawwata*, he surrounded, left a margin.

تحويط *tahweet*, circumference, land enclosed or embanked; dyke.

حائط - حيطان *háyit*, pl. *heetán*, wall. سور - جدار

احتاط *ihtáta*, he took precaution, kept in reserve.

احتياط *ihtiyát*, precaution; reserve of army.

احتياطي *ihtiyátiy*, precautionary, in reserve, provisory.

حبس احتياطي *habs ihtiyátiy*, precautionary imprisonment (before trial).

ضمان احتياطي *damán ihtiyátiy*, "*aval*" in French law, or additional and precautionary guarantee for a bill of exchange by a third party.

من باب الاحتياط *min báb el-ihtiyát*, as a measure of precaution, "to be on the safe side."

محيط - بحر محيط *moheet*, surrounding; *bahr moheet*, ocean.

محاط *mohát*, surrounded.

حافة *háfa*, edge, brim.

حال - حول *hál* (femin.), state, condition (see *hōl*).

حبّ or احبّ *habba*, or *ahabba*, he loved; preferred; wished. [cf. هبّ]

حبّ يعمل *habba y'amil*, he wished to do.

تحابّ *tahábba*, he loved mutually.

حبّ or محبّة *hibb*, or *hubb*, or *mahabba*, love, preference.

حبّي *hubbiy*, affectionate, relating to love.

حبيب - احباب or احبّاء *habeeb*, pl. *ahbáb*, or *ahibbá*, friend, lover, dear.

حبيبي - حبيبتي *habeebi*, femin. *habeebati*, my dear.

احبّ *ahabb*, dearer.

محبّ *mohibb*, lover.

محبوب *mahboob*, beloved; obsolete gold coin used as an ornament.

محابّ *mohább*, mutually loving, and beloved.

حبّ - حبوب or حبّات *habb*, pl. *hoboob*, or *hoboobát*, grain; in pl. cereals.

حبّة *habba*, a grain, 1-48th of a dirhem; pimple; pill.

حبر hibr, ink.

حبرة habara, lady's black silk cloak.

حبر habr, rabbi, Jewish priest.

حبس habasa, he put in prison, sequestered. [سجن]

حبس habs, prison, imprisonment; sequestration.

حبسخانه habs-khána (Persian), a prison, gaol.

احتبس ihtabasa, he restrained, contained.

محبوس – حبابيس mahboos, pl. mahábees, prisoner.

حبش habash, Abyssinia, the Abyssinians.

حبشي habashiy, an Abyssinian, Abyssinian.

حبك habaka, he made lace, interlaced.

حبل – حبال habl, pl. hibál, cable, rope.

حبائل habáyil, cordage, nets.

حبل habal, conception, pregnancy. [علوق]

حبلت habilet, (the woman) conceived. [حمل]

حبلى – حبالى hibla, pl. habála, pregnant.

حتة – حتت hitta, pl. hitat, piece, bit.

حتم hattama, he made obligatory.

تحتم tahattama, it became obligatory.

حتما hatmán, of necessity, without fail; "de plein droit."

حتى hatta, in order that; until, even then.

حج or حجّة hajj or hijja, the Great Pilgrimage to Mecca at the end of the Moslem year.

ذو الحجّة zoo l-hijja, the month of pilgrimage, the last lunar month.

حج hajja, he went on the pilgrimage.

حجّة – حجج hojja, pl. hojaj, good proof, sound argument, title-deed of property.

حاج – حجّاج hájj, pl. hojjáj, pilgrim to Mecca.

حاجي hájji (Persian), pilgrim.

احتج ihtajja, he relied on good proof.

احتجاج ihtijáj, reliance on good proof.

حجب hajaba, he veiled, guarded, cut off, disinherited.

حجاب hijáb, veil, amulet, diaphragm.

حاجب – حواجب hájib, pl. hawájib, eyebrow.

حاجب – حجّاب hájib, pl. hojjáb, guardian, beadle, usher, constable of a court.

محجوب mahjoob, veiled, timid, bashful.

حجر hijr, bosom, lap. [حضن]

حجر على hajr 'ala, interdiction against.

حجر (54) حديث

احجار - حجر *hajar,* pl. *ahjár,* stone, rock.

حجري *hajariy,* stony; mineral (coal).

حجرة *hujra,* cell, closet; the grave of Mahomed.

محجر *mahjar,* stony place, quarry; rocky bank.

حجز *hajaza,* he barred off, sequestered for debt.

حجز *hajz,* sequester, seizure for debt.

توقيع الحجز *tawqee'a el-hajz,* the imposing of a sequester.

حاجز *hájiz,* sequestrator, barrier; septum, diaphragm.

محجوز *mahjooz,* seized for debt.

الحجاز *El-Hijáz,* Hejáz, or Arabia Petræa, the mountain *barrier* between the low coast of Arabia and the *Najd* or plateau.

حجل *hajal,* partridge.

حجم *hajm,* bulk, mass, volume.

حجامة *hijáma,* a cupping, bleeding.

محجمة *mihjama,* a cupping instrument.

حدّ or حدّد *hadda,* or *haddada,* he delimited.

حدّ - حدود *hadd,* pl. *hodood,* edge, point; prohibition; limit, frontier.

حادّ *hádd,* sharp, pointed, vehement.

حداد *hidád,* grief, mourning. [آتم

حدّة *hidda,* vehemence.

حديد - سكّة الحديد *hadeed,* iron; *sikket el-hadeed,* railway.

حديدة - حدائد *hadeeda,* pl. *hadáyid,* pieces or tools of iron.

حدّاد *haddád,* blacksmith, ironmonger.

تحديد *tahdeed,* delimitation.

حدّب *haddaba,* he made convex.

حدبة *hadaba,* convexity.

احدب *ahdab,* convex, humpbacked.

محدّب *mohaddab,* convex.

حدث *hadasa,* it happened, befell.

احدث *ahdasa,* he made happen, caused.

حادث *hádasa,* he conversed with.

حدّث *haddasa,* he narrated.

حدوث *hodoos,* appearance, occurrence, birth.

حادثة - حوادث *hádisa,* pl. *hawádis,* accident; news.

حادثة قهرية *hádisa qahriya,* "cas fortuit," accident which could not be helped.

حداثة *hadása,* newness, youth, commencement.

حديث - حدثا *hadees,* pl. *hodasá,* new, new-born infant; young, recent.

حديث السنّ *hadees es-sinn,* young in years, child.

حديث - احاديث *hadees,* pl. *ahádees,* conversation; tradition; the traditions of Mahomed.

محدّث mohaddis, story-teller.

محادثة mohádasa, conversation.

حدج hadaj, colocynth, wild cucumber. [حدق]

حدر hadar, descent, slope.

حدس hads, a guessing; intelligence.

حدف hadafa, he threw, aimed at. [هدف]

حدقة hadaqa, eye-ball.

حديقة hadeeqa, orchard, garden.

حدق hadaq, aubergine, *solanum coagulans*. [باذنجان]

حادي عشر hádi 'ashar, eleventh.

حدوة hidwa, horse shoe. [نعل]

حذر hizr, caution, care.

احتذر ihtazara, he was cautious, took care.

محذور mahzoor, object of caution; danger.

حذق ـ حاذق hizq, sagacity; háziq, sagacious, piquant.

حذاء ـ احذية hizá, pl. ahziya, shoe, boot.

حذاية hazáya, dress, costume.

حرّ harra, it was hot, ardent.

حرّ ـ حرور harr, pl. horoor, heat; haroor, heat, especially heat of summer.

حرارة ـ حارّ harára, heat; hárr, hot.

حرّر harrara, he wrote; freed a slave. [قرّر]

تحرير ـ تحريرات tahreer, pl. tahreerát, a writing, document.

تحريراً or محرّر tahreerán, or moharrar, written.

محرّر moharrir, writer, author.

حرّ ـ احرار horr, pl. ahrár, free, free-born, honest, genuine, real.

بنّا حرّ banná horr, freemason.

حرّية horriya, freedom.

حرير hareer, silk.

حرب ـ حروب harb, pl. horoob (femin.), war.

حرب or حارب haraba, or háraba, he made war.

محاربة ـ محارب moháraba, war; mohárib, at war, warrior.

حربة harba, spear.

حرباً hirbá, chameleon. [ورن]

محراب ـ قبلة mihráb, the *qibla*, or niche at the end of a mosque, pointing to Mecca.

حرث harasa, he tilled, ploughed.

حرث or حراثة hars, or hirása, tillage, cultivation; field.

محراث mihrát, plough.

حراج haráj, auction. [مزاد]

حرز hirz, caution, care. [حذر]

احترز ihtaraza, he was cautious, guarded himself.

حرز haraz, purse; a valuable to be guarded.

تحرّز taharruz, care, precaution.

حرس harasa, he guarded, escorted.

حرس or حراسة hars, or hirása, guard, escort.

احترس (56) حركة

احترس *ihtarasa*, he was on his guard.

حارس - حرّاس *háris*, pl. *horrás*, guardian, military escort; bailiff.

محروس *mahroos*, guarded.

ممالك محروسة *mamálik mahroosa*, "guarded dominions," an official title of Turkey.

مصر المحروسة *masr el-mahroosa*, Cairo the Guarded, the usual title of Cairo. [عاصمة]

محترس *mohtaris*, cautious.

حرّش *harrasha*, he excited, provoked, incited.

حريش *harcesh*, coarse to the touch, prickly.

حرشة *hirsha*, a species of cucumber.

حرص - حريص *hirs*, covetousness; *harees*, covetous.

حرّص *harrasa*, he excited ambition, tempted.

حرّض *harrada*, he debauched, excited to debauchery.

حرف - حروف *harf*, pl. *horoof*, letter of alphabet; a grammatical particle or part of speech.

حروف الهجا *horoof el-hijá*, the alphabet.

حرف - حرف *harf*, pl. *hiraf*, edge, point; deviation.

حرفة - حرف *hirfa*, pl. *hiraf*, trade, profession. [صناعة]

حريف *hareef*, artisan, fellow-artisan; often as a term of contempt, "fellow," "chap."

حرفي *harfiy*, literal, word for word.

حرافة - حريف *haráfa*, piquancy; *harreef*, piquant.

حرّف *harrafa*, he tampered with the letters of a book, altered; transliterated.

تحريف *tahreef*, alteration, transliteration.

احترف *ihtarafa*, he followed a profession.

انحرف *inharafa*, he deviated, was indisposed.

منحرف *munharif*, oblique, indisposed.

حرف *horf*, a species of cress.

حرق *harq*, or *haraq*, fire, combustion.

حريقة *hareeqa*, conflagration.

احرق or حرّق *harraqa*, or *ahraqa*, he set on fire.

احترق *ihtaraqa*, it was on fire, took fire.

انحرق *inharaqa*, it was burnt.

تحريق *tahreeq*, a setting on fire; arson; the burnt up state of the soil during low Nile.

محروق *mahrooq*, burnt.

احتراق *ihtiráq*, lowest water-mark of Nile; a burning; a catching fire.

حركة *haraka*, motion, movement; action; agitation; a vowel-point ُ , َ , ِ .

تَحَرَّكَ *taharraka*, it was in motion.

حَرَّكَ *harraka*, he set in motion, excited; marked the vowel points.

تَحْرِيك *tahreek*, a setting in motion, exciting; marking the vowel-points.

حَرْكَشَة *harkasha*, agitation, commotion.

حَرَمَ *harama*, he forbad, deprived, excluded.

حَرَم or حِرْمَان *hirm*, or *hirmán*, deprivation, outlawry, prohibition.

حَرَام *harám*, forbidden, sacred; it is a sin to do it!

حَرَام عَلَيْكَ *harám 'alaik*, shame on thee! for shame!

حَرِمَ *harima*, it was unlawful.

حَرَّمَ *harrama*, he forbad, rendered sacred.

حَرَم - أَحْرَام *haram*, pl. *ahrám*, sacred, harem, wife; female kindred; a sanctuary, Mecca or Medina. [cf. هرم]

حُرْمَة *horma*, Moslem woman, wife.

حَرِيم - حَرِيمَات *hareem*, pl. *hareemát*, sacred, harem; in pl. women.

أَحْرَمَ *ahrama*, he went on pilgrimage to the sanctuary of Mecca.

أَحْرَام *ihrám*, rites, duties or dress to be observed by a pilgrim.

حَرَامِيّ - حَرَامِيَّة *harámiy*, pl. *harámiya*, robber, outlaw.

اِحْتَرَمَ *ihtarama*, he respected, venerated.

اِحْتِرَام - مُحْتَرَم *ihtirám*, respect; *mohtaram*, respected.

مُحَرَّم *moharram*, sacred; the first month of the Moslem year when war is *forbidden*.

مَحْرُوم *mahroom*, deprived.

مَحْرَمَة *mahrama*, handkerchief. [منديل]

السِتّ فاطمة هانم حرم المرحوم احمد بك *Es-sitt Fátma hánum, haram el-marhoom Ahmad Bey*, the lady Fatma, wife of the deceased Ahmed Bey.

حَرْمَل *harmal*, the herb rue.

حَرُون *haroon*, restive, vicious horse.

حَرِيّ *hariy*, worthy, excellent.

تَحَرَّى *taharra*, he sought out (the good); he investigated.

تَحَرِّيَات *taharriyát*, investigations.

حَزَّاز *hazzáz*, lecanora; hatred, spite. [حنّا]

حِزْب - أَحْزَاب *hizb*, pl. *ahzáb*, part, section; confederate.

حَزَرَ *hazara* he guessed; *hazr*, a guess.

حَزِيرَان *hazeerán*, Syrian month of June.

حَزَمَ *hazama*, he girt.

1

حزم - حِزام hizám, pl. hozom, girth, girdle.

مَحْزوم mahzoom, girt; waist-cloth, towel.

حازم házim, firm, resolute.

حازم الرأي házim er-ráy, a man of sound judgment.

حزن hazina, he was sad; huzn, sadness.

احزن ahzana, he saddened, vexed.

حزن or حزين hazeen, or hazin, sad.

حزانة huzána, family cares, maintenance of a young family. [cf. حضانة]

حس hassa, he felt, perceived by one of the senses.

حسّ بنفسه hassa binafsihi, he felt himself to be.

استحسّ istahassa, he detected, became aware of.

حسّس hassasa, he groped, felt for, manipulated.

حسّ hiss, voice, sensation.

طلّع ـ حسّك tallia' hissak, raise your voice!

حسّاس or حسيس hasees, or hassás, who feels; sensitive.

حاسّة ـ حواسّ hássa, pl. hawáss, a sense; the senses.

حاسّية hássiya, power of sense, sensibility.

محسوس mahsoos, perceptible to the senses; real.

حسب hasaba, he counted, calculated, reckoned.

حسب hasb, a sufficient portion; share.

حسبنا الله hasboná Allah. God is our trust!

حسبي ـ مجلس الحسبي hasbiy, relating to shares; Majlis el-hasbiy. Moslem Probate Court.

حسب hasab, quantity, ratio, proportion. [نسبة]

حسب or على حسب bi-hasab, or 'ala hasab, according to, in proportion to.

حساب ـ حسابات hisáb, pl. hisábát, calculation, account, bill.

علم الحساب 'ilm el-hisáb, arithmetic.

حاسب hásaba, he kept accounts, reckoned with, was on his guard.

حاسب hásib, (imperative) look out!

محاسب mohásib, accountant.

محاسبة ـ محاسبات mohásaba, pl. mohásabát, accounts, book-keeping.

محاسبجي mohásabaji (Turkish), accountant.

احتسب ihtasaba, he considered, reflected.

محتسب عليه mohtasab 'aleih, put to his charge.

حسد hasada, he envied, was jealous of.

حسد hasad, envy, jealousy.

حاسد or حسود *hasood*, or *hásid*, envious.

حسرة *hasra*, sigh, grief, regret, weariness.

حسوم *hosoom*, bad days, name of an unhealthy wind.

حسن - محاسن *hosn*, pl. *mahásin*, beauty, excellence ; in pl. good qualities or features ; charms.

حسن يوسف *hosn yoosuf*, white powder for the face.

حسن - حسان *hasan*, pl. *hisán*, handsome, excellent ; the proper name Hassan.

حسناء or حسنة *hasana*, or *hasná* (femin. of *hasan*), beautiful (woman) ; a good deed, act of charity.

احسن - حسنى *ahsan*, femin. *hosná*, better, more beautiful.

حسنى - حسنيات *hosna*, pl. *hosnayát*, good deed, charity.

حسين *hosain*, (diminutive of *hasan*), the proper name Hussein.

الحسنان *El-Hasanán*, the two sons of Ali and Fátma, Hassan and Hussein.

حسن or حسّن *hasona*, or *tahassana*, it was or became beautiful.

حسّن *hassana*, he beautified, approved of.

تحسين *tahseen*, praise, approval, decoration.

احسن *ahsana*, he bestowed, favoured.

احسان *ihsán*, favour, bounty.

استحسن *istahsana*, he approved of.

استحسان *istihsán*, approval.

محسن *mohsin*, benefactor.

حشّ *hashsha*, he cut grass.

حشيش *hasheesh*, grass, herbage ; an aphrodisiac prepared from hemp ; *cannabis indica*.

حشّاش *hashshásh*, grass-cutter or seller ; seller, or smoker of "*hasheesh*."

محششة *mahshasha*, "*hasheesh*" tavern.

حشر or حشّر *hashara*, or *hashshara*, he collected, loaded, inserted ; tampered with a document by inserting *interlinea*.

تحشير *tahsheer*, insertion of *interlinea*.

انحشر *inhashara*, it was inserted, thrust in.

حشر *hashr*, resurrection ; assembly, swarm.

حشرات *hasharát*, insects, swarming creatures.

حشار *hishár*, charge inserted into a gun.

حشفة *hashfa*, glans, gland.

حشم *hashima*, he blushed, took offence.

حشمة *hishma*, timidity, bashfulness ; modesty.

احتشم *ihtashama*, he showed respect, was awed.

محاشم *mahashim*, testicles.

حَشْمَة *hashma*, pomp, ceremonial, awe.

مُحْتَشِم *mohtashim*, venerable, revered.

حَشَا *hashá*, he stuffed, filled.

حَشْو *hasho*, stuffing, wadding.

حَشَا - احْشَاء *hashú*, pl. *ahshá*, entrails. [معى

حَاشِيَة - حَوَاشِي *háshiya*, pl. *hawáshi*, border, margin. [هَاشِى

لَحْم مَحْشِي *lahm mahshi*, stuffed meat; stew.

مَحْشُوّ *mahshoo*, stuffed.

حَاشَا *háshá*, excepted.

حَاشَا اللّٰه *háshá Allah*, God forbid!

حِصَّة - حِصَص *hissa*, pl. *hisas*, share, portion.

حَصْبَة - حَصْبَاء *hasba*, measles; *hasbá*, pebbles.

مَحْصُوب *mahsoob*, ill with measles.

حَصَد *hasada*, he reaped.

حَصَاد *hasád*, harvest.

حَصَاد المَحْصُول *hasád el-mahsool*, a gathering in of the crops.

حَصِيدَة *haseeda*, a crop.

حَصِر *hasira*, he felt constrained.

حَصَر *hasara*, he confined, restrained, limited.

حَصَرَهُ بِالجَرْد *hasaraho bil-jard*, he entered it in the inventory.

حَصَر شُبْهَتَهُ *hasara shubhatoh*, he suspected, he limited his suspicion to.

حَصْر *hosr*, retention of urine.

مَحْصُور *mahsoor*, taken ill.

حَصْر *hasr*, restriction, constraint.

حَاصَر *hásara*, he besieged.

مُحَاصَرَة *mohásara*, siege.

حِصَار *hisár*, castle, fortress.

حَصِيرَة - حَصَر *huseera*, pl. *hosor*, mat, matting.

حِصْرِم *husrum*, sour, acid fruit.

حَصَل *hasala*, it happened, resulted.

الحَادِثَة حَصَلَت *el-hádisa hasalet*, the accident happened.

حَصَّل *hassala*, he obtained; levied taxes.

حُصُول *hosool*, event, a befalling, attainment.

تَحْصِيل *tahseel*, success, attainment; collection of taxes.

تَحْصِيلدَار *tahseeldár* (Persian), tax-collector.

حَاصِل - حَوَاصِل *hásil*, pl. *hawásil*, result; end obtained; advantage; barn, court-yard.

تَحَصَّل عَلَى *tahassala 'ala*, he obtained, attained; it resulted from, was realized.

مَحْصُول - مَحْصُولَات *mahsool*, pl. *mahsoolát*, result; crops, produce; revenue.

حِصْن - حُصُون *hisn*, pl. *hosoon*, fortress; chastity.

حَصَنَة or حَصْنَاء *hasná*, or *hásina*, chaste woman. [cf. حَسْنَاء

مُحْصَنَة *mohsana*, chaste woman.

حصان ـ حصن ـ خيل hisán, pl. hoson, stallion, horse. Instead of hoson, the pl. in use is khail.

حصاة ـ حصيّ hasát, pl. hosiy; and حصوة ـ حصي haswa, pl. hasa, pebble, gravel, calculus.

احصى ahsa, he calculated.

حضيض hadeed, apogee; aphelion, furthest point.

حضر hadara, he was present, ready, he presented himself.

حضر haddara, he made ready, prepared.

احضر ahdara, he summoned, made appear.

احتضر ihtadara, he prepared himself, was on the point of death.

استحضر istahdara, he sent for, asked for the presence of, he brought forward (his witnesses).

حضرة hadra, presence; Excellency, Sir.

حضرتك or حضرتكم hadratak, or hadratkom, Thy or Your Excellency! Your Highness! Noble Sir!

حضراتكم hadrátikom, Your Excellencies! Gentlemen!

الحضرة الخديوية El-Hadrat el-Khedéwiya, H.H. the Khedive.

حضرتلري hazretleri (Turkish), His or Your Excellency.

حاضر ـ حاضرون hádir, pl. hádiroon (or hádireen), present, ready; domiciled (not nomad).

حضارة hadára, settled Arabs (not Bedouins).

احضار ihdár, a summons; a bringing forward.

محضر mohdir, "huissier," summons-server.

محضر ـ محاضر mahdar, pl. mahádir, report, minutes of proceedings, "procès-verbal."

حضن ـ حضون hidn, pl. hodoon, bosom, lap; interval of time.

حضانة hidána, maternal rights.

احتضن ihtadana, he embraced, took to his bosom.

حطّ hatta, he placed, put down, deposited.

انحطّ inhatta, it diminished, sank, was put down.

حطّ hatt, a putting down; reduction.

حاطّ or حططاط hátit, or hátt, he who places.

انحطاط inhitát, decline, decadence; a sinking.

محطّة mahatta, place where a thing is deposited; railway station.

وكيل المحطّة wakeel el-mahatta, station-master.

حطب ـ احطاب hatab, pl. ahtáb, firewood. Distinguish this from khashab, timber. [خشب]

حطم hatama, he broke in pieces.

حظّ hazza, he was delighted, glad.

حظّ ـ حظوظ hazz, pl. hozooz, delight, pleasure.

محظوظ *mahzooz*, gladdened, pleased.

محظوظيّة *mahzooziya*, happiness, joy.

حظي *hazia*, he succeeded in, obtained.

حظوة *hizwa*, success, advantage.

حظيّة ـ حظايا *haziya*, pl. *hazáyá*, concubine.

حفيد ـ حفدة *hafeed*, pl. *hafada*, grandson.

حفر *hafara*, he dug.

حفر ـ حفريّات *hafr*, pl. *hafriyát*, a digging; excavations.

حفرة *hofra*, hole, pit, hollow, well.

حافر ـ حوافر *háfir*, pl. *hawáfir*, hoof, digger.

حفّار *haffár*, digger, grave-digger.

محفر *mihfar*, spade.

تحفّظ or حفظ *hafiza*, or *tahaffaza*, he guarded, protected, was vigilant; reserved; learned by heart.

حفّظ *haffaza*, he taught (the Koran, &c.), made learn by heart.

حافظ *háfaza*, he guarded, watched over as a ruler.

استحفظ *istahfaza*, he sought protection.

حفظ *hifz*, guard, care, protection; faculty or power of memory.

حفظ و صيانة *hifz wa siyána*, guard and protection.

حفظ جميل *hifz jameel*, memory of a favour, gratitude.

حافظ *háfiz*, guardian; knowing by heart.

حافظة *háfiza*, faculty of memory.

محافظ *moháfiz*, guardian, governor of a town.

محافظة *moháfaza*, guardianship; township as apart from a "*mooderriya*;" governor's office or dwelling.

محفوظ *mahfooz*, guarded, reserved.

محفظة *mahfaza*, portfolio, case.

مستحفظ *mustahfiz*, reserve of police or of army; national guard.

حفل or احتفل *hafala*, or *ihtafala*, a crowd collected.

حفل or احتفال or محفل *hafl*, or *ihtifál*, or *mahfil*, crowd, procession, public ceremony, pomp.

احتفالي *ihtifáliy*, solemn, ceremonious, pompous.

حفلة *haflata*, nuisance, bore, embarrassment.

حفي ـ حفا *hafia*, he went barefoot; *hafán*, being barefoot.

حافي *háfi*, who is barefoot; unshod (horse).

حقّ ـ حقوق *haqq*, pl. *hoqooq*, truth; legal right.

حقّ عيني *haqq 'ainiy*, real property, "*droit réel.*"

مجرّد حقّ *mojarrad haqq*, personal property, "*droit incorporel.*"

الحقّ معك ـ عليك *el-haqq m'ak*,

you are in the right; *el-haqq 'alaik*, you are in the wrong.

حقّ الملكيّة *haqq el-malakiya*, right of property, "*propriété.*"

حقّ الانتفاع *haqq el-intifá'a*, usufruct.

حقّ الارتفاق *haqq el-irtifáq*, servitude.

حقّ الامتياز *haqq el-imtiyáz*, privilege.

حقّ رهن العقار *haqq rahn el-'aqár*, "*hypothèque,*" mortgage.

حقّ اختصاص بعقار *haqq ikhtisás bi-'aqár*, "*affectation.*"

حقّ الحبس *haqq el-habs*, "*rétention.*"

حقيقة ـ حقائق *haqeeqa*, pl. *haqáyiq*, a true statement, truth.

حقيقيّ *haqeeqiy*, true, real.

حقيقةً *haqeeqatán*, truly.

حقّق *haqqaqa*, he verified, investigated the truth; held a legal inquiry.

تحقيق ـ تحقيقات *tahqeeq*, pl. *tahqeeqát*, verification, legal inquiry, "*instruction.*"

قاضي التحقيق *qádi et-tahqeeq*, examining magistrate, "*juge d'instruction.*" [مستنطق]

حقّ ـ احقّ *haqq*, worthy; *ahaqq*, worthier.

احقّ *ahaqqa*, he obtained justice.

تحقّق *tahaqqaqa*, it came true, was proved correct.

استحقّ *istahaqqa*, he deserved; it fell due (as a bill, debt, interest, &c.).

استحقاق *istihqáq*, merit; the falling due of a debt, &c.

مستحقّ *mostahaqq*, deserved; fallen due.

محقّق *mohaqqaq*, verified, shown true.

حقّ ـ حقاق *hoqq*, pl. *hoqaq*, small box, snuff-box, casket; Indian "hookah."

حقب *hoqb*, epoch, century.

حقيبة *haqeeba*, camel's saddle-girth.

حقد *hiqd*, envy, malice.

حقر or حقّر or احتقر or استحقر *haqara*, or *haqqara*, or *ihtaqara*, or *istahqara*, he despised, treated with contempt.

حقارة ـ حقير *haqára*, contempt; contemptible.

حقل *haql*, cornfield, field. [غيط]

حقنة ـ محقان *hoqna*, clyster, enema; *mihqán*, syringe.

حقو *haqo*, waist, loins.

حكّ *hakka*, he scratched, rubbed.

حكّ ـ حكّة *hakk*, a scratching; *hikka*, itch.

محكّ *mihakk*, touchstone.

حكر or احتكر *hakara*, or *ihtakara*, he monopolised, bought up and held back corn, &c.

احتكار *ihtikár*, monoply.

حكر *hikr*, a waqf's ground-rent; a *real right* in favour of a legatee; quit-rent.

حكم - احكام *hokm*, pl. *ahkám*, judicial sentence, judgment, decision, order.

حكم *hakama*, he judged, passed sentence.

حكم عليه بالحبس *hakama 'aleih bil-habs*, he sentenced him to prison.

حاكم حكام *hákim*, pl. *hokkám*, judge, governor. [قاضي]

محكمة - محاكم *mahkama*, pl. *mahákim*, tribunal, court.

محكمة ابتدائية *mahkama ibtidáiya*, Tribunal of First Instance.

محكمة استئنافية *mahkama isteenáfiya*, Court of Appeal.

محكمة شرعية *mahkama shara'iya*, Court of Moslem law, Cadi's Court.

محكمة مختلطة - اهلية *mahkama mukhtalita*, mixed tribunal; *mahkama ahliya*, native tribunal.

محاكمة *mohákama*, trial, hearing. [مرافعة]

محكوم عليه - عليهم *mahkoom 'aleih*, pl. *mahkoom 'aleihim*, condemned man.

حكم *hakem*, wise, arbitrator.

حكم *hakkama*, he arbitrated, or sent to arbitration.

حكيم - تحكيم *tahkeem*, arbitration; *mohakkim*, arbitrator.

حكمة - حكم *hikma*, pl. *hikam*, science. [علم]

حكيم - حكماء *hakeem*, pl *hokamá*, physician.

حكيم باشي *hakeem báshi* (Turkish), chief doctor, surgeon-major.

استحكم *istahkama*, he fortified.

مستحكمات *mustahkamát*, fortifications.

محكم *mohkam*, firm, solid, well made.

حكى - يحكي *haka*, he narrated, said; *yihki*, he says. [روي]

حاكي *háki*, narrator.

حكاية *hikáya*, narrative, tale, statement.

محكي *mohka*, spoken of, mentioned.

حل *halla*, he unloosed, solved, absolved; alighted, descended; it was lawful.

حل محله *halla mahalloh*, he acted in his stead. [قام مقامه]

حل *hall*, an unloosing, solution.

حل *hill*, lawfulness.

حلال *halál*, a lawful thing; lawful.

حلول *holool*, descent, alighting; arrival of a date.

حلول الميعاد *holool el-mee'yád*, lapse or end of a fixed time, "*échéance*."

حللية or حلل *holal* or *holaliya*, robes, attire, cloak.

حلل ـ حُلّة *halla*, pl. *hilal*, saucepan; area, threshing-floor.

حليل ـ حليلة *haleel*, (femin.) *haleela*, lawful spouse.

احليل *ihleel*, urethra, duct, passage.

حلّل *hallala*, he analysed, rendered lawful.

تحليل *tahleel*, analysis, legalisation.

تحليلي *tahleeliy*, analytic.

محلّل *mohallil*, legaliser; he who marries a divorced woman only in order to divorce her after consummation, so that he may *make it lawful* for her first husband who divorced her to remarry her.

احتلّ *ihtalla*, he alighted, took up his residence; (the army) occupied (a country).

احتلال *ihtilál*, residence, occupation by an army.

جيش الاحتلال *jaish el-ihtilál*, Army of Occupation.

محلّ ـ محال *mahall*, pl. *maháll*, place, alighting place; district.

محلّة *mahalla*, village.

محلّي *mahalliy*, local, relating to a district.

مستحلّ *mostahill*, the same as *mohallil*.

محلول *mahlool*, unloosened, absolved, solved, vacant.

حلب *halaba*, he milked.

حليب *haleeb*, milked, milk.

لبن حليب *laban haleeb*, fresh, new milk.

حلب *halab*, Aleppo; milk.

حالب *hálib*, duct, ureter.

حلبة *holba*, fenugreek.

حلبي *halabiy*, native of Aleppo, gipsy, tinker.

محلب *mihlab*, milk-pail.

حلج *halaja*, he carded or ginned cotton.

حلاجة *hilája*, cotton-ginning.

حليج *haleej*, carded, ginned.

حلّاج *halláj*, cotton-ginner.

محلاج *mihláj*, cotton-gin; carding instrument.

حلزون *halazoon*, snail; deep well in a spiral; auger.

حلف يميناً or حلف *halafa*, or *halafa yameenán*, he took an oath (as a witness, &c., in court).

حلّف *hallafa*, he swore in, gave the oath.

حلف *half*, oath. [قسم]

حالف *hálif*, sworn in, under oath.

حلفا *halfá*, esparto grass; rushes.

وادي حلفاء *Wádi Halfá*, valley of rushes; the southern frontier town and province of Egypt on the Nile.

حلق *halaqa*, he shaved (the head, beard).

حلاقة ـ حلاقة *hiláqa*, a shaving; *halláq*, barber.

محلوق or حليق *haleeq* or *mahlooq*, shaven, shorn.

حَلقِي - حَاتق halq, throat; halqiy, guttural.

حَلقي - حَلْقة halqa, pl. halaq, bracelet, ear-ring, ring, circle; ring of men at an auction.

حلقة الاسماك halqat el-asmák, fish-market, or ring where fish is sold by auction.

حلقوم holqoom, throat.

راحة للحلقوم, ráhat lil-holqoom, "Rahat lakoum," peace to the throat, a sweetmeat.

حلم halama, he dreamed.

حلم - احلام holm, pl. ahlám, dream [رؤيا]

حلم - حليم hilm, gentleness; haleem, gentle.

حلّم hallama, he showed kindness.

حلمة halama, teat, nipple.

احتلام ihtilám, puberty.

حلا halá, it was sweet to the taste.

حلو - حلاوة haloo, or haláwa, sweetness; freshness of water; "baksheesh."

حلو - حلوة holo (femin.), holwa (usually pronounced haloo, halwa), sweet, nice.

ماء حلوة má holwa (mwai haloo), good water.

حلوى - حلاوى halwa, pl. haláwa, sweetmeat.

حلوجي halwaji (Turkish), confectioner.

حلوان halwán, fee, perquisite, "tip"; Helouan, a suburb of Cairo.

حلوى - احلى ahla, (femin.) holwa, sweeter.

حلّى or حلى hala, or halla, he adorned with jewels.

حلي - حلّي hali, pl. holiy, jewel, ornament.

حمّ or حمّم hamma, or hammama, he heated the bath.

حمّ homma, he was feverish, sick with fever.

استحمّ istahamma, he took a hot bath; (colloquially) he bathed (in hot or cold water).

حمّى - حمّيات homma, pl. hommayát, fever.

حمّام hammám, bath.

حمام hamám, dove, pigeon. [يمام]

محموم mahmoom, ill with fever.

حمد hamida, he praised; hamd, praise.

الحمد لله el-hamdo lillahi, Praise be to God!

الحمدلة el-hamdila, the phrase "el-hamdo lillahi."

محمدة - محامد mahmida, pl. mahámid, a praiseworthy action.

محمد Mohammad, praised, praiseworthy; Mahomet, pronounced in Turkish, Méhemet.

حميد hameed, praiseworthy, a title of God; Hameed.

احمد ahmad, more praiseworthy; Ahmed.

محمود mahmood, praised; Mahmoud.

حمودة or حامد hámid, or hamooda, names for men, similar to Hameed, Ahmed, Mohammad, Mahmood, &c.

حمرة homra, redness; red brick powder mixed with cement.

احمر - حمراء ahmar, (femin.) hamrá, red, brown.

الموت الاحمر el-mōt el-ahmar, red, bloody, violent death.

البحر الاحمر el-bahr el-ahmar, the Red Sea.

حمر homr, pl. of ahmar, red men, or things.

حمار - حمير himár, pl. hameer, ass. [جحش]

حمّار hammár, donkey-boy.

حميرة homaira, measles, red rash.

احمرار ihmirár, a turning red.

حميرى himmyariy, Himyaric, the old language of El-Yemen, in Arabia.

محمرة mahmara, machine for mixing "homra" cement.

حمز hamaza, he pricked. [همز]

حمز hamz, piquancy.

حماسة hamása, bravery, energy.

حمّص hammasa, he grilled, roasted peas, coffee, &c.

حمّص hommos, roasted peas.

حمص homs, or hims, the town of Emesa, in Syria.

تحميص البن tahmees el-bonn, the roasting of coffee-berries.

محمص mohammas, roasted.

حمض hamida, it was acid.

حمض or حموضة himd, or homooda, acidity; an acid.

حامض - حوامض hámid, pl. hawámid, chemical acid.

حميض hommaid, oseille, sorrel.

حمق or حماقة homq, or hamáqa, crass stupidity; insanity.

احمق or حمقان ahmaq, or hamqán, utter fool, thickhead, one who flies into a blind rage.

حمل himl, load, burden; 550 lbs., or 250 kilog., 200 oqes.

حمل hamala, he carried a load, bore; attacked; incited, caused.

حملت hamilet, she was pregnant. [حبلت]

حمل haml, a load, freight; act of carrying, pregnancy; woollen cloak.

حمل hamal, ram; Aries in the Zodiac.

حملة hamla, attack, onset; a load of 60 oqes, 75 kilog.; octroi on animals.

حمالة - حمائل himála, pl. hamáyil, sword-belt, sash.

حمّال hammál, a porter, carrier.

حمولة hamoola, cargo, freight, burthen.

حملى himaliy, water-carrier.

حامل hámil, bearer (of a bill of exchange), carrier; pregnant woman; cause, incentive.

حمّل hammala, he loaded.

تحمّل *tahammala*, he endured.

احتمل *ohtomila* (passive), it was probable.

محتمل - احتمال *ihtimál*, probability; *mohtamal*, probable.

محمل *mahmal*, litter, camel-load of the sacred carpet from Cairo to Mecca, and the return of the carpet of the previous year.

حماة - حمو *hamo*, (femin.) *hamá*, father-, mother-in-law.

حمى *hama*, he defended.

حامى *háma*, he defended, pleaded as a lawyer for his client.

حماية *himáya*, protection, consular protection, hence a foreign protected subject, not an Ottoman. [cf. رعيّة

حمية *himya*, diet for a sick person.

حميّة *hamiya*, wrath, anger.

حامي *hámi*, defender; hot; potent liquid.

حامي عنه *mohámi 'anoh*, his lawyer, defender.

محاماة *mohámát*, defence in court.

حنين *haneen*, sob.

حنون or حنّان *hanoon*, or *hannán*, sympathetic, tender.

حنّاء *hinná*, henna, *lawsonia alba*; a red stain for the fingers, hair, beard.

حنّا *Hanná*, John. [cf. يحيا

حنبل *Hanbal*. The Imám Abdullah Ibn Hanbal, founder of one of the four great Sunni schools of orthodox Islam, and the most fanatic and austere of the four. 780-855 A.D. Baghdad.

حنبلي *hanbaliy*, a follower of Hanbal; relating to his sect.

مالك - شافعي - حنيفة]

حانوت - حوانيت *hánoot*, pl. *hawáneet*, shop. [دكّان

حنث . حنث *hins*, perjury; *hanisa*, he broke his oath.

حنجرة *hanjara*, larynx.

حنش - احناش *hanash*, pl. *ahnásh*, snake, reptile.

حنطة *hinta*, wheat. [قمح

حناط *hinát*, balm, aromatics.

حنّط *hannata*, he embalmed the dead.

حانوطي *hánootiy*, a washer of corpses for burial. [مغسّل

حنف *hanafa*, he leaned, inclined.

حنفيّة *hanafiya*, tap, water-cock; metal jug; bath-room.

حنيف *haneef*, sincere in his inclination towards Islam, a true follower of Abraham.

حنيفة *Haneefa*, Aboo Haneefá Na'mán the Imam, founder of the most popular of the four great Sunni schools of orthodox Islam. 700-770 A.D. Baghdad.

حنيفي *haneefiy*, a follower of Aboo Haneefa, a Hanafee.

[شافعي - مالك - حنبل]

حنك *hanak*, palate, jaw, jowl.

حنايَة or حنو *hano*, or *hináya*, curve, curvature.

تَحَنَّى or حنى or حنا *haná*, or *tahanna*, it bent, was bent, curved.

حنّى *hanna*, he made bend, curved.

أنحنى *inhana*, it was bent, curved.

منحنى *munhani*, bent, curved.

حوب *hōb*, sin, regret, anxiety.

حوت - أحوات *hoot*, pl. *ahwát*, fish, large fish, whale; *Pisces* in the Zodiac.

حوّاتي *hawwátiy*, fisherman.

حويت *howait*, cunning, cheater.

حوج - حاجة *hōj*, necessity (see *hája*).

[حوز] - أستحوذ على (*hōz*); *istahwaza 'ala*, he obtained.

حور *hawar*, or *hōr*, poplar-tree.

أحور - حوراً - حور *ahwar*, (femin.) *hōrá*, pl. *hoor*, possessing beautiful black eyes.

الحور العين *el-hoor el-'ain*, pl., black-eyed (damsels) of Paradise, houris.

حوريَّة *hooriya*, (colloquial), houri, a black-eyed damsel of Paradise.

حوري *hoori* (Soudanese), "dug-out" canoe used on the coasts of the Red Sea.

حاور - محاورة *háwara*, he conversed; *moháwara*, conversation.

حواريّ *hawáriy*, apostle, disciple.

محار *mahár*, oyster, shell-fish.

محور *mihwar*, axis, cylinder, rolling-pin.

حوز or حيازة *hōz*, or *hiyáza*, possession, enjoyment.

حوزة *hōza*, sheep-fold; a kitchen, or other enclosure; possession, enjoyment.

حاز or أستحوز *háza*, or *istahwaza*, he possessed, obtained possession of. [حوذ]

حائز *háyiz*, possessor, holder, in possession.

حوش - حيشان - حوشة *hōsh*, pl. *heeshán*, enclosure, courtyard; *hōsha*, open space.

حَوَّش *hawwasha*, he collected, lumped together; put by (money), economised.

حوش الحرامي *hoosh el-harámiy*, seize the thief! stop him!

حوصلة *hōsala*, bird's crop, vesicle.

حوض - حيضان or حياض *hōd*, pl. *heedán*, or *hiyád*, dock for ships, reservoir; piece of cultivated land banked in for irrigation; pelvis.

حوطة - حاط *hōta*, care, guard (see *háta*).

حاك [حوك] - (*hōk*), *háka*, he wove. [نسج]

حول *hōl*, power, power of God.

حول or حوالى *hōla*, or *hawála*, around, round about.

حوال or حولان *hawál*, or *hawalán*, transition, change.

حوالة (70) حارة

حَوَالَة ḥawála, transfer; bill of exchange, money-order.

حَوَالِيّ ḥawáliy, changeable, versatile, cunning.

حَوِل - احْوَل ḥawal, squint; aḥwal, one who squints.

حَال - احْوَال ḥál, pl. aḥwál (femin.), condition, state, circumstances; trance, ecstasy.

احْوَال شَخْصِيَّة aḥwál shakhsiya, "Statut Personnel." Moslem law of marriage, successions, &c.

قَرَائِن الاحْوَال qaráyin el-aḥwál, probabilities, circumstances of the case; circumstantial evidence.

حَالَة - حَالات ḥála, pl. ḥálát, state, condition.

الحَالَةَ هٰذِهِ el-ḥáleto házihi, now, in fact.

حَالاً - فِي الحَال ḥálan, now; fil-ḥál, now, in fact, actually, at once.

حَالِيّ ḥáliy, actual.

حَائِل ḥáyil, changing; impediment.

حِيلَة - حِيَل ḥeela, pl. ḥiyal, ruse, trick; legal fiction.

احَالَ aḥála, he referred to, endorsed, transferred.

احَالَة iḥála, reference, transfer.

حَوَّلَ ḥawwala, he transferred, endorsed, converted, moved; turned aside.

تَحْوِيل - تَحْوِيلات taḥweel, pl. taḥweelát, transfer, endorsement, bank-note, money-bill or order.

تَحْوِيلَة taḥweela, reserve-bank of canal or river.

تَحَوَّلَ taḥawwala, it became transferred or converted.

احْتَال or تَحَايَل iḥtála, or taḥáyala, he was cunning; cheated.

احْتِيَال or تَحَايُل iḥtiyál, or taḥáyul, fraud, swindling.

احْتِيَالِيّ iḥtiyáliy, fraudulent, of false pretences.

اسْتَحَال istaḥála, it was absurd, impossible.

مُسْتَحِيل mustaḥeel, absurd. [cf. مُسْتَأْهِل

مُحَال moḥál, absurd.

مُحِيل moḥeel, transferor, endorser of a bill.

حَوَّاء Ḥawwá, Eve, the first woman.

حَوَى or احْتَوَى عَلَى ḥawa, or iḥtawa 'ala, it included. [شَمِل

حَاوِي or مُحْتَوِي عَلَى ḥáwi, or moḥtawi ala, including, containing.

حَوِيَّة ḥawiya, pad, camel-saddle.

حَيْث - مِن حَيْث ḥais, place where, whereas; min ḥais, whereas.

حَيْثِيَّة ḥaisiya, relevancy, status.

حَيَّد or حَوَّد ḥayyada, or ḥawwada, he made turn aside.

حَيْرَة or حَيْرَان ḥaira, or ḥayarán, astonishment.

حَار or تَحَيَّر ḥára, or taḥayyara, he was astounded.

حَائِر or حَيْرَان ḥáyir, or ḥairán, astounded.

حَارَة - حَارَات ḥára, pl. ḥárát, lane, narrow street.

حيض or محيض *haid*, or *maheed*, menses.

حيف *haif*, injustice.

حيل *hail*, strength; a standing erect.

قُم على حيلك *qom 'ala hailak*, stand upright! stand up!

حين ـ احيان *heen*, pl. *ahyán*, time, moment.

احياناً *ahyánán*, at times, sometimes.

حينئذ *heenayizin*, then, at that time.

حيانيّ *hayániy* (colloquial), ripe (fruit, dates, &c.).

حيي ـ يحيى *haya*, he was alive; *yaha*, he lives.

حياة or حيرة *hayát*, life.

في قيد الحياة *fi qaid el-hayát*, alive, in a state of life.

حيّ ـ احياء *haiy*, pl. *ahyá*, alive; *haiya*, hasten! look alive!

حياء ـ حييّ *hayá*, modesty; *haiy*, modest, chaste.

حيّة ـ حاوي *haiya*, snake; *háwi*, snake-charmer.

حيويّ *haiwaiy*, vital, pertaining to life.

حيوان ـ حيوانات *haiwán*, pl. *haiwánát*, animal, beast.

حيّا or احيا *hayyá*, or *ahyá*, he vivified, reclaimed waste land.

تحيّة or احياء *taheeya*, or *ihyá*, a vivifying, reclaiming waste land.

استحى *istaha*, he felt ashamed, blushed.

استحياء *istihiá*, shame, modesty.

مستحي *mostahi*, ashamed.

محيي *mohee*, (God) the Maker Alive.

يحيى or يحيا *Yahia*, John Baptist.

حيّ العالم *haiy el-'aálem*, sempervivum, calanchoë.

KH

خ *Khá*. Value = 600.

خاتون *khátoon* (Turkish), lady. [قادن]

خاض ـ خوض *kháda*, he forded (see *khōd*).

خاف ـ خوف *kháfa*, he feared (see *khōf*).

خاقان *kháqán* (Turkish), Sultan.

خال ـ خالة *khál*, (femin.) *khála*, maternal uncle, aunt (see *'amm*); suspicion, cloud; mole on the skin. [عمّ]

خال ـ خيال *khála*, he imagined (see *khayál*).

خام *khám* (Persian), raw; calico; novice.

خاميّ ـ موادّ خاميّة *khámiy* in *mawádd khámiya*, raw materials or stuffs.

خان ـ خون *khána*, he betrayed (see *khōn*).

خان *khán* (Persian), a title of the Sultan; prince; inn, hotel, bazaar.

خانم ـ هانم *khánum* (Turkish), lady (see *hánum*).

خانة *khána*, house, shop; stall, place, compartment, pigeon-hole.

خانوت *khánoot* (from *khána*), shop. [or حانوت]

خانية *khániya*, small canal by the side of a railway line. [جانبيّة]

خبا or خبىء *khabá*, he concealed. [خفى]

تخبّىء or استخبىء *takhabba*, or *istakhba*, he hid himself.

خبيئة *khabeeya*, a hidden thing.

خابية *khábiya*, jar, vat, dye-tub.

مخبا *makhbá*, hidden; a hiding-place.

خبث *khabusa*, he was base, behaved vilely.

خبث ـ خبيث *khabúsa*, infamy; *khabees*, infamous.

خبر ـ اخبار *khabar*, pl. *akhbár*, news.

علم خبر *'ilm-khabar*, receipt, invoice.

خبرة *khibra*, experience, expertise, survey.

اهل ـ ارباب الخبرة *ahl el-khibra*, pl. *arbáb el-khibra*, a professional expert or surveyor.

اخبر *akhbara* he informed, announced.

اخبار *ikhbár*, information.

اخبار بامر كاذب *ikhbár bi-amr kázib*, legal term for publishing a libel.

مخبر *mukhbir*, informant.

مخبر سرّيّ *mukhbir sirriy*, secret informant, police detective, spy.

خابر *khábara*, he exchanged news, corresponded.

مخابرة *mokhábara*, correspondence.

استخبر *istakhbara*, he wished to know, inquired.

اختبار *ikhtibár*, probation, on trial; the examination of candidates.

خبز *khobz*, bread. [عيش]

خبز *khabaza*, he baked.

خبّاز *khabbáz*, baker. [فرّان]

مخبزة *makhbaza*, bakery.

خبيزة *khobaiza*, geranium; mallow.

خبص *khabasa*, he mixed, muddled, trumped up, slandered.

خبص *khabs*, vice, bad conduct, slander.

خبط *khabata*, he knocked, made a noise.

خبطة *khabta*, noise of knocking; knock; noise in general.

تخبيط *takhbeet*, a making a noise.

خبل *khabal*, imbecility.

ختم *khatama*, he sealed the end of; ended.

ختم ـ اختام *khatm*, or *khitm*, pl. *akhtám*, seal, signet.

خاتم ـ خواتم *khátim*, pl. *khawátim*, seal-ring.

ختم ـ خاتمة *khitám*, or *khátima*, end, finis.

ختامى *khitámiy*, final.

خَتْمَة *khatma*, recitation of the Koran; the Koran.

خَتَّام *khattám*, engraver of seals. [نَقَّاش]

خَتَن *khatana*, he circumcised. [طهر]

خِتَان *khitán*, circumcision.

مَخْتُون *makhtoon*, circumcised.

خِجِل ـ خِجْلَان *khajal*, blush; *khajlán*, bashful.

خَخَام *khakhám* (Turkish), Jewish rabbi.

خَدّ ـ خُدُود *khadd*, pl. *khodood*, cheek. [وِجْنَة]

مِخَدَّة *mikhadda*, pillow, cushion.

خَدِيجَة *Khadeeja*, the first wife of Mahomed.

خَدِر *khadira*, he was torpid, benumbed.

خَدَّر *khaddara*, he made sleep by a soporific.

مُخَدِّر *mokhaddir*, a soporific, or strong liquor.

خَدَش *khadasha*, he scratched. [خربش]

خَدَع *khada'a*, he deceived.

خَدِيعَة or خَدَعَة or خِدَاع *khidá'a*, or *khoda'a*, or *khadee'a*, deceit, a ruse, trickery.

مَخْدَع *mikhda'*, alcove, bedroom.

خَدَم *khadama*, he served.

اِسْتَخْدَم *istakhdama*, he employed, took as servant.

خِدْمَة ـ خِدَامَة or خِدَامَة *khidáma*, or *khidma*, pl. *khidam*, service, duty.

خَدَّام *khaddám*, a servant.

خَادِم ـ خَدَمَة *khádim*, pl. *khadama*, servant; (in Turkish) eunuch.

مُسْتَخْدَم *mustakhdam*, employé; an official.

مَخْدُوم *makhdoom*, master, the person who is served; (in Turkish) a son.

خَدِيو *khadeev* (Persian), prince.

خِدِيوِيّ *Khedéwiy*, the Khedive, Khedivial.

الجِنَاب الخِدِيوِيّ *El-janáb el-Khedéwiy*, H.H. The Khedive.

الحَضْرَة الفَخِيمَة الخِدِيوِيَّة *el-hadrat el-fakheemat el-Khedéwiya*, His Exalted Highness The Khedive.

خُذ ـ اخذ *khud* (imperative of *akhaza*), take!

خَرِير *khareer*, murmur of running water.

خَرِىء ـ خَرَاء *kharia*, he went to stool; *khirá*, stools.

خَرِب *khariba*, it was in ruins.

خَرِب or خَرْبَان *kharib*, or *kharbán*, ruined, in ruins, spoilt, out of gear.

خَرَّب *kharraba*, he ruined, devastated.

خَرَاب *kharáb*, ruin, desolation; a ruin.

خَرُّوب *kharroob*, carob.

خَرْبَش *kharbasha*, he scratched.

خَرْبَشَة *kharbasha*, a scratch.

خَرَت *kharata*, he pierced.

خَرَج *kharaja*, he went out.

L.

اخرج *akhraja*, he took, sent, or drove out; exported.

استخرج *istakhraja*, he extracted, elicited.

خرج - اخراج *kharj*, pl. *akhráj*, expense, outlay.

خرج *khorj*, saddle-bag, wallet.

خراج *kharáj*, land-tax, tribute.

خراجي *kharájiy*, land paying the ordinary tax (see *'oshooriy*). [عشوري]

خرجة *kharja*, outlet, balcony.

خروج *khorooj*, a going out, issue, exit; exodus.

خارج *khárij*, he who goes out, external, exterior.

خارج عن *khárij 'an*, outside of, abroad; exclusive of.

خارجي *khárijiy*, foreign, external.

نظارة الخارجية *nazárat el-khárijiya*, Ministry of Foreign Affairs.

مخرج *makhraj*, place of issue, exit.

خريدة *khareeda*, a virgin, un-pierced pearl. [فريدة]

خردة - خردوات *khorda*, pl. *khordawát* (Persian), small ware, pedlar's haberdashery, trash; copper money.

خردجي *khordaji* (Turkish), pedlar, haberdasher.

خردل *khardal*, mustard.

خرز *kharaz*, chaplet of (glass) beads.

خرس *khirs*, hard bad soil, inferior land.

خرس *kharas*, dumbness.

اخرس *akhras*, dumb.

اخرس *ikhras* (imperative), hold your tongue!

خروس *khoros* (Turkish), cock; trigger.

خرشوف *kharshoof*, artichoke.

خرط *kharata*, he turned on a lathe.

خراط *kharrát*, a turner.

مخرطة *mikhrata*, lathe.

مخروط *makhroot*, turned, cone.

مخروطي *makhrootiy*, conic, conics.

خارطة or خريطة *khareeta*, chart, map.

خرطوم *khortoom*, proboscis, snout; the town of Khartoum in the Soudan where the two Niles meet after forming a narrow spit or snout of land.

خرع - اخترع *khara'*, (or better) *ikhtara'a*, he invented.

اختراع *ikhtirá'a*, invention, story, good idea.

خروع *kharwa'*, castor-oil tree.

خراف *kharáf*, a gathering of crops or fruit.

خريف *khareef*, harvest-time, autumn.

خروف - خرفان *kharoof*, pl. *khirfán*, sheep.

خرافة *khoráfa*, nonsense, false notion.

خرق *kharaqa*, he rent, tore.

خرق *kharq*, a rending, rent, tear.

خرقة *khirqa*, chemise; rag, ragged garment.

خرم *kharm*, or *khorm*, a short cut across, hole, a piercing.

خرنوب *kharnoob*, fruit of acacia nilotica. [قرظ]

خروشة *kharwasha*, rustle, rustling noise.

خزّ *khazz*, coarse silk. [تزّ]

خزر *khazar*, Caspian.

خيزران ـ خيازر *khaizarán*, pl. *khayázir*, cane, bamboo.

خزعبلة *khaza'bla*, quackery, humbug.

خزام *khizám*, nose-ring; twitch; seton.

خزامى *khozáma*, lavender.

خزّن *khazzana*, he stored in a magazine.

خزينة ـ خزائن *khazeena*, pl. *khazáyin*, treasury, cash or pay department; wardrobe.

مخزن ـ مخازن *makhzan*, pl. *makházin*, magazine; cesspool under a house.

مخزنجي *makhzanji* (Turkish), storekeeper.

خزية *khaziya*, humiliation.

خسّ *khassa*, (the Nile) fell; the liquid sank or decreased in a vessel.

خسّ النيل *khass en-neel*, low Nile.

خسّ *khass*, coss-lettuce.

خسيس *khasees*, miser; mean.

خستكة *khastaka* (Persian), sickness, indisposition.

مخستك *mokhastik*, sick, out of sorts.

خسر *khasira*, he suffered loss; it was damaged.

خسارة ـ خسائر *khasára*, pl. *khasáyir*, loss, damage. [ضرر]

خسران *khasrán*, one who has suffered loss; profligate, bankrupt.

خسوف *khosoof*, eclipse of moon. [كسوف]

خشّ *khashsha*, he entered. [دخل]

خشب ـ اخشاب *khashab*, pl. *akhsháb*, timber. [cf. حطب]

تخشيبة *takhsheeba*, wooden hut, hutting.

خشت *khisht*, dagger, pike.

خشخاش *khishkhásh*, poppy, opium. [ابوالنوم]

خشع *khasha'a*, he was humble.

خشاف *khusháf* (Persian *khosh áb*), a sweet drink.

خشم *khasham*, loss of sense of smell.

خيشوم *khaishoom*, cartilage of nose.

خشن *khashin*, coarse, rough to the touch.

خشونة *khoshoona*, coarseness.

خشي ـ يخشى *khashia*, he feared; *yakhsha*, he fears.

تخشّى or اختشى *takhashsha*, or *ikhtasha*, he felt ashamed.

مختشي *mikhtishi*, bashful, ashamed.

خشية *khashia*, shame.

خشّى *khashsha*, he terrified; growled at.

خشيةً من العار *khashiatan min el-a'ár*, from shame of the disgrace.

خصّ *khoss*, hut of straw; sentry-box. [خوص]

خصّ *khassa*, it was special.

خصوص *khosoos*, specialty; point in question.

خصوصي *khosoosiy*, special, private (as a letter).

خاصّ *kháss*, special, private; privy or royal.

دائرة خاصّة *dáyira khássa*, the Khedive's *private* property, household, or affairs.

خاصّة ـ خواصّ *khássa*, pl. *khawáss*, specialty, virtue, quality.

خاصّيّة ـ خصائص *khássiya*, pl. *khasáyis*, faculty, a special quality.

مخصوص *makhsoos*, special.

مخصوصًا *makhsoosán*, especially, specially.

خصّص *khassasa*, he designated, specialised.

مخصّص *mokhassas*, set apart; allowances.

اختصّ *ikhtassa*, he was, or thought himself, competent; it appertained.

اختصاص *ikhtisás*, competence (of a tribunal), special jurisdiction.

مختصّ *mukhtass*, competent.

خصوبة or خصب *khisb*, or *khosooba*, fertility of soil. [نبت]

اخصب *akhsaba*, it was fertile.

مخصب or خصيب *khaseeb*, or *mokhsib*, fertile.

خاصرة ـ خواصر *khásira*, pl. *khawásir*, waist, or narrow part of body.

اختصر *ikhtasara*, he abbreviated, was concise.

اختصار *ikhtisár*, brevity, summary, conciseness.

مختصر *mukhtasar*, summarised.

خصلة ـ خصال *khasla*, pl. *khisál*, nature, quality.

خصم *khasama*, he deducted.

خاصم *khásama*, he quarrelled, litigated.

خصم ـ اخصام *khasm*, or *khism*, pl. *akhsám*, enemy, opponent, adversary in a law-suit.

خصيم ـ خصماء or خصمان *khaseem*, pl. *khosamá*, or *khosmán*, opponent.

خصم ـ خصوم *khosm*, pl. *khosoom*, side; share.

خصومة *khosooma*, enmity, rivalry.

خصام or خصامية *khisám*, or *khusmániya*, enmity.

يخصم له *yokhsam laho*, it is to be deducted for him, he is entitled to the deduction.

اصول و خصوم *osool wa khosoom*, debit and credit.

اخصى or خصى *khasa*, or *akhsa*, he castrated.

خصيّ ـ خصيان *khasiy*, pl. *khisyán*, eunuch.

خصية *khosiya*, testicle.

خضب (77) خاطر

خضب khadb, verdure, vegetation.

خضاب khidáb, stain or dye from henna, &c., for the hair or fingers.

خضرة khodra, greenness.

اخضر ـ خضراء akhdar, (femin.) khadrá, green, grey.

خضر or خضار or بخضارات khodar, or khodár, or khodárát, greens, vegetables.

خضري khodariy, greengrocer.

خضر khadir, St. George, Elias. [روز ـ الياس]

خضع khada'a, he was humble.

خضوع khodooa', humility.

خاضع khádia', humble, obedient, subject.

خط ـ خطوط khatt, pl. khotoot, line, line of writing, handwriting, penmanship.

على الخط المستقيم 'ala l-khatt el-mostaqeem, in a straightforward manner.

خط الاستواء khatt el-istiwá, line of equator.

خط الاعتدال khatt el-ia'tidál, line of tropic.

خطي و ختمي khatty wa khitmy, my hand and seal.

خطّي khattiy, linear; of handwriting.

خطّاط khattát, calligrapher; a good "hand."

خطّ khatta, he drew a line, wrote in lines. [سطر

خطا khatá, error, accident. [غلط

خطأً khatá'an, by accident, by mistake.

خطاء و صواب khatá wa sawáb, corrigenda, errata.

خطية ـ خطايا khatiya, pl. khatáyá, error, sin.

خطب khataba, he preached, addressed a speech or letter; asked in marriage.

خطبة khitba, betrothal.

خطبة khotba, sermon, bidding prayer for the Sultan; betrothal; speech.

خاطب ـ خاطبة khátib, (fem.) khátiba, betrother; preacher.

خطيب khateeb, betrothed; preacher.

خطاب ـ خطابات khitáb, pl. khitábát, speech, epistle.

خاطب khátaba, he made a speech, addressed.

مخاطبة mokhátaba, correspondence. [مكاتبة]

مخاطب mokhátab, the person spoken to; 2nd person (in grammar).

خطر ـ اخطار khatar, pl. akhtár, danger, risk.

اخطر akhtara, he warned, reminded.

خطر or مخطر khatir or mokhtir, dangerous, risky.

مخطرة ـ مخاطر makhtara, pl. makhátir, a danger.

خاطر ـ خواطر khátir, pl. khawátir, mind; idea, pleasure, sake, memory.

خاطرة‎ *khátiroh* (colloquial), as he pleases; never mind!

خطّارة‎ *khattára*, bed of river; enclosure.

خطرف‎ *khatrafa*, he was delirious. [هذيان]

خطف‎ or اختطف‎ *khatafa*, or *ikhtatafa*, he kidnapped, eloped with, seized.

خطف‎ *khatf*, elopement, seizure, seduction.

خطّاف‎ *khattáf*, a large hook.

خطميّ‎ *khitamiy*, mallow, double mallow, "*guimauve*."

خطا‎ *khatá*, he took a step.

خطوة ـ خطوات‎ *khatwa*, pl. *khatwát*, a step, stride, pace.

خفّة‎ *khiffa*, lightness in weight, unimportance.

خفّف‎ *khaffafa*, he lightened, relieved, lessened a weight or penalty.

تخفيف‎ *takhfeef*, relief, indulgence, alleviation.

خفيف‎ *khafeef*, light, trifling, slight.

خفّ‎ *khuff*, slipper, shoe; camel's paw.

خفّيّة‎ *khiffiya*, lightness, light-heartedness.

استخفاف‎ *istikhfáf*, a desire to alleviate.

خفر‎ *khafara*, he guarded (especially by night). [غفر]

خفر‎ or خفارة‎ *khafar*, or *khifára*, guard, night-watch.

خفير ـ خفرا‎ *khafeer*, pl. *khofará*, night-watchman, village peasant police; *ghafeer*.

خافور‎ *kháfoor*, oats, rye; *avena fatua*.

خفض‎ *khafada*, he abased, hollowed out.

خفضة‎ *khifda*, "*kesra*," or "*i*" vowel-sound. [كسرة ـ جرّ]

خفق‎ *khafaqa*, it palpitated.

خفقان‎ *khafaqán*, palpitation.

خفي‎ or خفا‎ *khafá*, it vanished; or *khafia*, it was hidden. [خبا]

اخفى‎ *akhfa*, he hid a thing.

اختفى‎ *ikhtafa*, he hid himself.

خفيّ ـ خفايا‎ *khafiy*, pl. *khafáyá*, hidden, secret.

خفية‎ *khifiatán*, in secret.

مخفي‎ *makhfi*, stealth, by stealth; hidden.

لا يخفى‎ *lá yakhfa*, it is not hidden, it is well known.

خلل ـ خلال‎ *khalel*, pl. *khilál*, injury, vice, defect.

اخلّ ب‎ *akhalla bi*, he caused injury to.

اخلال‎ *ikhlál*, a doing injury.

مخلّ ب‎ *mokhill bi* injurious to.

اختلّ‎ *ikhtalla*, it was injured, disordered.

اختلال‎ *ikhtilál*, confusion, disorder, anarchy.

مختلّ الشعور‎ *mokhtall esh-sh'o-oor*, deranged in mind.

خلّ‎ *khall*, vinegar.

خِلال *khilál*, tooth-pick, a pricker.

خِلّ *khill*, sincere.

خَليل *khaleel*, sincere ; Charles.

خِلّة *khilla*, prickly shrub ; *khalla*, quality, nature.

خَلَب *khalaba*, he tore with the claws.

مِخلَب ـ مَخالِب *mikhlab*, pl. *makhálib*, claw, talon.

خَلبوس *khalboos*, liar ; buffoon ; lie, humbug.

خَليج خُلجان *khaleej*, pl. *khuljún*, strait, channel; Golden Horn ; Canal of Cairo.

اِختِلاج *ikhtiláj*, commotion of mind, nervous prostration, palpitation.

خَلخال ـ خَلاخيل *khalkhál*, pl. *khalákheel*, woman's anklet; convict's ankle-ring.

خُلود ـ خالِد *kholood*, eternity ; *khálid*, eternal, a dweller in paradise.

(خلس) ـ اختلس (*khalasa*), *ikhtalasa*, he defrauded.

اِختِلاس *ikhtilás*, fraud ; "*détournement*."

مُختَلِس *mukhtalis*, swindler.

خِلاسيّ *khilásiy*, mulatto, mixed.

خَلَص *khalasa*, it was pure, sincere, safe ; was finished.

خَلَص *kholos* (colloquial), it came to an end ; was completed.

خَلاص *khalás*, end, safety.

خُلاصة *khulása*, essence, pith, gist.

خُلوص *kholoos*, sincerity, salvation.

خالِص *khális*, pure, safe, thorough, quite.

خَلَّص *khallasa*, he completed ; saved.

تَخَلَّص من *takhallasa min*, he saved himself from, got out of a difficulty.

خالَص *khálasa*, he discharged a debt.

اِخلاص *ikhlás*, sincerity.

مُخلِص *mokhlis*, sincere.

مَخلَص *makhlas*, means of salvation or escape.

مُخالَصة *mokhálasa*, receipt, discharge of debt.

خَلَط *khalata*, he mixed.

خِلط ـ اخلاط *khilt*, pl. *akhlát*, mixture, humour.

خَلطة *khalta*, mixture.

اِختَلَط *ikhtalata*, it became mixed, it formed a mixture.

اِختِلاط *ikhtilát*, mixture, composition.

مُختَلِط *mukhtalit*, mixed, complex, compound.

مَخلوط *makhloot*, mixed, adulterated.

خَلَع *khala'a*, he undressed.

خَلَّع *khalla'a*, he sprained, dislocated.

اِنخَلَع *inkhala'a*, it was sprained, stripped.

خِلعة *khila'a*, robe of honour.

خُلوع *kholoow'*, a sprain, dislocation.

خُلع *khol'a* divorce, repudiation.

خليع or خالع *khália'*, or *khalee'a*, shameless, profligate.

خلف *khalafa*, it came next, succeeded to.

خلف *khalf*, after, next.

خلف *khalaf*, a successor, next man after.

خلف *khilf*, different, opposite.

خليفة – خلفاء *khaleefa*, pl. *khulafá*, "Caliph" or Khalif, successor of Mahomet; vicar, agent in charge.

خلافة *khiláfa*, Caliphate, successorship.

خلاف *khiláf*, contrary, other, besides. [غير

و خلافه *wa khiláfoh*, etcetera.

خلفة *khilfa*, a second crop; a quarrel.

خالف *khálafa*, he contravened, opposed.

مخالفة *mokhálafa*, opposition; "contravention," or petty offence.

مخالف *mokhálif*, opposing, contrary.

اختلف *ikhtalafa*, it differed from, varied.

اختلاف *ikhtiláf*, difference, variation.

مختلف *mukhtalif*, various, different.

مخلوفة *makhloofa*, camel-litter for women. [هودج

خلق *khalaqa*, he created.

خالق or خلاق *kháliq*, or *khalláq*, Creator.

اختلق *ikhtalaqa*, he lied, trumped up a story, invented a tale.

اختلاق *ikhtiláq*, lie, humbug, slander.

خلق or خلقة *khalq*, or *khilqa*, creature, people.

خلق كثير *khalq kateer*, a great crowd, mob.

خلق – اخلاق *kholq*, pl. *akhláq*, character, nature.

مخلوقات *makhlooqát*, created things.

خلقي *khalqiy*, congenital.

خلايق *khaláyiq*, (in Turkish) concubine, female slave.

خلا *khalá*, it was empty; he was alone.

خلي *kholia*, he was stripped or robbed of.

اخلى or خلّى *khalla*, or *akhla*, he evacuated, emptied.

خلّى السبيل *khalla es-sabeel*, he cleared the path, *i.e.* discharged a prisoner.

اختلى *ikhtala*, he retired into privacy.

خلاء or خلاة *khalá*, solitude, open deserted space; suburbs.

خلوّ *kholoo*, emptiness, immunity.

خلوة *khalwa*, retirement, inner private room, chapel.

خلاية النحل *khaláyat en-nahl*, beehive.

خالي *kháli*, empty, of no occupation; free from.

خلّي *khallee!* let it alone! never mind!

خلّي بالك *khallee bálak!* take care! look out!

خلى - يخلي *khala,* he cut forage; *yakhli,* he cuts.

مخلي *mikhla,* scythe, sickle.

مخلاة *mikhlát,* nose-bag for horses, receptacle for forage.

خمود *khomood,* numbness, debility.

خمر or خمّر *khamara,* or *khammara,* he made leavened bread, caused fermentation.

اختمر *ikhtamara,* the leaven rose; it fermented.

خميرة *khameera,* leaven, yeast.

خمر or خمرة *khamra,* or *khamr,* wine, any fermented liquor.

خمّارة *khammára,* tavern, hotel.

خمس *khoms,* one-fifth part.

خمس - خمسة *khamsa,* (femin.) *khams,* five.

خامس *khámis,* the fifth in order.

خمسون or خمسين *khamsoon,* or *khamseen,* fifty.

يوم الخميس *yōm el-khamees,* Thursday.

خماسين *khamáseen,* the *fifty* days between Easter and Pentecost; a hot sand-storm which blows during Spring.

خمّن *khammana,* he guessed, supposed.

تخمين *takhmeen,* a guessing, approximate idea.

تخميناً *takhmeenán,* approximately, at a guess. [تقريباً]

خنثى - خناث *khunsa,* pl. *khinás,* hermaphrodite, effeminate fellow.

تخنّث *takhannasa,* he was effeminate.

مخنّث *mokhannas,* effeminate, impotent.

خنجر *khanjar,* dagger, cutlass; hence our word "hanger."

خندق - خنادق *khandaq,* pl. *khanádiq,* ditch, trench.

خنزير - خنازير *khinzeer,* pl. *khanázeer,* pig.

داء خنازيريّ *dá khanázeeriy,* scrofula.

خنصر *khunsur,* little finger; penknife.

خنفسا - خنافس *khonfasá,* pl. *khanáfis,* beetle, scarab.

خنق *khanaqa,* he strangled. [شنق]

خنق *khanq,* strangulation, asphyxia.

اختنق *ikhtanaqa,* he felt choked, was strangled, died of asphyxia.

خناق *khunáq,* throat, larynx; laryngitis.

خناق *khináq,* quarrel, scuffle; throat.

خواجه *khawája* (Persian, *khōja,* professor), Sir, Mr., a European gentleman.

خواجه *khōja* (Persian), professor, teacher.

خوخ *khōkh,* peach.

خوخة (82) خياطة

خوخة *khōkha*, a wicket-gate or small door cut in a big gate, "*guichet*."

خور - أخوار *khōr*, pl. *akhwár*, dry water-course, nullah, ravine.

خوريّ *khooriy* (Syrian), Christian priest.

خوص *khoos*, palm-leaf, palm straw. [بوص]

احد الخوص "*Had el-khoos*," Palm Sunday. [شعانين]

خوض *khōd*, a fording, being fordable.

خاض *kháda*, he forded, waded.

مخاضة *makháda*, a ford.

خيفة or خوف *khōf*, or *kheefa*, fear.

خاف - يخاف *kháfa*, he feared; *yakhaf*, he fears.

خائف or خيّف *kháyif*, or *khiyyaf*, afraid.

اخاف or خوّف *khawwafa*, or *akháfa*, he frightened.

اخافة or تخويف *takhweef*, or *ikháfa*, intimidation.

مخافة *makháfa*, fear.

مخيف *mokheef*, terrific.

خول *khawal*, a man dressed up as a woman, an obscene dancer.

خوليّ - خوليّة *khōliy*, pl. *khōliya*, bailiff, gardener.

خون or خيانة *khōn*, or *khiyána*, treachery.

خائن *kháyin*, traitor.

خان - يخون *khána*, he betrayed; *yakhoon*, he betrays.

اوتمن فخان *o-otomina fa-khána*, he was trusted, and he betrayed; a legal term for breach of confidence or trust.

خيبة *khaiba*, disappointment, failure in hopes.

خائب *kháyib*, disappointed, unsuccessful.

خير *khair*, goodness, excellence, happiness; good, excellent; better, best.

كثّر خيرك *kattar khairak*, Thanks! May your happiness increase!

خيريّ *khairiy*, good, happy; pious, beneficent.

خيار *khiyár*, choice; cucumber.

اختار *ikhtára*, he chose; opted.

اختيار *ikhtiyár*, choice, option; an old man, a venerable senior.

اختياريّ *ikhtiyáriy*, optional.

مختار *mukhtár*, chosen; a village elder.

اخير or خير *akhyar*, or *khair*, better, best.

مخيّر بين و بين *mokhayyar bain wa bain*, he who has the option between this and that.

خيزران - خيازر *khaizarán*, pl. *khayázir*, cane, bamboo.

خيش *khaish*, coarse canvas or goats'-hair sacking; a sack; Bedouin tent.

خيط - اخياط *khait*, pl. *akhyát*, thread.

خياطة *khiyáta*, needle-work; a seam.

خاط - يخيط *khátu*, he sewed; *yakheet*, he sews.

خيّط *khayyata*, he sewed.

خيّاط *khayyát*, tailor.

خيّاطة *khayyáta*, sempstress; sewing-machine.

مخيط *mikhyat*, needle. [ابرة]

مخيّط or مخيوط *mokhayyat*, or *makhyoot*, sewn.

خيال *khayál*, shadow, phantom, spectre; imagination.

خيالي *khayáliy*, imaginary, unreal.

خال - يخال *khála*, he imagined; *yakhál*, he imagines.

تخيّل *takhayyala*, he imagined. [تصوّر]

خال *khál*, suspicion, cloud, mole on the face; maternal uncle.

خيل - خيول *khail*, pl. *khuyool*, horses, cavalry.

حصان - خيل *hisán*, horse; pl. *khail*, horses.

خيّال - خيّالة *khayyál*, pl. *khayyála*, cavalry. [سواري]

خيمة - خيام *khaima*, pl. *khiyám*, tent.

مخيّم *mokhayyam*, tented; a camp; covered with cobwebs, as it were spiders' tents.

D

د *Dál.* Value = 4.

داء - ادواء *dá*, pl. *adwá*, disease. [دوى]

داء الملوك *dá el-molook*, gout.

دادة *dáda*, nurse.

دار - دائرة - دور *dár*, house; *dáyira*, circle (see *dōr*).

داغ *dágh* (Persian), brand for cattle.

دام - دائمًا - دوام *dáma*, it endured; *dáyimá*, always (see *dawám*).

داي *dáy* (Turkish), uncle, senior, governor, "Dey" of Algiers.

داية *dáya*, midwife.

دبّ *dabba*, it crawled, moved the feet, kicked, made a noise.

دبيب *dabeeb*, noise of footsteps.

دبّ *dibb*, bear.

دابّة - دوابّ *dábba*, pl. *dawább*, quadruped, beast of burden, cattle. [مواشي]

ديباجة *deebája* (Persian), brocade, ornament; preface, illuminated preface, or opening chapter of book.

دبدب *dabdaba*, he made a noise. [دبّ]

تدبدب *tadabdaba*, it was pointed, conical.

مدبدب *modabdab*, conical, pointed.

دبر - ادبار *dubr*, pl. *adbár*, posterior, end, finis.

دبر - ادبر *dabara*, or *adbara*, he turned his back, fled.

دبار or ادبار *dabár*, or *idbár*, ruin, misfortune.

الدبران *Aldabarán*, a constellation in *Taurus*.

دَبَّرَ *dabbara*, he administered, managed.

تَدَبَّرَ *tadabbara*, he plotted, contrived.

تَدْبِير *tadbeer*, management; in Moslem law, freedom of a slave on the death of his master.

مُدَبِّر *modabbir*, a manager.

مُدْبِر *mudbir*, turning the back, fleeing.

دُبَارَة *dobára*, string, twine; trick, ruse.

دَبُّوس *dabboos*, pin, mallet.

دَبْش *dabsh*, rough blocks of building stone, "*moellons*." [دَقْشُوم

دَبَغ *dabagha*, he tanned.

دَبَّاغ *dabbágh*, tanner.

مَدْبَغ *madbagh*, tannery.

دِبْق *dibq*, bird-lime.

دِبْلَة *dibla*, finger-ring; tumour, boil.

دِبَّان or دُبَّان *dibbán*, flies.

دَجَاج - دُجُج *dajáj*, pl. *dujuj*, fowl. [فَرُّوج]

دَجَل *dajala*, he deceived, played the quack.

دَجَّال *dajjál*, Anti-Christ; false prophet; charlatan, quack.

دِجْلَة *dijla*, river Tigris, *Hidekel*. [فُرَات]

دَحْرَج *dahraja*, he rolled, revolved.

مُدَحْرَج *modahraj*, globular, round; rolled.

دَخَل *dakhala*, he entered.

دُخُول *dokhool*, entry, entrance.

دُخُولِيَّة *dokhooliya*, octroi at town gate.

دَخْل *dakhl*, income, manner.

دَخْلَة *dakhla*, right of entry, footing, interference.

دُخْلَة *dukhla*, consummation of marriage.

دَخِيل *dakheel*, enterer, guest.

دَاخِل *dákhil*, enterer, entering; interior, internal.

دَاخِلِيَّة *dákhiliya*, (ministry of) the Interior.

أَدْخَل or دَخَّل *dakhkhala*, or *adkhala*, he made enter, admitted, brought in, imported.

دَاخَل or تَدَاخَل *dákhala*, or *tadákhala*, he interfered, intervened.

مُدَاخَلَة *modákhala*, interference, intervention.

مَدْخَل *madkhal*, place of entry.

دَخَن *dakhana*, it gave out smoke. [بَخَر]

دُخَان *dukhán*, smoke; tobacco.

شَرِبَ دُخَان *sharaba dukhán*, he smoked tobacco, *i.e.* inhaled it, drank it in.

دَخَاخِنِيّ *dakhákhiniy*, tobacconist.

مَدْخَنَة *madkhana*, chimney, funnel.

دُخْن *dokhn*, millet, *panicum miliaceum*.

دُرَّة - دُرَر *dorra*, pl. *dorar*, pearl. [لُؤْلُؤ]

دُرِّيّ *dorriy*, brilliant, flashing, pearly.

اَلدُّرَّة or دُرَّة *idurra*, or *durra*, maize.

دَرَأ *dará*, he repulsed, refuted.

دَرْب ـ دُروب *darb*, pl. *doroob*, road, path, custom.

دَرَابْزون *darábzoon* (Greek *trapeza*), long desk, long counter; railings.

دَرَابُوكَّة *darábookka*, native drum. [دهلة]

دَرْبَكَة *darbaka*, noise, uproar.

دَرَج *daraja*, he inserted, inscribed, entered in the accounts.

اندرج *indaraja*, it was inserted, included.

دَرْج *darj*, insertion, registration.

دَرَّج *darraja*, he graduated, made go by degrees.

تَدْريج *tadreej*, graduation.

بالتَدْريج *bit-tadreej*, by degrees, gradually.

دُرْج ـ دُروج *dorj*, pl. *dorooj*, drawer, box, casket.

دَرَجَة ـ دَرَجات *daraja*, pl. *daraját*, degree, step.

اَوَّل دَرَجَة *awwal daraja*, first step; (court) of first instance.

دارِج *dárij*, common, in common use.

لِسان دارِج *lisán dárij*, common dialect or language.

دُرَّاج *dorráj*, francolin.

مُدْرَج *mudraj*, roll of paper, scroll.

مُنْدَرِج *mundarij*, contents, contained in.

دِرْدِيّ *dirdiy*, sediment, mud.

دِرْدار *dirdár*, elm tree.

دُرْزِيّ ـ دُروز *druziy*, pl. *dorooz*, Druse, a warlike pagan race in Mount Lebanon and the Hauran.

دَرَس *darasa*, he studied, threshed out.

دَرَّس *darrasa*, he taught.

دَرْس ـ دُروس *dars*, pl. *doroos*, lesson.

دِراسَة *dirása*, teaching, education; study.

مَدْرَسَة ـ مَدارِس *madrasa*, pl. *madáris*, school.

مُدَرِّس *modarris*, teacher.

دِراس *dirás*, a threshing.

دِريس *drees*, hay, dry *berseem* or clover; chaff, husks.

دِرْع or دِرَاعَة *dira'*, or *dorráa'a*, cuirass, smock.

دارِع or مُدَرَّع *dári'a*, or *modarra'a*, ironclad, cuirassier.

دَرْفَة ـ دِرَف *darafa*, pl. *diraf*, shutter.

دَرَق *daraq*, Adam's apple in the throat.

دَرَقَة *daraqa*, shield.

دَوْرَق or دُوراق *dōráq*, pitcher, ewer, long-necked bottle.

دَوْرَقْعَة *doorqa'a* (Persian), depression in floor, a sunken floor.

دَرَك *darak*, supervision.

دَرَكَة ـ دَرَك *daraka*, pl. *darak*, a

watchman's post or beat; a fixed station.

دركة الباب *darakat el-báb*, vestibule (see *dirka*).

ادرك *adraka*, he caught at, perceived, understood; arrived at age of puberty or discretion.

ادراك *idrák*, perception; age of discretion.

مدرك *mudrik*, intelligent, adult.

تدارك *tadáraka*, he provided for, equipped.

دركة *dirka* (for Persian *der-gyáh*), doorway, vestibule.

درهم - دراهم *dirhem*, pl. *daráhim*, (Greek *drachmé*) drachm, dram, 48·1 grains; 3·12 grammes; 400 dirhems equal an *oqqa*; an old name for silver money.

دراهم *daráhim*, money, cash. [نقود]

دروة *dirwa*, parapet; shelter-trench, low wall. [ذروة]

درويش - دراويش *darweesh*, pl. *daráweesh* (Persian), beggar at the door; monk, fanatic.

درى ب *dara bi*, he knew.

ادرى *adra*, he informed, explained.

دراية *diráya*, intelligence.

ما ادري اي *má adri ai* (*madri ó*), (colloquialism), "I don't know what not;" "etcetera."

مدرى *midra*, bar, pitchfork. [ذرى]

دزينة *dozeena* (European), dozen.

دسّ *dassa*, he hid, spied, touched, poked.

بالدسّ *bid-duss*, by stealth.

دسيسة - دسائس *daseesa*, pl. *dasáyis*, intrigue, plot.

دسيس or دسوس *dasees*, or *dásoos*, spy. [بصّاص]

دست *dast* (Persian), hand.

دستة *dasta* (Persian), packet, quire, bunch.

دستور *dastoor* (Persian), permission; break off! (military drill); register; code of law; cornerstone, foundation-stone; cut stone in general.

دسم *dasam*, Shrove Sunday, Quinquagesima.

دسمبر *Desember* (European), December.

دسنتريا *disenteriyá* (European), dysentery.

دشيشة *dasheesha*, bruised corn; inferior wheat.

دشت *dasht* (Persian), confusion, waste paper, rubbish.

دشّر *dashshara*, he dismissed, abandoned.

تدشير *tadsheer*, a getting rid of.

دعس *da's*, a treading, trampling. [دهس]

دعك *da'ka*, he rubbed. [فرك - عرك]

دعا *da'á*, he cried out, invited, prayed, named.

يدعو *yada'oo*, he cries out, names.

دعاء - ادعية *do'á*, pl. *adi'yia*, prayer.

دعوة *da'wa*, invitation, exorcism.

داعي *dá'iy*, he who calls, prays; a cause.

لداعي *li-dá'iy*, because, for the reason that.

دعوى - دعاوي *da'wa*, pl. *da'áwi*, law-suit.

اقام دعوى على *aqáma da'wa 'ala*, he brought an action against.

ادّعى *idda'a*, he asserted, claimed.

ادّعاء *iddi'á*, assertion, claim.

استدعى *istada'a*, he claimed.

تداعى *tadáa'a*, he called to another; he went to law.

مدّعي *modda'y*, plaintiff.

مدّعى عليه *modda'á 'alaih*, defendant.

مدعوّ *muda'oo*, named, whose name is.

يدعى *yoda'a*, he is called, his name is.

متداعي *motadáa'y*, a party to a law-suit.

دعة - ودع *da'a* tranquillity (see *wada'a*).

دغدغ *daghdagha*, he bruised, pummelled. [cf. زغزغ

دغري - طوغري *dooghri* (for Turkish *doghroo*), straight, direct, honest.

دفّ - دفوف *daff*, pl. *dofoof*, flap, shutter, drum.

دفّة *daffa*, rudder. [سكّان

دفي *dafia*, it was warm.

دفّأ *daffa*, he made warm.

دفا *dafá*, warmth.

دفي or دافئ *dáfi*, warm, tepid.

دفيّة - دفافي *daffiya*, pl. *dafáfi*, warm cloak.

دفّاية *daffáya*, stove, warming apparatus.

دفتر - دفاتر *daftar*, pl. *dafátir* (Persian), register, account-book, ledger.

دفتردار *daftar-dár* (Persian), accountant.

دفترخانه *daftar-kháne* (Persian), archives.

دفتريا *difteriyá* (European), diphtheria.

دفع *dafa'a*, he pushed; paid.

دفعة - دفعات *daf'a*, or *dof'a*, pl. *daf'át*, a push, payment; one time, once.

دفع *daf'*, a pushing, a paying.

دافع *dáfa'a*, he defended, contended.

دفاع or مدافعة *difá'*, or *modáfa'a*, defence.

دفاع عن نفسه *difá'a 'an nafsihi*, self-defence.

مدفوع *madfooa'*, paid; pushed.

مدفع - مدافع *madfa'*, pl. *madáfia'*, cannon. [طوب

دفن *dafana*, he buried.

دفن *dafn*, burial.

دفينة *dafeena*, buried treasure.

مدفون *madfoon*, buried.

دقّ *daqqa*, he pounded, knocked, hit; tattooed.

دقّق *daqqaqa*, he ground, made fine; ascertained accurately, went into minutiæ.

دقّة *daqqa*, tattoo-marks. [وشم

دقّة *diqqa*, fineness, exactitude, care; *daqqa*, herb-cake.

دقيق *daqeeq*, flour; fine.

دوقاق *doqáq*, cheap native soap.

دقيقة - دقائق *daqeeqa*, pl. *daqáyiq*, moment, minute.

تدقيق *tadqeeq*, precision, accuracy. [تحقيق]

مــدقَّق *modaqqaq*, exact, shown correct.

دقشوم - دبش *daqshoom*, small stone for building, smaller than *dabsh*.

دقهليّة - منصورة *Daq-haliya*, a province in the Delta, of which *Mansoora* is the capital.

دكّة *dikka*, bench, platform; waistband. [تكّة]

دكّان - دكاكين *dukkán*, pl. *dakákeen*, shop.

دلّ *dalla*, he indicated.

دليل *daleel*, guide, indication, proof.

ادلّة or دلائل *daláyil*, or *adilla*, proofs, indications. [بيّنة - برهان]

دلّال *dallál*, crier, auctioneer; an itinerant auctioneer in a bazar.

دلّالة *dallála*, female broker.

دالّ *dáll*, he who indicates, showing.

استدلّ *istadalla*, it became evident, inductive.

استدلال *istidlál*, induction; simple information, not sworn evidence.

دولاب - دواليب *dōláb*, pl. *dawáleeb* (Persian), chest of drawers, wardrobe; machine; wheel apparatus, trick, machination.

دلس or دلّس *dalasa*, or *dallasa*, he defrauded.

تدليس *tadlees*, fraud (especially in bankruptcy), "*dol*." [غشّ]

دلش *dalasha* (colloquial), he threw.

دلّع *dalla'a* he spoilt, pampered, petted.

مدلّع *modalla'* a spoilt (child).

دلع *dila'* insipid.

دلك or دلّك *dalaka*, or *dallaka*, he rubbed, used "*massage*."

تدليك *tadleek*, "*massage*."

دلو - دلي *dalo*, pl. *duliy* (femin.), bucket; Aquarius, in the Zodiac.

دم - دمو *dam*, blood (see *damo*.)

دمار *damár*, ruin.

دميرة *damaira* (Soudanese), rise of Nile.

دمس *dims*, ashes from the oven; dung.

مدمسة *madmasa*, dust-heap, ashheap, dung-heap.

دامس *dámis*, dark, cloudy; pitch-dark. [ظلام]

دمشق *Dimeshq*, Damascus.

دمعة - دموع *damu'a*, pl. *domooa'*, a tear.

دمع *dama'a*, he wept; *yadma'*, he weeps. [بكى]

تدمّع *tadamma'a*, it drizzled with rain.

دمعة *dima'a*, sauce, gravy, dripping.

دماغ ـ ادمغة *dimágh*, pl. *admigha*, brain. [مخ]

دمغة *damgha* (Turkish), stamp of a seal; impression. [see دمغة]

ورقة دمغة *waraqa damgha*, stamped paper for petitions and official documents.

دمغ *damagha* (from Turkish), he stamped with an official seal.

دمل ـ دمامل *dummul*, pl. *damámil*, boil, pimple.

دمن or ادمن *damana*, or more commonly *admana*, he persevered.

ادمان *idmán*, perseverance, assiduity.

مدمن *mudmin*, persevering assiduous.

دمنهور ـ بحيرة *Damanhoor*, a town near Alexandria, capital of the province of *Bahaira*.

دم ـ دماء or دمو *damo*, (or commonly) *dam*, pl. *dimá*, blood.

سفك دماء or اراقة دماء *safk dimá*, or *iráqat dimá*, a shedding of blood.

اولياء الدم or ذوي الدم *awliyá ed-dam*, or *zawee ed-dam*, owners of the blood, i.e. nearest relatives of a murdered man claiming vengeance.

دمياط *Damiát*, Damietta.

دنا *daná*, it was vile, ignoble.

دناءة *danáya*, vileness.

دني ـ ادناء *dani*, pl. *adná*, vile, base; glutton,

اشغال دنية *ashghál daniya*, hard labour.

دنا *dana*, it was near, he came near.

دني *dania*, it was vile; low, inferior.

دناية *danáya*, vileness, baseness, inferiority.

دني ـ ادنياء *daniy*, pl. *adniyá*, vile, base, low.

اشغال دنيّة *ashghál daniya*, hard labour.

دنى *danna*, he came near, approached.

دناوة *danáwa*, nearness.

دني ـ ادنياء *daniy*, pl. *adniyá*, near.

ادنى *adna*, nearer, viler, lowest, slightest.

ادنى دايل *adna daleel*, the slightest proof.

دنيا ـ دنى *dunyá*, pl. *dona*, this lower world of ours; the world; weather.

الدنيا ظلام *ed-dunyá zalám*, (it was) a dark night.

دنيوي *dunyawiy*, mundane, worldly.

دنج *danj* (European), dengue-fever.

دندش *dindish*, necklace.

دندن *dandana*, he hummed, sang.

دندرمة or درمة *dindirma*, or *dirdirma* (Turkish), ice cream.

دنس *danisa*, it was filthy. [نجس]

دنس ـ دناسة *danása*, filthiness, *danis*, filthy.

دنقلا *Donqolá*, Dongola in the Soudan.

دنقلاوي ـ دناقلة *Donqoláwiy*, pl. *Danáqla*, Dongolese.

دونانمة *donánma* (Turkish), fleet of ships.

دنكل *dinghil* (Turkish), axle-tree.

دهر ـ دهور *dahr*, pl. *dohoor*, epoch, age, century.

دهري *dahriy*, materialist, atheist.

دهس *dahasa*, he trod, trampled, ran over.

دهش *dahisha*, he took fright, was alarmed.

دهّش *dahhasha*, he frightened.

دهشة *dahsha*, fear.

دهشان *dahshán*, afraid, timid.

مدهش *modhish*, terrific.

دهلة *dohulla*, native drum.

دهليز *dihleez* (Persian), gallery, vestibule.

دهم *dahm*, a blackness, dark mass of people.

ادهم *adham*, a black horse; man's name.

دهن *dahana*, he anointed, besmeared.

دهن or دهان *dohn*, or *dahán*, ointment, paint, grease.

داهن *dáhana*, he flattered cajoled.

مداهنة *modáhana*, flattery, humbug.

دهاء *dahú*, shrewdness, strategy, finesse.

داهي or دهي *dáhi*, shrewd, deep, long-headed.

داهية ـ دواهي *dáhiya*, pl. *dawáhi*, calamity.

يا دوب *yá dōb*, almost.

دوخان *dawakhán*, giddiness, feeling sick.

دوخة *dōkha*, giddiness, feeling sick.

داخ *dákha*, he felt giddy, sea-sick.

دائخ *dáyikh*, giddy, sea-sick.

دوّخ *dawwakha*, he made unconscious, stunned.

دودة ـ دود *dooda*, pl. *dood*, worm, maggot; madder.

دوّادة *dawwáda*, she who extracts worms.

دور ـ ادوار *dōr*, pl. *adwár*, turn, circuit; story of house.

بالدور *bid-dōr*, by turns.

دوران *dawarán*, rotation, circulation.

دورية or داوريّة *dōriya*, or *dáwariya*, a patrol, going the rounds.

دار ـ يدور *dára*, it turned round; *yadoor*, it turns round.

دوّر *dawwara*, he made turn round, wound up, rounded, turned himself round.

دوّار *dawwár*, a (round) place or enclosure; block of farm buildings, out-houses.

دار ـ ديار *dár*, pl. *diyár* (femin.), house, province.

ديار مصريّة *diyár masriya*, Egyptian dominions.

دار السلام *dár es-Salám,* House of Peace; Heaven; a moslem country.

دار الحرب *dár el-harb,* House of War; the infidels.

دار الصناعة *dár es-saná'aa,* workshop, arsenal. [see ترسانة *tersána*]

دير ۔ ديورة *dair,* pl. *doyoora,* convent.

دائرة ۔ دوائر *dáyira,* pl. *dawáyir,* circle, circumference, department.

دائرة بلدية *dáyira baladiya,* municipality.

دائرة سنية *dáyira saniya,* royal department; administration of certain Khedivial estates mortgaged to bond-holders.

دوائر *dawáyir,* districts, provinces.

ادار *adára,* he governed, administered.

ادارة *idára,* administration.

اداري *idáriy,* administrative.

مدير *modeer,* administrator, governor of one of the 13 provinces of Egypt.

مديرية *modeeriya,* office of an administrator; one of the 13 provinces of Egypt.

استدارة *istidára,* rotundity.

مستدير *mustadeer,* round, roundish.

مدور *modawwar,* round, circular.

مدار *madár,* pivot, axis; means.

دوراق *dóráq,* long-necked water-bottle, ewer.

دوسة *dósa,* a treading, trampling.

داس ۔ يدوس *dása,* he trod upon; *yadoos,* he treads.

مداس *madás,* shoes.

دوشة *dósha,* row, a whining.

دوكة *dóka,* quarrel, uproar.

دول *dól,* a turning, return, change.

دولة ۔ دول *dawla,* pl. *dowal,* kingdom, empire, power, state; vicissitude.

صاحب الدولة or دوتلو *sáhib ed-dawla,* (or *derletlu,* Turkish), His Highness, a pasha of the highest rank.

دال ۔ يدول *dála,* it followed in turn; *yadool,* it follows.

داول *dáwala,* he deliberated with others, spoke in turn, dealt with questions in their turn.

مداولة *modáwala,* deliberation.

تداول *tadáwala,* it was current (coin).

متداول *mutadáwil,* current (coin); common.

دوم ۔ دوام *dōm,* or *dawám,* duration, permanence.

دائم *dáyim,* constant, enduring.

دائما *dáyimá,* always.

على الدوام *a'la ed-dawám,* constantly.

دوامة *dawwáma,* eddy, whirlpool. [شمية]

داوم *dáwama,* he persevered.

دام ۔ يدوم *dáma,* it endured; *yadoom,* it endures.

ما دام *má dám,* while, as long as.

ادام *adáma,* he perpetuated.

مداومة modáwama, perseverance.

مستديم mustadeem, continual, protracted.

دوم - دوم doom, or dōm, a species of forked palm tree, *Cucifera Thebaica*, with edible fruit like a cocoa-nut, called *moql hyphaëne*.

دون doon, low, under, less than; *minus*, without; vulgar, common, vile.

بدون bidoon, minus, without.

دونك doonak, on with you! forward!

دون سبع سنين doon saba' saneen, under seven years old.

دون غيره doon ghairoh, and no other.

دوّن dawwana, he inscribed, put down in writing.

مدوّن modawwan, inscribed, written down.

ادان adána, he accused, abased, held as vile.

ادانة idána, accusation, indictment; committal for trial.

مدين modeen, accuser, accusing.

مدان modán, accused; guilty.

دوى dawia, he was ill. [مرض]

داوى dáwa, he attended the sick. [عيادة]

دوى - ادواء dawa, pl. *adwá*, illness. [داء]

دواء - ادوية dawá, pl. *adwiya*, medicine. [علج]

مداواة modáwát, medical attention. [معالجة]

دواية dawáya, inkstand.

ديك - ديوك deck, pl. *doyook*, cock, male bird.

دين - ديون dain, pl. *doyoon*, debt.

ارباب الديون arbáb ed-doyoon, creditors.

دائن dáyin, creditor.

مداين modáyin, creditor.

مدين madeen, debtor.

مديون madyoon, indebted; debtor.

ديّان - ديّانة dayyán, pl. *dayyána*, creditor.

دين - اديان deen, pl. *adyán*, faith, religion.

يوم الدين yōm ed-deen, day of Judgment.

ديانة diyána, piety, creed.

دينار - دنانير deenár, pl. *danáneer* (Greek *denarion*), obsolete gold coin.

ديّوث dayyoos, pimp, cuckold. [معرّس]

ديوان - دواوين deewán, pl. *dawáween* (Persian), hall, ministry of state, office; divan; poems.

ديواني deewániy, imperial (as coin of the realm); a style of handwriting.

قرش صاغ or ديواني qirsh ságh, or *qirsh diwániy*, a full piastre, 2½d.

خطّ ديواني khatt diwániy, a beautiful style of handwriting used in Turkish official documents.

Z or D

(Or *th* as in *them*.)

ذ *Zál.* Value = 700.

ذا - ذاك *zá*, this; *zák*, that.

ذا - اولاء *zá*, this; pl. *oolái*, these.

ذاك - اولئك *zák*, that; pl. *ooláyik*, those.

ذلك - تلك *zálik*, (femin.) *tilk*, that.

هذا - هذه *házá*, (femin.) *házihi*, this.

هؤلاء *howlái*, these.

ذى *dee* (vulgarism for *zá*), this.

ذول *dól* (vulgarism), these.

دكها or دكهم *dik-há*, or *duk-hám* (vulgarism), those.

ماذا *mázá*, what?

كذا or هكذا or كذالك *kazá*, or *hakazá*, or *kazálik*, thus, like this, like that.

ذو - ذات *zát*, self, personality (see *zoo*).

ذباب - ذبّان *dobáb*, pl. *dibbán*, flies.

ذبح *dabaha*, he slaughtered.

ذبح *dabh*, a slaughtering.

ذبيح *dabeeh*, slaughtered; for slaughter, a victim.

مذبح *madbah*, slaughterhouse; altar of sacrifice.

ذخر *zakhara*, he stored grain.

ذخيرة - ذخائر *zakheera*, pl. *zakháyir*, grain, store of grain; priming or pinch of powder in pan of flint-lock musket; ammunition.

الذرّة or ذرّة *zurra*, or *durra*, or *idurra*, maize, sorgho. [ادرة]

ذرّ - ذرّة *zarra*, pl. *zarr*, atom, a grain.

ذرّية *zorriya*, posterity, family.

ذراع - اذرع *dirá'a*, or *zirá'a*, pl. *adru'a* (femin.), fore-arm, cubit, pic, ell.

ذراع بلديّ *dirá'a baladiy*, 23 inches; ·58 mètre.

ذراع نيليّ *dirá'a neeliy*, 21 inches; ·53 mètre.

ذراع استانبوليّ or اندازة or هنداسة *dirá'a istánbooliy*, or *endáza*, or *hendása*, 26 inches; ·66 mètre.

ذراع معماريّ *dirá'a mi'amáriy*, 29½ inches; ·75 mètre.

ذروة *dirwa*, apex; parapet, shelter-trench; low wall.

ذرى *dara*, he winnowed, tossed grain.

مذرى - مذاري *midra*, pl. *madári*, pitch-fork; fan for winnowing.

ذفر *zifr*, bad fishy smell.

ذقن - اذقان *daqan*, pl. *adqán*, chin, beard. [لحية]

ابو ذقن *aboo daqan*, a bearded man.

ذكر *zakara*, he remembered.

ذكر *zikr*, mention, memory; recital of prayer, act of devotion.

سالف الذكر sálif ez-zikr, above-mentioned.

مذكور mazkoor, above-mentioned.

ذاكر zákir, mindful, remembering.

ذكّر zakkara, he reminded.

ذاكر zákara, he consulted, discussed, studied.

مذاكرة mozákara, discussion, interview, study.

تذكار tezkár, a souvenir, memento.

تذكرة - تذاكر tazkara, pl. tazákir, ticket, letter, certificate, passport.

مذكّرة mozakkara, note, letter, memo.

تذكّر tazakkara, he remembered.

ذكر - ذكور zakar, pl. zokoor, a male; penis.

ذكور واناث zokoor wa inás, males and females.

ذكّر zakkara, he fertilised a female palm-tree; he put it into the masculine gender.

تذكير tazkeer, or tadkeer, impregnation, fertilisation; putting into the masculine gender.

مذكّر mozakkar, masculine (gender).

مذكرة muzkara, virago, amazon. [مسترجلة]

ذكيّ - اذكياء zakiy, pl. azkiyá, sagacious. [cf. زكيّ]

ذكاء zaká, sagacity.

ذلّ zill, or zull, vileness, abasement.

ذليل zaleel, vile, cringing.

مذلول mazlool, servile, cringing.

ذلك - ذا zálik (see zá).

ذمّ - يذمّ zamma, he blamed; yazomm, he blames.

ذمّ zamm, blame. [لوم]

ذمّة - ذمم zimma, pl. zimam, conscience, moral responsibility, hence a person under one's protection.

ذمّة zimmatán, conscientiously.

على ذمّة 'ala zimma, for the sake of.

ذمّيّ zimmiy, Christian subject of a Moslem power, whose safety is guaranteed by the honour of the Moslem ruler.

ذميم or مذموم zameem, or mazmoom, blameable.

ذنب - ذنوب zanb, pl. zonoob, sin, crime.

اذنب adnaba, he committed a crime.

مذنب modnib, guilty. [مجرم]

ذنب - اذناب danab, pl. adnáb, tail. [ذيل]

ذا - هذه - هذا zih in házihi, femin. of házá.

ذهب dahaba, he went away, departed.

ذهاب dahák, departure; act of going.

ذهاب واياب dahák wa iyák, a going and returning.

مذهب ـ مذاهب *madhab*, pl. *madáhib*, religion, creed.

ذهب *dahab*, gold, golden, of gold.

ساعة ذهب *sá'aa dahab*, a gold watch.

ذهّب *dahhaba*, he gilded.

ذهبية *dahabiya*, Nile "house-boat," sailing yacht.

استر دهبك و ذهابك و مذهبك *ostor dahabak wa dahábak wa madhabak* (proverb), "Conceal thy gold, the object of thy journey, and thy religion."

ذهول *zohool*, insanity, half-witted state of mind.

ذهل or انذهل *zahila*, or *inzahala*, he was astonished.

ذهن ـ اذهان *zihn*, pl. *azhán*, mind, intellect, prudence.

ذو ـ ذوون or ذوي *zoo*, pl. *za-oon*, (or commonly in construction) *zawy*, possessor, endowed with.

ذات ـ ذوات *zát*, pl. *zawát*, femin. of *zoo*, mistress, possessor; essence, personality, self.

ذو سوابق *zoo sawábiq*, a man of (bad) antecedents.

ذو القرنين *zoo l-qarnain*, the two-horned man, Alexander the Great (?), a legendary hero.

ذووه or ذويه *zawooh*, or *zaweeh*, his relations.

ذا ـ ذي *zá* and *zee*, accusative and oblique cases of *zoo*.

يوم من ذات الايّام *yóm min zát el-ayyám* one day, a certain day.

ذات ليلة *zát laila*, one night, a certain night.

ذاته *zátoh*, himself, one's self.

ذاتًا *zátan*, personally. [شخصًا]

محبّ ذاته *mohibb zátoh*, self-lover, selfish.

اشياء ذات قيمة *ashiá zát qeema*, valuables.

ذو القعدة *zoo l-Qa'da*, eleventh Moslem month (of Repose).

ذو الحجّة *zoo l-Hijja*, twelfth Moslem month (of Pilgrimage).

ذوبان *zawabán*, liquefaction.

ذاب ـ يذوب *zába*, it melted; *yazoob*, it melts.

ذوّب *zawwaba*, he melted, fused.

ذود ـ مذود (*dód*) *madwid*, manger, stall.

ذوق *zóq*, sense of taste, taste; good taste, refinement.

ذاق ـ يذوق *záqa*, he tasted; *yazooq*, he tastes.

مذاق *mazáq*, palate, seat of sense of taste.

ذا ـ ذي *dee* (vulgarism for *zá*), this.

الرجل ذي *er-rajil dee*, this man.

ذئب ـ ذئاب *deeb*, pl. *diyáb*, wolf.

ذوابة *zoowába*, tuft, mane.

كوكب ذو ذوابة *kawkab zoo zoowába*, comet.

ذيل ـ اذيال *dail*, pl. *adyál*, tail, shirt-tail, skirt; codicil, appendix.

R

, *Ré.* Value = 200.

راتينج *ráteenej*, resin.

رواح - راح *ráha*, he went (see *rawáh*.)

ريح - روح - رواح - راحة - راح *ráha*, repose (see *rawáh*, *rooh* and *reeh*).

رؤوس أرؤس - رأس *rás*, pl. *ro-oos*, head, promontory; bridle.

رأس المال *rás el-mál* (*rasmál*), capital stock; capital (of money).

رؤساء - رئيس *ráyis*, pl. *ro-osá*, chief, president; captain of a ship.

رياسة *riyása*, presidency, chiefdom.

ترأس *taraása*, he took the lead.

مترئيس *mutarayyis*, a leader.

مرؤوس *maro-oos*, a subordinate.

ترويسة *tarweesá*, heading (of a chapter).

راشيتسم *ráshitism* (French), *rachitisme*, rickets.

رأف *ráfa*, he was merciful.

رأفة *ráfa*, clemency, indulgence.

رؤوف *raoof*, clement, merciful.

راهوان *ráhwán* (Persian), roadster, hack; hence amble, quick walk.

راعوث *Rá'ooth*, Ruth.

يرى - رأى *ráa*, he saw; *yara*, he sees.

آراء - رأي *ráy*, pl. *aúrá*, opinion, view.

رؤية *rooya*, inspection, supervision, sight, attention to; looking for the new moon of Ramadan.

رؤى - رؤيا *rooyá*, pl. *rowa*, dream.

أرى - أرى *ara*, he showed (vulgarly written and pronounced *awra*).

ترآى *taráäa*, it appeared.

مراءاة or رئاء *riyá*, or *moráát*, hypocrisy.

مراء *morá*, a hypocrite.

رئات - رئة *riya*, pl. *riyát*, lung.

سل رئوي *sill riwaiy*, pulmonary consumption.

رايات - راية *ráya*, pl. *ráyát*, flag.

مرآة *miraát*, or *miráya*, mirror.

ورّيني *warreeni* (colloquial), show me!

رب *rabb*. The Lord God; possessor, owner.

رب العالمين *rabb el-a'álemeen*. The Lord of the Worlds, God.

يا رب *yá rabb*, O Lord!

رب البيت *rabb el-bait*, master of the house.

رب الدين *rabb ed-duin*, creditor.

أرباب *arbáb*, pl. of *rabb*, possessors; owners. [ذوي - أصحاب]

أرباب الديون *arbáb ed-doyoon*, creditors.

أرباب الخبرة *arbáb el-khibra*, experts, professional experts.

أرباب السوابق *arbáb es-sawábiq*, men of (bad) antecedents, old thieves.

ربّما *rubbamá*, perhaps.

رَبَّة *rabba*, femin. of *rabb*, mistress, possessor.

رباب *rabáb*, violin.

رَبَّانِيّ *rabbániy*, rabbi, rabbinical.

ربح - ارباح *ribh*, pl. *arbáh*, profit, money interest.

ربح or تربّح *rabiha*, or *tarabbaha*, he profitted.

رابح *rábih*, winner, gaining.

ربح و خسارة *ribh wa khasára*, profit and loss.

ربص *rabasa*, he expected.

تربّص *tarabbasa*, he awaited his opportunity.

تربّص و ترصّد *tarabbus wa tarassud*, a lying in wait (to commit a crime), a French legal term "*guet-apens*."

ربط *rabata*, he tied, bound, imposed.

ربط *rabt*, a binding, tie, connection.

ربط الاموال *rabt el-amwál*, imposing of taxation.

ضبط و ربط *zabt wa rabt*, "seize and bind;" organisation; a grip on (business); public security, police administration.

رباط or ربطة *rabta*, or *ribát*, tie, bond, station; head-dress.

رابطة - روابط *rábita*, pl. *rawábit*, rule, ordinance.

ارتبط *irtabata*, he became bound, dependent.

ارتباط *irtibát*, lien, dependence, connection.

مرتبط *murtabit*, attached, dependent.

مربوط *marboot*, bound, tied; attached to a religion, fanatic, "*marabout*."

مربط *marbat*, stable, place of fastening cattle.

ربع *roba'*, one-fourth part; Egyptian peck of 8¼ litres, or nearly 2 gallons; *raba'*, apartments.

اربعة - اربع *arba'a*, (femin.) *arba'*, four.

يوم الاربعاء *yōm el-arba'á*, Wednesday, fourth day of the week.

رابع *rábia'*, fourth in order.

رابعة النهار *rábia't en-nahár*, broad noon, noon-tide.

اربعون or اربعين *arba'oon*, or *arba'een*, forty.

اربعينيّات *arba'eeniyát*, forty days of winter (9th December to 17th January).

اربعة و اربعين *arba'a wa arba'een*, forty-four; centipede.

رباعيّ *robá'aiy*, four-lettered root of word.

ربيع *Rabeea'*, Springtime; *Rabeea'* I. and II., the third and fourth Moslem months.

ربّع - تربيع *rabba'a*, he squared; *tarbeea'*, a squaring.

مربّع *morabba'*, squared, a square.

مربع *marba'*, pasture-ground, plot of ground.

يربوع *yarboa'*, desert rat, jerboa.

ربقة *rabqa*, lasso, noose, halter.

ربل *rabal*, pulicaria undulata.

اربون or ربون *raboon*, or *arboon*, earnest-money, "arrhes."

ربا *rabá*, it grew up.

ربّى *rabba*, he trained up, disciplined.

تربية *tarbiya*, education, discipline.

مربّى *morabba*, preserve, jam.

مترّبي *motarabbi*, trained, disciplined.

ربو *raboo*, asthma.

رباء *ribá*, usury.

مرابأة *morábát*, usury, a taking of usury.

مرابي *morábi*, usurer.

رتب *rataba*, it was firm, settled.

رتّب *rattaba*, he organised.

ترتيب *tarteeb*, organisation, system, plan.

رتبة - رتب *rotba*, pl. *rotab*, rank, grade.

راتب *rátib*, pay, allowance; a certain spot, fixed.

ترتّب على *tarattaba 'ala*, it depended or resulted from; became organised.

مرتبة - مراتب *martaba*, pl. *marátib*, rank, high place.

مترتّبات *mutarattabát*, allowances, pay.

رتش *ratsh* (vulgar), bad, worthless.

رتق *rataqa*, he sewed up, repaired, shut.

رتق و فتق الامور *ratq wa fatq el-omoor*, "shut and open, (i.e. management of) business."

رتامة *ratáma*, snaffle, bit.

رثّة *riththa*, old clothes, rags.

رثاء - مراثي *rithá*, elegy; *maráthi*, lamentations.

رجّ or ارتجّ *rajja*, or *irtajja*, it trembled, shook.

ارتجاج *irtijáj*, commotion, shock.

رجب *Rajab*, honour, respect; the seventh Moslem month.

رجح *rajaha*, its weight told, it leaned.

رجّح *rajjaha*, he made preponderate, preferred.

مرجّح *morajjah*, preferred.

مرجيحة *marjaiha*, swing, see-saw, an Egyptian "merry-go-round."

ترجيح *tarjeeh*, preference.

رجز *rajaz*, a kind of rhyme or metre.

رجس *rajis*, vile, abominable. [نجس

رجاسة *rajása*, vileness, impurity.

رجع *raja'a*, he returned, turned back. [عود

رجوع or رجعة *rojooa'*, or *raja'a*, a return, recourse.

رجّع *rajja'a*, he sent back, made return, repeated.

راجع *rája'a*, he turned towards, had recourse to, referred, read over, controlled accounts.

استرجع istarja'a, he claimed back.

مراجعة moráju'a, control or inspection, recourse, reference.

راجع rájia', returning, intermittent or remittent (fever).

رجعي raja'iy, reversionary; revocable (divorce).

مرجع marja' a turning point.

رجل - ارجل rijl, pl. arjol (femin.), foot, leg. [ساق - قدم]

رجل - رجال rajil, pl. rijál, man, male.

رجّالة rajjála, men, troop, a band of men.

رجولية rojooliya, virility.

استرجلت istarjalat, she wished to be a man, mannish.

مسترجلة mustarjila, virago, amazon. [مذكّرة]

رجم rajama, he stoned to death.

رجيم rajeem, the Devil, (worthy to be stoned); in contrast to raheem, God the merciful. [رحيم]

رجا rajá, he hoped, begged.

رجاء rajá, hope, request.

ترجّى tarajja, he implored.

مرجوّ marjoo, (it is) requested; the favour asked.

رحب rahiba, it was spacious, there was room.

رحبة rahba, open space, courtyard. [فسحة]

or ترحّب, رحّب rahhaba, or tarahhaba, he welcomed, made room for.

مرحبا marhabú, welcome! [اهلاً و سهلاً]

ترحاب tarháb, a welcoming.

رحض rahada, he cleansed himself.

مرحاض - مراحيض marhád, pl. maráheed, latrine.

رحل rahala, he migrated, was nomad.

رحل rahal, nomads, Bedouins.

رحلة rihla, a journey, day's march.

رحيل raheel, a good mount (horse or camel); a bookstand.

ارتحل irtahala, he migrated, died, passed away (to heaven).

مرحلة marhala, resting-place.

رحم or ترحّم rahima or tarahhama, he had pity; (God) showed pity.

استرحم istarhama, he asked for pity.

رحمة or مرحمة rahma, or marhama, pity.

الرحمن الرحيم Er-Rahmán, Er-Raheem, (God) the merciful, the compassionate.

رحمن or رحمان rahmán, merciful.

مرحوم marhoom, deceased, at the mercy of God, the dear departed one.

رحم - ارحام rihm, or rahim, pl. arhám (femin.), womb, uterus, blood relationship.

ارحام *arhám*, blood relations.

ذوي الارحام *zawi el-arhám*, kindred, distant relatives.

رحى or رحاء *rahá*, a hand-mill. [جاروش]

رخص *rukhs*, cheapness. [بخس]

رخيص *rakhees*, cheap, trifling.

رخصة *rukhsa*, permission, leave of absence. [اذن]

رخصنامة *rukhsanáma* (Persian), licence, trade-licence.

رخّص *rakhkhasa*, he held cheap, permitted, authorised.

مرخّص *murakhkhas*, authorised, plenipotentiary.

مرخصة *markhasa*, bishop, dean.

رخام *rukham*, marble.

رخم *rakhm*, vulture.

رخى *rakhiu*, it was loose, flabby.

ارخى *arkha*, he loosened, let go.

ارتخى *irtakha*, it became loose, flabby.

رخاء or رخاوة *rakhá*, or *rakháwa*, looseness.

رخيّ *rakhiy*, loose.

ردّ *radda*, he restored, sent back, repaid, pushed back, answered.

ردّ *radd*, restitution, reply, repayment.

ارتدّ *irtadda*, he turned himself, became a convert.

تردّد *taraddada*, he went to and fro, repeated, frequented a place.

استردّ *istaradda*, he claimed back.

استرداد *istirdád*, a claiming back.

مرتدّ *murtadd*, convert, apostate.

مردود *mardood*, repaid, replied, returned.

ردّة *radda*, refuse, bran.

رداوة *radáwa*, badness.

ردي - ارديا *radi'*, pl. *ardiyá*, bad.

اردا *ardá*, worse. [العن]

اردب - ارادب *ardab*, pl. *arádib*, measure of grain, 5½ bushels; 198 litres.

ردع *rada'a*, he pushed away, prevented.

ردف - ارداف *ridf*, pl. *ardáf*, crupper, haunch.

رديف *radeef*, militia, army reserve.

ردم *radama*, he dammed, mended, blocked.

ردم *radm*, a blocking up; ruins.

رذع *raza'a*, he threw down.

رذالة *razála*, vileness, baseness.

رذيل *razeel*, vile, base.

ارز or رزّ *ruzz*, or *aruzz*, rice.

مرزّة *marazza*, rice-field.

رزّة - رزز *razza*, pl. *rizaz*, hinge.

رزب - مرزبّة (*razb*), *mirzabba*, pounder, beater, mallet.

رزق *razaqa*, he provided.

رزق *roziqa* (passive), he obtained; he was blessed with (children, &c.).

رزق - ارزاق *rizq*, pl. *arzáq*, food, provisions.

رزّاق razzáq, (God) the provider.

مرزوق marzooq, blessed, provided for (by God).

رزم - رزمة rizma, pl. rizam, bale, parcel. [طرد]

رزين - رزانة rezána, gravity; razeen, grave, serious.

رسوب rosoob, sediment.

راسب rásib, chemical precipitate. [عكارة]

راسخ rásikh, firm, solid.

رسغ rusgh, ankle, wrist. [معصم]

رسالة - رسائل risála, pl. rasáyil, something sent; message, missive, mission; means of transport, navigation.

رسيل - رسلاء raseel, pl. rosalá, messenger.

رسول rasool, prophet, bailiff.

رسول الله rasool Ullah, the prophet of God, a title of Mohammad.

ارسل arsala, he sent.

ارسال irsál, a sending.

مرسل mursil, sender; mursal, sent.

راسل rásala, he corresponded.

مراسل morásil, messenger, correspondent.

مراسلة morásala, letters, correspondence.

رسم rasama, he delineated, traced a plan, prescribed, ordained.

رسّام or راسم rásim, or rassám, painter, artist.

مرسوم marsoom, planned, traced; official order.

رسم - رسوم rasm, pl. rosoom, plan, tracing; tax, usage; address, title.

رسومات rosoomát, taxes.

رسميّ rasmiy, official, of government.

غير رسميّ ghair rasmiy, unofficial, private.

رسميّاً rasmiyán, officially.

رسى or رسا rasá, or risi, it was steady, at anchor.

رسى عند المورده risi 'and el-mawrada, he moored at the quay.

رسى المزاد عليه risi el-mazád 'aleih, the article at auction fell to him.

راسي rási, at anchor; successful bidder at an auction.

المزايدة على ذمّة الراسي عليه المزاد الأوّل el-mozáyada 'ala zimmet er-rási 'aleih el-mazád el-awwal, "folle-enchère," French legal term.

ارسى arsa, he cast anchor, came alongside.

مرساة mirsát, anchor. [باورة]

مرسى - مراسي marsa, pl. marási, port, anchorage.

رشّ rashsha, he sprinkled water.

رشّ rishsh, sprinkling, drizzle, small shot.

رشّ و كنس rishsh wa kens, watering and sweeping (of streets).

رشح rashaha, it oozed, sweated.

رَشَّ rashshaha, he formed, exercised.

ترشيح tarsheeh, formation.

مِرْشَحَة mirshaha, pack-saddle, felt saddle-cloth.

رُشْد rushd, righteousness; adult age.

راشِد, or رشيد, ráshid, or rasheed, pious, righteous, a true guide in faith.

هرون الرشيد Haroon el-Rasheed, Aaron the orthodox, "Haroun Al-Raschid."

رشيد Rasheed, Rosetta.

ارشد arshada, he showed the true path; indicated, pointed out.

ارشاد irshád, indication.

مرشد murshid, indicator; guide; teacher in faith.

رشف rashafa, he sipped, tasted.

رشيق rashiq, elegant, graceful, slender.

رشم rashm, halter, bit, nose-strap.

رشا rashá, he gave a bribe.

ارتشى irtasha, he took a bribe.

راشي ráshi, he who bribes.

مرتشى murtashi, he who takes the bribe.

رشوة rishwa, or rashwa, bribe.

رصّ rassa, he arranged, placed in order.

رصاص rasás, lead, bullet.

قلم رصاص qalem rasás, lead-pencil.

ترصيص tarsees, adjustment, arrangement.

رصد rasada, he watched with attention.

ترصّد tarassada, he lay in wait. [ربص]

رصد rasad, watching; observatory.

رصدخانة rasad-khána (Persian), observatory.

مرصد marsad, place of watching, observatory.

رصّع rassa'a, he set with jewels.

نشان مرصّع nishán morassa', order or decoration set in jewels.

رصيعة rase'eya, a set jewel.

رصيف - ارصفة raseef, pl. arsifa, quay, wharf, pavement, railway platform.

رصانة - رصين rasána, gravity; raseen, serious, grave. [رزانة]

رضّ radda, he bruised. [كدم]

راضّ rádd, who bruises; a hard weapon causing a bruise.

رضّ - رضوض radd, pl. rodood, a bruise.

رضع radia', (the infant) sucked.

ارضعت or رضّعت radda't, or arda't, (the mother) suckled.

رضيع radeea', a suckling; a babe.

رضاعة radáa'a, nursing.

مرضعة mordia'a, wet nurse.

رضى - يرضى radia, he was content; yarda' he is content.

ارضى arda, he made content or consent.

رضاء or رضوان ridá (rizá), or radwán, consent, contentment.

رِضاً ضِمْنِيّ *ridá dimniy*, tacit consent.

راضي *rádi*, he who is content or consenting.

ارْتَضَى *irtada*, he became content, consented.

بِالتَّراضِي *bit-tarádi*, by mutual consent, "à l'amiable."

رَطْب *ratb*, moist, fresh.

رُطَب *rutab*, ripe dates. [بَلح]

رَطِيب *rateeb*, moist fresh.

رُطوبة *rotooba*, moistness, moisture, damp.

رَطَل *ratala*, he poised, weighed in the hand. [وَزَن]

رِطْل - ارْطال *rotl*, pl. *artál*, pound weight, 144 dirhems; 15·85 ounces avdp.; 450 grammes; 3¼ gills liquid measure.

رَطانة or رَطَن *rotn*, or *ratána*, a strange lingo; patois; impure Arabic as spoken by negroes, berberines, &c.; foreign.

رَعَب or ارْتَعَب *ra'ba*, or *irta'ba*, he trembled with fear.

رُعْب *ro'ab*, fear, trembling.

رَعَد *ra'da*, it thundered; *ra'd*, thunder.

رَعْد و بَرْق *ra'd wa barq*, thunder and lightning.

ارْتَعَد *irta'da*, he trembled with fear.

رَعْرَع *ra'ra'a*, he refreshed himself (with a bath), was fresh, alert, beaming.

ارْتَعَش or رَعَش *ra'sha* or *irta'sha*, he shivered.

الرَّعْشَة الكُحُولِيّة *er-ra'sha el-kooliya*, delirium tremens.

رُعاف *ro'áf*, bleeding at the nose.

رَعونة *ra'oona*, culpable carelessness, folly.

ارْعَن *ar'an*, careless, flabby person, coward.

رَعَى - يَرْعَى *ra'a*, (the sheep) browsed; *yara'*, it browses.

ارْعَى *ara'a*, he led to pasture, tended sheep.

راعي *rá'ay*, shepherd. [غَنَّام]

راعَى *ráa'a*, he guarded, showed respect or care for.

رِعاية or مُراعاة *r'iáya*, or *morá'at*, respect, regard.

مُراعاةً لِلآداب *morá'atan lil-aadáb*, out of respect for morality or decency.

مَرْعَى *mará'ay*, pasture ground. [مَرْبَع]

رَعِيَّة - رَعايا *ra'iya*, pl. *ra'áyá*, sheep; Ottoman subject; Indian *ryot*.

رَعِيَّة و حَمايَة *ra'iya wa himáya*, Ottoman subjects and foreigners under (Consular) protection.

رَغِب *raghiba*, he desired. [رَجاء]

رَغْبة *raghba*, desire.

راغِب *rághib*, desirous.

مَرْغوب *marghoob*, thing desired, desire.

رَغيف - ارْغِفة *ragheef*, pl. *arghifa*, loaf.

رغم *raghm*, aversion, dislike.

رغماً عنه *raghmán 'anoh*, in spite of him or it.

رغى *ragha*, it foamed, bubbled, (hot or cold).

رغوة *raghwa*, foam, froth, a boiling over.

رف - رفوف *raff*, pl. *rofoof*, plank, shelf.

رفراف *rafráf*, splash-board of carriage.

رفروف *rafroof*, bandage, band.

رفاء *rifá*, peace, concord.

رفا or رفأ *rafá*, or *ráfá*, he conciliated, put straight.

رفت *rafata*, he dismissed, sent on.

رفت *raft*, dismissal from employment.

رفتيّة *raftiya*, Custom House permit for transit to another port in the same (Ottoman) country without repayment of dues; Customs' receipt.

مرفوت *marfoot*, dismissed, discharged.

رفس or رفص *rafasa*, he kicked out backwards; the horse kicked.

رفّاص *raffás*, kicker, screw of steamer.

رفض *rafada*, he rejected, refused.

رفض *rafd*, rejection, refusal.

رفع *rafa'a*, he lifted up, carried off elsewhere.

رفع عنه الاستئناف *rafa'a 'anoh el-istenáf*, he appealed (in law).

رافع *ráfa'a*, he contended in a tribunal.

ارتفع *irtafa'a*, it became high.

رفع *rafa'* a raising, lifting, carrying off; the *damma* or " ُ " vowel-sound. [ضَمَّة]

رفعة *rifa'a*, rank, position in society.

رفعتلو *rifa'tlu* (Turkish), a title for minor officials; honoured Sir.

ارتفاع *irtifá'a*, altitude, elevation.

مرافعة *morafa'a*, hearing of a case in court, proceedings in court; legal procedure.

رفيع *rafeea'*, or *rofaya'*, thin, slender, high.

مرفع *marfa'*, sideboard; carnival.

عيد المرافع *'eed el-maráfia'*, Fête of Carnival.

رفغ *rafgh*, the groin. [اربية]

رفق or ارفق *rafaqa*, or *ráfaqa*, he accompanied, helped.

ارتفق *irtafaqa*, he leaned on his elbows, relieved himself.

رفق *rifq*, gentleness, help.

رفاق or مرافقة *rifáq*, or *morafaqa*, companionship.

رفيق - رفقاء *rafeeq*, pl. *rofaqá*, comrade, accomplices.

احمد و رفقاه *Ahmed wa rofaquh*, Ahmed and his fellows (& Co.).

مرافق *moráfiq*, comrade; lover.

مرفق - مرافق *mirfaq*, pl. *maráfiq*, elbow. [كوع]

مرتفقات *mortafaqát*, latrines. [مرحاض]

رفه (105) ركب

رفَه‎ *rafaha*, he lived in luxury.

رفِيه‎ ـ رفاهَة‎ *rafeeh*, wealthy; *rafáha*, luxury.

رفا‎ *rafá*, he mended, darned.

رقَّة‎ *riqqa*, fineness, gentleness, delicacy.

رقيق‎ *raqeeq*, fine, delicate, compassionate.

رقيق‎ ـ رقاق‎ *raqeeq*, pl. *riqáq*, a newly-caught slave; slave in a slave gang; as distinct from 'abd, domestic slave.

رقيق‎ or رقّ‎ *riqq*, or *raqeeq*, slave-trade; *riqq*, tambourine.

استرقّ‎ *istaraqqa*, he caught, or traded in, slaves for sale.

رقّ غزال‎ *riqq ghazál*, parchment.

رقَب‎ *raqaba*, he observed, watched.

راقَب‎ *ráqaba*, he controlled, inspected.

مراقبة‎ *moráqaba*, inspection, control.

مراقب‎ *moráqib*, inspector, controller.

رقبة‎ ـ رقاب‎ *raqaba*, pl. *riqáb*, nape of neck; yoke.

رقبيّة‎ *raqabiya*, horse-collar.

مالك الرقبة‎ *málik er-raqaba*, owner of property which is held by another in usufruct; "nu-propriétaire."

رقَد‎ ـ راقد‎ *raqada*, he lay down; *ráqid*, recumbent.

ماء راقدة‎ *má ráqida*, stagnant water.

رقَّد‎ *raqqada*, he planted slips or shoots. [غرس]

رقَص‎ *raqasa*, he danced; *raqs*, a dance.

رقَّاص‎ *raqqás*, dancer; main-spring of watch.

رقعة‎ ـ رقاع‎ *roqa'a*, pl. *riqáa'*, patch; letter, note.

رقعة‎ *rōqa'a*, patch of ground, market-place.

رقَم‎ or رقَّم‎ *raqama*, or *raqqama*, he wrote, dated, numbered.

رقم‎ ـ ارقام‎ *raqm*, pl. *arqám*, figure, numeral.

رقيم‎ or مرقَّم‎ *raqeem*, or *moraqqam*, dated, numbered.

ترقيم‎ *tarqeem*, enumeration, dating, writing.

مرقوم‎ *marqoom*, written, aforesaid. [مذكور]

رقن‎ or رقَّن‎ *raqana*, or *raqqana*, he wrote, engrossed.

رقى‎ *raqia*, he mounted; *raqa*, he used magic.

رقية‎ *roqya*, magic. [سحر]

ترقَّى‎ *taraqqa*, he advanced, was promoted.

ترقِّي‎ *taraqqi*, promotion.

مرقى‎ ـ مراقي‎ *marqa*, pl. *maráqi*, a step forward.

ركّ‎ or ركاكة‎ *rekk*, or *rakáka*, fineness, weakness.

ركيك‎ *rakeek*, thin, weak.

ركِب‎ *rakiba*, he mounted (an animal to ride), rode, embarked.

رَكَّبَ rakkaba, he organised, composed. [رتب]

اِرْتَكَبَ irtakaba, he committed a crime, sin.

تَرَكَّبَ tarakkaba, it was organised, composed.

تَرْكِيب tarkeeb, organisation, composition.

رُكْبَة ـ رُكَب rokba, pl. rokab, knee.

رِكَاب ـ رُكُب rikáb, pl. rukub, stirrup.

رِكِبْدَار rikibdár (Persian), rough-rider, horse-breaker.

رَاكِب ـ رُكَّاب rákib, pl. rukkáb, rider, passenger by a train or ship.

رَكُوب rakoob, an animal for riding; a "mount."

عَرَبِيَة رَكُوب 'arabiya rakoob, a carriage (not a cart).

مَرْكَب ـ مَرَاكِب markab, pl. marákib, ship, barge; (in Asia Minor, ass, donkey).

مَرْكُوب ـ مَرَاكِيب markoob, pl. marákeeb, shoe.

مُرَكَّب murakkab, composed of, compound; (in Turkish, ink).

مُرْتَكِب murtakib, a criminal, sinner, guilty.

رَكَزَ rakaza, he set up a post, fixed a point, pitched a tent.

رَكِيز rakeez, post, nail, peg, pole set up.

مَرْكَز ـ مَرَاكِز markaz, pl. marákiz, centre of circle; arrondissement, head-quarters.

مَأْمُور المَرْكَز mámoor el-markaz, prefect of an arrondissement.

مَرْكَز رِيَاسَة الجَيْش markaz riyásat el-jaish, head-quarters of an army.

رُكُوز rokooz, reliance, belief in.

رَكَضَ rakada, he ran. [جرى]

رَكَعَ raka'a, he bent in prayer.

رَكْعَة raka'a, a prostration; a prayer.

رَكَمَ rakama, he heaped up.

اِرْتَكَمَ or تَرَاكَمَ irtakama, or tarákama, it formed a heap.

رُكْن ـ أَرْكَان rokn, pl. arkán, a solid corner or support, a corner, angle.

أَرْكَان الحَرْب arkán el-harb, staff of army.

رُكُونَة ـ رُكْنَة rokoona, solidity; rokna, proof, support.

رَكِين rakeen, solid.

اِرْتَكَنَ عَلَى irtakana 'ala, he relied upon, based his argument upon.

رَاكِيَة or رَكِيَة rakia, native oven, hole.

رَمَّ or رَمَّمَ ramma, or rammama, he mended, repaired.

تَرْمِيم or مَرَمَّة tarmeem, or maramma, a mending.

رِمَّة ـ رِمَم rimma, pl. rimam, rottenness, corpse.

رميم *rameem*, rotten, decayed.

رمّة *romma*, halter, bridle.

برمّته *birommatihi* (*bromto*), entirely; i.e. (an animal sold) halter and all.

رمح *ramaha*, he speared, galloped off.

رمح - ارماح *romh*, pl. *armáh*, spear. [حربة]

رمد *ramad*, ophthalmia.

رماد *ramád*, cinders, ashes.

رمز *ramaza*, he winked at; *ramz*, a wink. [غمز]

رمش - رموش *rimsh*, pl. *romoosh*, eyelashes. [هدب]

رمضاء *ramdá*, heat of summer.

رمضان *Ramadán*, or *Ramazán*, ninth Moslem month; the month of fasting.

رمق *ramaq*, dying breath, last gasp.

رمل - رمال *raml*, pl. *rimál*, sand; Ramleh.

رمّال *rammál*, fortune teller by sand.

مرملة *marmala*, sand-pot for drying ink.

ارملة - ارامل *armala*, pl. *arámil*, widow. [عازب]

رمّان *rommán*, pomegranate.

رمى - يرمي *rama*, he threw; *yirmi*, he throws.

رمي *rami*, a throw; jetsam.

رامي *rámi*, he who throws; *Sagittarius* in the Zodiac.

مرمى *marma*, distance of a throw; range.

مرمي *marmiy*, projectile, thrown.

رنّ *ranna*, it tinkled, re-echoed. [طنّ]

رنان or رنين *rinán*, or *raneen*, tinkle, ring, sob.

رنم *ranam*, a song.

رنم or ترنم *ranama*, or *tarannama*, he sang. [غنى]

رهبة *rahba*, fear, shyness.

رهّب *rahhaba*, he terrified.

ترهيب *tarheeb*, a terrorising.

رهيب *raheeb*, terrible.

راهب or رهبان *ráhib*, or *rohbán*, monk, recluse.

رهبانيّة *rohbániya*, monasticism.

رهج *rahaj*, arsenic, chemical precipitate. [زرنيخ]

رهز *rahaza*, he shook, trembled.

رهط *rahat*, leather fringe apron.

رهيف *raheef*, slender.

رهاق *riháq*, almost, very nearly.

مراهق *moráhiq*, almost adult youth; pubescent.

رهم - مرهم (*raham*) *marham*, ointment.

رهن *rahana*, he pledged, pawned, mortgaged.

رهن - رهون *rahn*, pl. *rohoon*, pledge, pawn.

رهن عقاريّ rahn a'qáriy, "hypothèque," mortgage of land.

رهنيّة rahniya, pledge, bond.

مرهونات marhoonát, things pledged, or mortgaged.

راهن ráhana, he betted with.

ارتهن irtahana, he bought a mortgage.

مداين مرتهن للعقار modáyin mortahin lil-'aqár, creditor of a mortgage.

راهوان or رهوان ráhwán (Persian), roadster; ambler.

روّى - روّية rawwá, he pondered; rawiya, attention.

روب - رائب rōb, curdling; ráyib, curdled.

رواج rawáj, circulation, currency, briskness (trade).

رائج ráyij, current, in circulation; brisk (trade).

على حسب الرائج 'ala hasab ar-ráyij, ad valorem, market rate.

روّج rawwaja, he put into circulation, made current, caused a briskness of trade.

رواح rawáh, a going.

راح - يروح ráha, he went; yarooh, he goes; roh, go thou!

روّح rawwaha, he went; (provincial) he came.

راحة ráha, repose, rest; fallow; palm of hand.

ريّح - تريّح rayyaha, he set at ease, convinced; taryeeh, a setting at ease, quieting fears.

تراويح taráweeh, prayers of rest; night prayers in the mosque during Ramadan.

ارتاح or استراح irtáha, or istaráha, he took his ease.

مرتاح or مستريح murtáh, or mustareeh, at ease, in repose.

مستراح mustaráh, water-closet, "lieu d'aisance."

استراحة istiráha, repose, a taking one's ease.

روح - ارواح rooh, pl. arwáh, soul, spirit; chamber of a revolver, or charge of a gun.

روحيّ roohiy, spiritual; spirituous (liquor).

روحانيّ roohániy, spiritual, ecclesiastical.

ريح - ارياح reeh, pl. riyáh, or aryáh (femin.), wind, evil spirit, ghost.

عليه ريح 'aleih reeh, he was an evil spirit.

مريوح mariooh, bewitched by an evil spirit.

ابو رياح aboo riyáh, scarecrow, weather-cock.

ريحة or رائحة - روائح reeha, or ráyiha, pl. rawáyih, odour, scent.

مرواح - مروحة marwáh, departure; mirwaha, fan.

ريحان raihán, basil-plant.

راود ráwada, he lusted for, disputed.

رويدأ roweedán, little by little, gradually.

اراد *aráda*, he wished.

اراده - اراد ة اراد *iráda*, desire, will, decree, fiat; *iráda saniya* سنيّة اراده, imperial decree.

مراد *murád*, desired, a desire; Murad or Amurath.

مريد *moreed*, desirous, candidate.

روز نامه *róz náma* (Persian), calendar, pension, office.

نوروز *naw-róz*, new year, autumnal equinox, Sept. 11.

روز قاسم *róz qásim*, feast of 7th November.

روز خضر و الياس *róz khadir wa Eliás*, St. George's Day.

روشن *róshan*, air-hole, sky-light.

روض - روضة *róda*, pl. *ród*, garden; island off Old Cairo.

رياضة or رياض *riyád*, or *riyáda*, training, discipline, "régime."

رياضات *riyádát*, mathematics.

روع - راع *rowa'*, awe, fear; *rúa'a*, he feared.

روق - رائق *róq*, limpidity; *ráyiq*, limpid.

روّق *rawwaqa*, he clarified.

اراق *aráqa*, he poured out; shed (blood).

ريق *reeq*, saliva.

رواق *rowáq*, gallery, cloister, porch.

تربيقة *tarweeqa*, breakfast.

روك or روكيّ *rók*, or *rókiy* (Coptic), general, common; undivided property.

روكيّة *rókiya*, the mass or total of an estate.

رول *ról* (French), "rôle," list, register. [جدول]

روم *róm*, desire.

رام - يروم *ráma*, he desired; *yaroom*, he desires.

مرام *marám*, desired; a desire.

روم *room*, Byzantium, the Roman Empire of the East; Asia Minor; a part of Asia Minor.

روم ايلي *room eeli* (Turkish), Roumelia.

روم ارام - روميّ *room*, pl. *arwám*, Greek Christian; *roomiy*, Romish; Greek Church.

فرخ روميّ *farkh roomiy*, a turkey.

روماتزم *roomátizm* (European), rheumatism.

رونق *rónaq*, splendour, beauty.

روى *rawa*, he narrated. [حكى]

راوي *ráwi*, narrator, story-teller.

رواية *riwáya*, narrative.

ريّ *raiy*, irrigation.

اروى *arwa*, he irrigated.

ريّة *rayya*, a canal for irrigation.

ريّة *riya*, lung.

ريب or ارتياب *raib*, or *irtiyáb*, doubt, suspicion.

راب or ارتاب *rába*, or *irtába*, he doubted, hesitated.

مرتاب *murtáb*, doubtful; suspected.

ريت - ليت *rait* (vulgar for *laita*), would that!

ريح - رواح‎ *reeh*, wind (see p. 108).

ريش - رياش‎ *reesh*, pl. *riyásh*, feather, plume.

ريف - ارياف‎ *reef*, pl. *aryáf*, riverain land, fertile land of Egypt by the Nile; the provinces, "in the country."

ريق - روق‎ *reeq*, saliva (see also *róq*).

ريال‎ *riál*, dollar, talari, Spanish reale.

ريم - تريم‎ (*reem*) *taryeem*, humbug, exaggeration.

بلا تريم‎ *bilá taryeem*, without exaggeration.

راية - رايات‎ *ráya*, pl. *ráyát*, flag.

Z

ز‎ *Zain*. Value = 7.

زاج‎ *záj*, vitriol.

زاد - زوّادة‎ *zád*, or *zowwáda*, victuals.

زاد - زيد‎ *záda*, it increased (see *zaid*).

زاده - بكزاده‎ *záda* (Persian suffix), born, -fitz, son of, as *beyzáda*, a boy's son, of good family.

زار‎ *zár*, negro incantations.

زار - زيارة‎ *zára*, he visited (see *ziyára*).

زأف - زيف‎ *záyif*, bad (money) (see *zaif*).

زبيب‎ *zabeeb*, raisins, liqueur from raisins.

زبدة‎ *zubda*, or *zibda*, butter, essence.

زبور‎ *zaboor*, Psalms of David. [مزمورا]

زبط‎ *zabat*, mire, street mud.

زوبعة‎ *zoba'a*, sandstorm, whirlwind.

زيبق‎ *zaibaq* (Persian), quicksilver.

زبل‎ *zibl*, pigeon manure. [سبلة]

زبّال‎ *zabbál*, dustman, scavenger.

مزبلة‎ *mazbala*, dust-heap, dung-heap.

زبون - زبائن‎ *zaboon*, pl. *zabáyin*, client, customer.

زجاج - قزاز‎ *zijáj* (colloquial = *qizáz*), glass; bottle.

زجر‎ *zajr*, prohibition; liquor licence.

زجل‎ *zajal*, vulgar tongue, ungrammatical speech, faulty metre.

حمل زجل‎ *himl zajal*, vulgar lampoon.

زحير‎ *zaheer*, dysentery, colic.

زحزح‎ *zahzaha*, he carried off, removed.

زحل‎ *zohal*, planet Saturn.

زحلق‎ *zahlaqa*, he slipped, rolled over. [زلق]

زحمة - زحم‎ *zahma*, crowd; *zahhama*, he crowded.

ازدحم or تزاحم‎ *izdahama*, or *tazáhama*, a crowd formed.

زخرفة‎ *zokhrofa*, ornament.

زخمة‎ *zokhma*, thong, strap; flogging.

زر‎ *zer* (Persian), gold, gold ornament.

زرّ‎ *zarra*, he buttoned.

زر - ازرار‎ *zirr*, pl. *azrár*, bud, tassel.

زِرار - زَرائِر *zorár*, pl. *zaráyir*, button.

زرب *zaraba*, he penned cattle.

زَرِيبة or زَرِيبَة *zarbiya*, or *zareeba*, cattle-pen, walled enclosure for cattle; lager, camp, night defence.

زَرْبة *zorba*, guardians, watchmen of cattle.

زرد - مزرود *zard*, flushing, choking; *mazrood*, red in face.

زرع *zara'a*, he tilled, sowed seed.

زرع or زراعة *zir'a* or *ziráa'a*, tillage.

انزرع *inzara'a*, it was tilled.

مزارع *mozári'a*, farmer.

زرافة *zoráfa*, giraffe.

زَرَّق - مِزْراق *zarraqa*, he pierced; *mizráq*, spear.

زرقة *zorqa*, blueness.

ازرق - زرقا *azraq*, (femin.) *zarqá*, blue.

مزرق *muzriq*, bluish, black and blue (bruise).

زركش *zarkasha*, he embroidered, brocaded.

مزركش *mozarkash*, (gold) brocade.

زرنيخ *zarneekh*, arsenic.

زرة *zirh* (Persian), mail, armour.

زرى - يزري *zara*, he despised; *yazri*, he despises.

ازرى ب *azra bi*, he made despicable, injured.

مزري *mozri*, injurious, bringing into contempt.

زعبوط *za'boot*, cloak, woollen cloak.

زعج - ازعج *za'aj*, anxiety; *aza'ja*, he annoyed.

مزعج *mozia'j*, annoying, embarrassing.

زعزع *za'za'a*, he shook, made tremble.

زعفران *za'furán*, saffron.

زعق - زعيق *za'qa*, he cried out; *za'eeq*, shout.

زعلة - زعلان *za'ala*, vexation; *za'alán*, vexed, angry.

ازعل *az'ala*, he angered, vexed.

زعم *za'm*, idea, notion, conjecture.

زعامة *za'áma*, authority, ancient feudal estate.

مزعم *maz'am*, doubtful, conjectural.

زغد *zaghada*, he pushed, poked.

زغر *zaghara*, he scrutinised.

زغاريت *zaghárcet*, shrill cries of joy.

زغزغ *zaghzagha*, he tickled.

زغطة *zoghotta*, hiccup, belch.

زغل *zaghala*, he adulterated.

زغل *zaghal*, bad (money).

زغلول *zaghlool*, young pigeon; large yellow date.

زفة or زفاف *zaffa*, or *zifáf*, festive procession at weddings, &c.

زفت *zift*, pitch, tar.

زي الزفت *zaiy ez-zift* (colloquial), like pitch, worthless.

زفر or ذفر *zifr*, bad, fishy smell.

زقاق - ازقة *zoqáq*, pl. *aziqqa*, street, lane.

زَقّ zaqqa, he pushed.

زَقَازِيق - شَرْقِيَّة Zaqázeeq, Zagazig, capital of the *Sharqiya* province of the Delta.

زَقْلَة zoqla, cudgel, staff.

زَكِيبَة - زَكَائِب zakeeba, pl. zakáyib, sack.

زُكَام zukám, influenza.

زَكَاء zaká, purity, piety.

زَكَاة zakát, alms as a religious duty.

زَكِيّ - اَزْكِيَاء zakiy, pl. azkiyá, pious. [cf. ذَكِيّ]

زَكَّى zakka, he purified, recommended as good.

تَزْكِيَة tazkiya, certificate of good character, recommendation.

زَلَّة zalla, slip, error, false step.

زُلَال zolál, slippery; *albumen*.

زَلْزَال or زَلْزَلَة zalzala, or zilzál, earthquake.

تَزَلْزَل tazalzala, it quaked, shook.

زَلَابِيَة zalábiya, galette, greasy sweet cake.

زَلَابَانِيّ zalabániy, seller of galette.

زَلَط zalt, nakedness; bare. [ملط]

زَلَّط zallata, he stripped bare.

زَلَط zalat, pebble.

زَلَط zalata, he swallowed.

زَلْعَة zala'a, urn, large jar.

زَلَق zalaqa, he slipped; zalq, slipperiness.

زَلْقَان zalqán, slipped, out of place, spoilt.

مَزْلَقَان mazlaqán, slope, slide, slippery place.

زِمَام - اَزِمَّة zimám, pl. azimma, bridle, reins, area within a bridle of control, hence control, arrondissement.

زَمْتَة zamta, gravity, seriousness; closeness of atmosphere, no wind.

زَمَّارَة or زَمْر zamr, flute; zammára, double reed pipe.

زَمَّار zammár, flute player.

مِزْمَار mizmár, glottis, flute.

مَزْمُور - مَزَامِير mazmoor, pl. mazámeer, Psalm. [زبور]

زُمْرَة - زُمَر zomra, pl. zomar, gang, clique.

زُمَّيْر zommair, oats, rye.

زُمُرُّد zumurrud, emerald.

زَمْزَم zamzam, a sacred well near Mecca.

زَمْزَمِيَّة zamzamiya, leather-bottle, pilgrim's water-bottle for filling at Zamzam.

زَمَع - اَزْمَع (zama') azma'a, he was constant, decided. [عزم]

مُزْمِع mozmia' resolute; thing decided upon.

زَمْكَان zamkán, angry, cross, vexed.

زَمِيل - زُمَلَاء zameel, pl. zomalá, comrade, colleague.

زَمْلَة zamla, family, reunion, "smala."

زَمَن - اَزْمَان zaman, pl. azmán, time, epoch.

زَمَان - اَزْمِنَة zamán, pl. azmina, time, epoch.

مِن زَمان *min zamán*, long ago, long since.

مُزْمِن *mozmin*, chronic (disease).

زَمْهَرير *zamhareer*, intense cold.

زَنْبور *zonboor*, wasp.

زَنْبَق *zanbaq*, lily, iris.

زَنْبيل *zanbeel* (Persian), basket.

زَنْج - زُنوج *zanj*, pl. *zonooj*, Ethiopian, negro.

زَنْجِيّ *zanjiy*, Ethiopian, an Ethiopian.

زَنْجِبار *Zanjibár*, Zanzibar.

زَنْجَبيل *zanjibeel*, ginger.

زِنْجير - جِنْزير *zinjeer* (Persian), chain (often pronounced *jinzeer*).

زَنْد *zand*, wrist, forearm.

زِناد *zinád*, gun-hammer, flint and steel. [شطفة]

زُنّار *zunnár*, girdle.

زَنْزَلَخْت *zanzalakht*, wild apple. [ذبق]

زَنَق *zanaqa*, he squeezed, held tight.

مَزْنَقة *maznaqa*, necklace.

زَنْقة *zanqa*, gonorrhœa.

زَنْقور - زَناقير *zanqoor*, pl. *zanáqeer*, recess, niche.

زَنَى - يَزْنِي *zana*, he committed adultery; *yazni*, he commits adultery.

زِناء *ziná*, adultery, fornication.

زاني - زُناة *záni*, pl. *zonát*, adulterer.

زانية - زَوانِي *zániya*, pl. *zawáni*, adulteress.

زِنة *zina*, a weighing (see وزن).

زِنْهار *zinhár* (Persian), Beware! Attention! (military).

زَهْد - زاهِد *zohd*, celibacy; *záhid*, celibate, ascetic.

زَهيد *zaheed*, few, trifling.

زَهَر *zahara*, it bloomed, shone with brilliance.

زَهْرة *zahra*, a flower.

زَهْر - زُهور or أزهار *zahr*, pl. *zohoor*, or *azhár*, flower; orange flower.

زُهْرة *zohra*, beauty; Venus.

داء زُهْرِي *dá zohriy*, venereal disease.

أزهر - زَهْراء *azhar*, (femin.) *zahrá*, brilliant, lovely.

الجامع الأزهر *el-jámia' el-azhar*, the brilliant mosque, mosque of "El-Azhar."

زَوْج - زَوْجة - أزواج *zōj*, (femin.) *zōja*, pl. masc. and femin. *azwáj*, spouse; husband, wife; pair, couple. (In vulgar Arabic written and pronounced *jōz*.) [جوز]

زَوْجات *zōját*, wives; pl. of *zōja*.

زَوْجِيّة *zōjiya*, fact or status of matrimony, matrimonial (affairs).

زَواج or ازدواج *zawáj*, or *izdiwáj*, marriage.

زَوَّج *zawwaja*, he gave in marriage.

تَزَوَّج *tazawwaja*, he took a wife, married.

مُتَزَوِّج *motazawwij*, married.

زور *zor*, throat; *zoor*, perjury, forgery, violence.

شهادة زور *shaháda zoor*, false testimony, perjury.

زوّر *zawwara*, he forged, falsified, perjured.

تزوير *tazweer*, act of forgery; perjury.

مزوّر *mozawwir*, forger, perjurer, falsifier.

سند مزوّر *sanad mozawwar*, forged document.

ازور – زوراء *azwar*, (femin.) *zorá*, oblique; a name for Baghdad.

مزور *mazwar*, made oblique, slanting.

زوراق *zoráq*, boat.

زيارة *ziyára*, visit, pilgrimage.

زار – يزور *zára*, he visited; *yazoor*, he visits.

زائر – زوّار *záyir*, pl. *zowwár*, visitor, pilgrim.

تزييرة *tazyeera*, lady's visiting dress.

مزار *mazár*, place visited, shrine.

زوّق *zawwaqa*, he adorned.

زوال *zawál*, decline, end, lapse; shadow.

زال – يزول *zála*, it ceased; *yazool*, it ceases.

ما زال or لم يزل *má zála*, or *lam yazol*, it did not cease; not yet.

زائل *záyil*, decadent.

زاوية – زوايا *záwiya*, pl. *zawáyá*, angle, corner; chapel, hermitage.

منزوي *munzawi*, hermit, recluse.

زيت – زيوت *zait*, pl. *zoyoot*, oil.

زيّات *zayyát*, oilman.

زيتون *zaitoon*, olive, olive-tree.

زيد – مزيد *zaid*, or *mazeed*, growth, surplus; *Zaid*, a man's name.

زيادة *ziyáda*, surplus, plus, more than.

بالزيادة *biz-ziyáda*, quite enough, too much.

زائد – ازيد *záyid*, superfluous; *aziad*, more abundant.

زاد – يزيد *záda*, it increased; *yazeed*, it increases, exceeds.

ازداد or تزايد *izdáda*, or *tazáyada*, it increased.

زيّد or زوّد *zayyada*, or *zawwada*, he made increase.

تزييد *tazyeed*, augmentation.

مزاد – مزايدة *mazád*, or *mozáyada*, auction.

مزيد *mazeed*, augmented, complex; growth.

ازدياد *izdiyád*, growth, increase.

زير – ازيار *zeer*, pl. *azyár*, very large pitcher.

زيطة – زاط *zaita*, uproar; *záta*, he shouted.

زائف or زيف *zaif*, or *záyif*, pl. *zoyoof*, bad money.

زيّف zayyafa, he adulterated; rejected as bad.

زيل - ازال - ازالة (zail) azála, he destroyed, ravished; izála, destruction. [cf. زوال]

زين - ازيان zain, pl. azyán, ornament.

زينة zeena, ornament, decorations; tattoo-mark; fête.

زيّن zayyana, he adorned.

تزيّن or ازدان izdána, or tazayyana, he adorned himself.

مزيّن mozayyin, barber, coiffeur.

زينب Zainab, a woman's name.

زيّ zee, or zaiy, aspect, fashion, dress; like.

أزيّ - زيّ ذي é-zaiy, how? zaiy dee, like this!

زيّ بعض zaiy b'ad, like one another.

زيّ الناس zaiy en-nás, in a human manner; call of nature.

تزيّا tazayyá, he dressed up, assumed a dress.

متزيّا mutazayyá, dressed up, dressed in.

S

س Seen. Value = 60.

س - سوف s, particle, prefix to aorist tense marking future signification; a contraction of sōf, afterwards.

سيصير sa-yaseer, it will be.

ساء - سو sá, it was bad (see sow).

ساج sáj, platane, teak.

ساجات sáját, castanets.

ساحة sáha, area, courtyard; status.

برأة ساحة baráa saha, innocence of status, the legal phrase for acquittal.

ساده sáda (Persian), simple, pure. [بسيط]

ساعة - ساعات sá'aa, pl. sá'aát, hour, the time, watch.

ساعة ذهب sá'aa dahab, a gold watch.

الساعة كم es-sá'aa kam, what is the time?

اكم ساعة akam sá'aa, a few hours.

الساعة اربعة es-sá'aa arba'a, four o'clock.

اربع ساعات arb'a sá'aát, four hours.

ساعاتي sá'átiy, watchmaker.

للساعة lis-sá'aa (lissa), up to now, not yet.

ساق - سياق sáqa, he went ahead, drove (see siyáq).

ساق sáq (feminine), leg, shank, stalk (see siyáq).

ساك - سوك sáka, he cleaned his teeth (see sōk).

سأل sáala, he asked.

يسأل yasál, he asks; yosál, it is asked.

سئل soo-ila, he was, it was asked.

سؤال - اسئلة soodl, pl. asila, question.

(116)

مسألة or مَسْئَلَة *masála*, pl. مسائل *masáyil*, question, topic, affair.

مسئول عن or مسئول *masool 'an*, asked about, responsible for.

مسئوليّة or مسئولِيّة *masooliya*, responsibility.

سائل *sáyil*, asker, beggar.

سل or اسأل *sal*, or *isál* (imperative), ask thou!

سال ـ يسيل *sála*, it flowed; *yaseel*, it flows. [contrast سأل

سيل ـ سيول *sail*, pl. *soyool*, torrent, flood, flux.

سيلان *sayalán*, flood, a flowing.

سائل or سيّال *sáyil*, or *sayyál*, fluid, liquid.

سوائل *sawáyil*, essences, fluids.

سيّالة *sayyála*, pocket, fob; small Nile canal, branch canal.

اسائة *isála*, a making flow, pouring out.

مسيل *maseel*, gutter, water-course.

سائر *sáyir*, other, remainder, rest; all.

سايس ـ سياسة *sáyis*, groom, running footman (see *siyása*).

سبّ *sabba*, he cursed, insulted grossly.

سبّ *sabb*, a curse, cursing, foul abuse.

سبيب *sabeeb*, horse-hair.

سبب ـ اسباب *sabab*, pl. *asbáb*, cause, reason, motive.

بسبب *bi-sabab*, by reason of, because of.

تسبّب *tasabbaba*, he caused; sold retail.

متسبّب *motasabbib*, causer, instigator; a pedlar, seller.

سبّابة *sabbába*, first or index finger.

سبت ـ سبد *sabat* (for Persian *sapad*), basket.

سبت or يوم السبت *sabt*, or *yōm es-sabt*, Saturday, the Jewish sabbath.

سبات *sobát*, lethargy.

سبتمبر *Sebtember* (European), September.

سبح *sabaha*, he swam. [عوم

سبّح *sabbaha*, he praised God.

سبحان الله *sobhán Allah*, Praise be to God!

تسبيح or سبحة *sibha*, or *tasbeeh*, eulogy or praise of God, hence rosary of beads.

سباخ *sibákh*, manure; artificial manure.

سبخة ـ سباخ *sabkha*, pl. *sibákh*, saline infiltration up to the surface of land, salt crust; shallow lagoon.

تسبيخ *tasbeekh*, a manuring of land.

سبط *sibt*, son, offspring, fruit.

سباطة *sabáta*, cluster of dates or bananas.

اسباط اسرائيل *asbát Isráyeel*, the tribes of Israel.

سبع ـ سباع *saba'*, pl. *sibáa'*, lion, beast of prey.

بركة السبع *Birkat es-saba'*, the lion's pool or lair.

سبع *suba'*, one-seventh part.

سبع - سبعة *saba'a*, (femin.) *saba'*, seven.

سابع *sábia'*, seventh in order.

سبعين - سبعون *saba'oon*, or *saba'een*, seventy.

اسبوع - اسابيع *osbooa'*, pl. *asábcea'*, week. [جمعة]

المثاني السبع - فاتحة القرآن *el-masáni es-saba'*, the seven eulogies or titles of God in the first chapter of the Koran, called the *Fátiha*.

سبق or سبرق *sibq, sabq*, or *sobooq*, priority, antecedence.

سبق الاصرار *sabq el-israr*, priority of determination, premeditation (in crime).

سبق *sabaqa*, it preceded, was previous.

سابق *sábiq*, previous, last.

اسبق *asbaq*, more previous, last but one.

سابقة - سوابق *sábiqa*, pl. *sawábiq*, an antecedent, precedent, (often in a bad sense).

عنده سوابق *'andoh sawábiq*, he has (bad) antecedents, "this is not his first offence."

ارباب سوابق *arbáb sawábiq*, men of (bad) antecedents, prisoners with previous convictions.

سابق *sábaqa*, he vied with, raced.

سباق or مسابقة *sibáq*, or *mosábaqa*, rivalry, race, horse-race.

سبك *sabaka*, he melted or founded metal.

سبيكة *sabeeka*, ingot.

سبّاك *sabbák*, founder, plumber.

مسبك *masbak*, foundry.

سبيل - سبل *sabeel*, pl. *sobol*, road, path, means; fountain.

على سبيل التعويضات *'ala sabeel et-ta'weedát*, in the way of damages, as compensation.

سبيل الله *sabeel Ullah*, God's path, for the sake of God, charity, a giving of water to thirsty Moslems; hence a fountain, as a pious gift erected in the street.

تخلية سبيله or اخلاء *ikhlá* or *takhliya sabeeloh*, clearing his path, releasing a prisoner. [افراج عنه]

سبلة *sabla*, dung of horse or cow. [زبل]

سبل *sabal*, ear of corn; indistinctness or dimness of vision. [سنبلة]

سبى *saba*, he took captive.

سبي سبايا *sabiy*, pl. *sabáyá*, captive in war. [اسير]

سبا *sabá*, Sheba in Yemen of Arabia.

ست - ستّات سيّدة - جدّة *sitt*, pl. *sittát*, (a corruption of *seyyida*), lady, Mrs.; a term of respect applied to a grandmother (colloquial for *judda*).

ستّ - ستّة *sitta*, (femin.) *sitt*, six.

ستّين - ستّون *sittoon*, or *sitteen*, sixty.

سدس *suds*, one-sixth part.

سادس *sádis*, the sixth in order.

ستور - ستر *sitr*, pl. *sotoor*, veil, veil of decency.

ستر *satara*, he veiled, covered.

تستّر *tasattara*, he veiled or hid himself, concealed the truth. [كتم]

ستائر - ستارة *sitára*, pl. *satáyir*, curtain.

سترة *sitra*, tunic, frock-coat.

مستور *mastoor*, veiled, covered.

سقف or تسقّف *satafa*, or *tasattafa* (colloquial), he took it easy.

است or ستة *sita*, or *ist* (femin.), anus.

سجد *sajada*, he prostrated himself in prayer. [عبد - ركع]

سجود *sojood*, adoration, prostration in prayer.

سجّادة *sajjáda*, prayer-carpet, rug.

مساجد - مسجد *masjid*, pl. *masájid*, mosque, the word from which "mosque" is corrupted. [جامع]

سجاير - سجارة *sijára*, pl. *sajáyir* (European), cigar or cigarette.

شجرة - سجرة *sajara* (vulgarism for *shajara*), tree.

تجيع or سجع *saja'*, or *tasjeea'*, rhythm, fine prose; cadence and rhyme in prose.

سجوق *sojooq* (Turkish), sausage; slow match.

سجلّ - سجلات *sijil*, pl. *sijilát*, scroll or roll of paper; register, archives.

سجّل *sajjala*, he registered, inscribed. [قيد]

تسجيل *tasjeel*, registration, inscription; registration of a letter by post.

مسجّل *mosajjal*, registered (per post, &c.). This word is vulgarly pronounced *musōgur*.

سجن *sajana*, he imprisoned. [حبس]

سجن - سجون *sijn*, pl. *sojoon*, prison, "détention."

سجّان *sajján*, gaoler.

مسجون - مساجين *masjoon*, pl. *masájeen*, imprisoned, a prisoner in gaol.

سحب *sahaba*, he drew, dragged; drew a cheque.

سحابة - سحاب *sahába*, pl. *saháb*, cloud.

تسحّب *tasahhaba*, he withdrew himself, was absent, had left a place.

صاحب الحوالة *sáhib el-hawála*, drawer of a bill of exchange.

استسحب *istas-haba*, he fetched, wished to fetch.

سحج *sahaja*, he excoriated.

سحاج *siháj*, a raw wound, excoriation

مسحوج *mas-hooj*, excoriated, raw.

سحر *sahara*, he bewitched.

سحر *sihr*, magic, sorcery.

ساحر or ساحِر *sáhir*, or *sahhár*, wizard.

سحر *sahr*, lung; *sahar*, dawn.

سحور *sahoor*, meal before dawn.

سحّارة *sahhára*, a large chest, trunk; witch; siphon of canal.

سحيفة *saheefa*, flood, rise of waters; a swamping.

سحق *sahaqa*, he rubbed hard, rubbed into small pieces, bruised.

اسحق *Is-haq*, Isaac.

ساحل ـ سواحل *sáhil*, pl. *sawáhil*, coast, river-bank; the cultivated banks watered by the Nile without canal irrigation.

غفير السواحل *ghafeer el-sawáhil*, coast-guardsman.

سحلية *sihliya*, lizard, garden-lizard. [برص]

سخر *sakhara*, he tyrannised, imposed "*corvée*."

سخّر *sakhkhara*, he subjugated.

سخرة *sokhra*, tyranny, especially "*corvée*."

تسخير *taskheer*, subjugation; legal fiction.

مسخّر *mosakhkhar*, a thing obtained by tyranny, injustice or legal fiction.

مسخرة *maskhara*, ridiculous; a mockery.

سخط *sakhata*, he turned to evil, debased in shape, spoke ill of.

مسخوطة *maskhoota*, ancient Egyptian statue, idol, supposed to be a man changed into stone as a punishment for sin.

سخل *sikhl*, kid, young goat.

سخم *sakham*, blackness, smut.

سخمة *sokhmat*, soot, "smut," filth.

سخمط *sakhmata*, he was licentious, he fornicated.

سخن *sokhn*, hot, warm (food, water); fierce.

سخنة or سخونة *sokhna*, or *sokhoona*, heat, fever.

سخّن *sakhkhana*, he heated, warmed.

اسخن *askhan*, hotter, fiercer.

سخاوة or سخاء *sakhá*, or *sakháwa*, generosity.

سخي *sakhiy*, generous.

سدّ *sadda*, he plugged, dammed a river.

سدّ ـ سدود *sadd*, pl. *sodood*, bar, dam of river.

سداد *sadád*, payment of money.

سدّد *saddada*, he paid a debt, paid in (money).

تسديد *tasdeed*, payment; paying off of debt.

سديد *sadeed*, just, honourable.

سدادة *sidáda*, cork, plug.

سدّة *sudda*, bench, threshold; dignity.

سدّة باباوية *sudda Bábáwiya*, Papal See.

سدر ـ نبق *sidr*, lotus-tree; like the *nabq*, "*viola arborea*."

سدر (120) سريح

سَدَر sadar, vertigo.

سدس - سُتّة suds, one-sixth part (see sitta).

سادِس sádis, the sixth in order.

سدل sadl, the hanging down of anything flexible (curtain, veil, hair, cloak, rope, &c.)

سذاب sadáb, the herb rue.

سذاجة sadája, simplicity.

سرّة - حبل السرّة surra, navel; habl el-surra, navel-string.

سرّ sarra, he gladdened.

سرور or مسرّة soroor, or masarra, joy, delight.

مسرور masroor, gladdened, glad.

مسروريّة masrooriya, gladness, a being gladdened.

سر sir (Persian ser), head, chief of a guild, &c.

سرّ - اسرار sirr, pl. asrar, mystery, secret; drinking a health, a "toast."

اسرار asrár, secrets; hasheesh or bang smoked in secret as being forbidden.

افشاء الاسرار ifshá el-asrár, revelation of (professional) secrets; breach of confidence.

كاتم الاسرار kátim el-asrár, concealer or keeper of secrets, a confidential secretary.

سرّيّ sirriy, confidential, secret.

مخبر سرّيّ mukhbir sirriy, secret informant, police spy, a detective.

سرير - سُرر sareer, pl. soror, bedstead, a flat desert plain, not sandy desert.

سرّيّة - سراري sorriya, pl. saráriy, concubine.

سرب - اسراب sarab, pl. asráb, pipe, drain, conduit.

سراباتي sarábátiy, cleaner of cesspools.

سرب saraba, he slipped away, got away.

تسرّب tasarraba, (the animal) escaped, slipped away, took its course.

سراب saráb (Persian?), mirage of desert.

مسرب masrab, path, course, pasturage.

سرج - سروج sarj, pl. sorooj, saddle, horse's saddle.

سرج or سرج saraja, or sarraja, he saddled (the horse).

سرّاج sarráj, saddler.

سروجي soroojiy, saddler.

سراج siráj (for Persian chirágh), lamp, illumination.

سرح saraha, he roamed, went early to the fields to work.

سرّح sarraha, he let free or loose (cattle), led to pasture; combed out his hair.

تسريح or تصريح tasreeh, a permit, pass, licence.

سارح sárih, pensive, absent-minded.

سريح sareeh, vagabond, pedlar.

سرقة سريكة soqa, or sawaqa sarecha, pedlars; mob.

أسرد or سرد sarada, or asrada, he narrated, set forth in order.

سرداب sirdáb (Persian), vault, secret passage.

سردار serdár (Persian), chief, leader, petty chieftain; in Egypt, Commander-in-Chief under the Khedive.

سرسب sarsaba (colloquial), he sprinkled.

سرطان saratán, crab, Cancer in the Zodiac; disease of cancer.

سرع saro'a, he was in haste, quick.

سرعة sora'a, haste, quickness.

سرعتيله sora'atila, (Turkish suffix ila, with) with haste; quick march!

سريع saree'a, quick, speedy.

سرع sora', reins for a horse.

أسرع asra'a, he hastened; was in a hurry.

أسرع بالجري asra'a bil-jari, he hurried away, running.

مسرع بالجري mosria' bil-jari, hastily running away.

أسرف or سرف sarafa, or asrafa, he squandered.

إسراف isráf, extravagance.

مسرف mosrif, spendthrift.

أسترق or سرق saraqa, or istaraqa, he stole.

أنسرق or سُرق soriqa, or insaraqa, it was stolen.

سرقة seriqa, theft.

سارق - سرّاق sáriq, pl. sorráq, thief.

مسروق masrooq, stolen.

سركي serghi (Turkish), a government bill of exchange or order for payment.

سرمد sarmad, eternal, very long. [صمد]

سرو sarw, or saroo, cypress-tree.

سروال - شلوار sirwál (for Persian shalwár), loose drawers, pantaloons.

سراي - سرايه seráya (for Persian serái), palace.

سرى sara, he travelled, it spread, was in force.

يسري عليه yasri 'aleih, it affects him, is of effect against him, injures him.

ساري sári, (a law) in force; contagious (disease).

سراية siráya, contagion, infection. [عدوى]

سطح or سطح satuha, or sattaha, he spread out flat, flattened.

سطح - سطوح satḥ, pl. sotooh, flat surface, flat roof, deck of ship.

سطحي sat-ḥiy, superficial, on the surface.

مسطح or مسطوح mastooh, or mosattah, flattened, flat.

مسطح or مسطاح mistáh, area, surface; threshing-floor.

مسطح mosattah, note showing area and limits of a piece of land.

سطر or سطّر *satara*, or *sattara*, he ruled lines, wrote out.

سطر ـ سطور *satr*, pl. *sotoor*, line, series.

ساطور *sátoor*, butcher's knife, chopper.

مسطّر *mosattar*, ruled (paper).

مسطرة *mastara*, ruler.

سطع *sata'a*, (the sun or moon) shone.

سطل *satl*, "hasheesh," lozenge of sugar and opium.

اسطوانة ـ اساطين *ostowána*, pl. *asáteen* (Persian; from Greek stoa), cylinder, column.

سطا ـ يسطي *satá*, he attacked, invaded; *yasti*, he attacks.

سطوة *satwa*, invasion, attack.

سطو *sato*, attack, burglary, brigandage.

ساطي ـ سطلة *sátí*, pl. *sotát*, brigand, burglar.

مسطي عليه *masti 'aleih*, victim of attack. [for مسطو *mastoo*]

سعة ـ وسع *sa'a*, capacity, width (see *wassa'a*).

سعتر *sa'tar*, herb thyme, pennyroyal.

سعد *sa'd*, good fortune, help from God.

سعيد *sa'eed*, fortunate; a man's name.

اسعد *asa'd*, more fortunate.

بورت سعيد *Bort Sa'eed*, Port Said,

named after the late Said Pasha of Egypt.

سعادة ـ عزّة ـ دولة *sa'ádet*, felicity; His Excellency, a title of second and third class Pashas, and also given by courtesy to Beys; inferior to *devlet*, superior to *'izzet*.

سعادتلو *sa'ádetlu*, Turkish form of above title.

سعادتلو افندم ـ ميرميران ـ لواء *sa'ádetlu efendim*, Turkish title for a third class Pasha, i.e. Liwa, brigadier, or civil *meeri-meerán*.

سعادتلو افندم حضرتلري ـ فريق *sa'ádetlu efendim hazretleri*, Turkish title for a second class Pasha, i.e. a *Fareey*, general of division, or Roumeli Beylerbey.

ساعد *sú'ada*, he assisted. [عاون]

مساعدة *mosáa'da*, help, goodwill, favour.

ساعد ـ سواعد *sú'yid*, pl. *sawá'yid*, fore-arm. [ذراع]

مسعود *masa'ood*, happy, lucky.

سعر ـ اسعار *sia'r*, pl. *asa'ár*, fixed price, legal tariff, rate.

سعر *so'r*, intensity, rabies.

سعران *sa'rán*, mad (dog.) [كلب]

سعف *sa'f*, palm-leaf or branch. [جريد]

سعفة *sa'fa*, ulcer on the head.

ساعفة *sá'afa*, he came to the rescue.

اسعاف *isi'áf*, aid, rescue, relief.

سعال *so'ál*, cough.

سعال ديكيّ so'ál deekiy, whooping-cough, *coqueluche*, " cock's cough."

سعن so'an, goatskin, bag.

سعى sa'a, he ran, exerted himself.

سعي sa'y, effort, a run.

مسعى ـ مساعي masa'a, pl. masá'ay, effort.

ساعي ـ سعاة sá'ay, pl. so'át, messenger, courier.

سفوف or سفّة saffa, or sofoof, dry grain, powdered stuff, especially medicinal powders.

سفّة saffa, basket of palm leaves.

سفح safaha, he shed blood. [سفك

سفّاح saffáh, bloodthirsty, name of a Caliph.

سفاح sifáh, debauchery.

سفد safada, (the animal) leaped.

سفر ـ اسفار safar, pl. asfár, voyage, journey, departure, travel.

سافر sáfara, he set out, departed.

سافر sáfir, traveller, departing.

مسافر mosáfir, traveller, guest.

مسافرة mosáfara, travel.

سفارة safára, mission, embassy.

سفير ـ سفراء safeer, pl. sofará, ambassador.

سفر ـ اسفار sifr, pl. asfár, book; one of the books of the Old Testament.

اسفر asfara, the sun rose, came up.

سفرة sofra, table, dinner-table.

سفرجي sofraji (Turkish), butler, waiter at table.

سفرجل ـ سفارج safarjal, pl. safárij, quince.

سفك safaka, he shed (blood). [سفح

سفك دماء sefk dimá, bloodshed, slaughter.

سفل sufl, lowness, under part; vileness.

سفليّ sufliy, low, inferior, under part.

سفلة ـ سفالة sifla, or safála, under part, baseness.

سافل ـ سفلة sáfil, pl. safala, low, base.

اسفل ـ اسافل asfal, pl. asáfil, lower, baser, under part.

اسافل النّاس asáfil en-nás, the lowest classes of people.

سفلى ـ اسفل sofla (femin. of asfal), lower.

سفلاق sifláq, toady, parasite. [طفيلي

سفينة ـ سفن or سفائن safeena, pl. sofon, or safáyin, ship, a smooth carvel-built ship. [مركب

سفنج or اسفنج sfinj, or isfinj, sponge.

سفه safiha, he was licentious, abusive.

سفاهة safáha, libertinism, insolence.

سفيه safeeh, insolent, licentious.

سقر saqar (femin.), hell-fire.

سقط saqata, he or it fell, it lapsed. [وقع

سقوط *soqoot*, fall, lapse (of a right).

اسقط *asqata*, he made fall, threw down, annulled, transferred a right, discounted; caused abortion; deducted.

اسقاط *isqát*, a causing abortion, throwing down, discount, transfer, annulling, deduction, subtraction.

سقّاطة - سقاقيط *saqqáta*, pl. *saqáqeet*, door-latch.

مسقط *masqat*, place of falling, place; Muscat.

مسقط اليه *mosqat ileih*, transferred or ceded to him; "concessionaire."

سقف - سقوف *saqf*, pl. *soqoof*, ceiling, roof.

سقيفة *saqeefa*, roof, roofing.

سقّف *saqqafa*, he roofed; he clapped, applauded.

تسقيفة - تساقيف *tasqeefa*, pl. *tasáqeef*, general repairs of houses, roofing.

اسقف - اساقف *usquf*, pl. *asáqif*, bishop, *episcopos*.

سقم - اسقام *saqam*, pl. *asqám*, disease.

سقيم *saqeem*, ill.

سقى or سقا *saqa*, or *saqqa*, he watered; gave to drink.

اسقى *asqa*, he watered (land, or cattle).

ساقي - سقاة *sáqi*, pl. *soqát*, cup-bearer.

ساقية - سواقي *sáqiya*, pl. *sawáqi*, (femin.) cup-bearer, water-wheel.

سقية الغيط *saqiyat el-ghait*, watering a field.

سقّاء - قربة *saqqá*, water-carrier of a *qirba*, or goatskin of water on his back. [حملي]

استقى *istaqa*, he drew water.

تسقية *tasqeeya*, irrigation.

استسقاء *istisqá*, dropsy.

مسقاة *misqát*, small canal, artificial rivulet.

مسقاوي *masqáwi*, land irrigated by a *sáqiya*, or water-wheel.

سكّ *sakka*, he slammed, hit hard, barred; shut.

سكّة - سكك *sikka*, pl. *sikek*, road. [طريق]

سكّة الحديد *sikkat el-hadeed*, railway.

سكّة - سكك *sikka*, pl. *sikek*, coined money.

مسكوكات *maskookát*, coined money.

مسكوك *maskook*, shut (door).

سكب *sakaba*, he poured, founded metal. [كبّ - سبك]

انسكب *insakaba*, it was poured.

سكت *sakata*, he ceased talking, became silent.

سكّت *sakkata*, he silenced (another).

سكوت *sokoot*, silence, reticence.

ساكت *sákit*, silent, reticent.

سكتة مخّية *sakta mukhkhiya*, apoplexy, brain stoppage.

سكات *sokát* (vulgarism for *sokoot*), silence.

سكر *sokr*, drunkenness.

سكران *sakrán*, drunk, intoxicated.

سكر *sakira*, or *sikira*, he got drunk.

اسكر *askara*, he made drunk, gave liquor.

مسكرات *muskirát*, intoxicating liquors.

سكّر *sakkara* (in Syria), he shut a door.

سكّر *sukkar*, sugar.

قصب سكر *qasab sukkar*, sugar-cane.

تكرير السكّر *takreer es-sukkar*, refining of sugar.

بول سكّري *bōl sukkariy*, diabetes.

سكّاف or اسكافي *sakkáf*, or *iskáfi*, cobbler.

سكن *sakana*, he kept quiet, dwelt.

سكّن *sakkana*, he pacified, settled a colony.

سكنى or سكن *sakan*, or *sukna*, dwelling-place.

سكون *sokoon*, rest, state of rest; the mark ٛ over a consonant showing that the consonant is at rest, and not followed by a vowel. [جزم]

سكّان - ساكن *sákin*, pl. *sukkán*, dweller, inhabitant; a consonant marked with the *sokoon*.

سكّان *sukkán*, tiller, rudder.

سواكن *Sawákin*, Suákin, a port on the west coast of the Red Sea.

مسكن - مساكن *maskan*, pl. *masákin*, dwelling-place.

مسكون *maskoon*, inhabited, or inhabitable.

مسكنة *maskana*, wretchedness, penury.

مسكين - مساكين *maskeen*, pl. *masákeen*, wretched, pauper, "*mesquin*."

سكّين - سكاكين *sikkeen*, pl. *sakákeen*, knife.

سكاكيني *sakákeeniy*, knife-maker, cutler.

سلّ *salla*, he unsheathed.

سلّ *sall*, an unsheathing.

سلّ or سلال *sill*, or *sulál*, phthisis, consumption.

سلّ - سلال *sell*, pl. *silál*, basket.

سلالة *sulála*, posterity.

مسلول *maslool*, unsheathed; consumptive.

مسلّة *misalla*, awl, bodkin; obelisk, e.g. Cleopatra's "needle."

مسلي or سلّى *silá*, or *masli*, clarified butter for cooking.

سلب *salaba*, he pillaged, stripped. [نهب]

سلب *salb*, pillage, nudity; negative answer.

اجاب بالسلب *ajába bis-salb*, he answered in the negative.

استلب *istalaba*, he pillaged, seized.

سلبة salaba, the bucket-rope of a well; rope.

اسلوب ـ اساليب usloob, pl. asáleeb, path, method.

سلجم or شلغم saljam, or shalgham, turnip. [لفت]

سلاح ـ اسلحة siláh, pl. asliha, arm, weapon.

اسلحة ناريّة asliha náriya, fire-arms.

حامل السلاح hámil es-siláh, carrying arms, armed.

سلّح sallaha, he armed, gave arms to.

تسلّح tasallaha, he armed himself.

مسلّح or متسلّح musallah, or mutasallih, armed.

سلحدار silihdár (Persian), armed attendant.

سلحفى solhafa (pronounced zihlifa), tortoise.

سلخ salakha, he skinned, stripped.

سلخ salkh, the cast-off skin, the peeled skin; the end of the month.

سلخ خانة or سلخانة salkh-khána (Persian), slaughter-house, where dead animals are skinned.

تسلّخ tasallukh, a raw wound, abrasion.

سلس salis, easy, gentle, suave.

سلاسة salása, suavity, facility of expression.

سلسبيل salsabeel, the fountain of Paradise.

سلسل salsala, he formed a chain, series.

تسلسل tasalsala, it formed a series, ran on in a series or consecutive numbers.

سلسلة ـ سلاسل silsila, pl. salásil, chain, series, zigzag, dynasty; bracelets.

متسلسل mutasalsil, consecutive, in series.

مسلسل بالحديد mosalsal bil-hadeed, (a prisoner) in chains; chained up.

ساط saluta, he was imperious.

سلّط sallata, he forced, urged, incited.

تسلّط tasallata, he lorded it, was domineering.

تسلطن tasaltana, he became ruler or Sultan.

سلطة or سلطنة sulta, or saltana, power, empire, tyranny.

سلطة مطلقة sulta mutlaqa, absolute, or discretionary power.

سلطة salta, woman's embroidered jacket.

سلطان ـ سلاطين sultán, pl. saláteen, dominion, power, proof. Hence, as a secondary meaning, powerful, Sultan, Sultana.

سلطان سليم Sultán Seleem, Sultan Selim.

فاطمة سلطان Fátma Sultán, Sultana Fatima.

سلطانيّ Sultániy, imperial.

طريق سلطانيّ tareeq sultániy, the public highway, the "King's highway."

سلطانيّة sultániya, vase, bowl.

سلف salafa, it was in advance, previous. [سبق]

سلف ـ اسلاف salaf, pl. aslâf, predecessor.

سلفي و خلفي salafi wa khalafi, my predecessor and my successor.

سالف sálif, previous, prior.

السالف ذكره es-sálif zikroh, above-mentioned.

سلف or سلفة salaf, or sulfa, advance of money, loan.

سلفيّات salafiyát, loans, advances of money.

سلّف sallafa, he lent, advanced money.

استلف istalafa, he borrowed, solicited.

تسليف و استلاف tasleef wa istiláf, a lending and borrowing.

سلف silf, brother-in-law.

سلق salaqa, he cooked by boiling.

مسلوق maslooq, boiled, cooked.

سلق salq, beetroot; green herb.

تسلّق tasallaqa, he climbed. [تسّ]

سلقى salqa, he threw another down on his back. [لقي]

استلقى istalqa, he lay on his back.

سلاقون saláqoon, red-lead, minium.

سلك salaka, he followed a path.

سلوك solook, course, conduct, behaviour, path or duty in life.

سيّء السلوك saiy es-solook, a man of evil life.

سلك ـ ساوك silk, pl. solook, wire, line, telegraph wire.

مسلك maslak, path.

مسلكة maslaka, drain-pipe; tube.

سلقع or سلكع salka'a, he slapped, whipped.

سلم silm, peace, quiet, orderliness of life.

سلم عمومي silm 'omoomiy, public peace or order.

سلام salám, the peace of God; salutation, a military salute.

سلاملك salámlik (Turkish), men's reception-room, "mandara."

سلامة saláma, peace, soundness, healthiness.

سلّم ـ سلالم sillim, (or sullam), pl. salálim, ladder, stairs, steps.

سلم salima, he was sound, healthy.

سالم ـ سلمة sálim, pl. salama, healthy, sound; name for a man, Sálim.

سليم ـ سلما saleem, pl. sulamá, healthy, sound; name for a man, Selim.

سليم الجسم saleem el-jism, able-bodied, sound in body.

اسلم aslam, sounder, better, more suitable.

سلّم sallama, he saluted, paid his respects; surrendered, delivered.

تسليم tasleem, surrender; payment, delivery.

استلم istalama, he received, took over.

استلام istilám, receipt, a taking over.

اسلم aslama, he surrendered to God, became Moslem.

اسلام islám, submission to God; Islam, the religion taught by Mahomed.

مسلم - مسلمون or مسلمين Muslim, pl. Muslimoon, or Muslimeen, he who has submitted to God, a Moslem, Mussulman, Mahomedan.

مسلّم musallim, surrendering, agreeing, yielding.

متسلّم mutasallim, responsible, a receiver of a trust; local governor.

سليمان Suleimán, Solomon.

سليماني suleimániy, sublimate, quintessence.

اسلامبول - استانبول Islámbol, a Turkish corruption of Istánbol, Stamboul.

اسلامبولي - استانبولي Islámboliy, Arabic adjective for Istánboliy, Constantinopolitan; applied to Turkish tobacco and to "Stambouline" coats.

سلامونية salámoniya, small crooked stick.

سلّى salla, he amused, consoled.

تسلّى tasalla, he amused himself, consoled himself.

تسلية tasliya, amusing another, diversion.

سلوة salwa, consolation.

سلوى salwa, quail, small bird.

[سماة]

سمّ or سمّ samma, or sammama, he poisoned.

سمّ - سموم samm, pl. somoom, poison.

سموم - سمائم samoom, pl. samáyim (femin.), a hot deadly wind, Simoom.

سامّ or سمّي sammiy or sámm, poisonous.

تسمّم tasammama, he poisoned himself, became poisoned.

مسامّ - مسامّات masámm, pl. masámmát, pore of skin.

سمت samt, direction, locality, address, conduct.

السمت es-samt, azimuth.

سمت الرأس samt er-rás, Zenith, point overhead.

سميت or سميد sameet, crisp biscuit made in rings; a sort of flour, "semolina."

سامح or سمح samaha or sámaha, he pardoned.

سماح simáh, forgiveness, pardon.

استسمح istasmaha, he asked pardon.

سماخ simákh, interior of ear, tympanum.

سمرة sumra, brown colour.

اسمر - سمراء asmar, (femin.) samrá, brown.

سمار samúr, fine reeds or rushes used for matting.

سمّر sammara, he nailed.

مسمار - مسامير *mismár*, pl. *masámeer*, nail, peg.

سمر *samar*, night talk.

سامر *sámara*, he conversed confidentially at night with.

سمير or سامر *sámir*, or *sameer*, the highest title of the Grand Vizier, applied to him by the Sultan as his confidential friend and sharer of his anxious *night thoughts* for the safety of the Empire.

سمّور *sammoor*, marten's fur.

سمسرة *samsara*, brokerage (Italian *senseria*).

سمسار - سماسرة *simsár*, pl. *samásira*, broker. [عميل]

سمسم *simsim*, sesame, millet.

سمع *sami'a*, he heard, listened.

استمع *istama'a*, he listened.

سمع or سماع *sama'*, or *samá'a*, hearing, sense of hearing.

سامع - سامعون *sámia'*, pl. *sámia'oon*, listener, audience.

سمّاق *sommáq*, porphyry, sumach.

سمك *samk*, thickness, solidity.

سميك *sameek*, thick, solid.

سمك - اسماك *samak*, pl. *asmák*, fish.

سمّاك *sammák*, fisherman, fishmonger.

حلقة الاسماك *halqat el-asmák*, fishmarket.

سمكات or سمكات *samakát*, or *samakát*, ornaments, trinkets.

سمن *samn*, fatness, lard, butter. [سلاء]

سمانة *samána*, fatness; calf of leg; quail.

سمين *sameen*, fat, stout.

تسمّن *tasamman*, he grew fat.

سمو *somoo*, elevation, highness, majesty.

سامي *sámi*, majestic.

سماء - سماوات *samá*, pl. *samáwát*, sky, heavens.

سماوي *samáwiy*, celestial.

سمو *somoo*, a naming.

سمّى *samma*, he named, gave a name to.

تسمية *tasmiya*, nomenclature, giving a name.

يسمى *yosma*, he is named; by name.

اسم - اسماء - اسامي *ism*, pl. *asmá*, or *usámi*, name.

بسم الله *Bism illah* in the name of God.

باسم الخديوي *bi-ism el-Khedéwiy*, in the Khedive's name.

مسمّى *mosamma*, named, by name. [المدعوّ]

سنّ *sanna*, he sharpened.

سنّان *sannán*, knife-grinder.

مسنّ *misann*, grindstone.

سنّ - اسنان *sinn*, pl. *asnán* (femin.), tooth; age; apex, point; powdered charcoal; inferior flour.

سنّة *sinna*, point, a tooth.

سنّ الفيل sinn el-feel, elephant's tooth, ivory. [عاج]

حديث السنّ hadees es-sinn, young in age.

طعن في السنّ t'ana fis-sinn, he was advanced in age, was an old man.

سنّ الرشد sinn er-rushd, majority, age of discretion. [تمييز]

مسنّ mosinn, old, aged.

سنّة ـ سنن sonna, pl. sonan, Moslem custom based on sacred tradition.

مسنون masnoon, customary, ordered by sonna.

سنيبرة sanaibra, necklace.

سنبوك ـ سنابيك sanbook, pl. sanábeek, dhow, sailing-boat of the Red Sea, &c.

سنبلة ـ سنابل sonbola, pl. sanábil, ear of corn; Virgo, in the Zodiac.

سنتي santi (French), centimètre.

سنجابي sinjábiy, grey, like squirrel's fur.

سنجق sanjáq (Turkish), banner, province. [لواء]

سنجة ـ سونكي sinja (for Turkish soongyoo), bayonet.

سنجة ـ سنج sinja, pl. sinaj, shop weights.

سنخ ـ اسناخ sinkh, pl. asnákh, root, alvéole.

سند ـ اسناد sanad, pl. asnád, support, prop; proof.

سندات ـ سند sanad, pl. sanadát, proof, title-deed, voucher, document, bill of exchange.

اوراق وسندات awráq wa sanadát, papers and documents.

سند sanada, he supported, helped.

اسند asnada, he made lean upon, propped up; imputed an offence against.

اسناد ـ اسانيد isnád, pl. asáneed, argument in support of a plea.

استند على istanada 'ala, he relied upon, based his argument upon.

مستندات mustanadát, bases, or arguments in proof.

مسند musnad, rest for arm, seat; throne.

سندرة sandara, garret, attic.

سندان or سندال sindán, or sindál, anvil.

سنديان sindiyán, oak, "yeuse."

سنّارة sinnára, fish-hook, fishing-tackle. [or صنّارة]

صنط or سنط sant, acacia, mimosa nilotica; acanthus; wart.

سنكري or سمكري sankariy, tinker, maker of tin-pots.

سنامة sanáma, camel's hump.

سنة ـ سنوات or سنون ـ سنين sana, pl. sanawát or sinoon, or sineen, year.

سنتين sanatain, two years.

ثلاث ـ اربع ـ خمس ـ ستّ ـ سبع ـ ثمان ـ تسع ـ عشر سنين talát, arba', khams, sitt, saba', tamáni, tisa', 'ashr sineen, 3, 4, 5, 6,

7, 8, 9, 10 years, *i. e. sana*, being feminine, takes a feminine numeral.

سنوي *sanawiy*, annual, yearly.

راتب سنوي *rátib sanawiy*, salary, annual income.

سناء *sanà*, majesty, grandeur; senna, senna Mekki, *cassia*.

سني *saniy*, majestic, royal, Khedivial.

ارادة سنيّة *iráda saniya*, imperial will, *fiat*, decree of Sultan.

دائرة سنيّة *dáyira saniya*, royal department; an administration of certain private Khedivial property under mortgage.

تسنّى *tasanna*, he felt at ease, found it easy, ready to be done.

سهر *sahira*, he watched by night, sat up at night.

سهر *sahar*, vigil.

سهرة *sahra*, evening party, ball.

ساهر or سهران *sáhir*, or *sahrán*, he who keeps vigil.

سهل *sahula*, it was easy, went smoothly.

سهولة *sohoola*, facility.

سهل *sahl*, easy, smooth.

اهلًا و سهلًا *ahlán wa sahlán*, welcome! [مرحبًا]

سهّل *sahhala*, he facilitated, smoothed the way.

تسهيل *tas-heel*, facilitation, help.

تسهّل *tasahhala*, it became easy, he found it easy.

تساهل *tasáhala*, he made mutual concessions, was accommodating.

اسهال *is-hál*, diarrhœa; giving a purge.

مسهل *mos-hil*, purgative; a purge.

سهيل *sohail*, constellation of Canopus.

سهم - سهام *sahm*, pl. *sihám*, arrow, gaming with arrows, casting lots; a share; share in a company; 1-144th part of a feddan or acre, 8¾ sq. yards; cosine.

ساهم *sáhama*, he took shares in a company.

مساهمة *mosáhama*, joint-stock (company), "*compagnie anonyme*." [شركة]

سهو *saho*, error, negligence, forgetfulness.

سهوًا *sahwán*, by mistake, through negligence. [خطأ]

سوء - ساء *sow*, or *soo*, badness, evil, bad; *sà*, it was bad.

سوأة *sawat*, vice, the worst part of a thing.

سيّئ *saiy*, bad, evil.

سيّئة - سيّئات *saiya*, pl. *saiyát*, evil quality, sin.

سوء القصد *soo el-qasd*, evil intent, malice.

سوء الاستعمال or المعاملة *soo el-istia'-mál*, or *soo el-mo'ámala*, ill-treatment, cruelty.

دفع سوء *dafa' sow*, a driving off of evil; scapegoat.

مساءة *masát*, evil deed.

سيّئ or رجل سو‎ rajil sow (or saiy), a bad man.

سيادة‎ siyáda, chiefdom, a title of respect.

سيّد - سادات‎ sayyid, pl. sádát, a descendant of the Prophet, aristocrat, lord, chief; master, Sir; the "Cid" of Spain.

سيد‎ seed, vulgarism for sayyid.

سيّدة - ست‎ sayyida (shortened into sitt), lady, Mrs.

سيّدة زينب‎ Sayyida Zainab, "Lady Zainab," the daughter of Khozaima, and wife of the Prophet, by reason of her charities called "the Mother of the Poor"; a mosque and district of Cairo named after her.

سيادتكم - سعادتكم‎ siyádetkom, your excellency, your *chieftainship*; distinguish this from sa'ádetkom; your *felicity*, excellency.

سواد‎ sawád, blackness; a black shape, shadow.

اسود - سوداء‎ aswad, or iswid, (femin.) sodá, black, dark blue.

سود‎ sood, black men or things.

سوداء‎ sodá, black bile, melancholy.

سودان‎ Soodán, the blacks, black men, Soudan.

ذهب سودا‎ dahaba soodán, it went wrong, was futile, in vain.

سوّد - بيّض‎ sawwada, he scribbled, wrote a rough draft; blackened; bayyada, he made a clean copy from the rough draft, whitened.

تسويدة‎ taswceda, a rough draft, memo.

مسوّدة‎ maswada, rough draft, memo.

سور - اسوار‎ soor, pl. aswár, wall of town, a boundary wall, garden wall. [جدار‎]

تسوّر‎ tasawwara, he climbed over a wall.

تسوّر الجدار‎ tasawwur el-jidár, "escalade," a French legal term for a form of burglary.

سوريّة‎ Sooriya, Syria, Shám. [شام‎]

سورة - سور‎ soora, pl. sowar, rank, series, sign from heaven; chapter of the Koran.

سوار - اساور‎ siwár, pl. asáwir, bracelet, bangle; linen cuff.

سواري‎ sowári (Persian), cavalry; also a captain of a man-of-war.

سوراخي‎ soorákhi (Persian), decanter, jug.

صواريخ‎ or سواريخ‎ sawáreekh, fireworks.

سياسة‎ siyasa, the art of governing a nation, or a horse; diplomacy, statesmanship.

ساس‎ sása, he governed, controlled.

سايس - سوّاس‎ sáyis, pl. sowwás, groom, running footman.

سياسيّ‎ siyásiy, diplomatic, cunning, shrewd.

ارباب السياسة‎ arbáb es-siyása, statesmen, diplomats.

سوس - سيسان‎ soos, pl. seesán, worm, ring-worm, caries or rottenness.

عرق السُّوس or سوس *soos*, or *'irq es-soos* (corrupted from the Greek), liquorice-water, a favourite summer drink.

تسوَّس *tasawwasa*, it became rotten, worm-eaten.

مسوَّس *mosawwas*, worm-eaten.

سوسن *soosan*, lily, white lotus, *nymphœa*.

السويس *Es-Sowayis*, Suez.

سوط *sōt*, whip, flogging. [cf. صوت]

سواغ *sawágh*, lawfulness, fitness. [جواز]

ساغ *ságha*, it was lawful.

يسوغ له *yasoogh laho*, he has the right, it is lawful to him.

سائغ *sáyigh*, lawful, proper.

سوف *sōf*, afterwards, later on, in the future.

مسافة *masáfa*, space of time, distance, interval.

بحر سوف *Bahr Soof*, Biblical name for the Red Sea.

سياق *siyáq*, course, driving; context of words.

سياقات *siyáqát*, conduits, drainage.

ساق - يسرق *sáqa*, he drove, pushed on; *yasooq*, he drives.

سُق *sooq* (imperative), drive on! be quick!

سائق or سواق *sáyiq*, or *sawwáq*, driver, drover.

ساق - سيقان *sáq*, pl. *seeqán* (femin.), leg, shank, stalk.

سوق - أسواق *sooq*, pl. *aswáq*, market, bazaar.

سويقة *sowaiqa*, small bazaar, fair; lane.

سوقة *soqa*, or *sawaqa*, common people, mob.

سوقة سريحة *soqa sareeha*, pedlars, vagabonds, mob.

مسواقة *maswaqa*, stick for driving cattle; cudgel.

سواك *siwak*, a picking of the teeth, as a religious cleansing of the mouth; tooth-pick.

سوَّك or ساك *sáka*, or *sawwaka*, he cleaned his teeth.

مسواك *miswák*, tooth-brush, toothstick.

سواك *sawák*, edges or sides of cut stone.

سوهاج - جرجا *Soháj*, a town on the Nile in Upper Egypt, in the province of *Girgá*.

سيمياء or سيم *seemyá*, or *seem*, magic, conjuring.

سيماء *seemá*, face, physiognomy.

سوي *sawia*, it was worth, equalled.

يسوى *yaswa*, it is worth, equals.

سوَّى *sawwa*, he made equal, settled a debt or claim, did, accomplished, smoothed.

تساوى or ساوى *sáwa*, or *tasáwa*, it was equal to.

استوى *istawa*, it was ripe, properly cooked, smooth, flat, equal.

استواء *istiwá*, ripeness, equality.

خط الاستواء *khatt el-istiwá*, line of the equator.

تسوية *taswiya*, equalisation, payment, settlement.

مساواة (134) سل السيف

مساواة mosáwát, equality.

مستوي mistíwi, ripe, smooth, cooked; of common gender.

متساوي or مساوي mosáwi, or mutasáwi, mutually equal.

سوى or سواء siwa, or sawá, equality, equal; other; either—or; both—and; except, same.

سواء سواء sawá sawá, together, with one another; the same, equal.

سوية sawiya, equality, totality.

سي seea, equal, similar.

لاسيما or لاسيّما lá-seeamá "nothing is equal to it," i.e. principally, especially.

سيب saib, a flowing, being left free to move.

ساب sába, it flowed, wandered, advanced.

سيّب sayyaba, he let go, left alone.

سيبه seeboh, or sayyiboh (imperative), let it go! never mind!

سايب sáyib, free, at large.

سيجة seeja, a native game like draughts.

سياج siyáj, hedge.

سيح saih, a flowing, melting of butter, &c.

ساح sáha, (the butter) melted; he roamed, travelled.

سياحة siyáha, travel.

سيّح sayyaha, he melted (the butter).

سايح sáyih, melted (butter).

سيّاح or سوّاح sayyáh, or suwwáh, traveller, tourist.

مسيّاح misyáh, melting-pot.

مساحة - مسح masáha, dimensions, survey, area (see also masaha).

سير - سيور sair, pl. soyoor, procedure, course, voyage, strap, cord.

سيرة - سير seera, pl. siyar, course, conduct, morals.

حسن السيرة or السلوك hasan es-seera, or es-solook, a man of good conduct or behaviour.

سار - يسير sára, he proceeded; yaseer, he proceeds.

سيّر sayyara, he sent, made proceed; took out a horse for exercise.

تسيير tasyeer, a sending, mission.

سائر sáyir, he who proceeds; other, remainder, rest, all.

سيّار - سيّارة sayyár, (femin.) sayyára, wanderer, planet.

تسيّر tasayyara, he relieved nature.

مسير or مسيرة maseer, or maseera, distance, course; mode of life.

مسير القطورات maseer el-qotoorát, train-service; railway guide-book.

سيسي seesi, pony.

سيف - سيوف saif, pl. soyoof, sword. [cf. صيف saif, summer.]

سل السيف or اشهار السيف sall es-saif, or ish-hár es-saif, a drawing or unsheathing the sword.

سيَّاف *sayyáf*, swordsman, headsman.

سيكورتة *sikoorta* (European), security, insurance.

سيل *sail*, torrent (see p. 116).

سينا *Seená*, Mount Sinai.

SH.

ش *Sheen*. Value = 300.

ش or شي *-sh*, or *-shi* (colloquial), negative suffix to a verb, like the French "*pas.*"

ما اعرفش *má a'arifsh*, I do not know.

ما شفتوهُ ش *má shuftooh-sh*, I did not see him.

شآء ‒ يشآء *sháá*, he wished; *yasháá*, he wishes.

ما شآء اللّٰه *má sháá 'lláh*, the will of God! Bravo! How fine!

ان شآء اللّٰه *in sháá 'lláh*, if God will; D.V.; I hope.

مشية *mashiya*, wish.

شيء ‒ اشياء *shai*, pl. *ashiá*, thing, something; in pl. goods, baggage.

ما فيش شيء *má feesh shai*, there is nothing.

اشياتهُ ‒ اشياء *ashiátoh* (vulgarism for *ashiáhó*), his things, his goods.

شوية *showaya* (diminutive), a little thing, a little of, few.

بشوية شوية *bi-showaya showaya*, little by little, slowly, gently.

شادر *shádir* (Persian *chádir*), tent, hut.

شاذّ *sházz*, differing, apart, aloof.

شاش *shásh*, muslin.

شاف ‒ يشوف *sháfa*, he saw; *yashoof*, he sees.

شف *shuf* (imperative), see thou! look!

تشرَّف *tashawwafa*, he "showed off," bragged.

شال ‒ شيلان *shál* (Persian), pl. *sheelán*, shawl.

شيلة *shaila*, small head-shawl.

شال ‒ يشيل *shála*, he carried, bore off; *yasheel*, he carries off.

شيَّال *shayyál*, porter, carrier. [حمَّال]

مشال *mashál*, removal, act of carrying.

شام *Shám*, Syria, Damascus.

شاميّ ‒ شوَّام *Shámiy*, pl. *Shuwwám*, Syrian, a Syrian.

شامة ‒ شيم *shama*, mole, beauty-spot (see *shaim*).

شوم or مشئوم *shóm*, or *mashoom*, left-hand, sinister, of evil augury.

شأن ‒ شؤون *shán*, pl. *sho'on*, affair, thing.

على شأن or من شأن or بشأن *bi-shán*, or *min shán*, or *a'la shán*, concerning, because, for.

شاورمة *sháwurma* (Turkish), a lamb roasted whole.

شاة *sháa*, sheep, animal.

شاه *sháh* (Persian), Shah, King.

شاهانه *sháhána* (Persian), royal, imperial.

شاهانيّ *sháhániy* (Arabic adjective formed from *sháhána*), royal, imperial.

شاهي *sháhi*, silk stuff.

شاهين *shaheen* (Persian), falcon.

شاويش - شاويشيّة *sháweesh*, pl. *sháweeshiya* (for Turkish *cháwush*), sergeant.

شاي *shái*, tea.

شبّ *shabb*, alum.

شبّ *shabba*, (the horse) reared up. [شلت]

شابّ - شبّان *shább*, pl. *shobbán*, lad; young of cattle.

شابّة - شوابّ *shábba*, pl. *shawább*, girl; young of cattle.

شباب or شبوبيّة *shabáb*, or *shaboobíya*, youthfulness.

شبشب *shibshib*, woman's slipper.

شبث or تشبّث *shabasa*, or commonly *tashabbasa*, he stuck to; set about, undertook.

شبر *shibr*, span of hand.

شابورة *sháboora*, morning mist, fog.

شبرا *Shoobrá* (Coptic), place, village; a suburb of Cairo.

شبريّة *shabriya*, camel-litter, cacolet.

شباراسات *shabárását* (for Persian *sipárish*), things ordered, debit accounts.

شباط *Shubát*, Syrian month of February.

شبع *shaba'*, satiety.

اشبع *ashba'*, he satiated another.

شبعان *shaba'án*, satiated, cloyed [cf. شعبان]

شبوق *shabooq* (for Turkish *chibook*), pipe, tube, rod.

شبق *shabaq*, lewdness.

شبّك *shabbaka*, he intertwined, implicated.

شبكة *shabaka*, net, network, entanglement.

شبّاك - شبابيك *shubbák*, pl. *shabábeek*, window; gridiron.

مشابك *mashábik*, a press, vice; fastenings.

شبل - شبلي *shibl*, lion's cub; *shibli*, species of cloth.

شبين *shebeen* (Coptic), place, village.

شبين الكوم - منوفيّة *Shebeen el-Kóm*, the capital of the *Menoofiya* province in Lower Egypt.

شبه or مشابية *shibh*, or *moshábaha*, resemblance.

شبه or شابه *shabaha*, or *shábaha*, it resembled.

يشبه *yishbih*, it resembles.

شبّه *shabbaha*, he likened to, compared to.

شبيه or مشابه *shabeeh*, or *mosháblh*, like, similar.

شبهة - شبهات *shubha*, pl. *shubuhát*, doubt, suspicion. [ريب]

حصر شبهته *hasara shubhatoh*, he suspected.

اشتبه في *ishtabaha fi*, he doubted, suspected.

اشتباه *ishtibáh*, doubt, suspicion.

مشتبه *mushtabih*, suspicious or obscure (affair).

شتّ *shatt*, dispersion, separation.

شتّت *shattata*, he dispersed.

شتيت ـ شتّى *shateet*, pl. *shatta*, diverse, sundry.

حوادث شتّى *hawádis shatta*, miscellaneous news.

شتل *shatl*, a plant.

شتم *shatama*, he insulted. [سفه ـ سبّ]

شتم *shatm*, an insulting.

شتيمة ـ شتائم *shateema*, pl. *shatáyim*, an insult.

شتوم or اشتوم *shotoom*, or *ashtoom*, gap, entrance between the sea and a lagoon.

شتاء ـ شتي *shitá*, pl. *shotiy*, winter; rain, rainy season.

شتوي *shitiwiy*, wintry, winter crop.

شتّى *shatta* (colloquial), it rained.

شجّ *shajja*, he wounded, fractured, split open.

شجر ـ اشجار *shajar* (vulgarly pronounced *sagar*), pl. *ashjár*, tree.

شجرة *shajara* (*sagara*), a tree.

شجّر *shajjara* (*saggara*), he grafted.

شاجر or تشاجر *shájara*, or *tashájara*, he quarrelled, had a "row" with.

مشاجرة *moshájara*, quarrel, brawl, row.

شجاعة *shajáa'a*, courage, bravery. [جسارة]

شجّع *shajja'a*, he encouraged.

شجيع ـ شجاع or شجعان *shajeea'*, or *shajáa'*, pl. *shijáa'*, brave.

شحت or شحذ *shahata*, or *shahada*, he begged for alms.

شحاتة *shiháta*, mendicity; a man's name.

شحّات *shahhát*, street-beggar.

شحم ـ شحوم *shahm*, pl. *shohoom*, grease, tallow, fat; pulp.

شحيم *shaheem*, fat, plump.

شحن *shahana*, he loaded, put in cargo.

شحن ـ شحنة or *shahn*, or *shohna*, cargo, load, burthen.

مشحون *mash-hoon*, laden.

مشحونات *mash-hoonát*, cargo.

سند المشحونات *sanad el-mash-hoonát*, bill of lading.

شحن or شحنة *shahna*, or *shihán*, a quarrelling.

شاحن *sháhana*, he quarrelled with, hated.

شخّ *shakhkha*, he relieved nature.

شخاخ *shikhákh*, fœces, urine.

شخشيخة *shukh-shaikha*, skylight for lighting the central court or well of stairs in a house.

شخص ـ اشخاص *shakhs*, pl. *ashkhás*, person, individual.

شخصاً shakhsán, personally. [ذاتاً]

شخصي shakhsiy, personal, individual.

شخصية shakhsiya, individuality, identity; medical diagnosis.

احوال شخصية ahwál shakhsiya, "Statut personnel," Moslem law of marriage, successions, &c.

وضع اشخاص wada' ashkhás, impersonation.

شخّص shakhkhasa, he identified, personated, attributed to a particular person, acted (on the stage).

تشخيص tashkhees, identification; drama.

شخط shakhata, he repelled, expelled in anger.

شدّ shadda, he tightened, intensified.

شدّد shaddada, he intensified, aggravated.

اشتدّ ishtadda, he or it became intense, firm, tight, vehement.

شدّة shidda, tightness, severity, intensity.

شديد shadeed, intense, tight, severe.

اشدّ ashadd, more intense, tighter, severer.

تشديد tashdeed, intensification; reduplication of a letter; the mark ّ over a letter.

شادوف shádoof, lever and bucket apparatus for raising water for irrigation.

شدّاف shaddáf, the man who works the shádoof.

شدق shidq, jowl, corner of mouth.

شديّاق shidiyáq, (Syrian) priest.

شذرات shazrát, sparkling atoms of ore, scattered beads, miscellanea.

شرّ or شرّ sharr, or shirra, rage, wickedness, enmity.

شرير ـ اشرار shareer, pl. ashrár, wicked, hostile.

شرّاني sharrániy, wicked, naughty.

شرارة sharára, spark.

شرّ sharra, it dripped, dribbled out.

شرب shurb, or shirb, a drinking.

شربة shorba, a drink, draught, potion, sherbet.

شربة shorba (Persian, chorba), soup.

شراب ـ اشربة sharáb, pl. ashriba, liquor, wine, syrup.

شرب shariba (shiriba), he drank; inhaled tobacco.

اشرب ashraba, he made drink; he accused.

شارب ـ شوارب sháril, pl. shawárib, moustaches. [شنب]

مشرب mashrab, source, temperament, disposition.

مشروبات mashroobát, drinkables, liquors.

مشربة or مشربية mishraba, or mushrabiya, a corruption of mushrifiya, a projecting window. [شرف]

شرج sharj, anus; crevice.

شرح *sharaha,* he cleft open, explained.

شرّح *sharraha,* he dissected anatomically.

انشرح *insharaha,* (his heart) was dilated; he was glad.

شارح *shárih,* pleasant, dilating (the heart); explaining.

شرح *sharh,* explanation, commentary.

شرحه *sharhoh,* used like our word "ditto."

تشريح *tashreeh,* anatomy; dissection.

اعمال تشريحية *a'amál tashreehiya,* anatomical operations.

مشرّح *mosharrih,* professor of anatomy, surgeon.

شرخة *sharkha* (Persian, *chárkh*), skirmishing.

شرد *shard,* intense trying heat, with simoom.

شرد *sharada,* or *sharata,* he fled, ran away; especially of animals.

شرش *shirsh,* a bundle of vegetables.

شرشر *sharshara,* he reaped, cut grass.

شرشارة *sharshára,* scythe, sickle; clasp-knife.

شرشير *sharsheer,* wild duck.

شرشف ـ شراشف *sharshaf* (Persian *charshaf*), with Arabic plural *sharáshif,* bed-clothes, sheets.

شرط *sharata,* he cut, slashed; indented a contract.

شرط ـ شروط *shart,* pl. *shoroot,* a cutting, indenture of contract, contract, conditions.

بشرط ان *bi-shart an,* on condition that.

شرطية *shartiya,* a written contract, deed.

شريط ـ شرائط *shareet,* pl. *sharáyit,* string, tape, cord, braid, facings of soldiers' coats; silk lace; rail of railway.

شارط or اشترط *shárata,* or *ishtarata,* he made a contract. [عقد ـ عهد]

مشارطة or اشتراط *moshárata,* or *ishtirát,* a mutual contract.

شرّط *sharrata,* he made incision, scarified, bled.

مشرط *mishrat,* scalpel, lancet.

شرع في *shara'a fi,* he began, attempted.

شروع في *shorooa' fi,* beginning, attempt.

شرع *shara'a,* he made a law.

شريعة or شرع *shara',* or *shariya'a,* Divine Moslem law, the *Sheri,* or *Sheriat.*

شرعي *shara'iy,* legal; of Moslem law.

طبّ شرعيّ *tubb shara'iy,* legal medical science; *i.e.* medical jurisprudence.

محكمة شرعية *mahkama shara'iya,* Court of Moslem law, a *sheri* tribunal.

شارع ـ شوارع *shári'a,* pl. *shawári'a,* street.

شِرَاع ‎ - شَرَع ‎ *shiráa'*, pl. *shoroa'*, sail.

شَرَف ‎ or شُرْفَة ‎ or شَرَافَة ‎ *sharaf*, or *shurfa*, or *sharáfa*, honour, nobleness of character, nobility.

شَرِيف ‎ - شُرَفَا ‎ or اَشْرَاف ‎ *shareef*, pl. *shurafá*, or *ashráf*, noble, aristocrat, descendant of the prophet; honourable, honest.

شَرَف القَمَر ‎ *sharaf el-qamar*, fullness of moon. [بدر]

شَرَّف ‎ *sharrafa*, he ennobled, showed or did honour to.

تَشْرِيفَات ‎ *tashreefát*, court ceremonies, levées.

تَشْرِيفَاتْجِي ‎ *tashreefátji* (Turkish), Lord Chamberlain, Master of the Ceremonies.

تَشَرَّف ‎ *tasharrafa*, he felt, or was, honoured.

اَشْرَف ‎ - شُرْفَى ‎ *ashraf*, (femin.) *shurfa*, nobler.

اَشْرَف ‎ *ashrafa*, it was eminent, prominent.

مُشْرِف ‎ *mushrif*, imminent, projecting.

مُشْرِفِيَّة ‎ *mushrifiya*, a projecting window, *mushrabiya*. [مشربية]

بِنَا مُشْرِف عَلَى السُّقُوط ‎ *binà mushrif 'ala es-soqoot*, edifice threatening to fall.

شَرْق ‎ *sharq*, sunrise, the east.

شَرْقِي ‎ *Sharqiy*, Eastern; (Saracen?)

شَرْقِيَّة ‎ - زَقَازِيق ‎ *Sharqiya*, the eastern province of the Delta, of which *Zaqázeeq* is the capital.

شُرُوق ‎ *shorooq*, sunrise.

شَرَق ‎ *sharaqa*, the sun rose.

اَشْرَق ‎ *ashraqa*, the sun shone.

شَرَاقِي ‎ *sharáqiy*, land exposed to the sun (without water); land not naturally watered by inundation of Nile, but requiring artificial irrigation.

شِرَاقَة ‎ *sharáqa*, female slave or concubine given in marriage as a present by her master to one of his courtiers or dependents.

اِشْرَاق ‎ *ishráq*, kindling wood, small pieces of resinous wood.

مَشْرِق ‎ *mashriq*, place of sunrise, the East.

شَرَّق ‎ *sharraqa* (colloquial), he went eastward, to Syria.

شِرْك ‎ *shirk*, association, *métayage* or farming with share of profits; idolatry.

شِرْكَة ‎ or شَرَاكَة ‎ *shirka*, or *sherika*, or *sharáka*, partnership, business, company, association.

شِرْكَة التَّضَامُن ‎ *shirka et-tadámun*, "*Société en nom collectif*."

شِرْكَة مُسَاهَمَة ‎ *shirka mosáhama*, joint-stock Co.; "*Société anonyme*."

شِرْكَة التَّوْصِيَة ‎ *shirka et-tawsiya*, "*commandite*," sleeping partnership.

شَرَك ‎ *sharak*, net, snare.

شَرِيك ‎ - شُرَكَا ‎ *shareek*, pl. *shuraká*, partner, accomplice.

اَحْمَد وَ شُرَكَاه ‎ *Ahmed wa shurakáh*, Ahmed and Co., Ahmed and his partners.

شريك shoraik (Turkish *choorek*), pastry, cake.

اشرك *ashraka*, he took as partner; he accused (another) of being his accomplice.

شارك or اشترك *sháraka*, or *ishtaraka*, he went shares or partners, was an accomplice.

مشاركة or اشتراك *mosháraka*, or *ishtirák*, partnership, complicity.

مشارك or مشترك *moshárik*, or *mushtarik*, partner, accomplice.

مشرك *mushrik*, idolator; accuser.

شرم *sharama*, he tore open, cut, split.

شرم - شروم *sharm*, pl. *shoroom*, creek, inlet, gulf; a cleft; an opening in a coral-reef. [شعب

شرمط *sharmata*, he tore.

مشرمط *mosharmat*, torn.

شرموطة - شراميط *sharmoota*, pl. *sharámeet*, rag, tatter; whore.

شراهة *sharáha*, gluttony, craving, lust.

شرهان *sharhán*, glutton, lustful, eager.

شروال *sharwál* (Persian, *shalwár*), loose drawers or *pyjámas*. [سروال

شراء *shirá*, a buying, purchase.

بيع و شراء *beea' wa shirá*, selling and buying; trade.

شاري *shári*, purchaser.

اشترى *ishtara*, he bought.

مشتري *mushtari*, purchaser; planet Jupiter.

مشترى *mushtara*, act of purchase; purchased.

شريان - شرايين *sharyán*, pl. *sharáyeen*, artery. [وريدة

شفلية *shodaliya* (colloquial), quarrelsome, rowdy fellows.

شط - شطوط *shatt*, pl. *shotoot*, shore, bank, coast.

شاطىء - شواطىء *sháti*, pl. *shawáti*, shore, bank, coast. [ساحل

شطب *shataba*, he ran his pen through, crossed out, cancelled.

شطب *shatb*, a cancelling, crossing out.

شطح *shataha*, he wandered as a vagabond.

شطر - شطور *shatr*, pl. *shotoor*, half, part, side.

شطارة *shatára*, cleverness, skill.

شاطر - شطار *shátir*, pl. *shottár*, clever, cunning.

شطرنج *shatranj* (Persian), game of chess.

شطفة *shutfa*, flint of flint-lock musket.

شيطان - شياطين *shaitán*, pl. *shayáteen*, Satan, devil; a cunning, deep rogue.

شظية *shaziya*, tibia, large bone of leg.

شعاع *sho'áa'*, pl. *shi'áa'*, ray of light; bars or trellis over a door.

شعب *sha'b*, coral-reef (on coasts of Red Sea).

شعب (142) اشغال شاقّة

شعب ـ شعوب sha'b, pl. sho'-oob, people, tribe.

شعب ـ شعبة sho'aba, pl. sho'ab, branch, bronchia; sho'abiy, bronchial; of bronchitis.

شعبان Sha'bán, eighth month of Moslem year. [cf. شبعان

شعر ـ شعور sha'r, pl. sho'-oor, hair.

شعرة shiu'ra, small hair, down.

اشعر asha'r, hairy, long haired on the head.

شعراني sha'rániy, hairy of body.

مشعراني masha'rániy, hairy, shaggy.

شعاري sha'áriy, official term for goats, sheep &c.; animals with hair or wool.

شعير sha'yeer, barley.

شعيريّة sha'yeeriya, vermicelli.

شعيرة ـ شعائر sha'yeera, pl. sha'áyir, religious rite.

شعر ـ اشعار shi'ar, pl. asha'ár, knowledge; poetry.

ليت شعري هذا الدنيا لمن laita shi'ari hazá ed-dunyá li-men, would that I knew to whom this world (belongs)!

شاعر ـ شعراء shá'yir, pl. sho'ará, poet.

شعرى shi'ra, Sirius, Dog Star.

شعور sho'-oor, intelligence, faculty of mind.

مختلّ الشعور mukhtall esh-sho'-oor, deranged in mind, insane. [خلل

شعر sha'ra, he knew, perceived.

ما يشعر الّا ان má yasho'r illá an, he does not know except that; before he knew (where he was) it happened suddenly that.

اشعر asha'ra, he informed.

اشعار ishi'ár, an informing, information.

استشعر istasha'ra, he inquired, it dawned upon him, he perceived. [cf. استحسّ

شعل or اشتعل sha'la, or ishta'la, it blazed, flamed.

اشعل asha'la, he lighted, set on fire.

شعلة shea'la, torch.

مشعل ـ مشاعل misha'l, pl. mashá'yil, torch, brazier.

شعانين sha'áneen, branches; Palm Sunday.

شغار shighár, marriage by "compensation," where two men exchange sisters or daughters in marriage.

شاغر sháyhir, camel pack-saddle. [غبيط

شغرتيّة shaghartiya, attendants of a singer.

شغف shaghaf, vehement passion of love.

شغل ـ اشغال shoghl, pl. ashghál, work, labour.

اشغال عموميّة ashghál o'moomiya, public works.

اشغال شاقّة ashghál sháqqa, penal servitude.

اشغال دنيّة *ashghál daniya*, vile, hard labour.

شغّال - شغّالة *shaghghál*, pl. *shaghghála*, labourer, navvy.

شاغل *shághil*, engaged in, occupying.

شغّل *shaghghala*, he employed labour, caused to work.

تشغيل *tashgheel*, a giving or making work.

اشتغل *ishtaghala*, he was busy, worked.

مشغول *mashghool*, busy, occupied.

شاغول *shághool*, main-sail; main-sheet.

شفّاف *shaffáf*, transparent.

شفر - اشفار *shifr*, pl. *ashfár*, edge, rim; labia.

شفط *shafata*, he sipped.

شفعة *shofa'a*, right of intervention; pre-emption: (*e.g.* of neighbour's land if for sale, according to certain conditions).

تشفّع *tashaffa'a*, he mediated, intervened.

شافعي *Sháfa'iy*, Mahomed Idris Sháfaiy of Cairo, d. 820, A.D., founder of one of the four great Sunni schools of orthodox Islam. [مالك - حنبل - حنيفة]

شفيع *shafeea'*, pre-emptor, who has a right to pre-emption.

شفقة *shafaqa*, compassion. [أنّ]

شفيق or شفوق *shafeeq*, or *shafooq*, compassionate.

شفة - شفاه *shifa*, pl. *shifáh*, lip of mouth.

شفاهاً *shifáhán*, verbally, *viva voce*.

شفة - شفوات *shafa*, pl. *shafawát*, lip.

الشفتين *esh-shifatain*, the two lips.

شفاء *shifá*, cure, convalescence.

شفي - شفي *shafa*, he cured; *shofia*, he was cured.

استشفى *istashfa*, he consulted a doctor.

مستشفى *mustashfa*, hospital.

[اسبتالية]

شقّ *shaqqa*, he split, caused pain.

شقّ - شقوق *shaqq*, pl. *shoqooq*, split, crevice; pain, toil.

شقّة *shiqqa*, piece, part; pain.

شقّة - شقاق *shoqqa*, pl. *shiqáq*, piece, part, set of rooms or flat in a house; note, *memo*.

شقيق - شقيقة *shaqeeq*, (femin.) *shaqeeqa*, split in half; a full brother or sister by the same parents.

شقائق *shaqáyiq*, anemone, peony.

شقاق *shiqáq*, a split, quarrel.

اشتقاق *ishtiqáq*, derivation, etymology.

انشقاق *inshiqáq*, schism, dissent.

منشقّ *munshiqq*, schismatic, dissenter.

شاقّ *sháqq*, splitter; toilsome, penal.

اشغال شاقّة *ashghál sháqqa*, penal servitude.

مشقّة - مشاقّ *mashaqqa*, pl. *masháqq*, difficulty.

مشاقّ *masháqq*, tow, refuse of hemp.

شَقْدَف *shaqdaf*, camel-litter, cacolet.

شُقْرَة - أَشْقَر *shoqra*, redness of hair; *ashqar*, red haired, roan.

شَقْفَة or شَقِيفَة *shaqfa*, or *shaqeefa*, bit, morsel; coarse salt, nitre.

شَقْلَب *shaqlaba*, he upset. [قلب]

شَقْلَبَان *shaqlabán*, changeable. [مقلبان]

شَقَاوَة or شَقَاء *shaqá*, or *shaqáwa*, wickedness; naughtiness; (in Turkish) a joke, chaff.

شَقِيّ - أَشْقِيَاء *shaqiy*, pl. *ashqiyá*, wretch, wicked, brigand, outlaw.

حَرَامِيَّة و أَشْقِيَاء *harámiya wa ashqiyá*, robbers, brigands, outlaws.

شَكّ - شُكُوك *shekk*, pl. *shokook*, doubt, suspicion.

بِدُون شَكّ *bidoon shekk*, undoubtedly, of course.

شَكَّ فِي *shakka fi*, he doubted.

شَاكِك or شَاكّ *shákik*, or *shákk*, he who doubts, hesitates.

شَكَّ نَقْدًا *shukuk*, on credit; *naqdán*, for cash.

مَشْكُوك *mashkook*, doubted, doubtful (affair).

شَكُوج *shakooj* (for Turkish *chekij*), hammer.

شَكَرَ or تَشَكَّرَ *shakara*, or *tashakkara*, he thanked.

شُكْر - شُكُور *shukr*, pl. *shokoor*, thanks.

شَاكِر - شَكُور *shákir*, or *shakoor*, thankful.

شَكْشُوكَة *shakshooka*, coquette, loose woman.

شَكْل - أَشْكَال *shekl*, pl. *ashkál*, shape, form, figure, sort. [نوع - جنس]

شَكْلًا - مَوْضُوعًا *sheklán*, formally, technically, on a point of law, (as apart from *mawdoo'án*, on the merits of the case); "à la forme," and not "au fond."

شَكِلِيّ *shikeliy*, quarrelsome, touchy.

شَكَّلَ *shakkala*, he fashioned, organised, composed. [رَكَّب - رَتَّب]

تَشْكِيل *tashkeel*, composition, organisation.

تَشَكَّلَ *tashakkala*, it took form, was composed of.

اِشْتَكَلَ *ishtakala*, it was ambiguous.

مُشْكِل *mushkil*, difficult, complex.

شِكَال *shikál*, foot-rope, tether.

شَكَمَ *shakama*, he slapped, flipped. [لَكَم]

شَكْمَجِيَّة *shakmajia* (for Turkish *chekmejé*), chest of drawers.

شَكَا or اِشْتَكَى or تَشَكَّى *shaka*, or more commonly *ishtaka*, or *tashakka*, he complained.

شَاكِي - مُشْتَكِي - مُتَشَكِّي *sháki*, or *mushtaki*, or *mutashakki*, complainant, plaintiff.

شِكَايَة *shikáya*, complaint.

شَكْوَى - شَكَاوِي *shakwa*, pl. *shakáwi*, complaint.

شلل *shalal*, paralysis, withered limb.

شلّال ـ شلّالات *shallál*, pl. *shallálát*, Nile cataract or rapids.

شلبي *shalabi* (for Turkish *chelebi*), a European or foreign gentleman, refined, polite.

شلتت *shalata*, the horse reared, bucked. [شبت]

شلاتي *shaláti*, species of native cloth.

شلح *shalaha*, he stripped.

شلفتت *shalfata*, he smudged out (fresh writing).

شليك *shulaik* (for Turkish *chilek*), strawberry.

شمّ or اشتمّ *shamma*, or *ishtamma*, he smelled at, sniffed.

شمّ *shamm*, a smelling, sense of smell.

شمّ النسيم *shamm en-naseem*, "sniff the breeze;" the Egyptian general spring holiday, which is celebrated on the Greek Easter Monday.

شمّام *shammám*, musk melon. [بطيخ]

شمّامات *shammámát*, perfumes.

شمشم *shamshama* (colloquial), he sniffed, smelled at.

شمبر *shambar*, circle, flange, ridge round.

شمتت *shamata*, he rejoiced at another's misfortune.

شمخ *shamakha* (vulgar), he sniffed a pungent odour.

شموخ *shomookh*, height, haughtiness.

شامخ *shámikh*, lofty, haughty.

شمر *shumar*, fennel.

شمار *shamár*, porter's knot, shoulder cord.

شمّر *shammara*, he girded up his loins; set about.

شمروخ ـ شماريخ *shamrookh*, pl. *shamáreekh*, long slender staff, stalk of bunch of dates.

شمس ـ شموس *shams*, pl. *shomoos* (femin.), sun.

شمسي *shamsiy*, solar; certain letters of the alphabet.

شمسيّة *shamsiya*, parasol, umbrella.

شمّاس *shammás*, acolyte, deacon.

تشمّس *tashámmasa*, he got sunstroke.

مشمّس *moshammas*, ill with sunstroke.

شمطة or شماطة *shamata* (Turkish), noise, uproar.

شمع ـ شموع *shama'*, pl. *shomooa'*, wax; candle.

شمّاع *shammáa'*, candlestick; pegs for clothes or hats.

شمعدان *shama'dán* (Persian), candlestick.

مشمّع *moshamma'*, waxed; oil cloth, waterproof.

شمعول *Shama'ool*, Samuel.

شمل *shaml*, the whole, reunion. [حوى]

شمول ب *shomool bi*, the including, inclusive of.

اشتمل على or شمل *shamala*, or *ishtamala a'la*, it included.

مشتمل على or شامل *shámil*, or *mushtamil a'la*, inclusive, including.

مشمول ب *mashmool bi*, including, containing.

شمال *shimál* (femin.) left hand side; north. [يسر]

شمالي *shimáliy*, northern.

شمندرة *shamandora* (Turkish), buoy, beacon.

شمية *shimya*, scouring of a stream, whirlpool. [دوّامة]

شنّ *shanna*, he sniffed.

شنب *shanab*, upper lip, moustache. [شارب]

شنتيان *shintiyán* (Turkish *chintiyán*), women's loose pantaloons.

شنتة or شنطة *shanta* (Turkish *chanta*), bag, valise, knapsack.

شنج *shanaj*, colic, gripes, convulsions.

تشنّج *tashannaja*, he was in convulsions.

شنيشة *shineesha*, hole in the wall.

شنيع *shaneea'*, infamous, heinous.

شناعة *shanáa'a*, infamy, depravity.

شنيف ـ تبن *shaneef*, large coarse net for carrying *tibn* or straw on donkeys or camels.

شنّف *shannafa*, he amused or interested by talk.

شنق *shanaqa*, he hanged (a murderer). [See خنق ـ عنق

قتل شنقاً *qatl shanqán*, death by hanging.

مشنقة *mashnaqa*, gallows, place of execution.

شنكل *shankal* (Turkish *chengel*), hook.

شهاب *shiháb*, brilliancy, ardour, zeal; meteor.

اشهب *ash-hab*, brilliant, whitish, grey.

شهد *shahida*, he gave evidence, witnessed.

شاهد *sháhada*, he saw, witnessed, interviewed.

استشهد or اشهد *istash-hada*, or *ash-hada*, he called witnesses to prove.

شهادة *shaháda*, evidence, written or oral; certificate.

شاهد ـ شهود *sháhid*, pl. *shohood*, a witness.

شاهد العين *sháhid el-a'in*, an eyewitness.

شاهد زور *sháhid zoor*, a false witness, perjurer.

شهادة زور *shaháda zoor*, false evidence, perjury.

شهيد ـ شهداء *shaheed*, pl. *shohadá*, witness for the faith, martyr, Moslem soldier killed in battle.

شوهد *shoohida* (passive of *sháhada*), he was seen, detected.

مشهد *mash-had*, funeral procession, shrine; publicity.

بمشهد خلق كثير *bi-mash-had khalq kateer*, in the presence of many people.

مشاهدة *moshàhada*, a seeing, interviewing.

شهداني *shahdànij*, hemp. [قنب]

شهر ‎ـ شِهْر or أشهر *shahr*, pl. *shohoor*, or *ash-hur*, month.

شهرة ‎ـ شِهير *shohra*, fame, notoriety; *shaheer*, famous.

شهّر or أشهر *shahhara*, or *ash-hara*, he made public; unsheathed (a sword).

مشاهرة *moshàhara*, a making public.

مشهور ‎ـ مشاهير *mash-hoor*, pl. *mashàheer*, famous.

أشهار *ish-har*, publication, declaration.

شهيق *shaheeq*, grunt, hiccup, sob.

شهل ‎ـ سهل *shahala* (for *sahhala*), he facilitated, carried off.

شهم ‎ـ شهامة *shahem*, wise; *shahàma*, wisdom, valour.

شهامتلو *shahàmetlu* (Turkish), valorous, royal.

شها or أشتهى *shahà*, or *i htaha*, he longed for.

أشتهاء *ishtihà*, appetite, a longing.

شهيّ *shahiy*, eager.

شهوة *shahwa*, carnal lust.

شهواني *shahwàniy*, sensual.

مشتهى *mushtaha*, desired, appetising.

شورى ‎ـ تشاور *shoora*, pl. *tashàwur*, council, counsel.

شورى القوانين *shoora el-qawàneen*, legislative council.

شورة *shora*, handkerchief; a desert shrub called the *Avicennia officinalis*.

شاور *shàwara*, he consulted with.

مشاورة *moshàwara*, consultation.

مشورة *mashwara*, consultation, deliberation.

أشار *ashàra*, he pointed out, indicated.

أشارة *ishàra*, indication, sign, gesture; demonstrative pronoun.

أشارجي *ishàraji*, signaller, signalman.

مشارٌ إليه *mushàrun ileih*, a polite way of expressing " aforesaid " when referring to high officials. [مذكور]

مشير *musheer*, leader, field marshal; a Pasha of the highest class.

أستشار *istashàra*, he asked advice.

أستشارة *istishàra*, an asking advice.

مستشار *mustashàr*, he whose advice is asked, councillor, adviser.

مشوار *mishwàr*, errand, course, walk.

شوشة *shoosha*, scalp lock, tuft.

شواش *shawàsh*, disorder, confusion.

شوّش *shawwasha*, he disordered.

مشوّش *mushawwash*, disordered.

تشويش *tashweesh*, a throwing into disorder; syphilis.

شوّط *shawwata*, he cooked up quickly.

أشواطة *ashwàta*, a mess, humbug, cooked up affair.

اشواق ـ شوق *shōq*, pl. *ashwáq*, desire.

شَوَّق *shawwaqa*, he excited desire.

تشويق *tashweeq*, an inciting or exciting.

اشتاق *ishtáqa*, he longed for.

اشتياق *ishtiyáq*, a longing for.

مشتاق *mushtáq*, desirous, eager.

شَيِّق *shayyiq*, desirous, eager.

اشواك ـ شوك *shōk*, pl. *ashwák*, point, thorn.

شوكك ـ شوكة *shōka*, pl. *shawák*, fork, spur; power, royalty.

شوكتلو *shevketlu* (Turkish), imperial, royal.

تين شوكي *teen shōkiy*, prickly pear, cactus fruit.

شاك ـ يشوك *sháka*, it pricked, was pointed; *yashook*, it pricks.

شَوَّل *shawwala*, the horse cocked its tail.

شوالات ـ شوال *sháwal*, pl. *shawálát* (Persian), sack.

شَوَّال *Shawwál*, tenth Moslem month.

اشول *ashwal*, left-handed.

شوم *shōm*, a hard wood used for staves.

زقلة شوم *zoqla shōm*, a cudgel of hard wood.

شونة ـ شوون or اشوان *shōna*, pl. *sho-on*, or *ashwán* (Coptic), storehouse, warehouse, barn.

شاُن ـ شوون *sho-on*, pl. of *shán*, affairs, things.

تشوّه ـ شَوَه *shawah*, deformity, *tashawwaha*, it was deformed.

شوى or اشوى *shawa*, or *ashwa*, he grilled, roasted.

مشوي *mashwi*, grilled (meat, fish, &c.)

شَيء ـ شَي *shai*, thing, (see *sháá*).

شيب *shaib*, grey hair.

شايب or اشيب *sháyib*, or *ashyab*, old, grey-haired.

شاب ـ يشيب *shába*, he grew old; *yasheeb*, he grows old.

شائبة ـ شوائب *sháyiba*, pl. *shawáyib*, petty vices or defects.

شيت *sheet* (Persian), calico, chintz.

شيح *sheeh*, fragrant desert plant, wormwood.

شيخ ـ شيوخ or مشايخ *shaikh*, pl. *shoyookh* or *masháyikh*, chief of tribe, elder, senior; a term of respect.

شيخ البلد *shaikh el-beled*, the head of the village, the officially recognised chief of a village.

شيخ الاسلام *Shaikh el-Islám*, the highest ecclesiastical dignity in Turkey; a Moslem Primate.

شيخوخيّة *shaikhookhiya*, old age, office of *shaikh*.

شياخة *sheyákha*, shaikhdom, office of *shaikh*.

شاخ ـ يشيخ *shákha*, he grew venerable; *yasheekh*, he grows venerable.

شيش sheesh (Turkish), skewer, thin rod; cross-lattice blind; venetian shutters.

شيشخانه sheesh-khána (Turkish), needle-gun, breech-loader.

شيشنة sheeshna (Persian cheshna), sort, sample.

شيشة sheesha (Persian), bottle, narghileh.

شيعة ـ اشياع sheea'a, pl. ashyá'a, sect, dissent; Persian sect; Metuali.

شيعيّ sheea'iy, dissenting, dissenter.

شاع ـ يشيع sháa'a, it was spread abroad; yasheea', it is spreading abroad.

شيّع shayya'a, he made public; he saw (a friend) depart; escorted a funeral; sent, forwarded.

تشييع tashyeea', a seeing a friend off; attendance at a funeral; a sending, forwarding.

اشاع ashá'a, he divulged, revealed. [افشا]

شايع ـ شاعة sháyia', pl. sháa'a, notorious.

شايعة sháyia'a, a female animal in heat. [عشرة]

مشاع musháa', divulged, public; a rumour.

شيّال ـ شال shayyál, porter, carrier (see shála).

شيم shaim, a being marked with a mole.

شيمة ـ شيم sheema, pl. shiam, character, disposition.

شامة shama, mole, beauty-spot.
مشيمة masheema, placenta.

SS.

ص Sád. Value = 90.

صابون sáboon (European), soap.
مصبنة masbana, soap-works.
صبّان sabbán, maker or seller of soap.
صاج sáj, sheet iron, oven plates.
صاح ـ صياح sáha, he cried out (see siyáh).
صار ـ يصير sára, it was, became; yaseer, it becomes.
صيرورة sairoora, a becoming; change of state.
مصير maseer, fact, matter of fact; place.
صاري sári, mast of ship or boat.
صاع ـ صيّع sáa'a, he wandered; sáya', vagabond.
صاغ ـ قرش صاغ ságh (Turkish), right hand, sound, well, excellent; qirsh ságh, a full piastre.
صاغ قول اغاسي ságh qōl aghási (Turkish), the agha, or chief of the right qōl or wing of a battalion; senior captain, or adjutant major.
صاغ ـ صوغ saghá, he fashioned (see sōgh).
صام ـ صوم sáma, he fasted (see sōm).

صان - صون sána, he protected (see sōn).

صائغ - صوغ sáyigh, jeweller (see sōgh).

صبّ sabba, he poured out. [كبّ]

مصبّ masabb, place of outpour; mould; river-mouth.

صبح - صبحيّة - صباح sobh, or sobhiya, or sabáh, morning.

صبيح sábih, matutinal; fresh (fish).

صبوح sabooh, morning drink.

صباحة sabáha, freshness, beauty.

مصباح misbáh, lamp.

صبر sabr, patience; aloes.

صبور or صابر sábir, or saboor, patient.

تصبّر tasabbara, he showed patience.

صبّر sabbara, he embalmed. [حنط]

صبّار - صبّيرة sobár, and sobbairá, cactus, prickly pear.

اصبع - اصابيع asbou', pl. asábeea', finger, toe.

صباع or صبع sobáa', or sábia' (colloquial), finger, toe.

صباعي or صباتي saba'iy, coarse reeds or rushes for mats.

صبغ sabagha, he dyed, soaked, immersed.

صباغ - مصبّغ sibágh, dye; sabbágh, dyer.

صبغة sibgha, a dyeing; baptism.

مصبغة masbagha, dyer's yard or shop.

صبا sabá (femin.), zephyr.

صبيّ - صبيان sabiy, pl. sobián, lad, apprentice.

صبيّة - صبايا sabiya, pl. sabáyá, girl.

صحّ sahha, it was right, proper, sound.

لا يصحّ lá yasahh, it is improper, wicked.

صحّة sihha, health; soundness, sanitation; accuracy, validity.

صحّتك sihhatak (usually pronounced sahhitak), thy health.

صحّة عمومية sihhat 'omoomiya, public health.

صحّي sihhiy, sanitary.

صحيح saheeh, true, accurate, valid.

صحّح - تصحيح sahhaha, he rectified, tas-heeh, rectification.

اصحاح as-háh, chapter of Bible.

صحبة sohba, society, friendship; nosegay.

صاحب - اصحاب sáhib, pl. as-háb, possessor, master, friend, comrade.

استصحب or اصطحب istahaba, or istas-haba, he accompanied, took as companion. [رفق]

صحراء - صحاري sahrá, pl. sahári, desert, Sahara.

صحف sahafa, he drew back, made room for.

صحيفة or صحائف sáheefa, pl. saháyif, or sohof, leaf, page of book.

المصحف el-mos-haf, the Koran.

صحن - صحون sahn, pl. sohoon, metal dish; dish. [طبق]

صحن الجامع sahn el-jámia', courtyard of mosque.

صحى or صحا *sihi*, he woke up. [يقظ]
أصحى or صحَّى *sahha*, or *as-ha*, he awoke another.
صحو *sahw*, sobriety, clearness of intellect.
صاحي *sáhi*, awake, sober, alert.
صخب *sakhb*, uproar, tumult.
صخرة *sakhra*, rock; sacred rock of Jerusalem.
صدد *sadad*, design, aim, object.
صديد ـ صديدي *sadeed*, pus; *sadeediy*, purulent.
صدأ ـ صدئ *sadá*, rust; *sadi*, rusty.
مصدَّئ *mosadda*, rusty, rusted.
صدى *sida*, or *sada*, echo.
تصدَّى *tasadda*, he undertook, took pains.
صدر *sadara*, it issued.
صدور *sodoor*, issue, source, emission.
صدارة *sadára*, source; pre-eminence.
صادر *sádir*, issuing, outgoing; export.
صدر ـ صدور *sadr*, pl. *sodoor*, chest of human body; source; seat of honour.
صدر اعظم *sadr aa'zam*, highest, noblest source of power; the Grand Vizier.
اصدر *asdara*, he made issue, promulgated, exported.
مصدر *masdar*, place of origin; infinitive mood.
صديري *sodairiy*, waistcoat, bodice.
صداع *sodáa'*, headache.

صدغ *sudgh*, temple of the head; door-post.
صدف *sadaf*, oyster-shell, mother-of-pearl.
صدفة *sodfa*, chance, coincidence.
بالصدفة *bis-sodfa*, by chance.
صادف or تصادف *sádafa*, or *tasádafa*, it chanced (mutually), he met by chance.
صدق or صداقة *sidq*, or *sadáqa*, truth, sincerity.
صدقة *sadaqa*, charity.
صادق or صديق *sádiq*, or *sadeeq*, true, sincere.
صدَّق *saddaqa*, he believed, approved, held to be true.
تصديق *tasdeeq*, belief.
صادق على *sádaqa 'ala*, he corroborated.
تصدَّق *tasaddaqa*, it came true, was believed.
مصدمة or صدمة *sadma*, or *mosádama*, shock, collision.
صادم or تصادم *sádama*, or *tasádama*, it collided.
صرَّة ـ صرر *sorra*, pl. *sorar*, bag of money, purse.
مصرور *masroor*, folded up in a bag or bundle.
صرير ـ صرّار *sareer*, creak, squeak, *sarrár*, cricket, cicada.
اصرّ ـ اصرار *asarra*, he persisted, *israr*, persistence.
مصرّ *mosirr*, persistent, determined.
مصارين *masárreen*, bowels.

صرح (152) مصروف

صرح ‎ *saroha*, it was clear, evident.

صراحة ‎ *saráha*, clearness; explanation.

صراحةً ‎ *saráhatan*, clearly.

صراح ‎ *sarah*, pure, clear; freedom.

صريح ‎ *sareeh*, clear, evident, categorical.

صرَّح ‎ *sarraha*, he explained; licensed; allowed.

تصريح ‎ *tasreeh*, explanation; permission, licence, diploma, passport.

مصرَّح ‎ *mosarrah*, permitted; licentiate.

صرخ ‎ *sarakha*, he cried out. [صاح]

صراخ or صريخ ‎ *sorakh*, or *sareekh*, cry, scream.

صاروخ ‎ *sárookh*, wailing spirit, ghost of a murdered man; rocket.

صواريخ ‎ *sawáreekh*, fireworks.

صرصر ‎ *sarsar*, cricket, cicada. [صرّار]

صراط - صرط ‎ *sirát*, pl. *sorot*, path, road to Heaven.

صرع - صارع ‎ *sara'a*, he flung down; *sára'a*, he wrestled.

مصروع - مصرع ‎ *sara'*, epilepsy; *masrooa'*, epileptic.

مصارعة ‎ *mosára'a*, a wrestling.

مصراع ‎ *misráa'*, valve, flap, shutter.

صرف ‎ *sarafa*, he spent, changed money; turned (a thing) aside.

صرف النظر عن ‎ *sarafa en-nazar 'an*, he disregarded, abandoned, dispensed with.

صرف ‎ *sarf*, turn, outlay, change of money; discharge or drainage; accidence.

صرف و نحو ‎ *sarf wa nahw*, accidence and syntax.

صرف ‎ *sirf*, sheer, mere, utter; pure, unalloyed.

صرَّف ‎ *sarrafa*, he inflected, &c. (in grammar).

تصريف ‎ *tasreef*, accidence, grammatical exercise in inflections, conjugations, &c.

صرَّاف - صيارف or صيارفة ‎ *sarráf*, pl. *sayárif*, or *sayárifa*, cashier, paymaster, accountant; provincial receiver of taxes; street money-changer.

صيرفيّة ‎ *sairafiya*, duty or office of a *sarráf*.

تصرَّف ‎ *tasarrafa*, he enjoyed as master, ruled, disposed of property, dispensed.

تصرّفات ‎ *tasarrufát*, rights of enjoyment of property or of its disposal.

متصرِّف ‎ *mutasarrif*, possessor; ruler; in Turkey, governor of a second-rate province under a Vali or governor general; (in grammar) relating to inflexion.

انصرف ‎ *insarafa*, it was spent; he departed, was absent.

مصروف - مصروفات or مصاريف

مصاريف منصرفة (153) صفار

roof, pl. *masroofát*, or *masáreef*, spent ; outlay, expenses, costs, expenditure.

مصاريف منصرفة *masáreef munsarafa*, expenses incurred.

مصرف *masraf*, outlay ; drainage canal.

صرم - صرماتي *sirm*, shape, shoe ; *saramátiy*, shoe-maker.

مصطب - مصطبة (*satab*) *mastaba*, dais, platform, bench.

صعب *sa'oba*, it was difficult, *sa'b*, difficult.

صعوبة *so'ooba*, difficulty.

يصعب علي *yasa'b a'layá*, it is difficult, hard for me.

مصائب *masáy'ib*, difficulties.

صعد *sa'ida*, he ascended.

صعود *so'ood*, ascent, the Ascension.

صاعد *sáy'id*, ascendant ; henceforth.

من الآن و صاعد *min al-aán wa sáy'id*, from now and in future, henceforth.

صعيد *Sa'eed*, Upper Egypt, to the South of Cairo.

صعيدي *Sa'eediy*, a native of Upper Egypt.

صاعقة *sá'yiqa*, thunderbolt, calamity.

صعلوك *so'look*, beggar, a "calendar" in the Arabian Nights' Entertainments.

صغر - صغران *sighar*, or *soghrán*, smallness, infancy, youth.

صغير - صغار *sagheer* (*soghayir*), pl. *sighár*, small, young.

اصغر - صغرى *asghar*, (femin.) *soghra*, smaller.

استصغر *istasghara*, he made little of, depreciated.

صغى or اصغى *sagha*, or *asghá*, he listened, paid attention.

اصغاء *isghá*, a listening, attention to.

صف - صفوف *saff*, pl. *sofoof*, row ; rank of troops.

صفة *soffa*, shelf, mantelpiece.

صفح *safaha*, he made flat ; pardoned.

صفح - صفاح *safah*, pl. *sifáh*, a flat surface.

صفيح *safeeh*, tin in sheets.

صفيحة - صفائح *safeeha*, pl. *safáyih*, tin plate, tin box ; can.

صفق *saffaha*, he clapped hands, applauded. [صفق]

تصفيح *tasfeeh*, a clapping, applause.

صفر *Safar*, the second Moslem month.

صفر - اصفار *sifr*, pl. *asfár*, cypher, zero.

صفرة - صفراء *sofra*, yellowness, *safrá*, bile.

اصفر - صفراء *asfar*, (femin.) *safrá*, yellow.

صفار الشمس *safár esh-shams*, yellowness of sun, just before sunset.

x

صفر (154) صلح

صَفَّر *saffara*, he whistled.

صفار - صفّارة *sofár*, cry, whistle, *saffára*, whistle (instrument).

صفير *safeer*, sapphire; cry, whistle.

صفصاف *sifsáf*, willow.

منصفطة *safsatu*, verbosity, balderdash.

صفق *saffaqa*, he slapped, clapped, applauded.

صفاق *sifáq*, peritoneum.

صفن *sofn*, bag, scrotum.

صفوة or صفو *safw*, or *safwa*, purity, choiceness.

صفاء *safá*, purity, peace of mind; bliss, æstheticism, voluptuousness; woman's hair ornament.

صافي *sáfi*, pure, clear.

اصطفى *istafa*, he chose; was pure, became pure.

صفى *saffa*, he purified, filtered; liquidated, or settled accounts.

تصفية *tasfiya*, liquidation; filtration.

مصفاة *misfát*, filter.

مصطفى *mustafa*, chosen, pure; a man's name.

صفة - وصف *sifa*, quality, attribute (see *wasf*).

صقر *saqr*, hawk.

صقعة - صقعان *saqa'a*, intense cold, frost; *saqa'án*, shivering.

صقل *saqala*, he polished, rubbed down.

مصقول or صقيل *saqeel* or *masqool*, polished, glossy.

صك - صكوك *sakk*, pl. *sokook*, authentic document.

صلب - اصلاب *solb*, pl. *aslab*, loins, lumbar region, i. e. the solid part of the body.

صلب *solb*, steel. [بولاد]

صلابة *salába*, solidity.

صلب *salib*, solid, firm, hard.

صليب *saleeb*, thwart, cross-wise; a cross.

صليبة *saleeba*, transverse dam or dyke.

اهل الصليب *ahl es-saleeb*, crusader.

صلبوت *salboot*, crucifix.

جمعة الصلبوت *joma'a es-salboot*, Good Friday.

صلب - صلب *salb*, crucifixion; *sallaba*, he crucified.

صلح *saloha*, it was good, fit or good for.

صلاح *saláh*, goodness, morality.

صلاحية *saláhiyah*, fitness, validity.

صالح - صوالح *sálih*, pl. *sawálih*, good, fit; profit, one's advantage or interest.

لصالحه *li-sálihihi*, to his advantage.

صوالح مختلفة *sawálih mukhtalifa*, conflicting interests.

اصلح or صلّح *sallaha* or *aslaha*, he rectified, repaired.

تصليح - اصلاح *tasleeh*, repairs; *isláh*, reform.

صالح *sálaha*, he made peace with.

صلح *solh*, peace after war, reconciliation.

مصالحة mosálaha, mutual reconciliation.

اصطلح istalaha, he made peace with, adapted himself to; was technical.

اصطلاح تجاري istiláh tijáriy, commercial usage.

اصطلاحات istiláhát, adaptations, usages, technical terms.

مصلح moslih, reformer, corrective; hence, salt as a corrective of food. [ملح]

مصلحة ـ مصالح maslaha, pl. masálih, attention to one's interests, transaction of business; a public department or administration.

صلع ـ اصلع sala', baldness; asla', bald.

صلاة ـ صلوات salát, pl. salawát, prayer.

صلّى ـ صلّى عليه salla, he prayed; salla a'leih, he prayed for him.

صلّى الله عليه وسلّم salla Allah a'leih wa sallam, May God bless him (Mahomet) and grant him peace.

صلعم a written (not pronounced) abbreviation of the above phrase.

صمّم sammama, he determined, persisted.

تصميم tasmeem, determination.

صميم sameem, interior, heart, pith.

صمام ـ صم simám, valve; samam, deafness.

اصمّ asamm, deaf.

صمت samata, he kept silent. [سكت]

سميت sameet, crisp biscuit in rings.

مسمط masmat, cook-shop.

سماخ simákh, cavity of ear. [سمخ]

صمد samad, eternal, God.

صومعة or صمعة soma'a, fellaheen's grain chest, bin, or recess in wall.

صمغ samgh, gum arabic.

صمولة samoola, rivet, nut of screw.

صمولي samooli, soldiers' bread. [جراية]

صنوبر sanobar, cone, fir, pine-tree.

صنج ـ اصنج sanaj, deafness; asnaj, deaf.

صندوق ـ صناديق sandooq, pl. sanádeeq, box, chest; safe, treasury, cash department.

صندل ـ صنادل sandal, pl. sanádil, large boat, sandal wood.

سنّارة or صنّارة sinnára, fish-hook, tackle.

صنط sant, acacia, mimosa nilotica; acanthus, wart.

صنطاوي santáwiy, species of small melon.

صنع sana'a, he manufactured, made. [عمل ـ فعل]

صنّع sanna'a, he invented, fabricated, trumped up.

تصنّع tasanna'a, he shammed, pretended to be.

اصطنع istana'a, it was artificial.

اِستصنع istasna'a he ordered to be made.

صناعة - صنائع sanáa'a, pl. sanáya', trade, profession. [كار - حرفة]

اهل الصناعة - ارباب الصناعة ahl es-sanáa'a, pl. arbáb es-sanáa'a, artisan, artificer.

تعاطى صناعته ta'áta sanáa'taho, he exercised his trade.

دار الصناعة dár es-sanáa'a, workshop, dockyard, arsenal. [See ترسانة tersana.

صنائعي sanáya'iy, artisan.

صناعي sanáa'iy, artificial.

تصنيع or تصنع tasneea', or tasannoa', artifice, intrigue.

مصطنع mostana', artificial, false.

صنعاء Sana'á, town of Sana in Arabia.

صنف - اصناف sinf (sanf), pl. asnáf, species, sort, kind.

اصناف asnáf, goods of all sorts, merchandise.

صنّف sannafa, he sorted out, compiled a book.

مصنّف mosannif, author, compiler. [مؤلّف]

صنفرة sanfara, emery paper.

صنم - اصنام sanam, pl. asnám, idol. [وثن]

رجل مصنّم rajil mosannim, a pensive man, one wrapped up in his own ideas.

صنو sino, nephew; part of a whole; sapling, shoot; like to, fellow to.

صنو الموز sino el-móz, young banana plant.

صنوان sinwán, pl. of sino, also kinship.

صهر sihr, son-in-law.

مصاهرة mosáhara, relationship by marriage.

صهريج - سرنج sahreej (Turkish, sarnij), cistern.

صهل - صهيل sahala, it neighed; saheel, a neigh.

صوب sob, the side which is exposed to view; aim, object, direction.

صوبة sóba, camel pack-saddle.

صائب sáyib, right, straight; proper thing to do.

صواب sawáb, rightness, accuracy, sobriety.

صواب وخطاء sawáb wa khatá, the right and the wrong, corrigenda, errata of a book.

اصاب asába, he hit the mark, wounded.

اصابة isába, a successful hit, accuracy of aim; a shooting, wounding.

اصابة العين isábat el-a'in, the "evil eye."

صائبه العيار sáyiboh el-'iyár, wounded by a shot.

مصاب mosáb, he who is hit.

مصيب moseeb, he who hits, assailant.

مصيبة - مصائب moseeba, pl. masáyib, blow, calamity.

استصوب istaswaba, he approved, thought it right.

صوت (157) صيد

صوت ـ اصوات sōt, pl. aswát, voice; cry.

صوات sawát, a crying out.

صوَّت sawwata, he shouted.

صوترى sotari, buffoon, vulgar fellow.

صور و صيداء Soor wa Saidá, Tyre and Sidon.

صورة ـ صور soora, pl. sowar, form, manner, copy, picture, face, shape.

صوَّر sawwara, he depicted, drew, painted.

تصوَّر tasawwara, he imagined, pictured to himself.

تصوير ـ تصاوير tasweer, pl. tasáweer, picture.

تصوير الشمس tasweer esh-shams, photograph, photography.

مصوَّر ـ مصوَّر mosawwir, artist, mosawwar, painted.

مصوَّراتي mosawwarátiy (colloquial), artist, photographer.

صوصوة sawsawa, murmur, coo.

صوغ sōgh, form, similarity of form.

صاغ or صوَّغ ságha, or sawwagha, he fashioned, made jewellery.

صيغة ـ صيغ seegha, pl. siagh, formula; shape; jewel.

صائغ or صيّاغ sáyigh, or sayyágh, jeweller, goldsmith.

مصاغ ـ مصاغات maságh, pl. masághát, jewel, jewellery.

صوف ـ اصواف soof, pl. aswáf, wool; woollen goods.

صوفي soofiy, (1) woollen; (2) (Greek, sophia, wisdom), Soofi, Moslem mystic, theosophist, quietist.

تصوَّف tasawwafa, he became a Soofi.

صوفان soofán, tinder, touchwood.

صول sōl (Turkish), left side; lieutenant.

صول اغاسي sōl aghási (Turkish), quartermaster, lieutenant.

صولة sōla, authority, influence, violence; rust.

صوم or صيام sōm, or siyám, fast, a fasting.

صام ـ يصوم sama, he kept fast, yasoom, he fasts.

صائم sáyim, he who fasts.

صون or صيانة sōn, or siyána, a guarding; chastity.

صان ـ يصون sána, he guarded, yasoon, he guards.

مصون ـ مصونة masoon, guarded; masoona, chaste woman.

صوَّانة sawwána, flint, granite, pebble.

اصوان Aswán, Assouan or Syene, on the Nile, near the first cataract; a rocky place, granite quarry.

صياح ـ صاح ـ يصيح siyáh, a shout, sáha, he shouted, yaseeh, he shouts.

صيد said, the chase, sport of any kind, fishing.

رشّ صيد rishsh said, small shot for a sporting gun.

صيّاد *sayyád*, sportsman, fisherman.

تصيّد or صاد or اصطاد *sáda*, or *tasayyada*, or *istáda*, he went out to shoot, fish, &c.

مصيدة *misiada*, trap, net, snare, pitfall.

صيداء و صور *Saida wa Soor*, Sidon and Tyre.

صيدلة *saidla*, science of pharmacy.

صيدلاني *saidlániy*, pharmaceutical chemist. [اجزاجي]

صيرورة ـ صار *sairoora*, change of state (see *sára*).

صيغة ـ صوغ *seegha*, formula, jewel (see *sogh*).

صيف ـ اصياف *saif*, pl. *asiáf*, summer. [cf. سيف]

صيفي *saifiy*, summery, summer crop.

صيف النيل *saif en-neel*, a canal not dry in summer.

صيّف *sayyafa*, he prepared for the summer crop; he gleaned.

صين ـ صيني *Seen*, land of China; *Seeniy*, Chinese.

صينية ـ صواني *seeniya*, pl. *sawáni*, large platter, tray.

صيوان *seewán*, large reception tent.

صيوان الاذن *seewán el-odon*, outer shell of ear, the *concha* or visible part of ear.

D or DH
(Sometimes Z).

ض *Dhadh*. Value = 800.

ضاع ـ ضيع *dáa'a*, it was lost, missing (see *daia'*).

ضاف ـ ضيف *dáfa*, he was hospitable (see *daif*).

ضأن ـ ضائن *dáyin*, pl. *dán*, sheep. [خروف]

لحم ضاني *lahm dáni*, mutton.

ضبّ *dabb*, lizard.

ضبّة الباب *dabbat el-báb*, door-latch.

ضبابة *dabába*, fog, mist.

ضبّ *dabba*, he seized, guarded.

ضبط *zabata*, he seized, arrested; recorded in writing.

ضبط *zabt*, arrest, grip; drawing up a report; organisation, police.

رجال الضبط *rijál ez-zabt*, men of the police.

ضبط و ربط *zabt wa rabt*, "a seizing and binding," public security, police.

ضبطية *zabtiya*, police, police-station; a policeman.

ضابط ـ ضبّاط *zábit*, pl. *zobbát*, officer of army, navy or police.

ضابطة ـ ضوابط *zábita*, pl. *zawábit*, rule, regulation.

انضبط *inzabata*, he was arrested, it was recorded.

مضبوط *mazboot*, arrested, recorded; firm.

مضبطة ـ مصابط *muzbata*, pl. *mazábit*, police report, document; written decision.

محضر ضبط الواقعة *mahdar zabt el-wáqia'a*, police report or "*procès verbal*" of a crime.

ضبع ـ ضبّع *dabo'a*, pl. *dibá'a* (femin.), hyena.

ضجّة *dajja*, tumult, groan.

ضَجَر ‎ dajar, anguish, anxiety.

اضطجع ‎ or ضجع ‎ daja'a, or idtaja'a, he lay down, reclined.

ضحك على ‎ dahika a'la, he laughed at, swindled.

ضاحك ‎ dáhaka, he mimicked, mocked.

اضحك ‎ ad-haka, he made laugh.

مضحك ‎ modhik, funny, ridiculous.

ضحى ‎ or ضحو ‎ or ضحاء ‎ dahá, or daho, or doha, morning sun, forenoon.

اضحى - اضحاة ‎ ad-hát, pl. ad-ha, sheep for sacrifice.

يوم الاضحى ‎ yōm el-adha, day of sacrifices, feast of Korbán Bairám, 10th of Zil-Hijja.

ضحيّة ‎ dahiya, victim, sheep for sacrifice.

ضاحية - ضواحي ‎ dáhiya, pl. dawáhi, outlying districts. [cf. ناحية‎]

ضخم - ضخام ‎ dakhm, pl. dikhám, gross, obese, bulky.

ضخامة ‎ dakháma, corpulence, bulkiness.

ضدّ ‎ didd, versus, contrary, against.

تضادّ ‎ or مضادّة ‎ tadádd, or modádda, mutual opposition, contrast.

اضرّ ب ‎ or ضرّ ‎ darra, or adarra bi, he injured.

ضرر - اضرار ‎ darar, pl. adrár, damage, injury.

اضرار ‎ idrár, a doing injury.

انضرّ ‎ indarra, he was injured.

اضطرّ ‎ idtarra, he felt injured; was compelled.

اضطرار ‎ idtirár, annoyance, compulsion.

تضرّر ‎ tadarrara, he complained of injury. [تظالم‎]

ضرورة ‎ daroora, urgent necessity, essential point; a call of nature.

ضروريّ ‎ daroriy, essential, indispensable, urgent.

مضرّ ب ‎ modirr bi, injurious.

مضرّة - مضارّ ‎ madarra, pl. madárr, injury.

ضرير ‎ dareer, injured (in sight), blind. [كفيف‎]

ضرّة - ضرائر ‎ darra (or dorra), pl. daráyir, fellow-wife; udder of cow; parrot.

ضرب - يضرب ‎ daraba, he struck, assaulted; multiplied (in arithmetic); struck coinage; imposed a tax; played a musical instrument; yadriba, he strikes, &c.

ضرب - ضروب ‎ darb, pl. doroob, blow, assault; multiplication; coinage; manner.

ضرب النار ‎ darb en-nár, musketry fire.

ضارب ‎ dáraba, he exchanged blows, fought.

مضاربة ‎ or تضارب ‎ modáraba, or tadárub, conflict, row.

اضطرب ‎ idtaraba, he felt beaten, anxious.

ضريبة - ضرائب ‎ dareeba, pl. daráyib, tax; measure of 8 ardebs of rice.

مضرب ‎ midrab, mallet; weaver's beam.

مضروب madroob, beaten.
مضطرب modtarib, anxious.
ضريح dareeh, tomb.
ضرس - اضراس dirs, pl. adrás, molar tooth.
ضرط darata, he broke wind.
ضرع - ضروع dara', pl. dorooa', udder, dug.
ضراعة daráa'a, humility.
مضارع modária', aorist or present tense.
ضعف da'f or do'f, weakness; di'f, the double.
ضعيف - ضعفاء du'yeef, pl. doa'fá, weak.
ضعفاء doa'fá, pl. weak, poor, footmen, infantry, not mounted Arab sheikhs, hence "zouaves."
اضعف ada'fa, he weakened.
ضعّف or اضعف or ضاعف du'a'fa, or ada'fa, or dáa'fa, he doubled.
تضاعف tadáa'fa, it doubled itself.
مضاعفة modáa'fa, the double, a doubling.
مضاعف modáa'f, doubled.
ضغط daghat, crush, squeeze; oppression.
ضغن daghina, he bore malice, plotted against.
ضغينة - ضغائن dagheena, pl. dagháyin, malice, intrigue.
ضفدع dafda', frog, toad.
ضفر dafara, he plaited, tressed.
ضفيرة - ضفائر dafeera, pl. dafáyir, tress of hair.

ضلّ dalla, he went astray, sinned.
ضلال dalál, perdition, error.
ضالّ dáll, sinner, gone astray, lost sheep.
ضلّة dilla, error, loss.
ضلع - ضلوع or اضلع dila', pl. dolooa', or adloa', rib.
ضليع dalcea', strong, well ribbed.
ضمّ damma, he collected, heaped up, added together; reaped a field.
ضمّ damm, addition.
انضمّ indamma, it was added up, collected, annexed.
ضمّة - مضموم damma, short ŏ vowel sound; madmoom, a letter marked with a damma; added up, collected. [رفع]
اضمحلّ or ضمحل damhala or idmahalla, it faded away, he grew weak, poor.
ضمد damada, he poulticed, bandaged.
ضمير - ضمائر damcer, pl. damáyir, conscience; secret thought; pronoun.
اضمر admara, he pondered, cogitated, plotted.
ضمور domoor, atrophy, skinniness.
ضمّارة dammára, female fortune-teller.
ضمن dimn, the inside, contents.
من ضمن min dimn inclusive.
ضمنيّ dimniy, inclusive; tacit, or understood, taken for granted.

شروط ضمنيّة *shoroot dimniya*, tacit conditions of a contract.

ضمن *damina*, he went bail, guaranteed. [كفل]

ضمّن *dammana*, (the magistrate) accepted bail; (the accused) offered bail; he bailed out; he inserted, included.

تضمّن *tadammana*, it included, contained.

ضمانة or ضمان *damán*, or *damána*, bail, guarantee.

ضامن - ضمّان *dámin*, pl. *dommán*, bailor, he who goes bail; responsible.

تضمين *tadmeen*, a bailing out, letting out on bail.

تضمينات *tadmeenát*, damages in law, "*dommages intérêts*." [تعويضات]

تضامن *tadámun*, mutual bail or solidarity in liability for debt, or costs.

شركة التضامن *shirkat et-tadámun*, "*société en nom collectif*," solidarity of partners.

مضمون *madmoon*, context, contents or tenour of a document; the thing which is guaranteed.

ضنانة *danáke*, narrowness, weakness, poverty.

ضهد or اضطهد *dahada*, or *idtahada*, he persecuted.

مضطهد *modtahid*, tyrannical, brutal.

ضهيّ *dahiy*, similar, like.

ضاهى *dáha*, he, it resembled.

مضاهاة *modáhát*, mutual resemblance.

مضاهي *modáhi*, similar, mutually resembling.

ضوّ - اضواء *dō (daw)*, pl. *adwá*, brilliancy, light.

ضو الشمس *dō esh-shams*, sunlight.

ضياء *diá*, brilliancy, light.

اضاءة *idát*, illumination, a giving light.

مضيء or ضوئي *dōiy*, or *modi*, brilliant.

ضياع or ضيع *daia'*, or *dayáa'*, loss. [فقد]

ضاع - يضيع *dáa'a*, it was lost; *yadeea'*, it is missing.

ضيّع or اضاع *dayya'a* or *adáa'*, he wasted, spoilt, lost.

ضائع *dáya'*, lost, missing.

ضيعة - ضياع *daya'a*, pl. *diyá'a*, village; lands.

ضيف - ضيوف *daif*, pl. *doyoof*, guest.

ضيافة *diyáfa*, hospitality.

ضاف - يضيف *dáfa*, he was hospitable; was a guest; *yadeef*, he is a guest.

مضيّف or مضيف *modeef*, or *midiáf*, hospitable, host.

اضاف *adáfa*, he joined, annexed, added to.

اضافة *idáfa*, junction, grammatical relation; conjunction.

اضافي *idáfiy*, relative, showing relation.

٢

اضافات *iláfát*, minor details, accessories.

مضاف *moláf*, added, annexed, related.

ضيق *deeq*, or *daiq*, narrowness, poverty, discomfort.

ضيّق *dayyiq*, narrow, strait, severe.

أضيق ـ ضيقى *adiaq*, (femin.) *deeqa*, narrower.

ضاق ـ يضيق *dáqa*, it was narrow; *yadeeq*, it is narrow.

ضيّق *dayyaqa*, he made narrow, constrained, compelled, showed severity.

تضايق *tadáyaqa*, he (mutually) annoyed, blocked up (a road), obstructed.

مضيقة ـ مضائق *madeeqa*, pl. *madáyiq*, embarrassment, straits.

T

ط *Tá*. Value = 9.

طاب ـ يطيب *tába*, he recovered health (see *tayyib*).

طابة *tába*, cork, stopper, ball.

طابو *tápoo* (Turkish), title-deed. [حِجّة]

طابور *táboor* (Turkish), battalion; used in different words of command, such as, Fall in! Deploy!

طابونة *táboona*, bakery, oven.

طابية *tábia* (Turkish), redoubt, fort.

طاح ـ يطرح *táha*, it was blown away (see *tawwaha*).

طار ـ طير *tára*, (the bird) flew. (See *tair*.)

طارة *tára*, round piece, circle, ornament.

طاس ـ طاسات *tás*, pl. *tását*, cup, bowl. [كأس]

طاعة ـ طوع *táa'a*, obedience (see *taw'*).

طاقة ـ طاق *táqa*, window; endurance (see *tŏq*).

طاؤوس *táwoos* (Greek), peacock.

طائفة ـ طوف *táyifa*, guild, crew (see *tŏf*).

طبّ ـ طبّي *tubb*, medical science; *tubbiy*, medical.

كشف طبّي *kashf tubbiy*, medical report, inquest.

شهادة طبّية *shaháda tubbiya*, medical certificate.

طبيب ـ اطبّاء *tabeeb*, pl. *atibbá*, physician. [حكيم]

طباشير *tabásheer*, chalk, crayon.

طبخ or طباخة *tabkh*, or *tabákha*, cookery.

طبخ *tabakha*, he cooked.

طبّاخ *tabbákh*, a cook.

مطبخ *matbakh*, kitchen.

مطبوخ or طبيخ *matbookh*, or *tabeekh*, cooked.

طبطب *tabtaba* (colloquial), he tapped, patted.

طبع *taba'a*, he printed, impressed.

طبع *taba'*, stamp, imprint, form, character.

طبيعة tabeea'a, natural character.

طبيعيّ tabeea'iy, natural, innate; physical.

طابع - طوابع tábi'a, pl. tawábia', postage-stamp.

انطبع intaba'a, it was printed.

مطبعة matba'a, printing-press.

مطبوع - مطبوعات matbooa', pl. matbooa'át, printed; (in pl.) prints, publications.

طبق tibq, conformity, coincidence; bird-lime.

طبق الاصل tibq el-asl, a true copy of the original.

طبقاً للقانون tibqán lil-qánoon, conformably to the law.

طبق or طبقة - اطباق tabaq, or tabaqa, pl. atbáq, layer, stratum, storey of house; pincers; dish, disk; earthenware plate.

طابق tábiq, valve, lid.

طبق tabaqa, it coincided, fitted, conformed to.

طبّق tabbaqa, he made coincide or conform; applied or adapted; shod a horse.

تطبيق tatbeeq, adaptation, application.

طابق or تطابق tábaqa, or tatábaqa, it coincided.

انطبق intabaqa, it was applicable, was made applicable.

مطابق - مطابقة motábiq, coinciding; motábaqa, a mutual conformity or applicability.

طبل - طبول tabl, pl. tobool, drum.

طبلة or طبليّة tabla, or tabliya, plate, platter; drum of ear; small table.

طبان tabán (Turkish, sole of foot), tire of wheel.

طبنجة tabanja (Turkish), pistol, revolver.

طبنجة بخمسة ارواح tabanja bi-khamsat arwáh, revolver with five souls, i.e. chambers.

طاجن tájin, small saucepan.

طحال tihál, spleen.

طحن tahana, he ground (corn, &c.)

طحين taheen, flour, ground corn; oil-cake.

طاحون - طواحين táhoon, pl. tawáheen, mill.

طرّ tarra, he snatched, pilfered.

طرّار tarrár, pickpocket, thief.

طرّة - طرر torra, pl. torar, tuft, edge, border.

طرة Toora, a village near Cairo, site of the chief convict prison.

طرأ - يطرأ tará, it mischanced; yatrá, it mischances, happens inauspiciously.

ان لم تطرأ عوارض in lam tatrá a'wárid, if no accidents happen; if all goes well (convalescence).

طرابزون trábizoon (Greek), long desk, railing.

طرابلس Tarábolus, Tripoli of Syria.

طرابلس الغرب Tarábolus el-gharb, Tripoli West (in Africa).

طرب (164) طراق

طَرِبَ *tariba*, he felt emotion (especially the effect of music.)

طَرَب *tarab*, emotion, delight; *tarib*, moved.

اطرب *atraba*, he excited (pleasant) emotion, by music or song.

مطرب *motrib*, musician, singer.

آلات مطربة *aālāt motriba*, musical instruments.

طربوش - طرابيش *turboosh*, pl. *tarābeesh*, red cap, fez.

طرابيشي *tarābeeshiy*, seller of tarbooshes.

طرح *taraha*, he flung; put up to auction; subtracted (in arithmetic).

طرح *tarh*, a fling, glance; subtraction; pronunciation, an uttering.

طرحة *tarha*, woman's light veil.

مطرح - مطارح *matrah*, pl. *matārih*, place, spot.

طرخون *tarkhoon*, estragon, artemisia dracunculus.

طرد *tarada*, he drove off, repelled, dismissed.

طرد - طرود *tard*, dismissal; pl. *torood*, parcel, piece of baggage.

طرّاد *tarrād*, repeller; breakwater; longitudinal dyke of canal.

استطرد *istatrada*, he pursued.

طريد *tareed*, repelled; tracked, object of chase.

طرز *tarz*, form, style, shape, manner.

طراز *tirāz*, embroidery, fashion.

طرش - اطرش *tarash*, deafness; *atrash*, deaf.

طرش *tarasha* (colloquial), he vomited. [قى]

طرطورة *tartoora*, cone, conical cap; fool.

طرطوفة *tartoofa*, apex, point; ground artichoke.

طرطير *tarteer*, lees, sediment; tartar or deposit.

طرف - اطراف *taraf*, pl. *atrāf*, side, edge, point.

اطراف *atrāf*, side issues, digressions, extremities.

طرف - طرفة *tarf*, glance, wink; *turfa*, novelty.

طرفاء *tarfā*, genus tamarisk.

طرق *taraqa*, he knocked, struck. [ضرب]

طرقة *tarqa*, a blow; once; pay or hire for a job.

طريق - طرق *tareeq*, pl. *toroq*, road, way, method.

طرق احتياليّة *toroq ihtiyāliya*, fraudulent means.

طريقة - طرائق *tareeqa*, pl. *tarāyiq*, sect, mode of life, course.

جبل الطارق *jebel et-Tāriq*, Tarik's mountain, Gibraltar.

مطرق *mitraq*, hammer.

شارع مطروق *shāria' matrooq*, beaten or frequented road.

طراق *tarāq* (Turkish), hoe, rake.

طرنبة *toronba* (for Turkish *tulumba*), pump, fire-engine.

طرنبيطة *tronbaita* (European, trumpet), drum.

طرو or طرى *taria*, or *taroa*, it was fresh, moist.

طراوة *tarawa*, freshness, moistness, dampness.

طرىّ *tariy*, fresh, moist, damp, cool.

طرّى *tarra*, he refreshed, seasoned.

طسّ *tass* (colloquial), downright; at one blow.

طشت or طست *tist*, or *tisht*, metal pan, tray, wash basin.

طاطورة *tatoora*, "datura," stramonium, a poison.

طعم *ta'ima*, he tasted, eat. [ذوق]

طعم - طعوم *ta'm*, pl. *to'oom*, taste, flavour.

طعم *to'm*, bait for fishing.

طعام - اطعمة *ta'am*, pl. *atia'ma*, viands, food.

طعّم *ta'a'ma*, he vaccinated; budded, baited.

تطعيم *tata'eem*, inoculation, vaccination; a budding or grafting.

طعميّة *ta'miya*, bean-paste, meat-ball. [فلافل - قريصة]

طعن *ta'na*, he stabbed, accused, attacked.

طعن في السنّ *ta'na fis-sinn*, he was advanced in age, very old.

طاعون *taa'oon*, plague, pestilence.

طغرا *tughra* (Turkish), the Sultan's cypher or sign-manual as seen on coins, public buildings, firmans, &c.

طغى or طغا *tagha*, or *taghia*, it burst its bounds, was outrageous, iniquitous.

طغيان or طغوى *tughiyan*, or *taghwa*, revolt, iniquity.

طاغى - طغاة *taghi*, pl. *toghat*, rebel, impious, tyrant.

طفيف *tafeef*, slight, trifling.

طفش - طفشان *tafasha*, he ran away; *tafshan*, fugitive.

طفى *tafia*, the fire went out.

طفو *tofoo*, extinction of flame or fire.

طفا or اطفا *atfa*, or *taffa*, he extinguished; slaked lime.

انطفا *intafa*, the fire was extinguished.

مطفى *motfi*, extinguisher, he who extinguishes.

مطفاية *mitfaya*, instrument for extinguishing.

طفاح *tifah*, overflow, eruption on skin; vomit.

طفل - اطفال *tifl*, pl. *atfal*, infant.

طفولية - طفلى *tofooliya*, infancy; *tifliy*, infantile.

طفال *tafal*, clay.

طفيلى *tofailiy*, fawner, cringer, lick-spittle; parasite, parasitic (disease).

طفا *tafa*, the water rose, overflowed. [سبحة]

طَقَّة or طَقْطَقَة **taqqa**, or **taqtaqa**, crack, cracking noise, cracking of knuckles in shampooing.

انْطَقّ **intaqqa**, it cracked, burst.

طَقْس ـ طُقُوس **taqs**, (Greek *taxis*), natural order or arrangement; weather, temperature, atmosphere; pl. **toqoos**, rites, liturgy.

طَقِم ـ طُقُوم **taqim**, pl. **toqoom** (Turkish), set of tools, gear, accoutrements, apparatus; harness.

طَقِيَّة or تَقِيَّة **taqiya**, cotton skullcap worn under the turban.

طَلّ على or اطَلّ على **talla 'ala**, or **atalla 'ala**, it was higher than, and dominated in view, looked out on.

شُبَّاك مُطَلّ على **shabbák motill 'ala** a window looking or giving out upon (a view).

طَلَب or تَطَلَّب **talaba**, or **tatallaba**, he asked, demanded.

طَلَب ـ طَلَبَات **talab**, pl. **talabát**, request, demand.

طَلْبَة **tolba**, (military) fatigue party.

طَالِب ـ طَلَبَة **tálib**, pl. **talaba**, claimant, student.

طَالِبَة العِشَار **tálibat el-i'shár**, bitch in heat.

انْطَلَب **intalaba**, it was asked, demanded.

طَالَب **tálaba**, he claimed repayment.

مُطَالَبَة **motálaba**, claim for payment.

مَطْلَب ـ مَطَالِب **matlab**, pl. **matálib**, problem, query.

مَطْلُوب ـ مَطْلُوبَات **matloob**, pl. **matloobát**, thing claimed, debt.

طَلْح or طَلْحَة **tal-ha**, acacia *seyál*.

طَلَس ـ اطْلَس (**tils**), **atlas**, smooth, satin; atlas.

طِلْسَم ـ طَلَاسِم **tilsam**, pl. **talásim**, talisman.

طَلَع **tala'a**, it rose, ascended, turned out, turned out well, succeeded, became.

اطْلَع فوق **itla' fóq**, go upstairs!

طُلُوع **toloo'a**, ascent, appearance.

طُلُوع الشمس **toloo'a esh-shams**, sunrise. [شرق]

طَلْع **tala'**, pollen, pollen of male palm.

طَالِع **táli'a**, ascending, star in the ascendant, good fortune.

طَلَائِع **taláy'a**, skirmishers.

طَلَّع **talla'a**, he made ascend or appear, raised.

طَلِّع حِسَّك **talli'a hissak**, raise your voice! speak louder!

طَالَع على or اطَّلَع على **tála'a**, or **ittala'a 'ala**, he studied, read.

اطِّلَاع على **ittilá'a 'ala**, study, perusal. [cf. تلاوة

مُطَالَعَة **motála'a**, study, attention, perusal.

طَلَق **talaqa**, he delivered.

طَلْق **talq**, parturition, discharge of a gun; eloquence.

طَلَاق ـ طَالِق **taláq**, divorce; **táliq**, divorced woman.

طَلَّقَ tallaqa, he divorced.

طلقة talaqa, discharge of gun, pull of trigger.

اطلق atlaqa, he drove out, fired a gun, generalised.

اطلق عِيار ناري atlaqa 'iyár náriy, he fired a shot.

اطلاق itláq, a driving out, firing a shot, generalisation, phraseology.

على الاطلاق a'la l-itláq, in general, absolutely.

مطلق ـ مطلقاً motlaq, absolute; motlaqán, absolutely.

سلطة مطلقة sulta motlaqa, discretionary power.

مطلقة motallaqa, a divorced woman.

طلمبة or طلنبة tulumba (Turkish), pump, fire-engine.

طلى or طلا tala, or talla, he anointed, gilded; was soft spoken.

طلاء tilá, varnish, gilding; pitch.

طمث tams, impurity, menses. [حيض]

طَمَّسَ tammasa, he inked over, blotted out.

طماطم tomátum (European), tomato. [قوطة]

طمع tamia'a, he coveted; tama', cupidity.

طمن tamn, tranquil.

طمأن منه tamána minoh, he relied on it, rested from.

اطمأنَّ اليه itmánna ileih, he relied on it, had confidence in.

اطمئنان itmeenán, confidence, trust.

مطمئنّ motmayinn, confident, tranquil.

طما or طمى tama, (the river) overflowed.

طمي tamiy, mud deposit left on fields after the subsidence of high Nile.

طنين taneen, tinkle, ringing. [رنين]

طنب ـ اطناب tonob, long rope; itnáb, prolixity.

طنبور tanboor, tambour, guitar.

طنجرة tanjara (Turkish), saucepan.

طنطنة tantana, noise, éclat, pomp.

طنطن به tantana bihi, he sang his praises.

طنطا ـ غربية Tanta, a large native town in the middle of the Delta, capital of the province of Gharbiya.

طه ـ ط ه Ta-ha, the two letters ta, ha, the title of chapter xx. of the Koran; used as a man's name like Ya-seen. [يس]

طهر or طهارة tohr, or tahára, purity; circumcision,

طهّر tahhara, he purified, circumcised.

تطهير tat-heer, purification, circumcision.

طاهر táhir, pure.

طهق معه tahaqa ma'ho (colloquial), he became disgusted with it.

طوبة ـ طوب tōba, pl. toob, brick.

طرّاب tauwáb, brick-maker.

طوبة *Tooba*, Coptic month of January.

طوب *toob* (for Turkish *top*), ball, cannon, artillery.

طوبجى , طوبجية *toobji*, pl. *toobjiya* (Turkish *topji*), artilleryman.

طوبخانة *toob-kháná* (Turkish *top-kháná*), arsenal, artillery.

طرّح *tawwaha*, he whirled, flung away.

طاح *táha*, it was blown away, vanished.

طور ـ اطوار *tōr*, pl. *atwár*, manners, conduct.

طوار *tawár*, area; circuit.

طوسة *tōsha*, noise, fuss, trifle.

طوّش *tawwasha*, he castrated.

طواشى ـ طواشية *tawáshi*, pl. *tawáshiya*, eunuch.

طوع *taw'*, obedient, willing.

طاعة or اطاعة *táa'a*, or *itáa'a*, obedience.

اطاع *atáa'a*, he obeyed.

مطاوعة *motáwa'a*, obedience.

مطيع *motea'*, obedient, obeying.

مطاع *motáa'*, person or law obeyed; king.

استطاع *istatáa'a*, he was able, capable.

استطاعة *istitáa'a*, capability.

طوغرى ـ دغرى *dooghri* (for Turkish *doghroo*) straight, upright, true, honest.

طوف *tōf*, turn, tour, patrol; raft.

طاف *táfa*, he patrolled, made a tour.

طوّف *tawwafa*, he patrolled, made turn.

طوّاف ـ طوّافة *tawwáf*, pl. *tawwáfa*, patroller; a patrol; chief of a patrol.

طوفان *toofán*, deluge.

طائفة ـ طوائف *táyifa*, pl. *tawáyif*, guild, crew, corporation; sex.

طوق ـ اطواق *tōq*, pl. *atwáq*, collar, power.

طوق or طاقة or اطاقة *tōq*, or *táqa*, or *itáqa*, power, power of endurance, capability.

طاق ـ طاقات *táq*, pl. *táqát*, arch, vault; layer.

طاقة *táqa*, arched window, air-hole; a "piece," or roll of cloth.

طول ـ اطوال *tool*, pl. *atwál*, length, height, longitude.

طولا or بالطول *toolán*, or *bit-tool*, lengthwise.

طوال *tawál*, duration, length of time.

طول *tōl*, power, superiority.

طويل ـ طوال *taweel*, pl. *tiwál*, long, tall; metre in poetry.

اطول ـ طولى *atwal*, (fem.) *tōla*, longer, taller.

طال ـ يطول *tála*, it was long, endured; *yatool*, it is long.

طالما *tála-má*, very often, for long since.

طوّل *tawwala*, he lengthened, made long, was prolix.

اطال اللسان *atála el-lisán*, he put out his tongue, abused.

تطاول على *tatáwala a'la*, he was rude to, insulted.

انطال *intála*, it was lengthened, it stretched; it reached, was adjacent.

تطويل *tatweel*, prolongation.

طائل *táyil*, profit.

على غير طائل *a'la ghair táyil*, in vain, without profit.

طاولة *tawla*, table; backgammon; stable, trough, manger.

مطاولة *motáwala*, insult, oppression.

مستطيل *mostateel*, oblong.

طونلاطة *tonaláta* (European), ton weight.

طوى ـ يطوي *tawa*, he folded, rolled up; *yatwi*, he folds.

طي *taiy*, a fold, roll, enclosure.

مرسل طيّة *mursal taiyoh*, sent (herewith), enclosed.

طويّة *tawiya*, conscience, heart; intention.

طوى *tawa*, rolled, folded.

مطوى *matwa*, penknife; folded, rolled.

مطوة *matwa*, penknife.

طيّب *tayyib*, good, excellent; well in health; honest; all right, very well.

اطيب ـ طوبى *atiab*, (femin.) *tooba*, better.

طيب *teeb*, perfume.

طياب *tiyáb*, the pleasant north wind in Egypt.

طاب ـ يطيب *tába*, he recovered health; it was excellent; *yateeb*, he is doing well, recovers.

طيّب *tayyaba*, he ameliorated; perfumed.

طير *tair*, flight, act of flying; birds.

طائر ـ طيور or طير *táyir*, flying; pl. *toyoor*, or *tair*, bird.

طار ـ يطير *tára*, it flew; *yateer*, it flies.

طيّار *tayyár*, volatile; pedlar who has no fixed shop.

طيّارة *tayyára*, child's kite.

طيرة or طيرورة *taira*, or *tairoora*, inconstancy, lightness.

طيز *teez*, rump, buttocks.

طيش *taish*, lightness; a trifle.

[طرشة]

طائش *táyish*, silly, trifler.

طيف *taif*, ghost, spectre; prism.

طين ـ اطيان *teen*, pl. *atyán*, earth, soil, land.

اطيان *atyán*, lands, landed property. [اراضي]

طينة *teena*, earthy nature of man.

طيّان ـ طيّانة *tayyán*, pl. *tayyána*, hodman, carrier of mud, mortar, &c.

Z or DH.

ظ *Za.* Value = 900.

ظبط *zabt*, vulgar inaccuracy for ضبط

Z

ظباطة – ظباطة *zabáta* (vulgarism for *sabáta*), cluster of fruit, dates, bananas.

ظرف – ظروف *zarf*, pl. *zoroof*, envelope; saucer; space of time; preposition; incidents or circumstances of an occurrence.

في ظرف الشهر *fi zarf esh-shahr*, in the course of the month.

ظروف التهمة *zoroof et-tohma*, circumstances or details of a crime.

ظرافة *zaráfa*, elegance, delicacy, refinement.

ظريف *zareef*, elegant, refined.

مظروف *mazroof*, envelope, portfolio.

ظفر *zafira*, he conquered.

ظفر *zafar*, victory.

مظفر *mozaffar*, made victorious (by God); a title of the Sultan.

ظفر – اظافر *dofr*, pl. *adáfir*, nail of finger or toe; paw, talon, claw, hoof.

ظفرة *zafara*, weakness of the eyes.

ظل – اظلال *dill*, pl. *adlál*, shade, shadow.

مظل or ظلل *modill*, or *modallil*, shady, shaded.

ظلفة الباب *dalfat el-báb*, wing or fold of a door.

ظلم – ظالم *zolm*, tyranny; *zálim*, tyrant.

ظلم *zalama*, he tyrannised, defrauded.

مظلوم – مظاليم *mazloom*, pl. *mazáleem*, victimised, victim of tyranny.

تظلّم من *tazallama min*, he sought redress, complained of tyranny.

ظلمة *zolma*, darkness, obscurity.

اظلم *azlama*, it was dark.

مظلم *mozlim*, dark, obscure.

ظلام *zalám*, darkness, dark.

ظمى or ظمآن *zamia*, or *zamáán*, thirsty, eager.

ظنّ – يظنّ *zanna*, he thought; *yazonn*, he thinks.

ظنّ – ظنون *zann*, pl. *zonoon*, opinion, idea, thought.

ظانّ *zánn*, thinker, thinking.

انا ظانن *aná zánin* (colloquial for *zánn*), I am thinking, I think.

مظنون *maznoon*, thought of, presumed, suspected.

ظهر – يظهر *zahara*, it appeared, seemed; *yazhar*, it seems.

اظهر *azhara*, he showed.

ظهور *zohoor*, appearance, aspect; Epiphany.

ظاهر *záhir*, apparent, visible, exterior; it seems.

ظهورات *zohoorát*, emergencies, unforeseen; provisional.

مظهر *mazhar*, place of view, or of manifestation.

تظاهر *tazáhara*, it appeared.

ظهر ‎ dahr, pl. dohoor, back of the body, &c.; menses.

ظهار ‎ dihár, a revolting form of divorce.

ظهر ‎ - اظهار ‎ dohr, pl. adhár, noon, mid-day.

عند الظهر ‎ a'nd ed-dohr, at mid-day.

بعد الظهر ‎ ba'd ed-dohr, afternoon.

ظهريّة ‎ dohriya, the afternoon in general; just after mid-day.

ع ‎ 'Ain. Value = 70.

(A guttural hiatus with any vowel-sound, as 'a, 'ee, 'i, 'ō, 'u or a'i.)

عاج ‎ - عوج ‎ a'áj, ivory (see ō'j). [سنّ الفيل]

عون ‎ - عادة ‎ a'áda, habit, custom (see ō'd).

عار ‎ a'ár, shame. عور ‎ - عيرًا ‎

عوّة ‎ - عاهة ‎ a'áha, calamity (see a'wwaha).

عباء ‎ or عباية ‎ a'báya, warm cloak.

عبّى ‎ a'bba, he packed up, filled up a sack.

عبوة ‎ o'bowa, sack, sacking.

عبث ‎ a'bs, a trifle, nonsense; cause for regret; error in judgment.

عبد ‎ a'bada, he worshipped, slaved for.

عبادة ‎ i'báda, worship.

عابد ‎ a'ábid, worshipper.

عابدين ‎ a'ábideen, pl., worshippers; a district in Cairo, containing the Khedive's palace.

عبد ‎ - عبيد ‎ a'bd, pl. a'beed, domestic (negro) slave.

استعبد ‎ ista'bada, he enslaved.

معبد ‎ - معابد ‎ ma'bad, pl. ma'ábid, place of worship.

معبود ‎ ma'bood, worshipped; idol.

عبر ‎ a'bara, he passed.

عبّر ‎ a'bbara, he defined.

تعبير ‎ ta'beer, definition; style.

اعتبر ‎ ia'tabara, he considered, estimated.

اعتبار ‎ ia'tibár, consideration, respect, esteem.

عبارة ‎ i'bára, phrase; affair, matter in hand.

هي عبارة عن ‎ hia i'bárat a'n, it consists in, of.

معبر ‎ ma'bar, place of passing, passage way.

معتبر ‎ moa'tabar, one who is respected, respectable.

عبري ‎ or عبراني ‎ i'biriy, or i'brániy, Hebrew, hebraic.

عبّاس ‎ - عبّاسي ‎ 'Abbás, (1) the uncle of Mahomed, whose descendants founded the great dynasty of the 'Abbásiy or Abbaside Caliphs of Baghdád, 750-1260 A.D.; (2) a pasha of Egypt, d. 1854.

عبّاسيّة ‎ 'Abbásiya, a suburb to the N.E. of Cairo named after 'Abbas Pasha.

عبيط ‎ a'beet, young; foolish, imbecile.

اعتباطًا ‎ ia'tibátán, blindly, foolishly.

عَبْقَرِيّ *a'bqariy*, excellent, handsome; falsehood.

عَبْكَة *a'baka*, bale of cloth, parcel.

عَبْل ـ اَثْل *a'bl*, tamarisk (see *atl*).

عِتَاب *i'tāb*, blame.

اِعْتَاب ـ عَتَبَة *a'taba*, pl. *aa'tāb*, threshold, foot of throne.

مَعْتُوب *ma'toob*, blamed.

عَتْرَس *a'trasa*, he snatched, carried off.

عَتَق or اِعْتَق *a'taqa*, or *aa'taqa*, he freed a slave.

مَعْتُوق or مُعْتَق *ma'tooq*, or *mo'taq*, freed, enfranchised.

عَتَاق *i'tāq*, enfranchisement.

عَتِيق ـ عَنْقَاء *a'teeq*, pl. *o'taqā*, ancient, antique.

عَتَقَة *a'taqa*, Ataka, a cliff near Suez.

عَتَلَة *a'tala*, iron crowbar.

عَتَل *a'tala*, he carried.

عَتَّال *a'ttāl*, carrier, porter. [شَيَّال]

عَتْمَة *a'tma*, darkness, obscurity. [ظَلَام]

مُعْتِم *mo'tim*, dark.

عَتَه or عَتْهَة *a'tāhu*, or *a'tah*, madness, dementia.

مَعْتُوه *ma'tooh*, mad, insane, demented.

عُتَّة ـ عُثْث *u'tta*, pl. *u'tat*, moth, maggot.

عَثَر *a'tara*, he stumbled over, groped or searched for.

عُثْمَان *'Osmān*, (1) the third caliph; (2) the founder of the Ottoman dynasty.

عُثْمَانْلِي *'Osmānli* (Turkish), a Turk, Ottoman.

عُثْمَانِيّ *'Osmāniy*, Turk, Ottoman.

دَوْلَة عَلِيَّة عُثْمَانِيَّة *dawlat 'aliya 'Osmāniya*, the exalted Ottoman Empire.

عِجَّة *i'jja*, omelet.

تَعَجَّب or عَجِب *a'jiba*, or *ta'ajjaba*, he was astonished.

اَعْجَب *aa'jaba*, he preferred, it pleased him.

عَجِيبَة ـ عَجَائِب *a'jeeba*, pl. *a'jāyib*, wonderful.

مُتَعَجِّب *motaa'jjib*, astonished.

عَجُور *a'joor*, long pumpkin.

عَجَز عَن *a'jaza a'n*, he was wanting in, incapable, weak.

عَاجِز *a'ājiz*, wanting, helpless, feeble, blind.

عَجُوز *a'jooz*, old, feeble.

عَجْز *a'jz*, weakness; deficit in accounts.

عِجْز ـ اَعْجَاز *u'jz*, pl. *a'ajāz*, buttocks. [اَلْيَة]

مُعَجَّزَة *mo'ajjaza*, deficit in accounts.

مُعْجِزَة *mo'jiza*, miracle. [كَرَامَة]

اِسْتَعْجَل or عَجِل *a'jila*, or *ista'jala*, he was in haste.

عَجَّل *a'jjala*, he accelerated.

عَاجِل or مُسْتَعْجِل *a'ājil*, or *mosta'jil*, in haste, urgent.

عَجْلَة ـ عَجُول *a'jala*, haste; *a'jool*, impatient, hasty.

عِجْل ـ عُجُول *i'jl*, pl. *o'jool*, calf, young of animal.

عَجَلَة _ عِجَل a'jala, pl. a'jal, wheel.

عَجَم _ عَجَمِيّ _ اَعجام a'jam, foreign, non-Arab; Persia, the Persians; a'jamiy, Persian, a Persian; aa'jám, Persians.

عَجَمِي a'jamiy, novice, foreigner, Persian.

عَجَن a'jana, he made paste.

عَجِين a'jeen, dough.

مَعجُون ma'joon, paste, hasheesh paste; putty.

عِجَان e'ján, perinæum.

عَجوَة a'jwa, date-fruit paste; dates stuck together.

عِدَة _ وَعَد i'da, a promise (see wa'da).

عَدَّ a'dda, he counted.

تَعَدَّدَ taa'ddada, it became numerous.

عَدَّدَ a'ddada, he numbered, counted.

اِستَعَدَّ istaa'dda, he was ready, capable.

اِستِعدَاد istia'dád, readiness, fitness.

عَدَد _ اعداد a'dad, pl. aa'dád, number, quantity.

عِدَّة _ عِدَد i'dda, pl. i'ded, number, several; equipment, tools, apparatus; period of purification. [اِداة]

عِدَّة مِرَار i'ddet mirár, several times, often.

عَديد a'deed, numerous.

مُتَعَدِّد mutaa'ddid, numerous.

مُستَعِدّ musta'idd, ready, capable.

مُعَدّ moa'dd, or moi'dd, ready, set apart for.

المَحَلّ المُعَدّ لِذَلِك el-mahall el-moa'dd li-zálik, the place set apart or used for that.

مَعدُود ma'dood, counted.

مُعَدِّدَة moa'ddida, a paid female mourner, who *counts up*, or chants the praises of the dead.

تَعدَاد taa'dád, census.

عَدَس a'ds, lentils, vetch.

عَدل or عَدَالَة a'dl, or a'dála, equity, justice.

عَدَلِيّ a'dliy, relating to justice.

عَدَّل a'ddala, he modified, rectified.

تَعدِيل ta'deel, modification, rectification.

اِعتَدَل ia'tadala, he was moderate.

اِعتِدَال ia'tidál, moderation, equilibrium, symmetry; equinox, tropic.

عَدُول a'dool, rectification, change.

عَادِل _ عُدُول a'ádil, pl. o'dool, just, impartial.

عَدِيل a'deel, brother-in-law.

مُعَدِّل moa'ddil, rectifier; average.

مُعَادَلَة mo'ádala, algebraic equation.

عَدِمَ a'dima, it was *nil*, non-existent.

عَدَم a'dam, *nil*; non-; un-.

عَدَم ثُبُوت a'dam soboot, want of proof, no proof.

عَدَم حُضُور a'dam hodoor, non-presence, absence.

عَادِم or عَدِيم a'ádim, or a'deem, non-existent; lost; *minus*, without.

اعدم aa'dama, he annihilated, put to death.

اعدام ia'dám, sentence of death.

انعدم ina'dama, it was destroyed, was used up.

عدن 'Adan, Eden; town of Aden.

معدن - معادن ma'din, pl. ma'ádin, mine, mineral, ore.

معدنيّات ma'diniyát, minerals, metals.

عدوان o'dwán, hostility, enmity.

عدا a'da, he was hostile; he crossed over.

عداوة a'dáwa, enmity, hostility.

عدوّ - اعداء a'dōō, pl. aa'dá, enemy, hostile.

تعدّى على ta'adda aa'la, he showed enmity, annoyed, opposed, encroached.

تعدّي على taa'ddi a'la, opposition, annoyance, trespass.

متعدّي mutaa'ddi, annoying; transitive verb.

اعدى aa'da, it was infectious; passed across.

عدوى or عدوة a'dwa, infection.

معدي mo'di, infectious.

امراض معدية amrád mo'diya, infectious diseases.

عدى i'da, shore, bank.

معدى - معادي ma'da, pl. ma'ádi, ferry, place of crossing.

معدية ma'diya, ferry-boat.

معدّي mo-a'ddi, ferryman.

ما عدا má a'dá, except.

عذب a'zb, sweet, delicious.

عذاب a'záb, torture.

عذّب a'zzaba, he tortured.

تعذيب ta'zeeb, infliction of torture.

عذر a'zara, he excused. [cf. عزر

عذرة or عذر o'zr, or i'zra, an excuse.

اعتذر ia'tazara, he excused himself, apologised.

اعتذر هذا العذر ia'tazara haza el-o'zr, he put forward this excuse.

العذر اقبح من الذنب el-o'zr aqbah min ed-danb, the excuse (is) worse than the offence.

معذور ma'zoor, excused, excusable; allowance should be made for him.

عذرة - عذراء o'zra, virginity; a'zrá, virgin, Virgo of Zodiac.

عرب - اعراب a'rab, pl. aa'ráb, Arab.

عربان o'rbán, Arabs of the desert, Soudanese Arabs of the hills.

ابن عرب ibn a'rab, son of an Arab; hence, in Egypt, a free-born native Egyptian.

عربيّ a'rabiy, Arabic, Arabian.

عربيّة - عربه a'rabiya (Turkish a'raba), cart, cab, carriage.

عربه جي a'rabaji (Turkish), cabman, carman.

عربدة a'rabada, row, uproar.

عربون a'rboon, earnest-money, arrhes.

عرج a'raja, he climbed, ascended.

معراج mia'ráj, ascent of Mahomed to Heaven; ladder.

عرج (175) عرافة

عرج a'raja, he limped, was lame.

اعرج aa'raj, cripple, lame; knave in cards.

عرس 'irs, spouse.

عرس u'rs, gaiety of a wedding. [فرح]

عريس a'rees, bridegroom.

عروسة - عروس a'roos, (fem.) a'roosa, bridegroom, bride; "fiancé, fiancée."

عروسته a'roosatoh (a'roostoh), his bride, his "fiancée."

العروسان el-a'roosain, the newly-married couple.

معرس mo-a'rras, cuckold, pimp.

عرسة i'rsa, weasel.

عرش a'rsh, throne. [كرسي - اريكة]

عريش a'reesh, shafts of a carriage.

العريش El-'Areesh, village of El-'Areesh on the Syro-Egyptian frontier.

عرصة a'rsa, open space, court-yard. [ساحة]

عرض a'rada, it happened, came athwart.

عارض a'árid, happening; cross-beam.

عارضة - عوارض a'árida, pl. a'wárid, accident. [قضاء - حادثة]

عرض a'rada, he presented a petition, pleaded; exposed, showed, set forth.

اعرض عن aa'rada a'n he turned himself aside, abandoned a plan.

عارض a'árada, he objected, opposed (in law).

اعترض ia'tarada, he objected.

تعرّض taa'rrada, he put himself in the way, tried to thwart.

استعراض istia'rád, review, parade.

عرض a'rd, offer, plea; (vulgarism for i'rd).

عرض - اعراض i'rd, pl. aa'rád, honour, modesty.

هتك العرض hatk el-i'rd, indecent assault (legal term).

عرض a'rd, width, breadth.

عريض a'reed, wide, broad.

عريضة a'reeda, petition; officer's commission of rank.

عروض a'rood (femin.), prosody, metre.

عرضحال a'rduhál (mostly used in Turkish), petition.

عرضحالجي a'rduhálji (Turkish), professional writer of petitions for illiterate persons.

معرض ma'rad, place of showing, exhibition.

معروض ma'rood, petition; half-witted, cracked.

معارضة mo'-árada, opposition (in law) against a sentence rendered in default.

عرف a'rafa, he knew. [علم]

عرفان i'rfán, knowledge.

عرافة i'ráfa, fortune-telling. [عيّنة]

عرفة ‎a'rafa,‎ vigil of feast of qorban or ‎adha,‎ on 9th of ‎Zil-Hijja;‎ hill, crest.

عرفات ‎a'rafát,‎ hill of recognition, Mount Arafat, near Mecca.

عرفيّ ‎o'rfiy,‎ arbitrary, unjust; customs not based on law or piety; private, unofficial.

عارف ‎a'árif,‎ knowing, aware of, wise.

عرّف ‎a'rrafa,‎ he informed, defined.

تعريف ‎ta'reef,‎ definition, tariff.

تعريفة ‎ta'reefa,‎ tariff.

اعترف ‎ia'tarafa,‎ he confessed.

اعتراف ‎ia'tiráf,‎ confession.

تعرّف ‎ta'arrafa,‎ he came to know.

استعرف ‎ista'rafa,‎ he recognised, identified.

عريف ‎a'reef,‎ school-monitor.

عرف البلد ‎o'rf el-balad,‎ local custom or usage.

معرفة ـ معارف ‎ma'rifa,‎ pl. ‎ma'árif,‎ science, knowledge; means, instrumentality.

بمعرفة البوليس ‎bi-ma'rifat el-bolees,‎ by means of the police. [واسطة]

معارف عمومية ‎ma'árif o'moomiya,‎ public instruction.

معرّف ‎mo-a'rrif,‎ inspector; toll-keeper.

معروف ‎ma'roof,‎ known; kindness, favour.

اعمل معروف ‎aa'mil ma'roof,‎ please! do the favour!

معرفة ‎ma'rafa,‎ horse's name.

عرق ‎a'riqa,‎ he sweated.

عرق ‎a'raq,‎ sweat; arrack, distilled liquor.

عرقيّة ‎a'raqiya,‎ skull-cap.

عرقان ‎a'rqán,‎ in a sweat, perspiring.

عرق ـ عروق ‎i'rq,‎ pl. ‎o'rooq,‎ vein, fibre; beam.

عرق السوس ‎i'rq es-soos,‎ liquorice-water.

عروق الشام ‎o'rooq esh-shám,‎ beams, poles, rafters, Syrian timber.

عراق عربيّ ‎i'ráq a'rabiy,‎ Mesopotamia.

عرك ‎a'raka,‎ he rubbed.

عارك ‎a'áraka,‎ he fought with.

معاركة ـ معركة ‎mo'áraka,‎ battle, ‎ma'raka,‎ battle-field.

عرّم ‎a'rrama,‎ he heaped up.

عرمة ـ عرم ‎o'rma,‎ pl. ‎a'ram,‎ heap.

عرا ‎a'ra,‎ it happened.

اعترى ‎ia'tara,‎ he seized, afflicted.

معتريه المرض ‎mo'atarihi el-marad,‎ his being afflicted with disease.

عروة ‎o'rwa,‎ button-hole.

عري ‎a'ri,‎ fellah's smock frock; "galabiya."

عري ‎a'ria,‎ he was naked, it was bare.

عرّي ‎arra,‎ he stripped, made bare.

عرية ‎o'ria,‎ nakedness.

عريان ‎o'rián,‎ naked.

عاري ‎a'ári,‎ bare, devoid, destitute of.

مُعَرَّى *moa'rra*, stripped, bared.

عَزَّ *a'zza*, it was noble, mighty, precious.

عِزَّةٌ or عِزّ *i'zz*, or *i'zza*, nobility, power; prime, intensity.

عِزّ الشِّتَاء *i'zz esh-shitá*, depth of winter.

عِزَّتلُو ـ سعادتلو *i'zzetlu*, Turkish title for the lower rank of bey, inferior to *sa'ádetlu*.

عَزِيز *a'zeez*, noble, mighty, precious, beloved.

عَزَّزَ *a'zzaza*, he ennobled, corroborated evidence.

مُعَزَّز *moa'zzaz*, corroborated (evidence).

أَعَزّ *aa'zz*, nobler, grander.

عَزَب *a'zab*, unmarried, celibate, solitary.

عُزُوبَة *o'zooba*, celibacy.

عَازِب ـ عَانِس *a'ázib*, widower; *a'ánis*, bachelor.

عَازِبَة *a'áziba*, unprotected female, divorced woman.

عَزْبَة ـ عَزْب *a'zba*, pl. *a'zab*, hamlet, village, farm.

عَزَّر or عَزَر *a'zara*, he blamed. [cf. عذر

عَزْر *a'zr*, blame.

تَعْزِير *ta'zeer*, blame, reprimand, punishment.

عَزْرَائِل *A'zráyeel*, the Angel of death.

عَزْف *a'zf*, music, sound.

عَزَقَ ـ مِعْزَقَة *a'zaqa*, he dug; *miu'zaqa*, hoe, spade.

عَزِيق *a'zeeq*, a digging, dug.

عَزَل *a'zala*, he dismissed; removed to another house.

عَزْل ـ عُزْلَة *a'zl*, dismissal; *ozla*, retirement, idleness.

عَزْلَة *a'zala*, family furniture for removal.

اِعْتَزَل *i'atazala*, he dissented, kept aloof.

مَعْزُول *ma'zool*, dismissed.

عَزَم *a'zama*, he decided; invited a guest.

أَنَا عَازِم *aná a'ázim*, I intend to.

عَزُومَة or عَزِيمَة *a'zeema*, or *a'zooma*, invitation, incantation, banquet, evening party.

عَزَى *a'za*, he accused, imputed, referred.

أَعْزَ or عَزْى *a'za*, grief, accusation; funeral.

عَزَّى *a'zza*, he condoled with.

تَعْزِيَة *ta'ziya*, sympathy, condolence; funeral.

مَعْزَاة *ma'za*, mourning for the dead.

عَسَر *a'sara*, it was difficult, strait.

عُسْرَة *o'sra*, difficulty, restraint.

عَسِير *a'seer*, difficult.

أَعْسَر *aa'sara*, he became insolvent.

إِعْسَار *ia'sár*, insolvency, in straits for money.

مُعْسِر *moa'sir*, insolvent.

مُعْسِر و مُوسِر *moa'sir wa moosir*, insolvent and solvent. [يسر

عَسْكَر ـ عَسَاكِر *a'skar*, army; *a'sákir*, troops.

A A

عسكريّ *a'skariy*, military, soldier, policeman.

عسكر *a'sker*, (in Turkish) a soldier.

لشكر - العسكر *lashkar* (Persian), army, "lascar," probably origin of *el-a'skar*.

معسكر *moa'skar*, camp.

عسل *'asal*, honey.

عسى *a'sa*, perhaps; I hope so; it is possible.

عشّة - عشاش *e'shsha*, pl. *i'shséh*, straw hut; nest.

عشب *o'shb*, green vegetation, grass.

عشر - عشرة *a'shara*, (fem.) *a'shr*, ten.

عشرون - عشرين *i'shroon*, or (colloquial) *a'shreen*, twenty.

عشر - عشور or اعشار *o'shr*, pl. *o'shoor*, or *áa'shár*, one-tenth part; tithes.

عشر *o'shar*, asclepias gigantea, calotropis procera.

عاشر *a'áshir*, the tenth in order.

عشوري *o'shooriy*, land paying tithes.

اعشاري *aa'sháriy*, decimal.

عاشوراء *a'ashoorá*, Feast of the 10th day of Moharram.

عاشورة *a'áshoora*, Arab plum-pudding.

عشيرة - عشائر *a'sheera*, pl. *a'sháyir*, small tribe; family. [قبيلة]

عشرة *i'shra*, gaiety, intimacy.

عاشر *a'áshara*, he was intimate, sociable.

معاشرة *mo'áshara*, intimacy.

اشعار *i'shár*, pregnancy of animals; being in foal, &c.

عشرة *i'shra*, an animal in foal or in calf, &c.

عشق *a'shiqa*, he loved (sexually).

عشق *i'shq*, sexual love.

عشيق or عاشق or عشّق *a'sheeq*, or *a'áshiq*, or *a'shsháq*, a lover.

معشوقة *ma'shooqa*, the woman beloved, sweetheart.

عشم *a'sham*, hope, longing. [امل]

عشم or تعشم *a'shima*, or *ta'ashshama*, he hoped for, coveted, longed for.

عشّم *a'shshama*, he made hope, encouraged.

متعشّم *mota'ashshim*, hopeful.

عشا *a'shá*, supper, evening meal.

عشيّة or عشا *i'shá*, or *a'shiya*, nightfall; after sunset; evening prayer.

تعشّى *ta'ashsha*, he passed the evening, supped.

عشاوة *a'sháwa*, dimness of sight by night.

عصعص or صص *o'so's*, tail-bone; coccyx.

عصب - اعصاب *a'sab*, pl. *a'asáb*, nerve.

عصابة *i'sába*, bandage.

عصب *a'saba*, he bound up, girded.

تعصّب *ta'assaba*, he bound himself, became rigid, fanatic.

عصبة *a'sba*, woman's kerchief.

عصب - عصبة *o'sba*, pl. *o'sab*, clique, gang.

عصبجي *o'sbaji*, a ruffian, one of a gang.

عصبات - عصبة *a'saba*, pl. *a'sabát*, father's relatives; agnates, residuaries.

عصبيّة *a'sabiya*, relationship of agnates.

عصيدة *a'sceda*, paste, starch; butter.

عصر *a'sr*, afternoon; 3 p.m.

عصر - اعصار *a'sr*, pl. *aa'sár*, epoch, century.

معاصر *mo'ásir*, contemporary.

عصّر *a'ssara*, he squeezed, distilled.

عصير *a'seer*, juice.

معصرة - معاصر *ma'sara*, pl. *ma'ásir*, pressing-machine.

عاصف *a'ásif*, violent, high, stormy.

عصفر *o'sfor*, carthamus. [قرطم]

عصفور - عصافير *o'sfoor*, pl. *a'sáfeer*, finch, sparrow.

عصمة *i'sma*, chastity. [عفّة]

عصمتلو *i'smatlu*, chaste; being the Turkish title for a princess.

عاصم *a'ásim*, chaste.

عاصمة *a'ásima*, chaste woman; capital town; an untaken fortress, "*pucelle;*" a title of Cairo.

معصوم *ma'soom*, infallible; above suspicion; not an outlaw, but in the enjoyment of civil rights.

معصم - معاصم *miu'sam*, pl. *ma'ásim*, wrist. [كرسوع]

عصا - عصيّ *a'sá*, pl. *o'siy* (femin.), stick, cane.

عصاية or عصاية *a'sáya*, stick, cane.

عصى *a'sa*, he revolted.

عصيان *'isyán*, revolt, mutiny.

عاصي - عصاة *a'ási*, pl. *o'sát*, rebel.

عضّ *a'dda*, he bit.

عضّة *a'dda*, a bite.

معضوض *ma'dood*, bitten.

عضد - اعضاد *a'dud*, pl. *aa'dád*, upper half of arm; help, succour.

ساعد *sáyi'd*, fore-arm, help, succour. [ذراع]

عضلة *a'dala*, muscle.

عضال *u'dál*, incurable.

عضو - اعضاء *a'dw*, pl. *aa'dá*, limb of body, member.

هو من اعضاء المجلس *hoa min aa'dá el-majlis*, he is (one) of the members of the council.

عطر - عطور *i'tr*, pl. *o'toor*, perfume, otto, *attar*.

عطّر *a'ttara*, he perfumed.

عطّار *a'ttár*, seller of perfumes, spices, drugs.

عطارد *o'tárid*, planet Mercury.

عطس *a'tasa*, he sneezed.

عطاس *u'tás*, a sneeze, sneezing.

عطش *a'tash*, thirst.

عطشان *a'tshán*, thirsty.

عطف *a'tafa*, he turned aside, leaned.

عطفة (180) عفق

عطفة a'tfa, side, by-street, lane.

عاطفة a'átifa, sympathy, leaning towards.

عطوفة u'toofa, benevolence, condescension.

عطوفتلو u'toofatlu (Turkish) title for Ministers of State and civilians of Bálá rank, condescending, gracious.

عطل o'tl, delay, obstruction, idleness, deprivation.

عطّل a'ttala, he hindered, obstructed; took holiday, procrastinated.

تعطيل ta'teel, holiday, off-day; injury caused by obstruction or delay; workmen's strike.

معطّل mo'attal, deserted, idle, shut up; rendered useless, injured.

عطن a'tana, it became spoiled, went bad (e.g. wine, water, &c.).

عطايا - عطيّة - اعطية or (2) عطاء a'tá, pl. aa'tiya; or (2) a'tiya, pl. a'táyá, gift.

اعطى - اعطاء a'ata, he gave; ia'tá, a giving.

اخذ و اعطاء akhz wa ia'tá, a taking and giving, trade, business.

معطي mo'ti, giver, God the Giver.

تعاطى táa'ta, he exchanged gifts; disputed, quarrelled, undertook, exercised.

تعاطى صناعته táa'ta sanáa'taho, he exercised his profession.

عظمة a'zama, grandeur; greatness.

عظيم - عظام a'zeem, pl. i'zám, grand, splendid; great, first-rate, capital.

والله العظيم walláhi el-a'zeem, by the Almighty God! the usual Moslem oath.

اعظم - عظمى aa'zam, (femin.) o'zma, greater, greatest.

بريطانيا العظمى Britániá el-o'zma, Great Britain.

صدر اعظم sadr aa'zam, the noblest source of power, the Grand Vizier.

عظّم a'zzama, he ennobled, magnified.

تعظيم ta'zeem, an ennobling, magnifying.

معظّم moa'zzam, exalted, imperial.

معظّمة moa'zzama, magnifying-glass.

عظم - عظام a'dthm, pl. ia'dthám, bone.

معظم mo'zam, majority, greater part.

عفّة - عفيف or عفوف iffa, chastity; a'feef, or a'foof, chaste.

عفرة a'fara, dust.

عفريت - عفاريت a'freet, pl. a'fáreet, demon, cunning.

عفش a'fsh, baggage, luggage.

عفص a'fs, gall-nut.

عفص a'fasa, he seized, flung, wrung.

عفق a'faqa, he seized, arrested.

[قفش

عفونة or عفن *a'fun*, or *o'foona*, stench of mildew.

تعفن *tu'affana*, it smelt rotten, decayed.

عفن *a'fin*, infectious disease. [عدوى

عفوني *o'fooniy*, malarious, pestilential.

عفا عن ـ يعفو *a'fá 'an*, he pardoned; *ya'foo* he pardons.

عفو *a'fw*, pardon.

عفو *a'foo*, merciful, pardoner.

استعفى *ista'fa*, he asked pardon, begged to be excused, resigned his post.

استعفا *istee'fá*, an asking pardon; resignation.

عافية *a'áfiya*, good health.

معافاة *mo'áfát*, exemption.

معفو or معاف *mo'áf*, or *ma'foo*, pardoned, exempted.

عقيق *a'qeeq*, agate, cornelian; a harbour near Suakin.

عقب *a'qaba*, he overtook, trod on one's heels.

عقب ـ عقبى *o'qb*, end; *o'qba*, retribution.

عقب ـ اعقاب *a'qb*, or *a'qib*, pl. *aa'qáb* (femin.), heel, axis, pivot, hinge.

عقبه *a'qiboh*, its heel, immediately after it, thereupon.

عقبة *o'qba*, once, one time.

عقيب or عاقب *a'áqib*, or *a'qeeb*, next after, successor.

عواقب ـ عاقبة *a'áqiba*, pl. *a'wáqib*, end, result.

عقبة *a'qaba*, hill; A'qaba, a place at the end of the narrow gulf on the eastern side of the Sinai Peninsula.

عقبة *a'qaba*, A monster barge dressed up as a ship at the ceremony of the cutting of the Khaleej or Canal of Cairo.

عقاب *o'qáb*, eagle. [نسر

عاقب *a'áqaba*, he punished (by legal sentence).

عوقب *o'oqiba*, he was punished (by legal sentence).

يعاقب *yo'áqab*, he shall be punished, is liable to be punished; it is punishable.

عقاب or معاقبة *i'qáb*, or *mo'áqaba*, punishment.

عقوبة ـ عقوبات *o'qooba*, pl. *o'qoobát*, punishment.

قانون العقوبات *qánoon el-o'qoobát*, Penal Code.

عقد *a'qada*, he knotted, contracted, made a contract; (the priest) united in marriage; (the liquid) congealed; it hardened.

عقد ـ عقود *a'qd*, pl. *o'good*, knot, contract, agreement. [عهد

عقد عرفي *a'qd o'rfiy*, private contract, *sous seing privé*.

عقدة ـ عقد *o'qda*, pl. *o'qad*, knot, plexus, joint, ganglion.

عقد *i'qd*, necklace.

عقاد *a'qqád*, lace-maker; knotter, maker of fringe and tassels.

عقيدة *a'qeeda*, creed.

تَعاقَد ta'áqada, he made a contract (mutually).

مُتَعاقِدين mota'áqideen, the contracting parties.

اِعْتَقَد ia'taqada, he tied himself to, believed in.

اِعْتِقاد ia'tiqád, belief in, reliance upon, "bona fides."

اِنْعَقَد ina'qada, it was knotted, assembled; it congealed, coagulated.

اِنْعِقاد المَجْلِس ina'qád el-majlis, the coming together of a council.

عَقْر o'qr, sterility. [عقم]

عاقِر a'áqir, sterile.

عَقار ـ عَقارات a'qár, pl. a'qárát, landed property.

البَنك العَقاري el-bank el-a'qáriy, land-bank, crédit foncier.

عَقّار ـ عَقاقير a'qqár, pl. a'qáqeer, drug, herb; simples.

عَقْرَب ـ عَقارِب 'aqrab, pl. a'qárib, scorpion; Scorpio of the Zodiac; hand of a clock, or watch.

عَقل ـ عُقول a'ql, pl. o'qool, mind, intelligence.

عَقْلًا aqlán, with reason, in reason.

عَقْلي a'qliy, intellectual, of the intellect.

عَقَل a'qala, he could think, conceive an idea; he tethered an animal.

لا يَعْقَل lá yo'qal, it is inconceivable, absurd.

عاقِل ـ عُقّال a'áqil, pl. o'qqál intelligent, clever.

عُقّال o'qqál, Druse priests, initiated men.

مَعقول ma'qool, intelligible; metaphysic.

عِقال i'qál, halter; foot-rope, tether; head-band.

عُقْلة o'qla, a knot in bamboo or cane.

أعْقَل ـ عَقْلاء aa'qal, (femin.) a'qlá, more intelligent.

عُقْم o'qm, sterility. [عقر]

عَقيم a'qeem, sterile.

عَكّة or عَكّا A'kká, Acre, a port in Syria.

عَكَر or عَكار a'kar or a'kár, sediment, dregs. [رسوب]

عَكروت a'kroot, cuckold, pimp.

عَكْس a'ks, upside down, reverse, wrong way round; back again.

بِالعَكْس bil-a'ks, on the contrary; vice versá.

اِنْعَكَس in'akasa, it was reversed.

مَعْكوس ma'koos, upside down, reversed.

عاكَس a'ákasa, he opposed, ran counter to, annoyed.

عاكِف ـ اِنْعَكَف a'ákif, persevering; ina'kafa, he persevered.

اِعْتَكَف ia'takafa, he prayed in seclusion.

عَكّام a'kkám, head camel man, leader of caravan.

عَكامة o'káma, muzzle, bridle.

عِكن ـ اعكان o'kan, or aa'kán, folds, wrinkles of the hips.

عِلّة ـ عِلَل i'lla, pl. i'lal, defect, disease; excuse.

عليل a'leel, unwell.

تعلّل taa'llala, he hesitated, made excuses.

معتلّ mo'tall, diseased, weak.

علبة ـ علاب u'lba, pl. i'láb, casket, small box.

علس a'lasa, he fought, beat.

علج ـ عالج (a'laja) - a'álaja, he treated medically.

علاج or معالجة i'láj, or mo'álaja, medical treatment.

علف a'laf, fodder, forage, hay. [grain = عليق

علّاف a'lláf, seller of hay or forage.

علق a'liqa, it hung, was in suspension.

علقت a'liqat, she conceived. [حبلت

علّق a'llaqa, he hanged up; (شنق) (shanaqa), he hanged (a murderer).

تعلّق ta'allaqa, he, it was attached, belonged to.

علاقة i'láqa, affection, attachment.

علق i'lq, unnatural love; sodomite.

علقة ـ علق a'laqa, pl. a'laq, leech.

علوق o'looq, conception, pregnancy. [حبل

عليق a'leeq, grain for horses. [hay = علف

علقة a'lqa, a couple of camels; a good flogging.

تعلّق ta'alluq, property of, belonging to.

تعليق ta'leeq, a hanging up; style of handwriting.

متعلّق mota'alliq, belonging to, dependent.

علقم a'lqam, colocynth, bryony, momordica elaterium.

علم a'lima, he knew. [عرف

أعلم a'alama, he informed, delivered judgment.

علّم a'llama, he taught, drilled.

تعلّم ta'allama, he learned.

استعلم ista'lama, he inquired. [استفهم

علم ـ علوم i'lm, pl. o'loom, science; -ology.

علم خبر i'lm khabar, receipt, memo.

دار العلوم dár el-o'loom, the ecclesiastical college at Cairo for students from the El-Azhar Mosque.

عليم ـ علماء a'leem, pl. u'lemá, learned, wise.

علماء u'lemá, Moslem priesthood, learned divines.

عالم a'álim, he who knows; wise.

عالمة ـ عوالم a'álima, pl. a'wálim, learned or wise woman; but only applied to a woman clever in singing; an "almeh," or singing girl (not dancing girl).

علم ـ أعلام a'lem, pl. aa'lám, flag.

اسم علم ism a'lem, a proper noun (grammatical term).

علامة ـ علامات a'láma, pl. a'lámát, sign, mark.

علّامة or علّام *a'llám*, or *a'lláma*, very learned, a title of divines or "*u'lemá.*"

اعلام شرعى *ia'lám shara'iy*, a judgment pronounced by a *Sheri'* tribunal.

عالم - عالمون *a'álem*, pl. *a'álemoon*, the universe.

تعليم *ta'leem*, teaching, instruction; drill.

تعليمات *ta'leemát*, instructions.

معلّم *mo-a'llim*, teacher, foreman.

معلوم *ma'loom*, known, of course! active voice of a verb.

معلوميّة *ma'loomiya*, information, knowledge.

علن *a'lana*, it was publicly known, open to the public.

اعلن *aa'lana*, he announced, advertised.

اُعلن *o'lina*, it was announced.

اعلان - اعلانات *ia'lán*, pl. *ia'lanát*, advertisement.

علنا or علانيةً *a'lanán*, or *a'lániyatán*, publicly.

علنى *a'laniy*, public, in public.

علا or تعالى *a'lá*, or *ta'ála*, it was high.

الله تعالى *Allah ta'ála*, God the High! how great He is!

علوّ or علاء *a'lá*, or *o'loo*, grandeur, height.

علىّ *a'liy*, noble, high; Ali.

دولة عليّة *dawlat a'liya*, the exalted empire, Turkey.

عالى or عال *a'áli*, or *a'ál*, noble, sublime; first-rate.

امر عالى or عالى *amr a'áli*, high order, Khedivial decree.

باب عالى *báb a'áli*, Sublime Porte.

علاوة *i'láwa*, surplus.

اعلى - عليا *a'ala*, (femin.) *u'lyá*, higher, upper.

على *u'la*, upon, at, against, according to.

تعال - ت *ta'ála*, come thou! for تى *ti*, which is the unused imperative of اتى

عمّ *a'mma*, it was universal, public.

عامّ - عامّة الناس *a'ámm*, common, public; *a'ámmat en-nás*, the general public.

عموم - عمومى *o'moom*, totality, generality; *o'moomiy*, general, public.

عميم *a'meem*, public, general.

عمامة - عمائم *i'máma*, pl. *a'máyim*, turban.

عمّ - عمّة *a'mm*, (femin.) *a'mma*, paternal uncle; aunt; patron or master.

ابن عمّه *ibn a'mmoh*, his cousin, uncle's son.

تعميم *tameem*, generalisation.

عمد *a'mada*, he propped up, intended, purposed.

عمد - عمدًا *a'md*, purpose; *a'mdán*, on purpose. [قصد]

تعمّد *ta'ammada*, he intended, determined.

اعتمد على i'tamada a'la, he relied upon, confided in.

عمود or عمود or عماد 'imád, or a'ámood, pillar, column.

اعمدة or عمد 'omod, or 'amad, or a'amida, pillars.

عمدة ‑ عمد 'omda, pl. 'omad, the officially recognised sheikh of a village.

عامودي a'ámoodiy, upright, perpendicular.

معتمد عليه moa'tamad 'aleih, trustworthy, trusted in.

عمر ‑ اعمار 'omr, pl. aa'már, age in years; lifetime.

عمرة 'omra, minor pilgrimage to Mecca.

عمر ‑ عمرو 'Omar, and 'Amroo, names for men.

عمران 'omrán, culture.

عمارة 'imára, cultivation, signs of life; fleet, expedition; edifice, repairs.

عامر a'ámir, flourishing, prosperous.

عمر 'ammara, he repaired; loaded a gun.

تعمير ta'meer, repairs; loading a gun.

معمر mo'ammar, repaired; loaded.

معمار mia'már, architect. [مهندس]

استعمر ista'mara, he colonised.

مستعمرات musta'marát, colonies.

عمش ‑ اعمش 'amash, blearness; aa'mash, blear-eyed.

عمق ‑ عميق o'mq, depth; 'ameeq, deep. [غمق]

عمل 'amila, he did, made. [فعل]

اعمل aa'mala, he caused to be done.

عامل a'ámala, he treated or behaved to.

استعمل ista'mala, he used, employed.

تعامل ta'ámala, he did business with, contracted with.

عمل ‑ اعمال 'amal, pl. aa'mál, work, act, deed.

عملية 'amaliya, work, practice, experience; surgical operation; medicine, purge.

عامل ‑ عملة 'aámil, pl. 'amala, doer, workman.

عملة 'omla, cash.

عمّال 'ammál, doing, in the act of doing; 'ommál, workmen.

عميل 'ameel, commission agent, broker.

عمولة 'omoola, commission, percentage, brokerage.

معمل ‑ معامل maa'mal, pl. ma'ámil, factory, workshop.

معاملة mo'ámala, treatment, conduct.

استعمال istia'mál, use, usage, employment.

مستعمل mosta'mal, used; second-hand; boatswain.

معمول ma'mool, done, executed, carried out.

قانون معمول به qánoon ma'mool bihi, a law in vigour.

عمان 'Omán, province of Muscat in E. Arabia.

D B

عمى - عميان 'ama, blindness; 'amyán, blind.

اعمى - عمياء - عمى aa'ma, (femin.) 'amyá, pl. 'omi, blind.

معمّى mo'amma, enigma, mystery.

عن 'an, out of, from, instead.

عمّا - عن ما 'an-má, written 'ammá, from that which.

عنان - عنن 'inán, pl. 'onon, reins.

عنّينة - عنين 'inneen, impotent; 'anína, impotence.

عنب - اعناب 'inab, pl. aa'náb, grape; vine. [كرم]

عنّاب 'onnáb, jujube.

عنبر 'anbar, ambergris.

عنبري 'anbariy, aromatic; raki.

عنبر - عنابر 'anbar, pl. 'anábir, barn, magazine. [انبار]

عنتري 'antariy, bodice, sleeved waistcoat.

عند 'and, at, near, with, upon, "chez."

عندي 'andi, with me, I have.

عندك 'andak, with thee, thou hast; stop!

عند الظهر 'and ed-dohr, at midday.

عند اللزوم 'and el-lozoom, in case of necessity.

عناد 'inád, obstinacy.

عنيد or عاند 'aneed, or a'ánid, obstinate.

عندليب - عنادل 'andaleeb, pl. 'anádil, nightingale. [بلبل]

عنز 'anz, she-goat.

عانس (عنس) ('anas), a'ánis, bachelor. [عزب]

عنصر - عناصر 'onsor, pl. 'anásir, element, principle of nature.

عنصرة 'ansara, Pentecost.

عنف 'anf, cruelty; violence; in turn.

عنيف 'aneef, cruel, violent.

عنق - اعناق 'onoq, pl. aa'náq, neck, throat. [cf. قفا]

تعانق or عانق a'ánaqa, or ta'ánaqa, he embraced.

عناق or معانقة 'ináq, or mo'ánaqa, caress, embrace.

عنقود 'onqood, cluster, bunch.

عنكبوت - عناكب 'ankaboot, pl. 'anákib, spider.

بيت العنكبوت bait el-'ankaboot, spider's web.

عنوان 'onwán, frontispiece, address of letter.

معنون ma'nwin, addressed (letter).

عنى 'ana, it meant, signified.

اعني or يعني aa'ni, or ya'ni, that is to say; viz.; it meant, it means.

معنى - معاني ma'na, pl. ma'áni, meaning, rhetoric.

علم المعاني 'ilm el-ma'áni, rhetoric.

اعتنى ia'tana, he was careful, anxious for.

عناية 'ináya, kindness, care for.

معنوي ma'nawiy, allegoric, unreal, virtual.

عهد 'ahida, he made a treaty or contract. [عقد]

عهد ـ عهود 'ahd, pl. 'ohood, treaty contract; will, testament; Old or New Testament of the Bible.

ولّي العهد waliy el-'ahd, heir-apparent.

عهدة 'ohda, responsibility, charge; also sometimes, the person responsible, as a sergeant of ghafeers; obsolete form of grant of lands in *fief*.

عاهد or تعاهد a'áhada, or ta'áhada, he made a treaty (mutually).

تعهّد ta'ahhada, he made a contract, undertook.

تعهّدات و عقود ta'ahhudát wa 'oqood, contracts and obligations.

متعهّد muta'ahhid, a contractor, responsible under contract. [مقاول]

معاهدة mo'áhada, treaty.

معهود ma'hood, contracted, provided for.

غير معهود ghair ma'hood, unexpected, not provided for, unforeseen.

عاهرة ـ عواهر a'áhira, pl. 'awáhir, whore.

عوج 'ōj, curvature.

عوج or تعوّج 'awija, or ta'awwaja, it was bent.

عوج 'awaj, curvature, curve.

اعوج aa'waj, cripple, crooked, drooping.

عاج a'áj, ivory, *bent* tooth of elephant.

عويجة 'awaija, a kind of *drooping* maize, or millet. [ذرّة]

عود 'ōd, a return, repetition, *recidive* in crime.

عودة 'awda, return, coming back.

عود ـ عيدان 'ood, pl. 'eedán, guitar, baton; a piece of sugar-cane; aloes.

عاد a'áda, he returned, came back; he did again, repeated. [رجع]

اعاد aa'áda, he came back, sent back, returned, repeated, restored.

أعيد oo'eeda, it was returned, repeated.

عوّد 'awwada, he made accustomed.

اعتاد or تعوّد ia'táda, or ta'awwada, he became accustomed.

عادة ـ عادات a'áda, pl. a'ádát, custom, habit.

عادي a'ádiy, usual, customary.

اعتياد ia'tiyád, custom, use, habit.

اعتيادي ia'tiyádiy, customary, usual.

اعادة ia'áda, repetition, a making return.

عيادة 'iyáda, a visiting the sick.

عائد a'áyid, returner, repeater; *recidiviste* in crime.

عائدة ـ عوائد a'áyida, pl. 'awáyid, tax, fee, profit.

عيد ـ اعياد 'eed, pl. aa'yád, fête, festival.

معتاد moa'tád, usual, customary.

عون بالله 'ōz billáhi, refuge in God.

تعوّذ ta'awwaza, he sought refuge.

تعويذ ta'weez, refuge, protection; amulet.

معاذ الله ma'áz Alláh, God forbid!

عور 'awar, loss of an eye; injury.

اَعْوَر (188) مَعْوَنَة

اَعْوَر *aa'war*, one-eyed.

عَوَّرَ *'awwara*, he injured, spoilt.

عَوْرَة *'awra*, nakedness, pudenda.

عَايَر ـ عَار *a'ár*, shame; *a'áyara*, he put to shame.

اَعَار ـ اِعَارَة *aa'ára*, he lent (money); *ia'ára*, loan.

عَارِيَّة ـ عَوَارِي *a'áriya*, pl. *'awáriy*, loan.

اِسْتَعَار *istaa'ára*, he borrowed.

مُسْتَعِير *mosta'yeer*, borrower.

عَوِز *'awiza*, he needed; wished for.

عَوِز or عَائِز *'awuz*, or *a'áyiz*, he who needs, wishes.

عوز or عَائِزْ اَنَا *aná a'áyiz*, or *'awuz*, I want, I wish.

عِوَض *'öd*, or *'iwad*, exchange, instead of.

عِوَضًا عَنْ ذَلِكَ *'iwadán 'an zálik*, instead of that.

عَاضَ *a'áda*, he gave in exchange.

عَوَّض *'awwada*, he indemnified, compensated.

تَعْوِيضَات *ta'weedát*, damages (in law), compensation.

عَاوَض *a'áwada*, he exchanged.

عِوَاض or مُعَاوَضَة *'iwád*, or *mo'áwada*, exchange.

اِسْتَعْوَض *ista'wada*, he appointed a substitute; replaced, gave instead.

عَوْف *'öf*, chance, condition. [عَيْف

عِيَافَة *'iyáfa*, fortune-telling.

عَوْق ـ عَاق *'öq*, obstacle; *'awwaqa*, he hindered.

تَعْوِيق *ta'weeq*, a causing delay, hindering.

تَعَوَّق or عَاق *a'áqa*, or *ta'awwaqa*, he loitered, was late.

عَائِق *a'áyiq*, hindering; rakish, debauchee.

عَوْل *'öl*, shriek, moan; misfortune.

عِوَل *'iwal*, confidence; cry for help.

عَوْل or عُوول *'u-ool*, paucity of an inheritance, insufficient for all the heirs.

عَوَّلَ عَلَى *'awwala 'ala*, he relied upon, believed in.

تَعْوِيل *ta'weel*, confidence, belief in.

عَيِّل ـ عِيَال *'ayyil*, pl. *'iyál*, family, child. [اهل]

عَائِلَة *a'áyila*, wife, family.

اَرْشَدْ العَائِلَة *arshad el-a'áyila*, eldest of the family.

عَوْم *'öm*, a swimming; river in flood, not fordable.

عَام *a'áma*, he swam. [سبح]

عَام ـ اَعْوَام *a'ám*, pl. *a'awám*, year.

عَوْن *'ön*, aid, succour.

عَوْنَة *'öna*, aid, succour; euphemism for *corvée*.

عَاوَنَ *a'áwana*, he assisted.

مُعَاوَنَة *mo'áwana*, assistance.

مُعَاوِن *mo'áwin*, assistant.

اَعَانَ *aa'ána*, he assisted.

اِعَانَة *ia'ána*, assistance.

اِسْتَعَانَ *ista'ána*, he asked for help. [اِسْتَغَاثَ]

اِسْتِعَانَة *isti'ána*, an asking for help.

مَعُونَة or مَغُونَة *ma'oona*, or *maghōna*, barge, lighter.

عانة a'ána, pubis.

عوّة 'awwaha, he injured; was injured.

عاهة a'áha, calamity.

معوّة mo'awwah, deformed, injured.

عوى 'awa (the dog) barked, howled. [نبح]

عواء or عوي 'awi, or 'owá, howl, bark.

عيوب ـ عيب 'aib, pl. 'oyoob, vice, stain, shame, defect.

عيب عليك 'aib 'alaik, shame on thee!

عيّب 'ayyaba, he stigmatised; stained, dishonoured.

عيبة or هيبة 'aiba (incorrectly haiba), valise, saddle-bag.

معيوب ma'yoob, disgraced, vicious, stained.

عود ـ اعياد ـ عيد 'eed, pl. aa'yád, fête, festival (see 'öd).

عيد الميلاد 'eed el-meelád, Christmas.

عيد الفصح 'eed el-fas-h, Easter.

عيد الصعود 'eed es-so'ood, Ascension.

عيد التثليث 'eed et-tathleeth, Trinity.

عيد جميع الاولياء 'eed jamee'a' el-awliyá, All Saints.

عيارات ـ عيار 'iyár, pl. 'iyárát, legal standard of coin, measures, &c.; calibre; the usual charge of powder and shot for a gun.

عيار نارّي 'iyár náriy, a shot or discharge from a gun.

عيّار 'ayyár, crane for lifting weights; cunning; rogue.

عار a'ár, shame, ignominy.

عيّر or عاير a'yyara, he put to shame, dishonoured.

عار ـ يعير a'ára (the horse) bolted; ya'yeer, it bolts.

معيار mi'yár, legal standard; law.

معيار شرعيّ mi'yár shara'iy, Moslem law or standard of right and wrong.

عيسى or حضرة عيسى 'Isa, or Hadrat 'Isa, Jesus Christ.

عيسوي 'Isawiy, Christian. [نصرانيّ]

يسوعي Yasooa'iy, Jesuit. (N.B. Mark the transposition of the letters عيسى.)

عيش 'aish, life, existence; bread.

عاش ـ يعيش a'ásha, he lived; ya'yeesh, he lives.

يعيش افندينا Ya'yeesh Efendeená, "Vive le Khédive!"

تعيّش ta'ayyasha, he lived, gained a living.

عيّاش a'yyásh, seller of bread in the streets.

عائشة A'áyisha, the favourite wife of Mahomed, and the Virago of the early Caliphate, after the Prophet's death.

معيشة ma'yisha, means of life, existence.

معاشات ـ معاش ma'ásh, pl. ma'áshát, means of life, monthly pay, wages; (in Turkey especially), pension, annuity.

عياط 'iyát, scream, cry; uproar.

عيّط 'ayyata, he screamed, shouted.

عيف 'aif, flight of birds. [عوف زجر]

عيافة 'iyáfa, fortune-telling, augury from flight of birds.

عول - عيال - عيّل 'ayyil, pl. 'iyál, family (see 'öl).

عيال صغير 'iyál sagheer, infant, small child.

عائلة a'áyila, family, wife.

عين or عيون - عين or اعين or اعيان 'ain, pl. 'oyoon, or aa'yun, and aa'yán, (femin.) eye, hole, source, fountain, essence; evil eye.

عيون 'oyoon, arches of bridge; spectacles, glasses.

اعيان البلد aa'yán el-balad, provincial notables.

اعيان منقولة aa'yán manqoola, moveables, furniture.

عينه or بعينه 'ainoho, or bi-'ainihi, he himself.

عين 'ain, self, same; the thing sold.

بعين الاسباب bi-'ain el-asbáb, for the same reasons.

بالاسباب عينها bil-asbáb 'ainihá, for the same reasons.

عين العقوبة 'ain el-'oqooba, the same penalty.

عين المعيّنة 'ain el-mo'ayyana, the identical thing.

عيناً 'ainán (payment) in kind, "en nature."

عيّنة or عينية 'ayyina (or 'ainiya), specimen, sample.

عيني 'ainiy, self, same; real.

عينية 'ainiya, self, same; sameness.

حقوق عينية hoqooq 'ainiya, real rights, "droits réels."

عيّن 'ayyana, he appointed, designated.

تعيين ta'yeen, appointment, designation.

تعيينات ta'yeenát, appointments, rations, allowances.

تعيّن ta'ayyana, he was appointed, it became evident, resulted.

عاين 'áyana, he examined, saw as an eye-witness.

معاين mo'-áyin, eye-witness, scrutiniser.

معاينة mo'-áyana, inspection, visit of the police to the scene of a crime.

معيّن mo'-ayyan, appointed, designated.

عوينات 'owainát, small eyes, spectacles.

معان ma'án, visible; Ma'án in Arabia Petræa.

عيى or عيّ 'ayya, he was weak, ill, incapable.

عيّا 'ayyá, he fatigued, made ill.

عياء 'ayá, illness, disease. [داء - مرض]

عيّان 'ayyán, ill, diseased.

GH
(a hard guttural G).

غ Ghain. Value = 1000.

غاب - غياب ghába, he was absent (see ghiyáb).

غاب - غابة ghába, forest; gháb, reeds, rushes.

مغارة or غار ghár, or maghára, cavern.

غور - غارة ghára, a raid (see ghör).

غار ghára, he was jealous (see ghaira).

غاغة or غوغاء ghágha (for Turkish ghóghá, or qavga), row, tumult, conflict.

غائش ghayish, a male dancer, khawal.

غائلة gháyila, calamity (see ghõl).

غاية gháya, extremity (see ghayyá).

غبّ ghibb, end; after.

غبّ السلام ghibb es-salám, after compliments.

غبّ مرور ٣ ايّام ghibb moroor talátat ayyám, after the lapse of 3 days; 3 days after sight (bill of exchange).

غبار ghobár, dust; aghbar, dust-coloured.

غبطة ghibta, Beatitude; title of a Patriarch.

غبيط ghabeet, dromedary-saddle for riding.

غبن ghabn, fraud, deceit.

غبن فاحش ghabn fáhish, gross fraud, "lésion."

غباني ghabániy, cashmere cloth.

غباوة ghabáwa, stupidity; غبي ghabiy, stupid.

غجر ghajar, or ghajariy, pl. aghjár (Persian), fortune-teller, gipsy, cheat; shameless buffoon.

غدّة ghudda, gland, tonsil; "goître," lupus.

غدر ghadara, he deceived, defrauded.

غدر ghadr, fraud, "concussion" in French law. [غرور - غبن - غشّ]

غدّارة ghaddára, pistol.

غداريف ghadáreef, vertebræ. [غضروف]

غدا ghadá (provincial, Bedouin), he came.

غد or غدا ghadá (or ghad), morning, midday meal.

غدًا ghadán, to-morrow.

تغدّى taghadda, he ate at midday; lunched.

غذا ghazá, he nourished.

غذاء - اغذية ghizá, pl. aghziya, food, nourishment.

تغذّى taghazza, he took nourishment.

غرّة - غرر ghurra, pl. ghurar, beauty; new moon, first day of lunar month.

اغرّ - غرّاء agharr, (femin.) gharrá, shining, glorious.

الشريعة الغرّاء esh-shariy'a el-gharrá, the glorious sheriat, or Divine Moslem Law.

غرّ - غرور gharra, he deceived; ghoroor, deceit.

مغرور maghroor, deceived; self-deceived, vain.

اغترّ ightarra, he was deceived.

غرار ghirár, sack.

غرب gharaba, he disappeared, went abroad, or westward; the sun set.

غروب ghoroob, sun-set.

غرب *gharb*, west; salivation.

غربيّ *gharbiy*, western.

الغرب *el-gharb*, the West; Algarve in Portugal.

طرابلس الغرب *Tarábolus el-gharb*, Tripoli West (in Africa).

غربيّة ـ طنطا *Gharbiya*, the central and largest province of Lower Egypt; capital, *Tantá*.

غريب ـ غرباء *ghareeb*, pl. *ghorabá*, strange, foreign, extraordinary.

غراب ـ غرابة *ghoráb*, crow, raven, bolt; *gharába*, strangeness.

استغرب *istaghraba*, he was astonished.

مغرب *maghrib*, place or hour of sunset; west.

مغربيّ ـ مغاربة *maghribiy*, pl. *maghárba*, Moor, Moorish.

غربل ـ غربال *gharbala*, he sifted; *ghirbál*, sieve.

غرّد *gharrada*, (the bird) warbled.

غرز *gharaza*, he stuck, it ran aground.

غرس ـ غراس *gharasa*, he planted; *ghirás*, a planting.

غرس ـ اغراس *ghars*, pl. *aghrás*, a plant, shoot.

غروش ـ قرش *ghroosh* (Turkish for Arabic *qirsh*), piastre, 2½d. ("*groschen*"?).

غرض *gharida*, he desired, aimed at.

غرض ـ اغراض *gharad*, pl. *aghrád*, desire, aim, object in view; malice, prejudice.

مغرض *moghrid*, prejudiced, partial.

غرغر ـ غرغرة *gharghara*, he gargled; *gharghara*, a gargle.

غرف *gharafa*, he ladled.

غرفة ـ غرف *ghorfa*, pl. *ghoraf*, pool, cell, cavity.

مغرفة *mighrafa*, ladle, scoop.

غرق *ghariqa*, he sank, was drowned, or wrecked.

اغرق *aghraqa*, he made sink, drowned; flooded a field.

انغرق *ingharaqa*, it was flooded, drowned.

استغرق *he was overwhelmed; it was exaggerated; it occupied much time.

غرق *gharaq*, act of sinking, drowning, shipwreck, flooding a field.

غريق *ghareeq*, drowned.

غارقة *gharooqa*, a ruinous form of mortgage; "*antichrèse*," abandonment of the usufruct to a creditor.

غرلة *ghorla*, prepuce.

غرم *gharima*, he owed money.

غرّم *gharrama*, he fined, made pay.

تغريم *taghreem*, imposition of a fine.

غرامة *gharáma*, money fine.

غريم ـ غرماء *ghareem*, pl. *ghoramá*, creditor; debtor.

غرام *gharám*, passionate love, penalty.

غري *gharia*, he coveted.

اغرى *aghra*, he excited desire, tempted, seduced.

اغراءُ الشيطان *aghráho esh-shaitán*, the Devil tempted him.

اغراء *ighrá*, temptation, seduction.

غراء *ghirá*, gum, glue; covetousness.

غز or غزغز *ghazza* or *ghazghaza*, he pushed in, plunged, thrust, dug.

غزة *Ghazza*, Gaza in Palestine.

غزارة *ghazára*, abundance.

غزل *ghazala*, he spun (wool, cotton, &c.)

غزل *ghazl*, spun yarn.

غزلية *ghazliya*, native stuff of silk and cotton mixed.

مغزل *mighzal*, spindle.

غزل *ghazal*, courtship, love poem.

تغازل *tagházala*, he flirted with, wooed.

غزال - غزلان *ghazál*, pl. *ghizlán*, gazelle.

رقّ غزال *riqq ghazál*, parchment.

غزا *ghazá*, he raided, attacked the enemy.

غزوة or غزاة *ghazwa*, or *ghazát*, raid, "razzia."

غازى - غزاة *ghází*, pl. *ghozát*, Moslem raider, champion of Islam.

غازية - غوازي *gháziya*, pl. *ghawázi*, a professional dancing girl of Upper Egypt; an obsolete gold coin.

غسّل or غسل *ghasala* or *ghassala*, he washed linen, a corpse, &c.

اغتسل *ightasala*, he washed himself.

غسل *ghasl*, or *ghusl*, a washing; a religious bathing of the whole body after certain pollutions. compare *wodoo*. [وضوء]

غسول *ghasool*, washing a dead body for burial.

غسيل *ghaseel*, washed; hence, clothes for the wash.

غسّال - غسّالة *ghassál*, (femin.) *ghassála*, washerman.

مغسل *maghsal*, laundry, lavatory.

مغسّل *moghassil*, a washer of corpses.

غشّ *ghashsha*, he cheated, adulterated, falsified.

غشّ *ghishsh*, fraud, adulteration.

مغشوش *maghshoosh*, adulterated (article); bad (coin).

غشيم - غشماء *ghasheem*, pl. *ghoshamá*, novice, awkward; recruit, a numbering off in drill, "by numbers."

الماس غشيم *almás ghasheem*, rough diamond.

غشوم *ghashoom*, ignorant, "*naif*."

غشاء - اغشية *ghishá*, pl. *aghshiya*, membrane, sheath.

غشي *ghushia*, he fainted.

غشيان *ghashayán*, a fainting.

غصب *ghasaba*, he used force, violated, ravished.

غصب *ghasb*, violence, force.

غصبًا عن *ghasbán 'an*, in spite of. [رغمًا]

اغتصب - اغتصاب *ightasaba*, he ravished; *ightisáb*, rape.

غصن ـ غصون *ghosn*, pl. *ghosoon*, branch, bough. [فرع]

غضب *ghadiba*, he was angry. [زعل]

غضب *ghadab*, anger.

غضبان or غضوب *ghadbán* or *ghadoob*, angry.

مغضوب عليه *maghdoob 'aleih*, object of wrath.

اغضب *aghdaba*, he provoked to anger, vexed.

غضروف ـ غضاريف *ghodroof*, pl. *ghadáreef*, cartilage, vertebra.

غضن ـ غضون *ghadan*, pl. *ghodoon*, fold, wrinkle.

فى غضون الشهر *fi ghodoon esh-shahr*, in the course of the month.

ظرف ـ [حرف]

غط ـ غطيط *ghatta*, he snored; *ghateet*, a snoring.

غطرش *ghatrasha*, (colloquial) he connived at, shut his eyes to.

غطس or غطّس *ghatasa*, or *ghattasa*, he plunged (another) into water, baptised.

غطاس or تغطيس *ghitás* or *taghtees*, a plunging; baptism; Epiphany.

مغطس *mightas*, tank for washing.

غطا or غطّا *ghatá*, or *ghatta*, he covered, put the lid on.

تغطّى *taghatta*, he covered or veiled himself.

غطاء ـ اغطية *ghitá*, pl. *aghtiya*, lid, cover.

مغطّى *moghatta*, covered; having a lid.

غفر *ghafara*, (God) pardoned.

استغفر *istaghfara*, he asked (God's) pardon.

استغفر الله *Astaghfir Ullah*, May God pardon me! Heaven forbid! You are too complimentary.

غفران or مغفرة *ghofrán*, or *maghfira*, God's pardon.

غفور or غفّار *ghafoor*, or *ghaffár*, God the Pardoner.

جمّ غفير *jamm ghafeer*, a vast crowd.

غفر or غفارة *ghafar*, or *ghafára*, the system of night-watch by peasants; post or beat of a night-watchman. [طرف ـ درك ـ نوبة]

غفير ـ غفراء *ghafeer*, pl. *ghofará*, night-watchman. This word is officially spelt *khafeer*. [خفير]

مغفر *mighfar*, helmet.

غفل *ghafala*, he was negligent, careless.

تغافل *tagháfala*, he was unready; shammed carelessness.

غفل or غفلة *ghafal*, or *ghafla*, negligence.

على الغفلة *'ala l-ghafla*, suddenly, by surprise.

غافل *gháfil*, negligent, careless.

غفوة *ghafwa*, a doze, nap, siesta.

غلّ ـ اغلال *ghill*, spite; *ighlál*, fraud, deceit.

غلّة ـ غلال *ghalla*, pl. *ghilál*, corn, cereals; revenue, crop.

استغلال *istighlál*, enjoyment of a right, taking the crops, &c.

غلب على *ghalaba 'ala*, he conquered, got the mastery over.

انغلب *inghalaba*, he was conquered.

تغلّب على *taghallaba 'ala*, he influenced, mastered.

غلبة *ghalaba*, victory; jabber, row.

غلبةلق *ghalabaliq* (in Turkish pronounced *qalabáliq*), row, crowd, confusion.

غلباوي *ghalabáwiy*, a jabberer, rowdy.

غلبان *ghalbán*, conquered; wrong; poor, pauper.

غالب *ghálib*, conqueror; probability, majority.

في الغالب or غالباً *ghálibán*, or *fi l-ghálib*, probably.

اغلب *aghlab*, more probable; majority.

اغلبيّة *aghlabiya*, majority, preponderance.

اغلبهم *aghlabohom*, most of them.

اغلبيّة الآراء *aghlabiyat el-aárá*, majority of votes.

مغلوب ـ مغلوبيّة *maghloob*, defeated; *maghloobiya*, defeat.

غاليبسيس *gháleebsees*, lamium purpureum.

غلس or غلص *ghilis*, cad, snob, vulgar fellow.

غلصمة *ghalsama*, uvula, pharynx.

غلط *ghalita*, he made a mistake, was in error.

غلط or غلطة *ghalat*, or *ghalta*, error, mistake. [خطاء]

غلطان *ghaltán*, in error, mistaken.

غلظة *ghilza*, coarseness, vulgarity.

غلاظة *ghiláza*, coarseness, thickness.

غليظ ـ غلاظ *ghaleez*, pl. *ghiláz*, coarse, thick, massive.

غلاف ـ غلفة *ghiláf*, sheath; *ghulfa*, prepuce.

اغلق or غلق or غلّق *ghalaqa*, or *ghallaqa*, or *aghlaqa*, he shut, closed. [قفل]

غلق *ghalaq*, small basket, pannier.

مغلوق or مغلق *maghlooq*, or *moghlaq*, shut, closed; dark.

مغلق *maghlaq*, enclosure, barn; timber-yard.

غلم or غلمة *ghalam*, or *ghulma*, sexual lust.

غلام ـ غلمان *gholám*, pl. *ghilmán*, lad, small boy.

غلينة *ghaleena* (Greek), calm; gentle wind.

غلاء ـ غالي *ghalá*, dearth, dearness; *gháli*, dear, expensive.

غلى ـ يغلي *ghala* (the water) boiled; *yighli*, it boils.

غلّى or اغلى *ghalla*, or *aghla*, he made boil, he boiled.

غليان *ghalayán*, ebullition.

غلّاية *ghalláya*, kettle.

مغلي or مغلّي *maghulli*, or *maghli*, boiled; a decoction.

غمّ - غموم *ghamm,* pl. *ghomoom,* sadness.

مغموم *maghmoom,* saddened, sad.

غمد *ghamada,* he sheathed; *ghimd,* a sheath.

غمر *ghamara,* he covered over.

غمرة *ghamra,* abundance, great quantity.

غمز or تغامز *ghamaza,* or *taghámaza,* he winked at, connived.

غمزة *ghamza,* wink, hint, connivance.

غماز *ghamáz,* trigger.

غمس *ghamasa,* he soaked, dipped. [غطس]

غمص *ghamas,* blearness, weakness of eyes.

غمض *ghamada,* he shut his eyes, kept dark, connived at.

غامض *ghámid,* dark, obscure, secret.

غمق *ghomq,* depth. [عمق]

غامق *ghámiq,* deep. [غريط]

غمّى *ghamma,* he covered.

غنج *ghunj,* indecent posturing or gait.

تغنّجت *taghannajet,* she solicited by her gait.

غندر *ghandar,* foppishness, coquetry.

غندور - غندورة *ghandoor,* fop; *ghandoora,* immodest woman.

تغندر *taghandara,* he flirted.

غنغرينة *ghangharcena* (European), gangrene.

اغتنم or غنم *ghanima,* or *ightanama,* he took booty, profited by.

غنيمة - غنائم *ghaneema,* pl. *ghanáyim,* booty, spoil.

غنم - اغنام *ghanam,* pl. *aghnám,* sheep.

غنّام *ghannám,* shepherd. [راعي]

غنى or غذاء *ghaná,* or *ghina,* wealth, luxury.

غنيّ - اغنياء *ghaniy,* pl. *aghniyá,* rich, wealthy.

استغنى عن *istaghna a'n,* he was rich enough to do without, he dispensed with.

غذوة - غذاً - اغاني *ghinwa,* or *ghiná,* pl. *aghání,* song.

غنّى or تغنّى *ghanna,* or *taghanna,* he sang.

مغنّي *moghanni,* singer.

غوث or غياث *ghōs,* or *ghiyás,* help, succour, salvation.

اغاثة - اغاث *aghása,* he helped, rescued; *ighása,* rescue.

استغاث *istaghása,* he cried for help.

غور - غارة (ghōr) *ghára,* raid, incursion. [غزا]

غار *ghár,* or *maghára,* cavern.

غويشات *ghowaishát,* glass bracelets.

غوّش *ghawwasha,* he jabbered, was vulgar.

غوص *ghōs,* a plunging, diving.

غوط *ghōt,* a depression, hollow.

غائط *gháyit,* fœces.

تغوّط *taghawwata*, he went to stool.

غويط *ghaweet*, deep.

غيط ـ غيطان *ghait*, pl. *gheetán*, field, lowland.

غاغة or غرغاء *ghōghá* (*gágha, gargá*), row, tumult.

غول ـ غيلان *ghool*, pl. *gheelán*, vampire, foul demon.

غائلة ـ غوائل *gháyila*, pl. *ghawáyil*, calamity.

غوى *ghawa*, he lost his way, desired.

أغوى *aghwa*, he led astray, seduced.

غيّة *gheeya*, desire, error, seduction; flock of decoy pigeons.

غيب or غياب *ghaib*, or *ghiyáb*, absence, alibi.

غيبة *ghaiba*, or *gheeba*, absence; back-biting.

على الغائب or غيباً *ghaibán*, or *a'la l-gháyib*, a knowing by heart. [حفظ]

غائب *gháyib*, absent, absentee, defaulter; third person in grammar.

غيابيّ ـ غيابيّاً *ghiyábiy*, or *ghiyábiyán*, by default (legal term).

تغيّب or غاب *ghába*, or *taghayyaba*, he absented himself, disappeared.

متغيّب *mutaghayyib*, absentee.

غيّب *ghayyaba*, he made disappear.

غاب ـ غابة *ghába*, forest; *gháb*, reeds, rushes.

غيث *ghais*, rain as a blessing from God.

غيرة *ghaira* (or *gheera*), jealousy; zeal.

غيور *ghayoor*, jealous, zealous.

غار or تغاير *ghára*, or *tagháyara*, he was jealous.

غيار *ghiyár*, otherness, change, relief.

غير *ghair*, other, another, different; not, except, without.

غير صحيح *ghair saheeh*, not true.

و لا غيره *wa lá ghairoh*, only he, and no other but he.

بغير or من غير ذلك *bi-ghair* (or *min ghair*) *zálik*, without that.

غير مرّة *ghair marra*, more than once.

غيّر *ghayyara*, he made change, altered.

تغيّر *taghayyara*, it became changed.

مغاير *mogháyir*, contrary, opposed to.

غيط ـ غيطان *ghait*, pl. *gheetán*, field, lowland. [غوط]

غيظ or غياظ *ghaiz*, or *ghiyáz*, anger.

انغاظ or اغتاظ *ingháza*, or *ightáza*, he became angry.

اغاظة ـ اغاظ *agháza*, he made angry; *igháza*, provocation.

اغتياظ *ightiyáz*, anger.

غيلة *gheela*, guile, treachery. [حيلة]

غائلة ـ غوائل *gháyila*, pl. *ghawáyil*, calamity. [غزل]

غيم ـ غيوم *ghaim*, pl. *ghoyoom*, cloud. [سحابة]

مغيّم (198) فاتحة

مغيّم *moghayyam*, clouded over.

غيّا *ghayyá*, he set up a staff, flag, limit.

غاية *gháya*, limit, extremity, aim, end in view.

بغاية *bi-gháya*, extremely, excessively.

لغاية ذلك *li-gháya zalik*, as far as that, to that end.

F

ف *Fé*. Value = 80.

ف - فقال *fa*, and, then; *faqála*, and he said.

فات - فوت *fáta*, he passed (see *föt*).

فاح - فوح *fáha*, it exhaled a smell (see *föh*).

فار - فور *fára*, it began to boil (see *för*).

فأر - فئران *fár*, pl. *fcerán*, rat, mouse; a carpenter's plane.

فارّ - فرّ *fárr*, a fugitive (see *farra*).

فأس - فؤوس *fás*, pl. *fo-oos* (femin.), pick-axe, adze; the town of Fez in Morocco.

فاق - فوق *fáqa*, it surpassed (see *föq*).

فأل - فؤول *fál*, pl. *fo-ol*, a good omen taken from a good name, word, book, &c.

تفاءل *tafáála*, he sought a good omen.

فائدة - فيد *fáyida*, advantage (see *faid*).

فبراير *Febráyir* (European), February.

فتّ *fatta*, he broke up small.

فتيت *fateet*, small, tiny, fragment.

تفتّت *tafattata*, it was broken up small.

فتح *fataha*, he opened, began; conquered.

افتتح *iftataha*, he opened (an assembly), inaugurated.

فتح - فتوح *fat-h*, pl. *fotooh*, opening; victory.

نصرٌ من الله وفتحٌ قريب *nasrun min Allah wa fat-hun qareeb*, Help from God and a speedy victory.

فَتحة *fat-ha*, orifice; vowel-sound of short *a*, the mark ‍ above a letter. [نصبة]

فاتح or فتّاح or مفتّح *fátih*, or *fattáh*, or *mofattih*, Conqueror; God, he who opens salvation, or a conquered country.

لون فاتح or مفتوح *lōn fátih*, or *maftooh*, light tint or colour.

محمّد الفاتح *Mohammad el-Fátih*, Mehomet II. of Turkey, the Conqueror of Constantinople, A.D. 1453.

مفتّح الابواب *mofattih el-abwáh*, God, the opener of the doors (of salvation).

فاتحة *fátiha*, the first short or opening chapter of the Koran, corresponding to our Lord's Prayer.

افتتاح الجلسة *iftitáh el-jalsa*, the opening of a sitting of a Court.

استفتاح *istiftáh*, the opening of a day's work; a shopkeeper's first sale or money taken in in the morning.

مفتاح - مفاتيح *miftáh*, pl. *mafátih*, key.

مفتاح مصطنع *miftáh mostana'*, false key.

مفتوح *maftooh*, opened, open, light tint; a consonant marked with *fat-ha*.

فتر *fitr*, half a span, from thumb to fore-finger. [شبر]

فاتر *fátir*, lukewarm, tepid.

فاتورة *fátoora* (European, *fattura*), sample of cloth.

فتّش *fattasha*, he inspected, investigated.

تفتيش - تفاتيش *tafteesh*, pl. *tafáteesh*, inspection; the area of inspection, duty of an inspector.

مفتّش *mofattish*, inspector.

فتق *fataqa*, he split open. [فلج - فلق]

فتق *fatq*, rupture, split; hernia.

فتاق *fitáq*, hernia.

رتق و فتق الامور *ratq wa fatq el-omoor*, the shutting and opening, *i.e.* the transaction of business. [cf. ضبط و ربط]

فتك ب *fataka bi*, he attacked, wounded, killed.

فتك *fatk*, violence.

فتل *fatala*, he twisted, made thread.

فتيلة - فتائل *fateela*, pl. *fatáyil*, thread, wick, cord.

فتن or افتن *fatana*, or *aftana*, he excited to revolt, stirred up, plotted.

فتنة *fitna*, plot, sedition.
[sagacity = فطنة]

مفتن *moftin*, plotter, demagogue.

فتنة *fotna*, acacia blossom.

مفتون *maftoon*, excited, seduced, mad.

فتاء *fatá*, youthfulness.

فتى - فتيان *fata*, pl. *fityán*, lad, boy, brave youth. [صبي]

فتاة - فتيات *fatát*, pl. *fatayát*, girl, maidservant.

فاتية - فواتي *fátiya*, pl. *fawáti*, prostitute.

فتوّة *fotoowa*, youth, brave exuberance of male youth.

فتوّتلو افندم *fotoowatlu efendim*, a Turkish title applied in addressing letters to junior officials, captains, lieutenants, &c.

فتوى - فتاوى *fatwa*, pl. *fatáwa*, or *fatáwi*, a jurist's decision in Moslem sacred law.

افتى *afta*, he gave a decision or *fatwa*.

مفتي *mufti*, Moslem judge who delivers the *fatwa*, jurisconsult.

استفتى *istafta*, he asked the *mufti* for a *fatwa*.

فج *fijj*, unripe (fruit). [see ني]

فج *fajj*, ravine.

فاجأ or فجأ *fajá*, or *fája*, he surprised, caught in the act.

فجأةً *fojátan*, suddenly. [بغتةً]

فجر or فجرة or فجريّة *fejr*, or *fajr*, or *fijriya*, dawn; aurora; bugle-call of *réveille*.

فجور or فجر *fajr*, or *fojoor*, debauchery, libertinism.

فاجر *fájir*, debauchee.

فجل - فجّال *fijl*, radish; *fajjál*, greengrocer.

فجّالة *fajjála*, greengrocers; market gardens; a suburb to the N.E. of Cairo.

فجر or فحت or فحت *fahata*, or *fahasa*, or *fahara*, he dug. [حفر]

فحش or فحش *fohsh*, or *fahshá*, lust, prostitution.

فاحش *fáhish*, outrageous, glaring, atrocious.

ثمن فاحش *taman fáhish*, an outrageous price.

غبن فاحش *ghabn fáhish*, gross fraud, lésion.

فاحشة - فواحش *fáhisha*, pl. *fawáhish*, prostitute.

فحص *fahs*, scrutiny.

فحص or تفحّص *fahasa*, or *tafahhasa*, he scrutinised, inquired carefully into.

فحل - فحول *fahl*, pl. *fohool*, stallion, he-camel; male palm; fine and large specimen.

فحل جاموس *fahl jámoos*, a fine buffalo.

فحل بصل *fahl basal*, a large onion.

فحولة *fohoola*, virility.

فحم - فحوم *fahm*, pl. *fohoom*, charcoal, coal.

فحم حجري *fahm hajariy*, mineral coal.

فاحم *fáhim*, black (hair), black as coal.

فحوى *fahwá*, sense, meaning of word.

فخّة *fakhkha*, a trap, snare.

فاختة *fákhita*, a cooing dove, ringdove.

فخذ - افخاذ *fakhd*, pl. *afkhád* (femin.), thigh; leg (of mutton).

فخّارة *fakhkhára*, pottery, china.

فاخورة *fákhoora*, a pottery, place for making pots.

فخيرة *fakheera*, hole, pit, depression.

تفخّر or افتخر or فاخر or فخر *fakhara*, or *iftakhara*, or *fákhara*, or *tafakhkhara*, he boasted, took pride in, showed off.

افتخار *iftikhár*, pride, boasting.

فخفخ *fakhfakha*, he bragged, vaunted.

فخامة *fakháma*, illustriousness, pomp, pride.

فخامتلو *fakhámetlu*, Turkish title for a Prime Minister; Grace or Highness.

مفخّم or فخيم *fakheem*, or *mofakhkham*, illustrious.

دولة فخيمة - دولة علّية *dawla fakheema*, official Turkish title for any European Power, "the illustrious state," in contradistinction from *dawlat 'aliya*, Turkey, the Exalted State.

أفدنة ـ فدّان or فدادين *feddán*, pl. *afdína*, or *fadádeen*, Egyptian acre, a little larger than an English acre; *i.e.* 166 rods instead of 160; 4200 square metres.

فدن *fidn*, one feddán.

فدا or فدية *fidá*, or *fidiya*, ransom.

فذلكة *fazlaka*, sum total, summary, gist.

فرّ ـ يفرّ *farra*, he fled; *yafirr*, he flees.

فرار *firár*, flight, escape.

فارّ or فرّار *fárr*, or *farrár*, a fugitive.

ولّى الفرار *walla el-firár*, he fled, took to flight.

فرّ هارباً *farra háribán*, he fled as a fugitive (*e.g.* from justice).

فرات و دجلة *Furát wa Dijla*, Euphrates and Tigris.

الفراتان *El-Furátán*, the two Euphrates, *i.e.* the Euphrates and Tigris; Mesopotamia.

فرّج *farraja*, he opened, laid bare.

تفرّج *tafarraja*, he opened his heart, amused himself, walked about sightseeing.

افرج عنه *afraja 'anho*, he released (him, a prisoner), set him at liberty. [اخلا سبيله]

فراجة *ferája*, Turkish lady's cloak.

فراجيّة *farajiya*, a Cadi's loose robe. [فروبة]

فرّوج ـ فراريج *furrooj*, pl. *faráreej*, chicken, hen. [فرخ]

فرارجيّ *farárjiy*, chicken-seller.

فرجة *forja*, a show, sight.

فرج ـ فروج *farj*, pl. *forooj*, fissure, cleft, vulva.

فرج *faraj*, joy, relief.

انفراج *infiráj*, a being wide open.

زاوية منفرجة *záwiya munfarija*, obtuse angle.

فرح *fariha*, he was glad, gay.

فرّح or افرح *farraha*, or *afraha*, he gladdened.

فرح *farah*, gaiety; wedding fête.

فرح or فرحان *farih*, or *farhán*, glad, gay.

مفرح *mofrih*, gladdening.

فرخ ـ فراخ *farkh*, pl. *firákh*, chicken, fowl.

معمل الفراخ *maa'mul el-firákh*, incubator, oven for the artificial hatching of chickens.

تفريخ *tafreekh*, a hatching.

فرخ ورق *farkh waraq*, a sheet of paper.

فرّاخ *farrákh*, poulterer.

فرد ـ افراد or فرود *fard*, unit, odd number, one piece, bale, basket, half-load; pl. *afrád*, units, *forood*, pieces.

فرد و جوز *fard u jōz*, odd and even.

فرد طبنجة *fard tabanja*, a pistol.

فريدة ـ فرائد *fareeda*, pl. *faráyid*, pearl; quire of paper.

D D

انفراد infrád, isolation, solitude.

مفرد or منفرد mofrad, or monfarid, alone, solitary; kept apart; the singular number.

فردوس ـ فراديس firdáws, pl. farádees (Persian), Paradise.

فرز farz, choice, selection.

فرز or فرّز faraza, or farraza, he chose, picked out, distinguished between.

مفروز or مفرّز mafrooz, or mofarraz, chosen, élite.

فرس or افترس farasa, or iftarasa, (the animal) was ferocious, spirited; (the dog) flew at.

فريسة fareesa, prey, victim (to a wild beast, &c.).

فرس ـ افراس faras, pl. afrás, mare.

فارس ـ فرسان fáris, pl. forsán, cavalier, good horseman.

فراسة farása, skill in horsemanship; firása, sagacity.

فرس النبيّ farus en-nabiy, the Prophet's mare; mantis insect.

فوارس fawáris, cavalry.

فرس Fors, Persia, the Persians.

فارسيّ fársiy, a Persian, Persian.

مفترس moftaris, fierce, spirited (animal).

فرش farasha, he furnished a house, laid down carpets, bedding; spread out articles for sale; he brushed.

فرش ـ فروش farsh, pl. foroosh, bed, bedding.

فراش ـ فرش firásh, pl. forosh, bed; a wife; farásh, moth.

فرّاش farrásh, sweeper, valet; upholsterer, decorator for festivals.

فرشة fursha (Turkish fircha), brush.

مفروشات mafrooshát, furniture, especially soft furniture, upholstery, carpets, &c.

فراشة العجلة farúshat el-'ajala, tire of wheel. [طبان]

فرصة ـ فرص forsa, pl. foras, opportunity.

انتهز الفرصة intahaza el-forsa, he took the opportunity.

مرتعد الفرائص morta'yid el-faráyis, trembling with fear.

فرض ـ فروض fard, pl. forood, Divine precept; moral obligation, duty, share; tax.

فرضة forda, notch, inlet.

فريضة ـ فرائض fareeda, pl. faráyid, inheritance, share of inheritance.

فرض or افترض farada, or iftarada, he supposed, allowed a supposition.

افتراض iftirád, hypothesis.

مفروض mafrood, supposed, hypothesis.

فرط farata, he surpassed.

فرط fart, excess, negligence; death.

افراط ifrát, excess, abuse of authority.

تفريط tafreet, omission of duty, falling short, imprudence.

مفرط mofrit, excessive.

فرط فيه الفرط farata fihi el-fart, he met with a fatal accident.

فرع ـ فروع faru', pl. forooa', branch. [غصن]

فَرعيّ *fara'iy*, incidental, minor (detail).

فرعون - فراعنة *Fira'oon*, pl. *Farú'yina*, Pharaoh, tyrant.

فرغ *faragha*, it was empty; he was at leisure.

فراغ *farágh*, emptiness, leisure, cession.

فارغ *fárigh*, empty, idle, bootless (talk).

افرغ or فرّغ *afragha*, or *farragha*, he emptied, ceded, unloaded.

استفرغ *istafragha*, he vomited.

فرق or فرّق *faraqa*, or *farraqa*, he divided, separated, distinguished between; distributed.

فارق *fáraqa*, he withdrew himself, departed.

فرق - فروق *farq*, pl. *forooq*, difference, line of parting, separation; synonym.

فراق or مفارقة *firáq*, or *mofáraqa*, departure, separation.

فرقة - فرق *firqa*, pl. *firaq*, division or corps of army, sect, congregation; set.

فريق *fareeq*, General of Division, Lieut.-General.

فرقان *forqán*, distinction between good and evil; the Koran.

متفرق *mutafarriq*, various, dispersed, scattered.

فقع or فرقع *farqa'a*, or *faqa'a*, it exploded, burst, cracked.,

فرقعة *farqa'a*, explosion, a cracking.

فرقلة *firqilla*, a whip of twisted cords.

فرك *faraka*, he rubbed, rubbed to pieces.

فرك *fark*, friction.

فرك *firk*, conjugal hatred.

فريك *fareek*, corn-cake.

فرم *farama*, he minced, chopped.

فرّام *farrám*, professional cutter of tobacco.

مفروم *mafroom*, mince.

فرمان - فرمانات *farmán*, pl. *farmánát* (Persian), Imperial order, brevet, or letters patent.

فرن - فرّان *forn*, oven, bakery; *farrán*, baker.

افرنج or فرنج or افرنك *franj*, or *afranj*, or *afrank*, Frankish, European, Europeans.

فرنساوي - فرنسا *Fransáwiy*, French, Frenchman; *Fransá*, France.

بنتو فرنساوي *binto fransáwiy*, a napoleon or 20 (*vingt*, *venti*) franc piece.

فرهد *farhada*, he alarmed, confounded, prostrated or overpowered.

فرهدة *farhada*, confusion, nervous prostration.

مفرهد *mofarhad*, confounded, shaken.

فروة *furwa*, fleece, fur.

فروية *forwiya*, a furry article, fur cloak, judge's robe.

افتراء or فرية *firiya*, or *iftirá*, lie, slander.

افترى *iftara*, he slandered. [قذف

مفتري *moftari*, slanderer.

فرة *fira*, abundance (see *wafr*).

افتز or فزّ *fazza*, or *iftazza*, he leaped, trembled. [هزّ]

فزّة *fazza*, a jump.

استفزّ *istafazza*, he provoked.

فزع *faza'*, fright.

فزع مائي *faza' máiy*, hydrophobia, fear of water.

فزع على *faza'a 'ala*, he rushed at, attacked. [فرس]

فس ـ طربوش *fes*, fez, red cap, tarboosh.

فستق *fistiq, fustuq*, pistachio.

فستان *fistán* (Turkish), petticoat; kilt.

فسح *fasoha*, it was spacious.

فسحة or فسخة *fos-ha*, or *fasáha*, an open space, or room.

تفسّح *tafassaha*, he strolled, took his ease, promenaded.

فسخ *fasakha*, he abolished. [لغو]

فسخ *faskh*, abolition, dissolution of contract.

فسيخ *faseekh*, dried stinking fish, mostly from Damietta, and considered a great relish by the fellaheen.

فسخاني *fasakhániy*, seller of *faseekh*, or rotten fish.

فساد *fasád*, moral corruption, intrigue, conspiracy, nullity.

افسد *afsada*, he corrupted, vitiated.

مفسد *mofsid*, corrupter, conspirator.

فسّر or فسر *fasara*, or *fassara*, he explained, commented upon. [شرح]

تفسير ـ تفاسير *tafseer*, pl. *tafáseer*, commentary.

فسطاط ـ مصر عتيقة *Fostát*, a large tent; the first Moslem settlement at Cairo; *Masr 'Ateeqa*, or Old Cairo near Roda.

فسق ب *fasaqa bi*, he fornicated with; sodomised with.

فسق ب *fisq bi*, indecent assault (legal term).

فسقيّة *fisqiya*, tomb; fountain; "jet d'eau." [فوّارة]

فسل *fasl*, vile, vulgar.

فسولية *fasooliya*, French beans.

فشك or فشنك or فشيك *fishenk*, or *fisheik*, or *fishek* (Turkish), cartridge; squib; rocket.

فشا *fasha*, it was revealed.

افشى *afsha*, he revealed (the secret).

افشاء الاسرار *ifshá el-esrár*, a revealing of secrets, professional breach of confidence (legal term).

فصّ ـ فصوص *fiss*, or *fass*, pl. *fusoos*, stone of a ring, lobe of the ear.

فصح *fas-h*, Easter.

فصاحة *fasáha*, eloquence.

فصيح *faseeh*, eloquent. [بليغ]

فصد *fasada*, he bled (surgically). [حجم]

فصادة *fisáda*, phlebotomy.

مفصد *mifsad*, lancet. [مشرط]

فصل ـ فصول *fasl*, pl. *fusool*, division, chapter, season; dismissal from office.

فصيلة ـ فصائل *faseela*, pl. *fasáyil*, species, genus.

فيصل *faisal*, decision, interruption.

نصل or فاصل *fasala*, he divided, decided, dismissed from office; weaned; bargained.

فصال *fisál*, bargain, agreement on price; weaning, separation.

فصّل *fassala*, he detailed.

انفصل *infasala*, he was separated; departed, ceased.

فاصل *fásil*, a divider, dividing.

تفصيل ـ تفاصيل or تفصيلات *tafseel*, pl. *tafáseel*, or *tafseelát*, details, particulars.

مفصل ـ مفاصل *mafsil*, pl. *mafásil*, joint, articulation.

مفصلات *mofassilát*, hinges. [رزّ]

فضّ *fadda*, he broke into little pieces; ended.

فضّة *fadda*, silver; one para, of which 40 equal one piastre or 2½d.

فضّي *faddiy*, silvery, made of silver.

انفضّ *infadda*, it came to an end.

فضيع *fadeeh*, atrocious, vile. [فظيع]

فضل ـ فضول *fadl*, pl. *fodool*, surplus, favour; a work of supererogation.

فضلاً عن ذلك *fadlan 'an zálik*, moreover, in addition to that, besides that.

فضل *fidila*, he remained; it remained over as surplus.

فضّل *faddala*, he favoured, preferred.

تفضّل *tafaddala*, he deigned, condescended.

فضيلة ـ فضائل *fadeela*, pl. *fadáyil*, virtue, merit.

فضولي *fodooliy*, officious, without authority.

فاضل *fádil*, virtuous, superfluous.

فضلات *fadlát*, fœces, excrement.

[قذر]

فضا *fada*, it was empty, spacious.

افضى الى *afda ila*, it led to, caused. [سبب]

ضرب مفضي الى الموت *darb mufdi ila l-mōt*, a blow causing death (legal term); manslaughter.

فضي *fádi*, empty, at leisure, not engaged.

فضاء or فضاوة *fadá*, or *fadáwa*, blank space, areola.

اراضي فضاء *arádi fadá*, waste or unoccupied lands.

فطر or افطر *fatara*, or *aftara*, he ate after fasting.

فطر or افطار *fitr*, or *iftár*, evening meal during the fast of Ramadan.

فطور *fotoor*, breakfast, morning meal.

فطر *futr*, mushroom.

فطير *fateer*, unleavened bread; biscuit, pastry.

فطاطري *fatátriy*, biscuit-seller, pastrycook.

فطرة *fitra*, nature, constitution.

فطس *fatasa*, he smothered.

فطيس *fatees*, expired, dead, without breath; carrion.

فطمت *fatamet*, she weaned (the infant).

سيّدتنا فاطمة *sayyidetná* (*sittná*) *Fátma*, "Our Lady Fatma," daughter of Mahomet, wife of Ali, and mother of Hassan and Hussein.

فطنة *fitna*, intelligence, sagacity. [فتنة = plot.

فطين *fateen*, intelligent.

فظيع *fazeea'*, vile, atrocious.

فعل ـ افعل or نعال *fi'al*, pl. *afa'ál*, or *fi'ál*, the verb; an act or deed.

فعلاً or بالفعل *fi'alan*, or *bil-fi'al*, actually, in fact.

فعل *fa'ala*, he did, acted; made, executed. [عمل

افتعل *ifta'ala*, he concocted, cheated.

افتعال ـ افتعالة *iftia'ál*, or *iftia'ála*, trickery, intrigue.

انفعل *infa'ala*, he was affected, impressed by.

فاعل ـ فعلة *fá'yil*, pl. *fa'ala*, actor, doer, agent; workman; active participle.

فاعليّة *fá'yiliya*, efficacy.

مفعول به *mafa'ool bihi*, done by, passive.

افعى ـ افاعي *afa'a*, pl. *afá'iy*, viper.

فغفور *faghfoor*, chinaware, porcelain. [فجّار

فقد ـ فقود or فقدان *faqd*, or *foqood*, or *fiqdán*, loss.

فقد *faqada*, he lost; *foqida*, it was lost.

افقد *afqada*, he caused the loss.

فاقد *fáqid*, lost, missing; loser.

فقيد *faqeed*, lost; especially dead, deceased (of a murdered man).

مفقود *mafqood*, lost.

تفقّد *tafaqqada*, he searched for a lost thing, inspected.

افتقد *iftaqada*, he visited the sick. [عيادة

فقر *faqr*, poverty.

فقير ـ فقراء *faqeer*, pl. *foqará*, poor; a "fakir."

فقير الحال *faqeer el-hál*, poor, poor in state.

فقرة ـ فقر *fiqra*, or *faqra*, pl. *fiqar*, tale; paragraph, clause, vertebra.

عامود فقاريّ *a'ámood faqáriy*, spinal column, backbone.

فقس *faqs*, a hatching, breaking the shell.

فقّوس *faqqoos*, a kind of gourd plant, pumpkin.

فقط *faqat*, only, not more; that is all. [قط

تفقيطة *tafqeeta*, the total of a sum written down in *words*.

فقع or فرقع *faqa'a*, or *farqu'a*, it burst, exploded.

فقه ـ فقاهة *fiq-h*, or *faqáha*, the dogmatic theology of the Moslems, jurisprudence.

فقيه ـ فقهاء *faqeeh*, pl. *foqahá*, theologian; teacher or reciter of the Koran.

فقي or فقّي *fiqy* or *fiqqy*, vulgarism for *faqeeh*.

فكّ *fakka*, he unloosed, untied, relieved. [حلّ]

مفكوك *mafkook*, loosened, unfastened.

فكّ - افكاك *fakk*, pl. *afkák*, jaw; an unloosing. [حنك]

فكر - افكار *fikr*, pl. *afkar*, thought, opinion. [بال]

فكّر *fakkara*, he reminded, made think.

تفكّر *tafakkara*, he thought, reflected.

افتكر *iftakara*, he thought, was of opinion, remembered.

فاكر *fákir*, mindful, remembering, thinking.

فكاهة *fukáha*, gaiety.

فاكهة - فواكه *fákiha*, pl. *fawákih*, fruit. [ثمر]

فاكهاني *fákihániy*, fruiterer.

فلّ *full*, jasmine, white scented blossom.

فلّ - فرّ *falla*, vulgarism in Upper Egypt for *farra*, he fled.

فلت *falata*, he ran away, escaped.

فلّت *fallata*, he smuggled, allowed to escape. [هرّب]

مفلوت عيارة *mafloot 'iyároh*, broken or spoilt calibre (of gun).

فلت *falat*, debauchery.

فلاتي - فلاتية *falátiy*, pl. *falátiya*, debauchee, blackguard; robber.

فلاتية و حرامية و اشقياء *falátiya wa harámiya wa ashqiyá*, robbers, ruffians, brigands, &c.

تفليتة *tafleeta*, contraband, smuggling.

فلج *falaja*, he split in two.

فلج *falj*, split, one-half.

فالج *fálij*, hemiplegia, paralysis. [شلل]

مفلوج *maflooj*, paralytic; split in two.

فلاح *faláh*, God's blessing, prosperity.

فلاحة *faláha*, tillage. [حراثة]

فلاّح *falláh*, peasant, "fellah."

فالح *fálih*, useful, beneficial. [صالح]

فلذ *filiz*, bit, morsel.

فلوذق *falozaq*, pudding of sugar and starch, gelatine. [بالوظة]

فلس - فلوس *fals*, pl. *foloos*, mite, atom, scale of fish; rubbish, nonsense.

فلوس *foloos*, money, cash. [عملة - نقد]

افلس or فلّس or تفالس *aflasa*, or *fallasa*, or *tafálasa*, he became bankrupt, failed. [اعسار]

افلاس or تفليس or تفالس *iflás*, or *taflees*, or *tafálus*, failure of a non-trader; bankruptcy of a trader.

تفليسة *tafleesa*, a bankruptcy case.

وكيل التفليسة *wakeel et-tafleesa*, administrator of a bankrupt's estate.

افلاس بالتقصير *iflás bit-taqseer*, simple bankruptcy of a trader.

افلاس بالتدليس *iflás bit-tadlees*, fraudulent bankruptcy.

مفلس or متفالس *muflis*, or *mutafális*, bankrupt.

مدين مفلس *madeen muflis*, bankrupt debtor.

فلسفة or فیلسفة *filsafa*, or *feelsafa* (Greek), philosophy.

فیلسوف or فلیسوف *filsoof* (Greek), philosopher, atheist.

متفلسف *mutafalsif*, sophist.

فلاطون or افلاطون *Flátoon*, or *Iflátoon* (Greek), Plato.

فلع - فلعة *fala'a*, he split; *fila'a*, a split, slice.

فلفل *filfil*, pepper.

فلافل *faláfil*, bean paste, condiment.

فلق *falaqa*, he split open.

فلقة *filqa*, slice, crack in a wall, fissure.

فلقة *falaqa*, a cleft stick; stocks to hold the feet; hence a pole and loops of string for holding up the soles of the feet for the torture of the *bastinado*.

فلق - افلاق *falaq*, pl. *afláq*, split trunk of a palm-tree; beam.

مفلوق *maflooq*, split, cleft open.

فلك or فلك *falaka*, or *fallaka*, the breast swelled out.

فلك - افلاك *falak*, pl. *aflák*, the convex sky; globe, firmament.

علم الفلك *'ilm el-falak*, astronomy. [رصد - نجم]

فلكيّ *falakiy*, astronomer.

فلك *fulk* (femin.), boat.

فلوكة - فلائك *falooka*, pl. *faláyik*, felucca, boat.

فلائكيّ *faláyikiy*, boatman. [مراكبيّ]

فلمنك *Filemenk*, Flemish, Holland.

فلان or فلان *folán*, or *folániy*, So and So; such a one, a certain person or thing.

فلّين *falleen*, cork.

فم - افواه *fum*, pl. *afwáh*, mouth, orifice. [فوهة]

افمام *afmám* (as if pl. of *fumm*), mouths of canals.

فنّ - فنون *funn*, pl. *fonoon*, species, art, trickery.

دار الفنون *dár el-fonoon*, academy.

تفنّن *tafannana*, he invented, trumped up; was an adept.

فنتازيا *fantázia* (Italian), fantasia, a public show, rejoicings.

فنجان - فناجين *finján*, pl. *fanájeen* (Persian), cup, vulgarly pronounced *fingál* or *filyán*.

فنّخ *fannakha*, he overcame, made a fool of.

فند - افناد *find*, pl. *afnád*, species; troops.

فنّد *fannada*, he criticised, ridiculed.

فندق - بندق *funduq* (Italian, *fondaco*), store, hotel; also *bunduq*, (Venetian) gold sequin; filbert nut.

فنار *fanár*, lighthouse.

فانوس - فوانيس *fánoos*, pl. *fawánees*, lantern.

فنش *fanasha*, he took up much room, swaggered.

فنى *fania*, it faded.

فانى *fáni*, fading, evanescent, mortal.

فَنَاء *faná*, a fading away, a being mortal.

دار البقاء and دار الفَناء *dár el-faná*, this lower world which passes away; *dár el-baqá*, the abode of permanence, heaven.

فهد *fahd*, lynx, leopard.

فهرست *fihrist* (Persian), index, catalogue.

فهرسة *fahrasa*, index, catalogue.

فهق *fahaqa*, he wounded in the neck, half-strangled.

فهِم *fahima*, he understood.

فهم *fahm*, the understanding.

فهمي or فهيم *faheem*, or *fahmiy*, intelligent.

فاهم *fáhim*, one who understands.

مفهوم *mafhoom*, understood; of course.

فهّم *fahhama*, he made understand, explained.

استفهم *istafhama*, he wished to understand, interrogated.

استفهام *istifhám*, interrogatory, inquiry.

فوت or فَوات *föt*, or *fawát*, a passing away; interval.

فوات الميعاد *fawát el-mee'yád*, lapse of an interval.

فات ـ يفوت *fáta*, he passed; *yafoot*, he passes.

فوّت *fawwata*, he made or let pass.

تفاوت *tafáwut*, interval of time.

فوج ـ افواج *föj*, pl. *afwáj*, troop, band, crowd.

فوح *föh*, exhalation of smell.

فاح ـ يفوح *fáha*, it gave out a good smell; *yafooh*, it smells nice.

فوّح *fawwaha*, it smelled strong, stank.

فؤاد ـ افئدة *fooád*, pl. *afida*, heart, soul, spirit.

فور ـ فوران *för*, or *fawarán*, ebullition, impetuosity.

فوراً *fawrán*, at once, quickly, forthwith.

فار *fára*, it began to boil; gushed, bubbled.

فوّارة *fawwára*, fountain.

فار ـ فيران *fár*, pl. *feerán*, mouse, rat.

فارة *fára*, carpenter's plane.

دار فور *Dár Foor*, the land of the Foor, Soudanese Darfour.

فوز *föz*, victory, safety.

فوزي *fözíy*, victorious; proper name for a man.

فاز *fáza*, he succeeded in, escaped.

فائز ـ فائض *fáyiz*, interest on money (see فيض).

فوّض *fawwada*, he gave power or jurisdiction, he left a matter to another's judgment.

انا افوّضه اليك *aná ofawwidho ileik*. I leave it to you to decide.

فوضى *föda*, communism, anarchy.

تفويض *tafweed*, giving jurisdiction, delegation of power.

مفاوضة *mofáwada*, community of interests.

فوطة ‎- نوط‎ *foota*, pl. *fo-at*, towel, duster.

فوق ‎*foq*, on, upon; above, upstairs; over; more than.

فوقاني ‎*foqániy*, upper, uppermost.

فوق تحت ‎*foq taht*, up down; upside down.

فاق ‎*fáqa*, he surpassed, was preeminent.

فائق ‎*fáyiq*, pre-eminent, superior, excelling.

افاق ‎*afáqa*, he recovered health, became sober, wide awake.

افاقة ‎*ifáqa*, convalescence, recovery.

فواق ‎*fooáq*, sob, death-agony.

فول ‎*fool*, broad beans.

فوّال ‎*fawwál*, seller of (cooked) beans.

فولية ‎*foolaya*, wild thyme, mint.

فوهة ‎- فوهات ‎*fooha*, pl. *foohát*, orifice. [فم]

فوّه ‎*fowwah*, madder, "*garance.*"

تفاوه ‎*tafáwuh*, interview, mouth to mouth.

فيّ ‎*fiya*, my mouth.

فوه ‎- فاه ‎- فيه ‎*foho*, *fáho* and *fehi*, his mouth. [Nom., Accus., Genit.]

في ‎*fee*, in, into, at, among, concerning.

في المائة ‎*fil-máya*, per cent.

عشرة في عشرة ‎*'ashara fi 'ashara*, 10 times 10.

فيه ‎*feeh* (colloquial), there is, there are.

كان فيه ‎*kán fih* (colloquial), there was, there were.

فيه ‎*feehi*, in him, in it.

ما فيه ش ‎- ما فيش ‎*má feesh* (colloquial), there is not, there are not.

في ‎- افياء ‎*fay*, pl. *afyá*, shade. [ظلّ]

فيات ‎*feeát*, at so much; price (more used in Turkish than in Arabic).

فيد ‎*faid*, endurance, disappearance. (This verbal root is not used.)

فائدة ‎- فوائد ‎*fáyida*, pl. *fawáyid*, advantage, benefit; interest on money; commentary or scholiast of text; moral to be drawn from a story or legal opinion.

فوائد متجمّدة ‎*fawáyid mutajammida*, compound interest.

افاد ‎*afáda*, he informed; it benefitted.

يفيد ‎*yofeed*, he informs, it is useful, beneficial.

افادة ‎*ifáda*, information, statement; benefit.

مفيد ‎*mofeed*, informer, informing; useful, interesting.

استفاد ‎*istafáda*, he inquired, derived benefit.

يستفاد من ‎*yostafád min*, it is ascertainable from.

فيروزي ‎*fairooziy* (Persian, *fairooza*), turquoise.

فيض ‎*faiz*, or *faid*, abundance, exuberance.

فيضان *fayadán*, overflow, flood.

فيضان النيل *fayadán en-Neel*, Nile in flood, time of high Nile.

فاض ـ يفيض *fáda*, it abounded; *yafeed*, it is in flood.

فائض ـ فاض ـ فائز *fáyiz*, surplus, overflow, interest on money, often incorrectly written فائظ and فائز.

فوائض *fawáyiz*, pl., interest, profits on money.

فيفاء ـ فيافي *faifa*, pl. *fayáfi*, desert.

فيل ـ افيال or فيلة *feel*, pl. *afyál*, or *fiala*, elephant.

سنّ الفيل *sinn el-feel*, elephant's tooth, ivory. [عاج]

فيّوم *Fayyoom*, a province in Upper Egypt, a large oasis to the W. of the Nile.

Q.

ق *Qáf*. Value = 100.

(Q. (1) A strong guttural, a *k* pronounced low down in the throat; (2) sometimes *unsounded*, as a hiatus; and (3) *vulgarly*, as a *g* in *go*, *get*. Thus حقيقة " the truth," *haqeeqa*, becomes *ha-ee-a*, or vulgarly *hageega*.)

قِ ـ وقى *qi* (imperative), guard thou! (see *waqa*.)

قاء ـ تقيّأ *qá*, or *taqayyá*, be vomited.

قى or قىء *qay*, or *qoyá*, vomit.

مقىّ *moqayya*, or *moqeey*, emetic.

قادن ـ خاتون *qádin* (Turkish), lady.

قازمة *qázma* (Turkish), pick-axe.

قاعة ـ قوع *qáa'a*, inner private room (see *qóa'*).

قاف *qáf*, the letter *qáf*; Mt. Caucasus.

قاقلة *qáqola*, cardamum.

قال ـ قول *qála*, he said (see قيل).

قام ـ قوم *qáma*, he stood (see *qōm*).

قامة ـ قوم *qáma*, height, stature (see *qōm*).

قامشي *qámshi* (Turkish), whip.

قاموس *qámoos*, ocean; Arabic Lexicon.

قانون ـ قوانين *qánoon*, pl. *qawáneen*, (Greek *kanon*), law, canon, code of law; statute; fee; musical instrument like a harpsichord.

قانوناً *qánoonán*, according to law.

قانوني *qánooniy*, legal, statutory.

قانونيّة *qánooniya*, legality.

قاوق *qáwuq* (Turkish), large cap like a football.

قاون *qáwoon* (Turkish), melon (not *water* melon).

قائم مقام ـ قوم *qáyim maqám*, *locum tenens*, lieutenant-colonel (see *qōm*).

قبّة *qabba*, collar. [ياقة]

قبّة ـ قبب *qubba*, pl. *qubab*, dome, cupola.

قبوة *qabwa*, a little arch, vault.

مقبّب *moqabbab*, domed, convex.

قبح *qaboha*, it was vile, abominable.

قبّح *qabbaha*, he stigmatised, blamed.

قباحة qabáha, vileness, fault; (in Turkish law) a contravention. [مخالفة]

قبيح qabeeh, base, vile.

قبر qabara, he interred, buried the dead. [دفن]

قبر qabr, pl. قبور qoboor, tomb.

مقبرة - مقابر maqbara, pl. maqábir, cemetery.

قبرص qibris, island of Cyprus.

قبس or اقتبس qabasa, or iqtabasa, he learnt (eagerly).

قبشة qobsha (Turkish, qopcha), hook and eye.

قبض في qabada fi, he seized. [ضبط - مسك]

قبض qabd, seizure.

قبضة qabda, grip, handle, hilt.

انقبض inqabada, he was costive, griped.

مقبوض maqbood, seized; (money) encashed.

قبط or اقباط qibt or aqbát, the Copts, Jacobite Christians of Egypt.

قبطى qibtiy, a Copt, Coptic; Jacobite Christian; linen.

قبقاب - قباقيب qabqáb, pl. qabáqeeb, pattens, sandals.

قبل qabala, he received, accepted.

قبّل qabbala, he kissed. [باس]

قابل or تقابل qábala, or taqábala, he was face to face, met, equalled as a set-off.

اقبل aqbala, it approached, was prosperous.

استقبل istaqbala, he went to meet, welcomed.

قبل qabl, before (of time).

قبلا or من قبل qablán, or min qabl, previously.

قبل qubl, front part; pudenda.

قبلة qubla, a kiss. [بوسة]

قبل qibal, power, presence; a facing towards, as regards.

من قبله min qibalihi, as regards him.

قبلة - محراب qibla, a facing towards Mecca for prayer; hence the niche or altar-place of a mosque, the mihráb.

قبلىّ qibliy, south, southern.

الوجه القبلىّ - صعيد el-wajh el-qibliy, the southern part, i.e. Upper Egypt, or Sa'eed.

قبول qabool, receipt, acceptance, consent.

على قبول 'ala qabool, on the understanding that; on his accepting the condition.

ايجاب و قبول eejáb wa qabool, offer and acceptance.

قبيل qabeel, category, class, ancestry.

قبيلة - قبائل qabeela, pl. qabáyil, tribe, "Kabyle."

اقبال iqbál, auspicious arrival, prosperity; an imperial concubine.

استقبال istiqbál, a welcome, a going out to meet; the future.

قابل qábil, an acceptor, comer; possible; capable; next or coming (week, &c.).

قابِليَّة qábiliya, capability, possibility.

قابِلة qábila, midwife, she who receives the new-born infant.

هو قابل للانفصال hoa qábil lil-infisál, he can be dismissed; it is possible to dismiss him.

قبالة qibála, piece of land in a [حوض] hōd.

مقبل muqbil, coming, next (week, month, &c.), prosperous.

مستقبل mustaqbil, future.

مقابل moqábil, equivalent, provided for.

مقابلة moqábala, an equivalent; quid pro quo, a set-off.

مقبول maqbool, accepted, received, popular.

تقبيل taqbeel, a kissing.

قبانة qabána, official weighing of goods.

قبّان qabbán, steelyard, Roman balance.

قبّاني qabbániy, official weigher.

قبّة ‐ قبوة qabwa, a little arch, vault (see qubba).

قبودان qaboodán (European), ship captain.

قبودان باشا qaboodán Báshá (Turkish), Admiral.

قبوط qaboot (European), capote, cloak.

قتب qatab, hump, load; pack.

ابو قتب aboo qatab, a humpback.

قتل qatala, he killed, put to death; also (provincial) he "kilt," wounded, hit.

قتل نفساً qatala nafsán, he killed a soul, he killed a man.

قتل نفسه qatala nafsaho, he killed himself.

قتل عمداً qatala 'amdán, he killed with intent.

قتل مع سبق الاصرار qatala ma' sabq el-isrár, he killed with premeditation (French jurisprudence).

قتل شنقاً qotila shanqán, he was executed by hanging.

قاتل qátil, murderer, killer.

القاتل يقتل el-qátil yoqtal, the slayer shall be slain.

قتيل ‐ قتلي qateel, pl. qatla, slain, killed.

مقتول ‐ مقاتيل maqtool, pl. maqáteel, slain, killed.

قاتل qátala, he fought, battled with.

قتال qitál, battle, mutual killing.

قثّاء quttá, cucumber, gourd, pumpkin.

مقاث or مقثاء maqútt, or maqtá, kitchen garden, cucumber garden.

قح qohh, purity of race.

قحة ‐ وقح qiha, impudence (see waqih).

قحبة ‐ قحاب qahba, pl. qiháb, whore; cough.

قحط qaht, drought.

قحط وغلاء qaht wa ghalá, drought and dearth.

قحم or اقتحم qahama, or iqtahama, he rushed at, charged on horseback.

قحوان qohwán, camomile.

قد qad (an emphatic particle), indeed, in fact.

قد كان qad kána, and indeed it was so.

قد ـ قدود qadd, pl. qodood, a cutting into strips; hence the human figure, stature; a fixed quantity.

قد qadd (vulgarism), so much, how much.

قد شهر qadd shahr, about a month.

قد اي qadd aiy, what quantity? about what?

قدح qadh, criticism, blame.

قدح ـ اقداح qadah, pl. aqdáh, goblet, cup, glass; Egyptian pottle of 1¾ quarts, or 2 litres.

قدر qadara, he could; it was worth.

اقدر aqdir, I can, am able to.

قدّر qaddara, he estimated, valued.

تقدير taqdeer, valuation, assessment; fate, predestination; meaning, hypothesis.

اقتدر iqtadara, he was capable of, had the power to.

اقتدار iqtidár, ability, capacity.

مقتدر muqtadir, able, capable.

قدر qadr, fixed quantity; power.

قدر qadar, destiny, power, value, quantity; (qadr and qadar, are practically the same).

قد و قضاء qadar wa qudá, destiny and fate.

ليلة القدر lailat el-qadr, Night of Power, 27th of Ramadan.

على قدر الامكان 'ala qadar el-imkán, as much as possible, to the utmost possible.

قدرة qidra, saucepan, earthen pot. [حلّة]

قدرة qudra, power.

قادر or قدير qádir, or qadeer, able, powerful.

مقدار ـ مقادير miqdár, pl. maqádeer, a quantity, a certain amount.

مقدرة maqdara, power, wealth.

قدس quds, sanctity, saintship; Reverend, as a title for a priest.

القدس el-quds, the holy place, Jerusalem.

الروح القدس er-rooh el-quds, the Holy Ghost.

قديس qadees, holy, pious; saint.

قدّاس quddás, Liturgy; the Sacrament.

قدّس qaddasa, he consecrated.

مقدس maqdis, a holy place.

كتاب مقدّس kitáb moqaddas, Holy Bible.

قادوس ـ قواديس qádoos, pl. qawádees, the jars tied on the wheel of the sáqiya.

قدم ـ اقدام qadam, pl. aqdám, (femin.) foot.

قدم qidem, seniority, precedence, priority.

قدّام qoddám, in front of. [امام]

قُدَّامِي *qoddámiy*, front part, the van.

قدوم *qadoom*, adze.

قدوم *qodoom*, arrival.

قدم *qadama*, he arrived, advanced.

قدّم *qaddama*, he put forward, presented.

قدّم بلاغ *qaddama balágh*, he presented a petition.

اقدم *aqdama*, he persevered boldly.

تقدّم *taqaddama*, he came forward.

اقدام *iqdám*, energy, perseverance.

تقديم *taqdeem*, a presenting, presentation.

قادم *qádim*, a comer, next (week, month, &c.).

قديم - قدماء *qadeem*, pl. *qodamá*, ancient. [عتيق]

اقدم *aqdam*, more ancient, prior, senior.

اقدميّة *aqdamiya*, precedence, seniority.

مقدم *muqdim*, front part, prow, or bow of ship; previous.

مقدّم *moqaddim*, overseer, foreman; the old man-servant of a harem.

مقدّمة *moqaddama*, preface, promiss in logic.

مقدّم or متقدّم *moqaddam*, or *motaqaddim*, previous, in advance, prior.

متقدّم فى السنّ *motaqaddim fi s-sinn*, advanced in age, old.

قدوة *qidwa*, sample, model, pattern.

قدة - وقد *qida*, combustion (see *waqada*).

قذر or قاذورات *qazar*, or *qázoorát*, sewage.

قذر *qazir*, fetid, drainy smell, foul.

قذف *qazafa*, he ejaculated, hurled; slandered; accused of adultery.

قذف *qazf*, slander, accusation of adultery.

مقذوف *maqzoof*, projectile. [مرمى]

مقذاف *miqdáf*, oar.

قرّ *qarra*, it was fixed, rested firm.

قرار *qarár*, stability, decision, resolution.

قرّر *qarrara*, he fixed, deposed to, put down in writing. [حرّر]

تقرير *taqreer*, a fixing, deposition, letter, document, memorandum.

اقرّ *aqarra*, he confessed. [اعترف]

اقرار *iqrár*, confession.

تقرّر *taqarrara*, it was fixed; it was laid down as a rule.

استقرّ *istaqarra*, it was fixed, certain, permanent.

مقرّ *moqirr*, he who confesses.

مقرّ *maqarr*, a fixed place, post.

مقرّر *moqarrar*, certain, established; direct (of taxation); permanent (domicile).

محلّ مستقرّ *mahall mostaqarr*, fixed abode, domicile.

ارض قارّة *ard qárra*, continent of land.

اقرأ - قراء *qará*, he read; *aqrá*, he made read.

قرأة *qiráat*, a reading.

قاري٠ (216) قرص

قَرَّاء - قاريء *qári*, pl. *qorrá*, reader.
القرآن *el-qorán*, the Koran, the book for reading par excellence, Moslem bible.
انقرأ *inqará*, it was read, legible.
قُرّ - اقراء *qur*, pl. *aqrá*, interval of purification after divorce.
مقراء *maqrá*, a reading, or group of readers of the Koran.
قراغول or تراقول *qaràghol*, or *qaráqōl* (Turkish), mainguard; police station.
قره كوز *qara ghyooz* (Turkish), black eye; Punch and Judy.
قرب *qariba*, it was near (of time or place).
قَرَّب *qarraba*, he came near, brought near; approached, approximated.
تقرَّب *taqarraba*, he came near; he took the Sacrament.
قرب *qorb*, vicinity, nearness.
قريب *qareeb*, near, soon, speedy.
عن قريب *'an qareeb*, soon, shortly.
قريب - اقرباء *qareeb*, pl. *aqribá*, relative, kinsfolk.
اقرب - اقارب *aqrab*, pl. *aqárib*, nearer; near relative.
قرابة *qaráha*, relationship, kinship.
قربان *qorbán*, an approaching to God by sacrifice; a sacrifice, deodand; Eucharist.
قربان بيرام or عيد الاضحى *qorbán Bairám*, 10th day of Zil Hijja, the day of sacrifice at Mina near Mecca, the greatest Moslem festival, also called *'eed el-adha*.

تقريب *taqreeb*, approximation.
تقريبا *taqreebán*, approximately, nearly.
قربة - قرب *qirba*, pl. *qirab*, goatskin sack for water; about 14½ gallons.
قارب - قوارب *qárib*, pl. *qawárib*, small boat.
مقربة *maqriba*, vicinity.
قربانة or قرابينة *qarbána*, or *qarabána*, or *qarábeena* (European), carbine.
قربيصة *qorbaisa*, large brick.
قرح - قروح *qarh*, pl. *qorooh*, ulcer.
اقترح *iqtaraha*, he proposed, voted for.
قرد - قرود *qird*, pl. *qorood*, monkey. [نسناس]
قراد *qurád*, a tick on animals.
قرز or قرص *qaraza*, or *qarasa*, he pinched.
قرش - قروش - غروش *qirsh*, pl. *qoroosh* (from Turkish *ghroosh*, which is from German *groschen*), piastre, 2½d.
قرش صاغ or قرش ديواني *qirsh ságh* or *diwániy*, a good or government piastre, 2½d.
على دائر القرش الواحد *'ala dáyir el-qirsh el-wáhid*, (cash paid down) piastre by piastre.
قريش - قراش *qoraish*, pl. *qorásh*, a famous tribe of Mecca, kindred of Mahomet.
قرص *qars*, a cutting, piercing, stinging.
قرص *qarasa*, he cut open, he pinched, pricked; (the serpent) bit; (the scorpion) stung.

قرص ‒ اقراص *qors*, pl. *aqrás*, disk, round cake; small metal disk used as a female ornament for the head.

قرصة *qarsa*, a sting, insect-bite, prick, pinch.

قرّاصة *qarrása*, pincers, hand-cuffs.

قريصة *qareesa*, bean paste. [طعميّة]

قرصان ‒ قراصين *qorsán*, pl. *qaráseen*, corsair.

مقراص *miqrás*, pincers, knife.

قرض *qarada*, he cut off a piece; lent money.

قرض ‒ قروض *qard*, pl. *qorood*, loan. [سلف]

اقترض or استقرض *iqtarada*, or *istaqrada*, he borrowed.

انقرض *inqarada*, it was cut off, became extinct.

اقتراض بحريّ *iqtirád bahriy*, bottomry, *contrat à la grosse*.

استقراض *istiqrád*, a loan, public loan.

مقراض *miqrád*, scissors. [مقصّ]

قرط *qort*, bunch, ring, girt, trifolium, leek.

قرط *qarata*, he cut in pieces.

قيراط ‒ قراريط *qeerát*, pl. *qaráreet*, 1-24th part; 175 sq. mètres or 209 sq. yards; ·197 grams; 1-16th of a dirhem; about one inch; half a gill.

قرطاس ‒ قراطيس *qirtás*, pl. *qaratees*, paper, documents, scrip, consols, stocks.

قرطم *qortom*, carthamus, safflower, wild saffron, a food for camels.

قرع *qara'a*, he knocked at a door; cast lots.

قرعة *qara'a*, baldness.

اقرع *aqra'*, bald.

قرع كوسة *qara' koosa*, a small vegetable marrow.

قرعة *qora'a*, a casting of lots, ballot.

قرعة عسكريّة *qora'a 'askariya*, conscription.

فرز القرعة *farz el-qora'a*, a choosing by ballot.

مقرعة *miqra'a*, whip, a flogging.

قرفة *qirfa*, skin, bark; cinnamon.

قرفة *qarafa*, nausea, loathing.

قرافة *qaráfa*, cemetery, tomb.

قرفان *qarfán*, disgusted.

اقترف *iqtarafa*, he committed a crime. [ارتكب]

استقرف *istaqrafa*, he loathed, hated.

مقرف *moqrif*, cross, bad tempered, disgusted.

قراقة *qaráqa* (Italian?), hoe, rake; dredger.

قرمزيّ *qirmiziy*, crimson, scarlet.

قرمزيّة *qirmiziya*, scarlet fever, scarlatina.

قرن *qarana*, he joined, attached.

قارن *qárana*, he joined himself to; he compared, set side by side; was in conjunction.

اقترن ب *iqtarana bi*, he joined himself to, was connected with, adjacent.

قرن ‒ اقران *qiru*, pl. *aqrán*, equal, peer, rival.

قرين (218) تقسيط

قرين *qareen*, near, touching; a comrade.

قرينة ـ قرائن *qareena*, pl. *qaráyin*, a near thing, inference, context.

قرائن الاحوال *qaráyin el-ahwál*, probabilities of the case; circumstantial evidence.

قران *qirán*, auspicious approach; the conjunction of planets.

قرآن ـ قراء *qorán*, the Koran (see *qará*).

اقتران *iqtirán*, union.

مقارنة *moqárana*, comparison, coincidence.

قرن ـ قرون *qarn*, pl. *qoroon*, horn; age, epoch; bit, piece, morsel.

ذو القرنين *Zoo l-qarnain*, the two-horned one; a title applied to Alexander the Great as the reputed son of the horned Ammon (see Koran, chap. xviii.).

قرنة *qorna*, corner; scullery-sink.

قرنب *qoronb*, cabbage. [كرنب]

قرنبيط *qarnabeet*, cauliflower.

قرنافة *qornáfa*, stock or butt-end of rifle.

قرنفل *qaranful*, "girofle," clove, spice, carnation.

قرنطينة *qaranteena* (Italian), quarantine.

قرة *qara* (Turkish), land, mainland; black; used in words like *qaraqol*, *qaraqyooz*, &c.

قرةقول *qaraqol* (Turkish), main-guard, police-station; vulgarly *qaraqon*. [or قراقون]

قرية ـ قرى *qariya*, pl. *qora*, village.

قروط *qarwata*, he cut, clipped, snipped.

قز ـ دود القز *qazz*, raw silk; *dood el-qazz*, silk-worm.

قزاز *qazzáz*, seller of raw silk.

قزازة ـ قزائز *qizáza*, pl. *qazáyiz*, bottle. [زجاج]

لوح قزاز *lōh qizáz*, pane of glass.

قزح *qozah*, cloud-angel.

قوس قزح *qōs qozah*, Qozah's bow, rainbow.

قزدير or قصدير *qazdeer* (Greek, *kassiteros*), tin.

قزعة *qoza'a*, a small piece; dwarf.

قزمة ـ قزم *qazma*, pl. *qizam* (from Turkish *qázmaq*, to dig), pickaxe.

قزان ـ قزغان *qazán* (Turkish *qazghán*), cauldron.

قس *qass* or *qiss*, a Christian priest, Reverend.

قسيس ـ قسس *qasees*, pl. *qosos*, a Christian priest, a Reverend.

قيسارية *qeesáriya*, street in a bazar, khan.

قسط ـ اقساط *qist*, pl. *aqsát*, justice; share, portion, instalment.

قسّط *qassata*, he portioned off, paid by instalments.

تقسيط *taqseet*, instalment, paying instalments; a kind of title-deed.

قسطاس *qustás*, balance of justice; scales.

قسطنطينيّة *Qostantiniya*, Constantinople.

قسم or قسّم *qasama*, or *qassama*, he divided, classified, apportioned.

اقسم بالله *aqsama billáhi*, he swore by God.

قسم - اقسام *qasam*, pl. *aqsám*, oath. [حلف - يمين]

قسم - اقسام - مركز *qism*, pl. *aqsám*, portion, part, district; the "*qisms*" of Upper Egypt corresponded to the "*markazes*" or arrondissements of Lower Egypt, but this official term (*qism*) has lately been abolished in favour of *markaz* throughout Egypt.

ناظر القسم or مأمور المركز *názir el-qism*, former official title of Prefect of arrondissement in Upper Egypt, now abolished in favour of *mámoor el-markaz*.

قسمة *qisma*, share, fate, "*kismet*"; division.

قاسم *qásim*, he who divides; a man's name.

قسيم *qaseem*, a fellow sharer, equal.

قسيمة - قسايم *qaseema*, pl. *qasáyim*, receipt-foil which is torn out of a book of counter-foils.

تقسيم *taqseem*, division; classification.

مقسوم *maqsoom*, dividend, divided.

مقسوم عليه *maqsoom 'aleih*, divisor.

خارج القسمة *khárijel-qisma*, quotient, result.

قسا *qasá*, he was hard, cruel.

قساوة or قسوة *qasáwa*, or *qaswa*, cruelty, harshness.

قسيّ - قسيان *qasiy*, pl. *qisyán*, cruel, harsh.

قشّ *qashsha*, he swept up, collected.

قشّ - قشوش *qashsh*, or *qushsh*, pl. *qoshoosh*, straw, thatch.

قشّة *qushsha*, a bit of straw, rubbish, chaff; nest.

مقشّة *miqashsha*, broom.

قشبر *qoshbor*, scurf of hair.

قشر *qashara*, he peeled, barked, shelled.

قشرة or قشر - قشور *qishr*, or *qishra*, pl. *qoshoor*, rind, peel, husk, crust; egg-shell.

قشط *qashata*, he scratched out, erased. [شطب]

قشّط *qashshata*, he robbed, stripped.

قشط *qisht*, erasure, scratching out. [كشط]

قشطة *qishta*, cream; custard-apple; (pine-apple?).

قشطيّ *qishtiy* (medical), aphthous, of thrush.

قشعر *qash'ara*, he shivered, had "goose flesh."

قشعريرة *qosha'reera*, a shivering.

قشف *qashaf*, chap, chilblain, sore.

قشلاق‎ *qishláq* (Turkish), barracks, winter quarters.

قصّ‎ *qassa*, he cut, narrated.

قصّة‎ - قصص‎ *qissa*, pl. *qisas*, piece, story, tale.

قصّاص‎ *qassás*, a professional clipper of donkeys, horses, camels, &c.

قصّ‎ or قصص‎ *qass*, or *qasas*, sternum, chest.

قصاص‎ *qisás*, retribution, *lex talionis*.

اقتصّ‎ *iqtassa*, he took vengeance, pursued, tracked.

مقصّ‎ *maqass*, scissors.

مقاصّة‎ *maqássa*, a mutual cutting, compensation.

قصب‎ - اقصاب‎ *qasab*, pl. *aqsáb*, cane, rod, flute; gold thread or embroidery, gauze embroidery.

قصب سكّر‎ *qasab sukkar*, sugar-cane; *qasab muss*, sugar-cane for sucking.

قصبة‎ *qasaba*, pole, measure of 11⅔ feet, 3·55 mètres.

قصبة‎ *qasaba* (in Turkish), town, village.

قصّاب‎ *qassáb*, land-surveyor. [مسّاح‎

قصّاب‎ *qassáb* (in Turkish), butcher. [جزّار‎

قصد‎ *qasada*, he intended, tended towards.

قصد‎ *qasd*, intention, motive, aim. [عمد‎]

قصدا‎ or بقصد‎ *qasdán*, or *bi-qasdin*, on purpose.

سوء القصد‎ *soo el-qasd*, evilness of intention.

قصد سيّئ‎ *qasd saiy*, evil intention.

قصيدة‎ *qaseeda*, sonnet, short poem.

قصّاد‎ *qossád*, in front of, facing.

تقصّد‎ *taqassada*, he intended, determined.

اقتصاد‎ *iqtisád*, economy, moderation.

مقصد‎ - مقاصد‎ *maqsad*, pl. *maqásid*, aim, object in view.

مقصود‎ - مقاصيد‎ *maqsood*, pl. *maqáseed*, the same as *masqad*.

قصدير‎ or قزدير‎ *qasdeer* (Greek *kassiteros*), tin.

قصر‎ *qasara*, he shortened, confined; failed in, fell short; he bleached linen.

قصّر‎ *qassara*, he shortened, made fall short; he bleached linen.

قصور‎ *qosoor*, defect, shortcoming, neglect.

تقصير‎ *taqseer*, a making defective, negligence.

افلاس بالتقصير‎ *iflás bit-taqseer*, simple bankruptcy, not fraudulent. [cf. دلس‎

تقصيرة‎ *taqseera*, short stick.

قصير‎ *qaseer* (vulgarly *qosayir*), pl. *qisár*, short.

قاصر‎ - قصّر‎ *qásir*, pl. *qossar*, minor, under age.

قصر‎ - قصور‎ *qasr*, or *qosoor*, defect, shortcoming, exception.

قصر‎ - اقصر‎ or قصور‎ *qasr*, pl. *aqsor*, or *qosoor*, palace, castle, citadel; Alcazar.

الاقصر‎ *El-Aqsor*, Luxor, i.e. the

temples or castles, of Luxor, and Karnak.

قنا ـ قصير *Qosair*, Kosair, a port on the Red Sea, east of Kena.

قيصر *qaisar* (Latin), Cæsar, Kaiser.

قيصر الهند *qaisar el-Hind*, Emperor or Empress of India.

قصريّة *qasriya*, chamber-pot.

اقصر ـ قصرى *aqsar*, (femin.) *qosra*, shorter.

مقصور *maqsoor*, shortened, shut up; bleached linen.

مقصورة *maqsoora*, inner chamber; shut up; a recluse virgin of Paradise; railed enclosure.

قصعة ـ قزعة *qosa'a*, or *qoza'a*, dwarf; *qasa'a*, large bowl, platter.

مقصع *maqsa'*, stunted, dwarfed.

قصف *qasafa*, he snapped, broke.

قصا *qasá*, distance, the far distance.

اقصى ـ قصيّ *qasiy*, pl. *aqsá*, distant.

اقصى *aqsa*, more distant.

المغرب الاقصى *el-maghrib el-aqsa*, the most distant or extreme West, Morocco.

المسجد الاقصى ـ صخرة *el-masjid el-aqsa*, the most distant mosque (of importance, from Mecca), the *Sakhra*, or Rock Mosque of Jerusalem.

اقصى الحدّ or اقصى المدّة *aqsa el-hadd*, or *aqsa el-modda*, the extreme limit, maximum of interval.

اقصى العقوبة *aqsa el-'oqooba*, the extreme penalty.

استقصاء *istiqsá*, investigation, inquiry.

قضّ ـ انقضّ على (*qadda*), *inqadda a'la*, he attacked.

قضبة *qadba*, wand, staff, rail.

قضيب ـ قضبان *qadeeb*, pl. *qodbán*, bar, staff; rail; penis.

قضى *qada*, he judged, decided, executed; died.

قضى حاجته *qada hájataho*, he accomplished his business.

انقضى *inqada*, it came to an end, was accomplished.

انقضى نحبه *inqada nahboho*, he died.

اقتضى *iqtada*, it became necessary.

قضاء *qadá*, the office of a judge; a sitting in judgment; fate; accident; province.

قضاءً *qadáan*, by accident, fatally.

قضاء و قدر *qadá wa qadar*, fate and destiny.

قضائي *qadáiiy*, judiciary, judicial.

ضبطيّة قضائيّة *zabtiya qadáiiya*, judiciary police, "*police judiciaire*."

قضيّة ـ قضايا *qadeeya*, pl. *qadáyá*, law-suit; case for trial; a dossier.

قاضي ـ قضاة *qádi*, pl. *qodát*, judge, cadi.

قاضي شرعي *qádi shara'iy*, a judge of the Moslem sacred law or *sheri'at*.

قاضي التحقيق *qádi et-tahqeeq* "*juge d'instruction*."

قاضي الحكم *qádi*, in *el-*

حكم القاضي *hukm el-qádi*, the sentence *which judges*, i.e. the sentence *to the effect that*, &c.

انقضاء *inqidá*, end, completion.

اقتضاء *iqtidá*, necessity.

مقتضى *moqtada*, necessary, to the effect that; the tenour or purport (of an order).

بمقتضى *bi-moqtada*, in consequence of, because of, according to.

قط *qat*, only, solely. [فقط]

قطّ *qatt*, not at all, never.

قطّ - قطاط *qitt*, pl. *qitát*, cat.

قطب - قطوب *qotb*, pl. *qotoob*, axis, pole of globe, pivot; sanctity, his reverence; chief, leader.

قطر *qatara*, it dripped; he attached, towed.

قطر - قطر *qatr*, pl. *qitar*, distillation, drop.

قطرة *qatra*, one drop.

قطّر *qattara*, he distilled.

تقطّر *taqattara*, it dripped; was towed.

قطر - قطار *qotr*, pl. *aqtár*, side; diameter; country, dominions of a kingdom.

اقطار مصريّة *aqtár masriya*, Egyptian dominions.

قطر *qotr*, aloes-wood.

قطر - قطورات *qatr*, pl. *qotoorát*, railway train.

قطار *qitár*, string of animals; railway train; a file of two soldiers.

قطرميز *qatrameez*, jar, vase.

قطران *qatrán*, tar, goudron.

قطيرة - قطائر *qateera*, pl. *qatáyir*, sailing boat, "dhow."

مقطور *maqtoor* (boats) in tow; (animals) in string; towed.

قطرب *qotrob*, demon, incubus.

قطع *qata'a*, he cut, interrupted; he brought; sometimes used like our idioms with "get."

قطعة - قطع *qita'a*, pl. *qita'*, piece, morsel.

قطع *qata'*, a cutting, interruption, decision.

قطعيّ *qata'iy*, final, decisive, incisive.

قطعًا *qata'án*, decidedly, decisively.

انقطع *inqata'a*, it was cut off, ceased.

استقطع *istaqta'a*, he wished to cut off; he deducted part of a servant's wages.

قاطع - قطّاع *qátia'*, pl. *qottáu'*, a cutter, incisive; a decisive (speech, sentence, &c.).

قاطع الطريق *qátia' et-tareeq*, highway robber.

قطيع *qatee'a*, flock, herd.

مقطعة *maqta'a*, piece, syllable; the dam of a canal or rivulet.

مقاطعة *moqáta'a*, province, district, shire.

مقطوع *maqtoo'a*, cut, cut off.

قطاعيّ وبالجملة *qitáa'iy wa bil-jumla*, retail and wholesale.

اقتطف or قطف qatafa or iqtatafa, he plucked fruit, gathered a vintage.

مقتطف moqtataf, collected, gathered in; an Arab magazine or miscellany.

مقطف ـ مقاطف maqtaf, pl. maqátif, basket.

قطيفة ـ قطائف qateefa, pl. qatáyif, velvet; in pl. a sort of pastry.

قطم or قطّم qatama, or qattama, he cut.

مقطّم moqattam, cut, sheer; name of the abrupt cliffs to the south of Cairo.

قطن qatana, he dwelt. [سكن]

قاطن ـ قطّان qátin, pl. qottán, a dweller, inhabiting.

قطن qatan, crupper, haunches, loins.

قطن ـ اقطان qotn, pl. aqtán, cotton. [cf. كتّان]

قطنيّة qotniya, cotton cloth, cotton goods; grain, pulse, beans.

قاطون ـ خليج qátoon, house sewer or underground canal into the *khaleej* in Cairo.

قعد qa'ada, he sat down (after standing); he rested, remained; continued. [جلس]

قعود qo'ood, act of sitting, sitting posture.

قاعد qá'yid, a sitter, seated, sitting down.

قاعدة ـ قواعد qá'yida, pl. qawá'yid, (fem.) something steadfast; a rule, principle.

قعدة in ذو القعدة qa'da, in the phrase *zoo l-qa'da*, the month of *repose* before the Hajj or pilgrimage, the 11th lunar Moslem month.

قعود ـ قعدان qá'ood, pl. qia'dán, young camel just fit to be used for riding.

تقاعد taqá'yada, he sat apart, he retired on a pension. [استودع]

تقاعد ـ معاش taqá'yud, pension; more commonly *ma'ásh*.

متقاعد motaqá'yid, retired, pensioner.

مقعد maq'ad, seat, place of sitting; storey, room.

مقعد moqa'id, cripple, who cannot stand.

قعر ـ قعور qa'r, pl. qo'oor, a hollow; bottom of a well, box, &c.

قعير qa'eer, deep, hollow.

قاعرة السكّة qá'irat es-sikka, in the open street.

مقعّر moqa'a'r, hollowed out, concave. [اجوف]

قفّة ـ قفف qoffa, pl. qofaf, basket.

قفتان qoftán, cassock, gown, long robe.

قفّاز ـ قفيز qaffáz, glove; qafeez, hasp of lock.

قفش qafasha, he seized, collared hold of.

قفص *qafas*, cage, wicker work, wicker bedstead, clothes-basket, lattice.

قفل *qafala*, he locked up, shut, ended, returned.

قفل ـ قفول *qofl*, pl. *qofool*, padlock; closing or "*clôture*" of an assembly, finis.

قافلة ـ قوافل *qáfila*, pl. *qawáfil*, caravan, return caravan.

قفاء *qafá*, nape of neck, back of head. [رقبة]

قفا or اقتفى *qafá*, or *iqtafa*, he pursued, followed.

اقتفى اثره *iqtafa asaraho*, he followed up his track, pursued him.

قافية ـ قوافي *qáfiya*, pl. *qawáfi*, rhyme.

مقفى *moqaffa*, rhymed, in rhyme.

قاقلى *qáqolla*, cakile maritima, alcali plant, cardamum.

قل *qalla*, it was few.

قلل *qallala*, he lessened, made diminish.

تقليل *taqleel*, diminution.

استقل *istaqalla*, he was independent.

قلة *qilla*, paucity.

قليل *qaleel*, few, little of, slight.

اقل *aqall*, less (emphasis on final *ll*).

الاقل *al-aqall*, the least, at the least.

قلته احسن *qillatho ahsan*, better without it; worse than nothing.

قلة ـ قلل *qolla*, pl. *qolal, qoola*, an earthen water-bottle; peak, spire.

استقلال *istiqlál*, independence.

مستقل *mustaqill*, independent.

قلب *qalaba*, he turned a thing the other way round; upset, overturned. [عكس]

انقلب *inqalaba*, it was upset, overturned; was transformed.

قالب ـ قوالب *qálib*, pl. *qawálib*, a mould.

قلب ـ قلوب *qalb*, pl. *qoloob*, heart, kernel, gist, essential part, centre.

مقلوب ـ مقلبان *maqloob*, or *maqlabán*, upset, reversed.

مقلب *maqlab*, a place for emptying carts, shooting rubbish.

قليوبية ـ بنها *Qalioobiya*, a province in the Delta, the chief town of which is *Benha*.

قلد *qalada*, he encircled, enwreathed.

قلادة *qiláda*, necklace.

قلد *qallada*, he girt (another with a sword of honour), conferred (a decoration).

قلد *qallada*, he counterfeited, imitated.

تقليد *taqleed*, conferring an honour; imitation, counterfeiting.

تقلد ب *taqallada bi*, he assumed to himself a rank; put on a decoration.

قلزم or بحر القلزم *qulzum*, or *Bahr*

قلزم *el-qulzum* (*Clysma*), the Gulf of Suez; north part of the Red Sea.

قلع *qalu'a*, he uprooted, tore off, stripped. [cf. خلع

قلع ‐ قلعة *qala'a*, pl. *qilúa'*, castle, fortress; square formation of troops.

القلعة *el-qala'a*, the citadel of Cairo.

قلع ‐ قلوع *qila'*, pl. *qolooa'*, sail. [شراع

قلاوز or قلغوز *qilághoz* (Turkish), pilot, auger, gimlet.

قلف *qilf*, bark or rind of a branch.

قلفة *qolfa*, prepuce.

اقلف *aqlafa*, he circumcised.

قلف *qalafa*, he caulked a boat or ship.

قلفطة *qalfata* (Italian *calafato*), caulking.

قلفة or خليفة *qalfa* (for *khaleefa*), female house-keeper; head woman-servant in a harem.

قلقيلة *qolqaila*, clod of earth.

قلق *qalaq*, agitation, nervous excitement, sleeplessness.

قلق or قلقان *qalqán*, or *qaliq*, anxious, nervous, sleepless.

قلقاس *qolqás*, colocasia, arum; a sort of potato.

قلقل or تقلقل *qalqala*, or *taqalqala*, he shook, trembled.

قلم or قلم *qalama*, or *qallama*, he clipped, cut a pen, snipped.

قلم ‐ اقلام *qalem*, pl. *aqlám*, a reed pen which is cut; hence a place where the pen is used, a bureau, office; a slap on the face.

اقليم ‐ اقاليم *iqleem*, pl. *aqáleem*, climate, rural provinces of Egypt, as distinct from the towns of Cairo, Alexandria, &c.

قلندر *qalendar*, a wandering dervish, an ascetic.

قلي or قلى *qalá*, he fried; he hated; he calcined, made alcali.

مقلي *maqli*, fried.

مقلى *miqla*, a frying-pan.

قلي *qily*, alcali, cinders of plants.

قمة ‐ قمم *qimma*, pl. *qimam*, crown of head, summit.

قمح *qamh*, wheat.

قمحة *qamha*, a grain of wheat, half gramme.

قمحي *qamhiy*, ripe corn coloured, the usual colour of the Egyptian complexion.

قمّاح *qammah*, seller of corn.

قمر ‐ اقمار *qamar*, pl. *aqmár*, moon. [هلال ‐ بدر

قمري *qamariy*, lunar; lunar letters.

قمري *qomri* (Turkish), dove.

اقمر *aqmara*, the moon shone.

مقمرة الدنيا *ed-dunyá moqmira*, a moonlight night.

قمر الدين *qamar ed-deen*, dried apricot paste.

قامر *qámara*, he gambled.

قمار or مقامرة *qimár*, or *moqámara*, gambling.

قمرية *qimariya*, hole for light, small window.

قمراتي qimarátiy, glazier, seller of window-panes.

قمّر qammara, he toasted bread.

قمس qamasa, he plunged into water, dived.

قاموس qámoos, Ocean, Arabic lexicon.

قماش ـ اقمشة qomásh, pl. aqmisha, cloth, stuff.

تقمّش taqammasha, he dressed up in fine clothes.

قميص ـ قمصان qamees, pl. qomsán, chemise, shirt.

قمّص qommos, Coptic priest.

قمع qama', funnel, cone; qama'a, he knocked down.

قمقم ـ قماقم qomqom, pl. qamáqim, flagon, flask.

قمقام qomqám, ringworm.

قملة ـ قمل qamla, pl. qaml, louse, lice.

قمّل qommal, ringworm.

قمين qameen, oven, bakery.

قنا Qená, Kena, a town and province in Upper Egypt.

قنينة or قنيذيّة qineena, or qonainiya, bottle, glass.

قنّب qonnab, hemp, cannabis indica.

قنبرة ـ قنبلة ـ قنابل qunbura, or qunbula, pl. qanábil (Persian khumbara), bomb-shell.

قنجة ـ قنج qanja, pl. qinaj, river boat.

قنداق qondáq (Turk), butt-end of rifle.

قنديل ـ قناديل qandeel, pl. qanádeel, lamp, illumination.

قنص qans, chase, sport.

قنصل ـ قناصل qonsol, pl. qanásil (European), Consul.

قنصلاتو qonsoláto (European), consulate.

قنطرة ـ قناطر qantura, pl. qanátir, bridge, arch.

قناطر خيريّة qanátir khairiya, the Barrage, or Beneficent Arches.

قنطار ـ قناطير qintár, pl. qanáteer, "qantár"; hundredweight of 99½ lbs., or 100 rotls, or 45 kilog.; the qintar of Alexandria equals 140 kilog.

قنع or اقتنع qania'a, or iqtana'a, he became content or was convinced.

قناعة qanáa'a, contentment.

اقنع aqna'a, he convinced, contented.

مقنع ـ مقتنع moqnia', convincing; moqtania', convinced.

قنفذ qonfoz, beaver, otter, water-rat.

قنا ـ قنوة qaná, he acquired; qinwa, acquisition.

قناة ـ قناوات qanát, pl. qanáwát, small canal.

قنال السويس qanál es-Sowayis (European), Canal of Suez.

اقنوم oqnoom (Greek), principle of nature.

قهر qahara, he forced, conquered.

قهرًا *qahrún*, by force, by violence. [كرهًا]

قهريّ *qahriy*, violent, beyond control, "*force majeure.*"

قاهر *qáhir*, conqueror; planet Mars. [مرّيخ]

القاهرة *El-Qáhira*, The Victrix, Cairo.

قهقرة *qahqara*, retreat, rout.

تقهقر *taqahqara*, he retreated beaten.

قهقهة *qahqaha*, loud laughter.

قهوة *qahwa*, prepared coffee, coffee; a coffee shop, *café*. This word originally meant a drink, wine.

قهوهجي *qahwaji* (Turkish), coffee-seller.

قهوة بنّ *qahwa bonn*, coffee-berry.

قهاوي *qaháwi*, coffee-shops, *cafés*.

قوب *qoob*, skin disease, plague, *dartre*; chicken.

قوت ـ اقوات *qoot*, pl. *aqwát*, food, nourishment.

قات *qáta*, he nourished.

تقوّت *taqawwata*, he nourished himself, subsisted on.

قود or قياده *qōd*, or *qiyáda*, a leading, control.

قاد ـ يقود *qáda*, he led, ruled over; *yaqood*, he leads, rules.

انقاد *inqáda*, he was led; he obeyed.

انقياد *inqiyád*, obedience, a being led.

قائد ـ قوّاد *qáyid*, pl. *qowwád*, leader, governor; *qawwád*, pimp.

مقود *miqwad*, halter.

قوّارة *qawwára*, a kitchen instrument, scoop.

قوس ـ اقواس *qōs*, pl. *aqwás* (femin.), bow, arc, metal spring; *Sagittarius* of the Zodiac.

قوس قزح *qōs qozah*, rainbow, bow of Qozah the Cloud Angel.

قوّاس *qawwás*, bowman, archer.

قوّاص *qawwás*, constable, consular guard.

قوطة ـ قوط *qoota*, pl. *qoot*, tomato.

قوع *qōa'*, open space, depression.

قاع ـ قيعان *qáa'*, pl. *qee'yán*, hollow, low ground.

قاعة *qáa'a*, private inner room.

قوقعة *qōqa'a*, small shell, cowry; snail.

قول ـ اقوال *qōl*, pl. *aqwál*, speech, talk, a saying.

قال ـ يقول *qála*, he said; *yaqool*, he says.

قل *qul* (imperative), say thou! speak!

قاول *qáwala*, he bargained, made a contract.

مقاولة *moqáwala*, bargain, contract.

مقاول *moqáwil*, a contractor.

مقولة *maqoola*, category, subject.

قائل *qáyil*, speaker, saying.

قوّال *qawwál*, impromptu rhymster, jabberer.

مقال *maqál*, speech, talk.

مقالة *maqála*, treatise, discourse.

قول qōl (Turkish), wing of battalion; arm, branch.

قول اغاسي qōl aghási (Turkish), wing commander, adjutant-major. [صغ]

قيل ـ يقال qeela, it was said; yoqál, it is said, he is named; by name.

القيل و القال el-qeel wa el-qál, gossip, town talk; literally, "what is said and what they say."

قوم or قيّم qōm, or qiyám, the act of standing up.

قوم ـ اقوام qōm, pl. aqwám, nation, people.

قام ـ يقوم qáma, he stood up, acted for, fulfilled; yaqoom, he stands up, &c.

قم qum! (imperative) stand thou up!

قام مقامه qáma maqámaho, he acted instead of.

قامة qáma, height of body, stature. [قدّ]

قاوم qáwama, he resisted.

مقاومة moqáwama, resistance.

اقام aqáma, he made stand, set up.

اقام دعوى على aqáma da'wa 'ala, he brought an action against, prosecuted.

اقامة iqáma, a setting up; bringing an action; celebrating or exercising; a residence, abode.

استقام istaqáma, he or it was upright; he went straight in life.

استقامة istiqáma, uprightness, rectitude.

تقويم taqweem, almanac; register; valuation.

قائم qáyim, erect, holding; a right angle; perpendicular.

قائم مقام ـ ثالثة qáyim maqám, locum tenens; lieutenant-colonel, Bey of sálisa rank.

قائمة ـ قوائم qáyima, pl. qawáyim (femin.), erect; a right angle; "bordereau;" paper money; memoes, bills, scrip; a telegraph post, mast.

قوّام qawwám, erect, alert; quick.

قوّام qawwám! (interjection or exclamation) Be quick!

قوّم qawwama, he drew up, compiled, fixed, estimated value.

قيّوم qayyoom, the Eternal God.

قيام qiyám, a standing up; prayer.

قيامة qiyáma, resurrection; uproar, bustle.

قيّم qayyim, substitute, guardian.

قيمة ـ قيم qeema, pl. qiyam, value. [ثمن]

ذو قيمة zoo qeema, valuable.

اشياء ذات قيمة ashyá zát qeema, things of value, valuables.

مقام muqám, place, seat of office.

مقيم moqeem, resident, dweller, setter up.

مستقيم mostaqeem, straight; rectum.

قوّة ـ قوى qowwa, pl. qowa, force, strength, power, faculty, sense.

قوي ‎ـ‎ اقوياء qawiy, pl. aqwiyá, strong; very.

اقوى aqwa, stronger.

كثير قوي kateer qawiy, very much, very many.

قوي كثير qawiy kateer, very strong.

قوّى qawwa, he strengthened, encouraged.

تقوية taqwiya, a strengthening, encouragement.

تقوّى taqawwa, he strengthened himself, grew strong.

مقوّى moqawwa, strengthened; cardboard.

تقاوي taqáwi (provincial), seed-corn; seed for sowing.

قى ‎ـ‎ قاء qay, vomit; see qá.

قيح qaih, pus, matter.

قيد ‎ـ‎ قيود qaid, pl. qoyood, a tying down, fettering a prisoner; entering in the accounts, inscription in a register; chain, bond, status.

فى قيد الحياة fi qaid el-hayát, in a state of life, alive, fact of life.

قيديّة qaidiya, registration.

قيد و تسجيل qaid wa tasjeel, registration and inscription.

قيّد qayyada, he bound, fettered; registered.

مقيّد moqayyid, registrar, guardian.

مقيّد moqayyad, registered, bound down.

مقيّد بالحديد moqayyad bil-hadeed, bound with fetters.

قيراط ‎ـ‎ قراريط qeerát, pl. qaráreet, 1-24th part; 175 sq. mètres or 209 sq. yards; 1·975 grains; 1-16th of a dirhem; about one inch.

قياس qiyás, measure, standard of measure; comparison.

قاس ‎ـ‎ يقيس qasa, he measured; yaqees, he measures.

مقايسة moqáyasa, comparison.

مقاسات maqását, dimensions.

مقياس ‎ـ‎ مقاييس miqyás, pl. maqáyees, instrument for measuring.

قياسة qiyása, Nile boat of Wadi Halfa district.

قياض or مقايضة qiyád, or moqáyada, exchange, barter.

قيطاس qaitás (Latin), cetacea, whale, whalebone.

قيطان qeetán, cord, braid.

قيظ qaiz, dog-days, intense heat of summer.

قيلة or قيلولة qaila, or qailoola, siesta, mid-day halt.

اقال aqála, he forgave, annulled a contract.

اقالة iqála, pardon, remission, a let-off.

بيع الاقالة beea' el-iqála, "vente à réméré."

استقال istaqála, he sent in his resignation.

اوقّ or اقّ or وقّ waqqa, or oqqa,

2¾ lbs. avdp., 36 okes equal the qintar of 99 lbs.

اوقية *oqqiya*, ounce, 1⅓ ounces avdp.

K.

ك *Káf*. Value = 20.

ك *ka* (prefix), like, as, similar to.

كرجل *ka-rajil*, like a man.

كذا or كذلك *kazá*, or *kazálik*, thus, like that. [كيت]

ك *-ak*, (femin.) *-ik*, as a suffix, thee, thy, thine. [for *ka, ki*.]

كتابك *kitábak*, thy book.

انا ضربتك *aná darabtak*, I beat thee.

كابي *kábi*, pale, wan; humble.

كاد ـ كود *kád*, almost, all but, just (see *kōd*).

كاد ان يقع *kád an yaqa'*, he almost fell.

كار ـ كارات *kár*, pl. *kárát* (Persian), work, profession.

ارباب الكارات *arbáb el-kárát*, artisans, craftsmen.

كارخانة *kár-khána* (Persian), brothel.

كأس ـ كأسات *kás*, pl. *kását*, (femin.) cup; cymbal.

كان ـ كون *kána*, he was, existed (see *kōn*).

كأنّ *ka-anna*, as if.

كانون *kánoon*, hearth, stove; Kanoon I. and II., the Syrian months of December and January.

كبّ *kabba*, he poured out, upset.

كبّب *kabbaba*, he roasted.

كباب *kabáb*, roast meat, meat roasted on a spit.

كبد *kibd*, liver.

كبّاد *kabbád*, bitter orange for preserve.

كابد *kábada*, he endured.

مكابدة *mokábada*, endurance.

كبر *kibar*, or *kubr*, greatness, old age.

كبّر *kabbara*, he made great, declared to be great.

تكبّر or استكبر *takabbara*, or *istakbara*, he was proud, talked big.

كبير ـ كبيرة *kabeer*, (femin.) *kabeera*, great, large.

اكبر ـ اكابر *akbar*, pl. *akábir*, greater, greatest.

كبار *kibár* (pl. of *kabeer*), great.

كبرى ـ كبر *kubra*, pl. *kubur* (femin.), greater, greatest.

الله اكبر *Allah akbar*, God is greater (than all), God is the greatest.

تكبير *takbeer*, a making great; the saying "God is the greatest."

متكبّر *mutakabbir*, proud, haughty, pompous.

كبريت *kibreet*, sulphur, lucifer. [كفريت]

كبس على *kabasa 'ala*, he seized, fell upon.

كبس *kibs*, mud hut of wattles, reeds and mud.

كَبَّسَ *kabbasa*, he shampooed. [دلك]

كابوس *káboos*, nightmare.

كَبِيسَة *kabeesa*, leap year.

كَبَّاس *kabbás*, valve.

كبسول *kabsool* (European), capsule, cap for gun, "*amorce*."

كبش *kebsh*, ram.

كَبْشَة *kabsha*, ladle, a ladleful, handful.

كبش *kabasha*, he scooped up with both hands.

كَبَك *kabak*, barge, lighter, pontoon.

كبيكج *kabeekaj*, genus *ranunculus*.

كِبْل ـ كَبُول *kibl*, pl. *kobool*, chain, fetter. [قيد]

كَبَّل *kabbala*, he put in chains, pinioned.

مُكَبَّل *mokabbal*, chained, pinioned.

كِبَّايَة *kibbáya*, a glass tumbler.

كَتَب *kataba* (pronounced *kitib*), he wrote.

اكتتب *iktataba*, he subscribed, enlisted.

كَاتَب *kátaba*, he corresponded by letter.

كِتَاب ـ كُتُب *kitáb*, pl. *kutub*, a book, epistle, letter.

كتبخانه *kutub-khána* (Persian), library.

كتبي *kutubiy*, book-seller.

كِتَابَة *kitába*, writing, in writing.

كتابات *kitábát*, letters, epistles.

كاتب or كَتَبَة *kátib*, pl. *kataba* or *kuttab*, clerk.

كَتِيبَة *kateeba*, a squadron or force of cavalry.

كُتَّاب ـ كَتَاتِيب *kuttáb*, pl. *katáteeb*, elementary school.

اكتتاب *iktitáb*, subscription, enlistment.

مُكَاتَبَة *mukátaba*, correspondence.

مُكَاتِب *mukátib*, correspondent.

مَكْتَب ـ مَكَاتِب *maktab*, pl. *makátib*, school, office.

مَكْتَبَة *maktaba*, desk.

مَكْتُوب ـ مَكَاتِيب *maktoob*, pl. *makáteeb*, written, a letter.

كَتَع ـ اكتع *kata'*, *akta'*, a twisted limb.

كتخدا ـ كياحيا or كحي *ket-khudá* (Persian; corrupted into *kiáhiá* or *kihia*), steward of an estate, manager.

كَتِف ـ اكتاف *kitf*, pl. *aktáf* (femin.), shoulder.

كتف *katafa*, he seized by the shoulder, pinioned.

كَتْكُوت ـ كَتَاكِيت *katkoot*, pl. *katákeet*, chicken. [فرّوج]

كُتْلَة *kutla*, mass, bulk, lump, bunch, trunk of human body or tree.

كتم *katama*, he concealed, kept silence or a secret.

تَكَتَّم *takattama*, he kept silence, withheld the truth.

كتم or كتمان *katm*, or *kitmán*, concealment.

كاتم الاسرار *kátim el-asrár*, concealer of secrets, a confidential secretary.

كتّان - قطن *kattán*, linen, flax; *qotn*, cotton.

كتينة *kateena* (Italian), watch-chain, *catena*.

كثيث or كثيف *katheeth*, or *katheef*, thick, dense (hair, foliage, liquid).

كثرة or كثر *kisr*, or *kasra*, abundance.

كثير - كثار *kateer*, pl. *kitár*, many, much, numerous.

اكثر - الاكثر *aktar*, more; *el-aktar*, the most, at most.

كثّر *kattara*, he made increase, augmented.

كثّر خيرك *kattar khairak*, thanks! may your happiness increase!

تكثّر or تكاثر *takassara*, or *takásara*, it became abundant.

كحال or كحل *kohl*, or *kihál*, powder of burnt frankincense or almonds used as a black dye for the eyelids.

كحيل *kaheel*, black-eyed, kohl-eyed.

عين كحيلة *'ain kaheela*, eye adorned with kohl.

مكحلة *mik-hala*, kohl-bottle.

الكحول *al-kohol*, alcohol. [كوحول]

كحيل *kohail*, thoroughbred horse.

كاحل - كواحل *káhil*, pl. *kawáhil*, ankle.

كخيا - تكخدا *kihia*, steward (see *ket-khudá*).

كدّ *kadd*, fatigue.

كدر *kadr*, grief, annoyance.

كدّر *kaddara*, he vexed, caused grief.

تكدّر *takaddara*, he felt grieved.

مكدّر - متكدّر *mokaddar*, vexed, aggrieved; *motakaddir*, feeling grieved.

كدم *kadum*, bruise, contusion.

كذا or كذلك *kazá*, or *kazálik*, thus, like that.

كذب *kidb*, lie, falsehood.

اكذوبة *akzooba*, lie, lying.

كذب *kazaba*, he told a lie; (the gun) missed fire.

كاذب - كذّاب *kázib*, or *kaddáb*, liar.

امر كاذب *amr kázib*, slander, libel.

اخبر بامر كاذب *akhbara bi-amr kázib*, he uttered a libel.

كذّب *kazzaba*, he contradicted, gave the lie to.

امر مكذوب *amr makzoob*, falsehood, an affair which has been *lied* about.

كرّ or تكرّر *karra*, or *takarrara*, it recurred.

كرّر *karrara*, he made recur, repeated; he refined sugar.

تكرار *takrár*, repetition, recurrence.

تكرير *takreer*, a causing of repetition; a refining of sugar.

كرّة - كرّات *karra*, pl. *karrát*, a time, once. [مرّة]

مكرّر mokarrar, repeated; refined sugar.

أوامر مكرّرة awámir mokarrara, repeated orders.

كرّاريّة kurráriya, bobbin, reel of cotton, &c.

كروب kroob (European), croup; a Krupp gun.

كرب karb, distress, indigence.

كرب karab, yoke-pin of plough.

كرباج korbáj, courbash, hippopotamus-hide whip; a flogging, bastinado.

كربال korbál, vine-trellis; raft-frame. [رويس

كارو káro (European), car, cart.

كرّات korrát, leek, garlic.

كرد ـ اكراد kurd, pl. akrád, Koord, Koordistan.

كردان kerdán (Persian gerden, neck), necklace.

كرز karaz, cherry.

كرازة kiráza, church service, sermon.

كرّاسة ـ كراريس korrása, pl. karárees, folio, pamphlet, copy-book; several sheets sewn together.

كرسوع korsooa', wrist. [رسغ ـ معصم

كرسف korsof, a piece of cotton wool.

كرسيّ ـ كراسي kursiy, pl. karási, chair, throne, locus.

كرسيّ المملكة kursiy el-mamlaka, capital town.

كرش karasha, he drove off, chased out.

كرش kirsh (femin.), paunch, tripe; wrinkle.

تكرّش takarrasha, it was wrinkled.

كرشوني karshooniy (Syriac), Arabic written in Syriac characters.

كريشي koreishiy, a sort of muslin.

كراع ـ كوارع koráa', pl. kawária', trotters of sheep or ox.

كوارعي kawária'iy, a seller of trotters.

كرفس karafs, celery.

كرك kurk (Turkish), fur, fur-coat. [فروة

كركي kurkiy, crane, stork.

كركة karaka, calico.

كرّاكة karráka (Italian), dredger, rake. [or قرافة

كركب karkaba, he threw into disorder, confused.

كركبة karkaba, confusion, commotion, uproar.

كراكيب karákeeb, lumber, confusion of rubbish.

كركدنّ karkadann, rhinoceros. [مرميس

كرم karam, nobleness, respect, favour, generosity.

كرامة karáma, miracle, benevolence.

كرّم karrama, he honoured, showed favour.

كريم ـ كرام kareem, pl. kirám, noble, gracious.

عفو كريم 'afw kareem, gracious pardon, or amnesty by the king.

مكرّم mokarram, ennobled, held in honour; a title of Mecca.

كريمة *kareema* (used in Turkish), daughter.

كرم - كروم *karm*, pl. *koroom* (Syrian), vine. [عنب]

كرنب or قرنب *kurunb*, cabbage, cauliflower.

كرنافة *kurnáfa*, butt-end of rifle.

كره or استكره *karaha*, or *istakraha*, he abhorred, loathed.

كراهة *karáha*, abomination.

اكره *akraha*, he showed violence, violated.

اكراه *ikráh*, violence. [قهرا]

كريه *kareeh*, hateful, detestable.

مكروه *makrooh*, hated; hence, a sin hateful to God.

كرة - كرى *kora*, pl. *kora*, ball, globe.

كرة الارض *korat el-ard*, globe of the world.

كروى *korawiy*, globular.

كرويا *karawiyá*, carvi, food given to an invalid.

كروينة *karawaita*, bedstead, sofa.

كروان *karawán*, partridge.

كرا *kirá*, hire. [اجر]

كارى *kára*, he let on hire.

اكترى *iktara*, he took on hire.

يكرى *yokra*, it is to let.

مكرى *mokra*, let, hired.

مكارة *mokárát*, hire.

مكارى *mokári*, he who lets on hire, especially one who lets out animals on hire.

مكر *mokir*, muleteer.

كوروسكو *Korosko*, a village on the Nile about half-way between Assouan and Wady Halfa.

كزاز *kozáz*, a shivering from cold.

كزبرة or كزبرة *kusbura*, coriander.

كس *kuss*, vulva.

كسب or اكتسب *kasaba*, or *iktasaba*, he gained, profited.

كسب or اكتساب *kasb*, or *iktisáb*, gain, profit.

كسبان *kasbán*, he who gains, successful in trade.

مكسب *maksab*, profit, gain.

مكسوب *maksoob*, gained, the profit gained.

كسبة *kusba*, paste of sesame oil, fattening food.

كستبان *kustabán* (Turkish), thimble.

كسح or مكسح (كسح) *kasah*), *mokassah*, or *aksah*, cripple, maimed, paralytic.

كساد *kasád*, dulness of trade, nothing doing.

كاسد *kásid*, dull trade.

كسر or كسر *kasara*, or *kassara*, he broke, broke into, defeated.

انكسر *inkasara*, it was broken, he was defeated.

كسر - كسور *kasr*, pl. *kosoor*, a breaking, fraction.

كسر الباب *kasr el-báb*, a breaking in of the door (a legal term for burglary).

كسرة *kasra*, short "i" vowel-sound. [جرّة - خفضة]

مكسور *maksoor*, broken, broken in heart or spirit, sorry; marked with the "kasra."

مكسَّر *mukassar*, broken; a broken or irregular plural.

تكسيرة *tukseera*, a breakage, break.

اكسير or الاكسير *ekseer*, or *el-ekseer*, elixir, the philosopher's stone.

كسع *kasa'*, it sailed down with the current, came down the Nile.

كسوف ـ خسوف *kosoof* (see also *khosoof*), eclipse of sun.

كسف *kasafa*, he shamed, disappointed.

مكسوف *maksoof*, sorry, ashamed, disappointed.

كسفة *kasfa*, disappointment, vexation.

كسفريت ـ كبريت *kasfareet*, lucifer match. Evidently a corruption of phosphorus and *kibreet*, sulphur.

كسكس *kaskasa*, he drew back, recoiled. [كش]

كسل *kasal*, laziness, idleness.

كسلان *kaslán*, lazy.

تكاسل *takásala*, he became lazy.

كسلا *Kasalá*, a town in the E. Soudan.

كسوة ـ كساوى or كسى *kiswa*, pl. *kasáwi*, or *kisa*, dress, style of dress, dress or cover of the Ka'aba at Mecca; hence a religious ceremony at Cairo at the making of this cover. [كعبة]

اكتسى *iktasa*, he dressed himself, wore.

كشّ *kashsha*, he recoiled, shrank; it was wrinkled.

تكشيشة *taksheesha*, wrinkle.

كشح *kashah*, flank, short ribs.

كشرى *kushari*, lentils and rice, "kidgeree."

كشر *kashshara*, he frowned, showed anger.

كشط *kashata*, he scratched out, erased. [قشط]

كشف *kashafa*, he revealed, laid bare, examined.

انكشف *inkashafa*, it was revealed, examined.

اكتشف *iktashafa*, he revealed himself.

استكشف *istakshafa*, he inquired into, or wished to uncover.

كشف ـ كشوف or كشوفات *kashf*, pl. *koshoof*, or *koshoofát*, revelation, discovery, inquiry, "reconnaissance;" official list or report.

كشف طبّى *kashf tubbiy*, medical report.

كشف على اعيان ثانتة *kashf 'ala aa'yán sábita*, "visite des lieux," legal inspection of a place.

فى الكشف *fi l-kashf*, in the open, in the open air.

كشّاف *kashsháf*, census. [تعداد]

كاشف or كشّاف *káshif*, or *kashsháf*, official searcher, superintendent.

كشك *kishk*, wheat and milk paste.

كظم *kazam*, throat, gullet.

كظم *kozima* (passive), he was silent.

كاظم *kázim*, reticent.

كعب ـ كعوب *ka'b*, pl. *ko'oob*, ankle, knuckle, dice, cube.

كعبة *Ka'ba*, the Ka'aba or shrine at Mecca.

كاعب ـ كواعب *ká'yib*, pl. *kawá'yib*, virgin of Paradise.

مكعّب *moka'ab*, cubed, cubic.

كعك *ka'k*, cake.

كفّ ـ كفوف *kaff*, pl. *kofoof*, (femin.) palm of hand; glove, slap, blow; a hem.

كفّة *kiffa*, platter of a pair of scales; sling; *kuffa*, hem.

كفيف *kafeef*, blind, almost blind.

كفّ عن *kaffa 'an*, he kept aloof, withdrew his hand, ceased from.

كفّ بصره *kaffa basaroho*, he became blind, his eyesight ceased.

تكفّف *takaffafa*, he kept putting out his hand to beg, was a beggar.

كفيّة or كوفيّة *kufiya*, head-shawl.

كفتة or كوفته *kufta* (Persian), meat-ball.

كافّة *káffa*, the whole, all. [جميع ـ كلّ]

كفاءة or كـفـاء *kafá*, or *kafáia*, equality.

كفو *kafw*, equal, similar.

كانأ or كافأ *káfá*, it was equal to, he rewarded.

كفاء or مكافأة *kifá*, or *mokáfát*, equality; a reward, compensation.

كفاية *kifáya*, sufficiency.

كـفـيّ or كافي *kafiy*, or *káfi*, sufficient.

كفى ـ يكفي *kafa*, it sufficed; *yakfi*, it suffices, is enough.

كفى or كفّى *kaffa*, or *kúfa*, it sufficed.

كافى *káfa*, he rewarded. [كافأ]

اكتفى *iktafa*, he was content, satisfied.

مكافأة ـ مكافآت *mokáfát*, pl. *mokáfát*, reward, prize at school.

كفح or كافح *kafaha*, or *káfaha*, he made war. [حرب]

كفاح *kifáh*, mutual war.

كفر *kafara*, he disbelieved in Allah.

كـفـر *kufr*, disbelief in Allah; ingratitude.

كافر ـ كفرة or كفّار *káfir*, pl. *kafara*, or *kuffár*, disbeliever.

كاور *ghiáour* (Turco-Persian for *káfir*), disbeliever.

كفّر *kaffara*, he expiated his own sin; forgave another.

تكفير *takfeer*, expiation, forgiveness.

كفّار *kaffár*, very impious, atheist.

كفّارة *kaffára*, expiation, funeral offerings of charity.

كفر ـ كفور *kafr*, pl. *kofoor*, village.

كافور *káfoor*, camphor.

كفل *kafala*, he went bail for another, guaranteed. [ضمن]

كفيل ـ كفلاء *kafeel*, pl. *kufalá*, he who goes bail.

كفالة *kafála*, guarantee, fact or amount of bail.

كفل ـ اكفال *kafal*, pl. *akfál*, haunch. [ردف]

كفن *kafan*, winding-sheet, shroud.

كَفَّن *kaffana*, he shrouded a dead body.

كل ـ اكل *kul*, (imperative) eat thou! (see *akala*).

كُلّ ـ كاهْ *kull*, all; *kulloh*, all of it.

كل منهم *kull minhom*, every one of them.

كل واحد *kull wáhid*, each one.

كُلّيّ *kulliy*, universal.

كُلّيّة *kulliya*, totality.

بالكُلّيّة or كُلّيّة *kulliyatan*, or *bil-kulliya*, altogether, totally.

كُلّما *kullamá*, whenever, whatever, all that.

اكليل *ikleel*, crown, diadem; rosemary.

كلّل *kallala*, he crowned.

تكليل *takleel*, coronation; Coptic marriage ceremony.

كلّا *kallá*, not at all, an emphatic negative. No! on the contrary.

كلا ـ كلتا *kilá*, (femin.) *kiltá*, both.

كلب ـ كلاب *kelb*, pl. *kiláb*, dog.

ابن الكلب *ibn el-kelb*, son of a dog, a term of abuse, exactly the same as the Turkish "*Kyoopōl.*" [كوپك اوغلى]

كلب *kaliba*, the dog went mad; the man had hydrophobia. [سعران]

كلاب *kaláb*, rabies, "*rage*," hydrophobia.

مكلوب *makloob*, bitten by a mad dog; rabid.

كلّابة *kullába*, pincers, hook.

كلبش *kalabsh*, handcuffs.

كلرا or كولرا *kolará* (European), cholera. [هيضة]

كلس ـ تكليس *kils*, lime, calcium; *taklees*, calcination.

كلف *kalifa*, he undertook.

كلفة *kulfa*, responsibility, anxiety, undertaking, expense.

كلّف *kallafa*, he consigned, entrusted a task to; it cost; he invited, legally summoned.

تكليف ـ تكاليف *takleef*, pl. *takáleef*, burden, imposition, ceremony, bother, fuss; invitation; legal summons; official receipt for, or acknowledgment of, amount of land held by a taxpayer (see *mokallafa*).

تكليف بالحضور *takleef bil-hodoor*, a legal summons to appear.

تكلّف *takallafa*, he held or made himself responsible, undertook, put himself to trouble.

مكلّف *mokallaf*, held responsible; invited, capable; summoned legally.

مكلّفة ـ ورد ـ قسيمة *mokallafa*, schedule or register of land tax, *i.e.* the amount of land for which a man is *responsible* (see *wird* and *qaseema*).

كلّاف ـ علّاف *kalláf*, seller of fodder for cattle (see *'alláf*).

كلف ـ اكلاف *kulaf*, or *kalaf*, pl. *akláf*, expenses.

تَكَلَّم or كَلَّم *kallama*, or *takallama*, he spoke. [قول]

كَلَام *kalám*, speech, affair spoken of.

كَلِمَة - كَلِمَات *kilma*, or *kelima*, pl. *kelimát*, word.

كَالَم *kálama*, he spoke with, interviewed.

مُكَالَمَة *mukálama*, interview.

مُتَكَلِّم *mutakallim*, speaker; first person singular.

كِلِيم *kileem* (Turkish), carpet, rug.

كُلْوَة - كَلَاوِي *kilwa*, or *kulwa*, pl. *kaláwi*, kidney.

كُلْوِيّ *kilwiy*, renal, of the kidneys, nephritic.

كِلَا - كِلْتَا *kilá*, (femin.) *kiltá*, both.

كَم *kam*, how many? how much?

اكَم يَوم *akam yōm* (colloquial), a few days.

كَمَا *kamá*, as, in the same way as.

كَمَان *kamán*, also, more, again. [ايضًا]

كُم - كُنَّ *kom*, (femin.) *konna*, ye, your.

كُمَا *komá*, ye two.

كَمِّيَّة *kammiya*, quantity.

كُمّ - اكْمَام *kumm*, pl. *akmám*, sleeve, cuff.

كِمّ - كِمَام *kimm*, pl. *kimám*, calyx, bud.

كِمَام or كِمَامَة *kimám*, or *kimáma*, muzzle, bit.

كَمَاة *kamát*, truffles.

كَمْبِيَالَة *kambiála* (Italian), bill of exchange.

صَاحِب الكَمْبِيَالَة *sáhib el-kambiála*, drawer of a bill.

قَابِل الكَمْبِيَالَة *qábil el-kambiála*, acceptor of a bill.

حَامِل الكَمْبِيَالَة *hámil el-kambiála*, bearer of a bill.

مُحِيل الكَمْبِيَالَة *moheel el-kambiála*, transferor, endorser of a bill.

كَمْبِيَالَة تَحْت اذن *kambiála taht izn*, bill (payable) to order.

كَمَّتْرَى *kommatra*, pear, pear tree.

كَمَر *kamar* (Persian, waist), girdle, belt.

كُمْرُك - كَمَارِك *kumruk*, pl. *kamárik* (from Greek, through Turkish *gyoomruk*), Custom-house, the Customs.

تَهْرِيب مِن الكُمْرُك *tahreeb min el-kumruk*, smuggling, contraband. [فلّت]

كُمْسَارِي *komsári* (European), commissionaire, commissary, railway guard.

كَمَّاشَة *kammásha*, tongs.

كَمَال *kamál*, perfection, entirety.

كَامِل *kámil*, perfect, entire, whole, complete.

كَمَّل or اكْمَل *kammala*, or *akmala*, he completed.

تَكْمِيل or اكْمَال *takmeel*, or *ikmál*, a completing.

تَكْمِيل *takmeel*, the whole.

تَكْمِيلِيّ *takmeeliy*, supplementary, for the completion of.

تكملة takmila, complement, balance.

استكمل istakmala, he tried to complete or attain.

كمنجة kamanja (Persian), fiddle, long thin viol.

كمين kameen, ambush.

كامن kámin, a man in ambush.

كمّون kammoon, herb cummin.

كنّ - كم konna, femin. of kom, ye, your.

كنّ kanna, he concealed, covered over.

كنّة - كنائن kanna, pl. kanáyin, daughter-in-law.

كانون kánoon, stove, hearth; Kanoon I. and II., Syrian months of December and January.

كنز - كنوز kinz, or kanz, pl. konooz, hidden treasure.

كنس kanasa, he swept.

كنس or كناسة kans, or konása, a sweeping.

مكنسة miknasa, broom.

كنيسة - كنائس kaneesa, pl. kanáyis, church.

كنيف kaneef, latrine, w.c.

كنافة konáfa, sweetstuff, a special dish of fine macaroni much eaten during Ramadan.

كناية or كنية kináya, or kunya, allusion, metonymy; nickname. [لقب]

كهربا kahrubá (Persian, kah, a straw, and rubá, snatching; hence straw-snatcher), amber.

كهربائية kahrubáiya, electricity.

كهرمان or كارم kahramán, or kárim (colloquial), amber.

كهف kahf, cave.

كعك or كهك kahk (better ka'k), cake.

كهل - كهول kahl, pl. kohool; middle aged; elderly.

كهانة kiháne, fortune-telling. [عيافة]

كاهن - كهنة káhin, pl. kahana, augur, Levite, priest.

كهنة kohna, rags, tatters. [خرقة]

كوب - اكواب koob, pl. akwáb, bowl.

كوبري koobri (for Turkish kyupru), bridge.

كوخ kookh, hut.

كود - كاد ان يقع kód, a wishing, a being on the point of; as kád an yaqa', he almost fell.

كوذة (كوز) kooz), káza, groin.

كور koor, large bellows of forge.

كورك korak (Turkish kyurek), spade.

كوز - اكواز kooz, pl. akwáz, pitcher.

كوز ادرّة kooz durra, a head of maize.

كوستكة koostaka (Turkish), long watch-chain.

كوسلة koosala, sole-leather.

كوسة koosa, small vegetable-marrow. [قرع]

كوشة or امينة kosha, or ameena, lime-kiln.

كوشك kooshk (Persian kyooshk), kiosque.

كوع - اكواع kooa', pl. akwáa', elbow. [مرفق]

كوفة Koofa, ancient town on Euphrates, rivalled by Baghdad.

كوفيّ *Koofiy*, Koofic, a style of Arab writing, named after *Koofa*.

كوفيّة *koofiya*, head-shawl.

كوكب - كواكب *kawkab*, pl. *kawákib*, star. [نجم]

كوؤل - الكوؤل *ko-ol, al-ko-ol*, alcohol. [كحل]

كوم - اكوام - شَبينِ الكوم *kōm*, pl. *akwám*, heap, mound, village often built on high ground, as *Shebeen el-kom*.

كوّم *kawwama*, he heaped up.

كون *kōn*, existence, the fact of, because; viz., i.e.

كونه *kōnoho*, his existence, while he was.

حالة كون *hálet kōn*, although, while that.

لكون - مع كون *li-kōn*, because; *ma' kōn*, although.

كونيّ *kōniy*, real, actual.

كان - يكون *kána*, he was, existed; *yakoon*, he, it is. [صار]

كوّن *kawwana*, he created, put together.

تكوين *takween*, creation, genesis.

تكوّن *takkawwana*, it took form, became formed.

كاين *káyin*, existing, he who is.

كان ... او *kána ... aw*, either ... or; whether it be ... or.

مكان - اماكن *makán*, pl. *amákin*, place. [مكن]

كيّ *kaiy*, cautery; ironing linen, &c.

كوى *kawa*, he cauterized, ironed clothes.

اكتوى *iktawa*, he burnt or cauterized himself.

مكوة *mikwa*, flat iron.

كي or لكي *kai*, or *li-kai*, in order that.

كيت وكيت - كذا *kait wa kait*, thus and thus (a colloquialism for *kazá*).

كيد or مكيدة *kaid*, or *makeeda*, plot, ruse, intrigue. [حيلة]

كيس - اكياس *kees*, pl. *akyás*, purse, bag, sack, hair glove.

كيس نقود *kees noqood*, a purse of money.

مكيّساتي *mokayyisátiy*, professional rubber with the hair glove in the Turkish bath.

كويّس *kowayyis* or *kwice*, nice, pretty, excellent.

اكوس *akwas*, nicer, better.

كيف *kaif*, how? in Turkish it has the special meaning of taking one's ease, *dolce far niente*; exhilaration.

كيفيّة *kaifiya*, the howness, quality; details or state of the case.

كيفنجه *kaifinja* (Turkish military term), stand easy!

كيالة *kiyála*, a measuring of grain.

كال - يكيل *kála*, he measured grain; *yakeel*, he measures.

كيلة *kaila*, a measure of nearly 2 pecks, or 3⅔ gallons; 16½ litres, or 1-12th of an ardab.

كيّال *kayyál*, a professional measurer of grain.

مكيال - مكاييل *mikyál*, pl. *makáyeel*, a standard of measure for grain.

كيلون *kailoon*, the plate-lock of a door or box. [قفل]

كوالينيّ *kawáleeniy*, lock-maker.

كيمياء or كيميّة *keemiya*, chemistry, perhaps derived from *kem* or *khem*, an old name for Egypt; alchemy, rational magic as opposed to *seemiyá*, false magic. [سيمياء]

كيماويّ *keemáwiy*, chemical.

تحليل كيماويّ *tahleel keemáwiy*, chemical analysis.

كيهك *kiahk*, Coptic month of December.

L.

ل *Lám.* Value = 30.

ل - لهُ - لك *la*, to, for; *laho*, to him; *lak*, to thee.

ل - لي *li*, to, for, because of; in order to; *lee*, to me.

للّٰه *lillah*, to God.

لاجل - لايّ *li-ajl*, because; *l-áiy*, why? for what?

لهذه الاسباب *li-hazihi 'l-asbáb*, for these reasons.

لعدم حضوره *li-'adam hodoorihi*, owing to his absence.

لكون *li-kōn*, because, for the fact that.

لماذا *li-mázú*, why? for what?

للايجار - لمبيع *lil-eejár*, for hire; *li-mabee'a*, for sale.

للسّاعة *lis-sáa'a* (*lissa*), up to now, not yet.

ليكون معلومًا *li-yakoon ma'loomán*, let it be known!

لو - لِ *law - li*, if - then (coordinate conjunctions).

لو جاء لنظرته *law já li-nazartoh*, if he had come I should have seen him.

لا *lá*, not.

لاسيّما *lá-seeyamá*, nothing is equal to it; especially.

لاّك - ملاك - ملائكه (*láka*) *malák*, pl. *maláyika*, messenger, angel (see also ملك).

لام - لوم *láma*, he blamed (see *lōm*).

لأم *láma*, he repaired, joined the pieces together.

التأم *iltáma*, it collected, came together.

التئام *iltiyám*, a coming together, crowding.

ملتئم *multayim*, collected, joined.

لوح - لائحة *láyiha*, note, circular (see *lōh*).

لؤلؤ - لآلىء *looloo*, pl. *lááli*, pearl. [درّة]

لبّ - لبوب *lubb*, pl. *luboob*, pulp, kernel, heart.

لبابة *libába*, crumb, gruel.

لبيب *labeeb*, gentle, sincere.

لبب *labab*, martingale, breast strap.

لبّة *libba*, necklace; *labba*, bosom, chest.

لبلاب *lablab*, creeping plant.

لبلبى *leblebi* (Turkish), parched Indian corn.

لبوة *lubwa*, lioness. [اسد]

لولب *lawlab*, metal spring, watch spring. [يايى]

لبث

لَبِث labita, he remained, stayed. [مكث]

لَبْخة labkha, poultice (Turkish? lápa).

لَبَّخ labbakh, the common acacia of Egypt; albizzia labbakhi; acacia mimosa.

لَبَد labada, he lurked, lay in wait for.

لِبْدة libda, felt; peasant's felt cap.

لَبَّادة labbáda, felt horse-cloth.

لَبِس - يلبس labisa, he dressed himself; yalbis, he dresses.

لِبْس libs, clothing, dress.

لِباس - البِسة libás, pl. albisa, drawers, clothing.

مَلْبوس malboos, clothed; inspired, devotee; mad, epileptic.

مَلْبوسات or مَلابس malboosát, or malábis, clothes.

اِلْتَبَس iltabasa, it was muffled up, ambiguous.

اِلْتِباس iltibás, ambiguity, doubt.

مُتَلْبِس multabis, ambiguous, obscure in meaning.

تَلَبَّس talabbasa, he was implicated in, was in the act of doing.

شوهد مُتَلَبِّساً بالجناية shoohida mutalabbisán bil-jinaya he was seen in the act of crime; he was detected *flagrante delicto*.

مُلَبَّس mulabbas, sweetmeats, comfits.

لِبْش libsh, bundle of brushwood for dams.

تَلْبيشة talbeesha, embanking a canal, or making a dam with libsh.

لجلج

لَبْلِبة labliba, piece of soft stuff, dough. [لبابة]

لَبَن laban, milk.

لبن حليب laban haleeb, fresh (milked) milk.

لَبَّان labbán, milkman.

لَبون laboon, milch, giving milk; also a suckling, young camel, &c.

لُبان lubán, gum mastic for chewing; resin for pastilles or incense.

لِبان libán, tow-rope for boats.

جبل لبنان Jebel Lubnán, Mount Lebanon.

لَبَّيْك labbaik, Lo! Here I am before Thee, Oh God! "Adsum" (pilgrim's ejaculation).

لَبَّى الدَّعوة labba ed-da'wa, he died; he said "Labbaik," "Adsum," to the call of God.

تَلْبية talbiya, the phrase "labbaik," &c.

لَتّ latta, he bruised, shook.

لَتَم or لتم latama, he slapped. [لطش]

لَثْمة lathma, a kiss.

لِثام lithám, woman's veil over the mouth; mask.

لَثَّم or تَلَثَّم laththama, or talaththama, he wore a mask, muffled his face (brigand, robber).

لِثة - لثات lisa, pl. lisás, gums of the mouth.

لَجّ lajja, he persisted, repeated.

لَجْلَج or تَلَجْلَج lajlaja, or talajlaja, he kept on repeating, faltered, hesitated in speech.

لُجَّة *lujja*, sea; large tract of land inundated by the Nile.

الْتَجَا or لَجَأ *lajá*, or *iltajá*, he sought refuge.

الْجَأ *aljá*, he forced, induced.

مَلْجَأ *maljá*, place of refuge.

مُلْتَجِى *multaji*, seeker of refuge.

لِجَام *lijám*, bit, curb.

لَجْنَة *lajna*, committee.

لَحّ - الْحّ (*lahha*) *alahha*, he insisted, encouraged.

اِلْحَاح *ilháh*, insistance, an urging.

لَحْد *lahd*, niche inside a Moslem grave.

لَحِس *lahisa*, he licked with the tongue.

لَحْس *lahs*, a lick, licking.

لَحَظ *lahaza*, he glanced at, observed.

لَحْظَة *lahza*, a glance, a moment.

لَاحَظ *láhaza*, he inspected, superintended.

مُلَاحِظ *moláhiz*, inspector; petty police-officer.

مُلَاحَظَة *moláhaza*, inspection, remark, supervision.

مَلْحُوظ - مَلْحُوظَات *malhooz*, pl. *malhoozát*, observed, seen; a remark, note, annotation.

لِحَاف *liháf*, bed-sheet, wrapper. [ملاية

لَحِق *lahiqa*, it reached, was in touch with.

اَلْحَق *alhaqa*, he overtook, reserved.

اِلْحَقْنِى *ilhaqni*, Help! reach me! [انجدنى

مُلْحَق *mulhaq*, annexe, attached, belonging to.

لَاحِق *láhiq*, attacher, in possession; next in turn.

لَحْمَة *lahma*, piece of meat; flesh.

لَحْم - لُحُوم *lahm*, pl. *lohoom*, meat, flesh.

مُلَحَّم *molahham*, fleshy, obese.

لِحَام *lihám*, solder.

لَحْن *lahn*, sound, melody, accent, tone.

الْحَى - لَحَى *alha*, he sinned; *ilhá*, sin, bad conduct.

لِحْيَة - لِحَى *lihia*, pl. *liha*, beard. [ذقن

لَخْبَطَة *lakhbata*, confusion, mixture.

لَخْبَط *lakhbata*, he mixed, confused.

تَلَخْبَط *talakhbata*, it was mixed, in confusion.

لَخّص - (*lakhasa*), *lakhkhasa*, he picked out the pith, summarised.

تَلْخِيص *talkhees*, summary, epitome.

مُلَخِّص *molakhkhis*, epitomiser; reporter on a case.

لَخْلَخ *lakhlakha*, he made shake, loosened.

لَخَمَة - تَلَخَّم *lakhma*, embarrassment; *talakhkhama*, he embarrassed himself.

لِدَة - ولد *lida*, birth (see *walada*).

لَدُن or لَدَى *ladon*, or *lada*, at, in presence of.

لَذَّة - لَذَّات *lazza*, pl. *lazzát*, pleasure, delight.

لذيذ *lazeez*, delightful, delicious.

لذيذة - لذائذ *lazeeza*, pl. *lazáyiz*, pleasure; delights, charms.

الذّ *alazz*, more delightful.

تلذّذ or التذّ *iltazza*, or *talazzaza*, he delighted in, enjoyed.

ملذّات *malazzát*, delights, sensual pleasures, "*délices.*"

لزّ على *lazza 'ala*, he pushed, pressed.

لزج or لزق or لصق *lazija*, or *laziqa*, or *lasiqa*, it stuck to, was gummy.

لزّق *lazzaqa*, he gummed, pasted up.

لزم - يلزم *lazima*, it was necessary, attached to; *yalzam*, it is necessary.

لزوم *lozoom*, necessity.

لازم *lázim*, necessary.

لازمة - لوازم *lázima*, pl. *lawázim*, a necessary article.

لوازمات *lawázimát*, necessaries, stores (for army, &c).

الزم *alzama*, he necessitated, held responsible, adjudged (costs) against.

لازم *lázama*, he attended upon, was dependent.

ملازمة *mulázama*, attendance upon, dependence.

ملازم *mulázim*, subaltern, lieutenant, attaché.

التزم *iltazama*, he undertook, contracted for.

التزام *iltizám*, responsibility, contract, lease, feudal grant of land.

ملتزم *multazim*, contractor, lease-holder.

ملزوم ب *malzoom bi*, responsible for.

ملزومية *malzoomiya*, responsibility.

ملزمة *malzama*, quire; clip, vice.

ملزم *molzam*, responsible.

لسعة *lasa'a*, sting; bite of serpent.

لسان - السنة *lisán*, pl. *alsina*, tongue, language. [لغة]

لسان دارج *lisán dárij*, vernacular, or common dialect.

لسان الحال *lisán el-hál*, day's doings; news, topics of the day; *i.e.* if things could speak for themselves.

عن لسان *'an lisán*, from hearsay.

لشا - تلاشى (*lashá*), *talasha*, it was ruined, spoilt; *taláshi*, destruction.

لصّ - لصوص *luss*, pl. *losoos*, robber, burglar, brigand. [حرامي - سارق]

لصق *lasiqa*, it adhered; *lassaqa*, he made adhere.

لاصق or التصق *lásaqa*, or *iltasaqa*, it was in contact; adhered.

ملتصق *multasiq*, adherent, contiguous.

لضم *ladama*, he threaded beads, a needle, &c.; joined.

لطش *latasha*, he slapped.

لطف - الطاف *lotf*, pl. *altáf*, kindness, grace.

لطافة *latáfa*, grace, elegance; wit.

لطيف *lateef*, gracious, courteous, witty.

لطيفة - لطائف *lateefa*, pl. *latáyif*, witticism, epigram.

تلطيف *talteef*, affability, a showing kindness.

لطم *latama*, he slapped, beat.

تلاطم *talátum*, mutual collision, dashing together.

لعب *la'iba*, he played.

لاعب *láa'ba*, he fondled, played with another.

لعب - العاب *lia'b*, pl. *ala'áb*, a game, play.

لعاب *lo'áb*, saliva.

ملعب *mala'b*, playground, circus.

لعس *la'sa*, he bit, chewed.

لعق *la'iqa*, he licked, sucked.

ملعقة - ملاعق *mila'qa (mala'qa)*, pl. *malá'yiq*, spoon.

لعل *laa'll*, perhaps. [ربما]

لعل *la'l*, garnet; ruby; carmine colour.

لعن *la'na*, he cursed, blasphemed.

لعان *li'án*, imprecation; a form of divorce.

لعنة *la'na*, a curse, cursing.

ملعون *mala'oon*, accursed, damned.

لعين *la'een*, accursed.

العن - بطال *ala'n*, literally, more accursed, but used in Egypt merely for "worse," as the comparative of *battál*, bad.

لغز *lughz*, enigma, mystery.

لغط *laght*, noise, uproar.

لغيف *lagheef*, receiver or concealer of stolen goods.

لغم - لغوم *lagham*, pl. *loghoom* (Turkish), sewer, drain; military mine of powder; blasting charge for quarrying.

لغمط *laghmata* (colloquial), it was smeared, stained.

لغو *laghw*, nullity. [فسخ]

لاغي *lághi*, null, void.

الغى *algha*, he annulled, abolished.

الغاء *ilghá*, a making null and void.

ملغى *mulgha* (or *malghi*), annulled, obsolete.

ملغات *mulghát*, nullities, errors annulled.

لغة - لغات *lugha*, pl. *lughát*, language, phraseology. [لسان]

كتاب اللغة *kitáb el-lugha*, dictionary.

لغوي *laghawiy*, linguistic, pedantic, verbose.

لف *laffa*, he wrapped up.

لفافة *lifáfa*, wrapper, bandage.

لف *laff*, a wrapping up.

لفيف *lafeef*, complex, wrapped.

لفاف *laffáf*, professional *roller* of cigarettes.

ملفوف *malfoof*, wrapped up; vague; a cabbage.

ملف *milaff*, envelope, cover.

لفت *lafata*, he turned to look.

لفت *laft*, glance, a turning towards.

التفت *iltafata*, he turned his attention to, took care, paid attention.

التفات *iltifát*, courtesy, pains, attention to.

ملتفت *multafit*, painstaking, attentive.

استلفت *istalfata*, he asked (another) to pay attention, drew his attention to.

لفت *lift*, turnips.

لفّاح *luffáh*, mandrake.

تلفظ or لفظ *lafaza*, or *talaffaza*, he uttered, pronounced, spoke.

لفظ ـ الفاظ *lafz*, pl. *alfáz*, word, phrase, pronunciation.

لفّق *laffaqa*, he hemmed, sewed together, trumped up a story; humbugged.

تلفيق *talfeeq*, humbug; a trumped-up case, a false accusation.

ملفّق *molaffaq*, sham, trumped-up, falsified.

لقب ـ القاب *laqab*, pl. *alqáb*, surname, nickname.

ملقّب *molaqqab*, surnamed, *alias*.

لقح على *laqaha 'ala*, he ejected at, uttered abuse, insult.

لقح or لقاح *laq-h*, or *laqáh*, pollen, fecundation.

لقّح *laqqaha*, he impregnated, vaccinated. [طعّم]

لقط *loqata*, he picked up by chance, gleaned.

لقطة *loqta*, treasure-trove.

لقيط *laqeet*, a foundling, exposed infant.

لقف *laqifa*, he seized, caught at.

ملقف *malqaf*, air-shaft on roof, sky-light.

لقلق *laqlaqa*, he made shake, agitated.

لقلاق *laqláq*, stork.

لقمة ـ لقم *loqma*, pl. *loqam*, morsel.

لقمان *Loqmán*, the Oriental Æsop; a fabulist.

تلقيم *talqeem*, ceiling, panelled ceiling.

لقّن *laqqana*, he instructed, prompted, suggested, dictated.

تلقين *talqeen*, suggestion, a prompting; funeral oration.

ملقّن *molaqqan*, prompted (speech); not one's own genuine evidence or ideas.

لقاء *liqá*, the face; a meeting face to face.

لقي or التقى *laqia*, or *iltaqa*, he found; met with.

القى *alqa*, he threw down, charged, accused.

لاقى or تلاقى *láqa*, or *taláqa*, he met, interviewed.

تلقّى *talaqqa*, he went to meet, anticipated.

تلقاء *tilqá*, in front of.

من تلقاء نفسه *min tilqá nafsihi*, of his own accord or right.

ملاقاة *muláqát*, a meeting face to face, interview.

ملقى *mulqa*, or *mulqi*, thrown down.

استلقى ـ سلقى *istalqa*, he threw himself down, reclined (see also *salqa*).

لك ـ لكم *lak*, to thee; *lakom*, to ye.

لكم or لكد *lakaha*, or *lakada*, he slapped, struck.

لكز or لكم *lakaza*, or *lakama*, he struck. [لطم]

لكمية or لكميّة *lakamiya*, fist. [بنية]

لكاكيم *lakákeem*, blows with the fist.

لكن ـ لكنّ *lakin*, but; *lakunna*, to ye (femin.).

الكن ـ لكن *lakina*, he stammered; *alkan*, stammerer.

لكي *likai*, in order that. [كي]

لم *lam*, not (past sense with aorist tense).

لم يكن *lam yakon*, it was not.

لم يلد و لم يولد *lam yalid wa lam yoolad*, (Allah) did not beget and was not begotten.

ما لم يكتب *má lam yiktib*, unless he should write.

لمّا *lammá*, when that, since that.

لمّ *lamma*, he gathered, picked up.

التمّ *iltamma*, it formed a crowd, they collected in a crowd.

ملموم *malmoom*, gathered, collected.

لمح *lamaha*, he glanced at; it shone, sparkled. [لمع]

لمّح *lammaha*, he hinted or alluded to.

لمحة *lamha*, glance, sparkle, hint.

لمح البصر *lamh el-básir*, an object clearly seen, distinct view.

تلميح *talmeeh*, allusion, a hinting.

لمس *lamasa*, he touched, handled. [مسّ]

لمس *lums*, touch, a touching.

لامس *lámis*, he who touches.

قوّة لامسة *qowwa lámisa*, sense of touch.

لامس *lámasa*, he touched mutually.

ملامسة *mulámasa*, caress, fondling.

التمس *iltamasa*, he besought, asked humbly.

التماس *iltimás*, supplication, request.

التماس اعادة النظر *iltimás ia'ádet en-nazar*, Requête Civile, plea for a new hearing of a civil suit.

لمع ـ يلمع *lama'a*, it shone, sparkled; *yalma'*, it sparkles.

لامع *lámia'*, brilliant.

ملمّع *molamma'*, diverse; mixed speech.

لملم *lamlam*, atriplex halimus.

لمة *luma*, help-meet, wife; equal, one of a pair.

لن ـ لن تنظر *lan*, not; *lan tanzor*, thou wilt not see.

لهب *lahiba*, it flamed.

التهب *iltahaba*, it was inflamed.

لهيب or لهلوبة *laheeb* (vulgarism, *lahlooba*), flame.

التهاب *iltihúb*, inflammation.

ملتهب *multahib*, inflamed.

لهجة *lahja*, tongue, language. [لغة]

لحس or لهس *lahasa*, he licked with the tongue.

لهف *lahf*, regret, complaint.

تلهّف or لهف *lahifa*, or *talahhafa*, he longed for, regretted.

لِهِم - الْهِم (luhima) ilhám, divine inspiration. [وحي]

مُلْهَم mulham, inspired by God.

لَهَّم lahhama, he passed on, handed secretly.

لها or الَّتهى lahá, or iltaha, he amused himself.

لهو lahw, play, amusement. [لعب]

تلاهى taláha, he amused himself.

ملهى - ملاهي milha, pl. maláhi, plaything; musical instrument.

لَوْ - لِ law - li, if - then (co-ordinate conjunctions).

لو عمله لنظرته law a'malaho li-nazartoh, if he had done it, I should have seen it.

لو لا law lá, unless.

و لو wa law, although.

لوبية or لوبياء loobiya, haricot beans; dolichos lubia.

لَوَّث lawwasa, he soiled, besmirched.

تَلَوَّث talawwasa, it became soiled, stained.

ملوَّث بالدم molawwas bid-dam, (clothes, &c.) stained with blood.

لوح - الواح lóh, pl. alwáh, tablet; sheet or piece of metal; plank, board; pane of glass; wooden shovel for grain.

لوحة lóha, one piece, a plank; notice board.

يلوح talawwaha (colloquial), he sickened, grew feeble.

لائحة - لوائح láyiha, pl. lawáyih, note, circular, decree, statute.

لوز - لوزة lóza, an almond; tonsil, gland; lóz, almonds.

لوط Loot, the patriarch Lot.

لوطيّ - اواطة lootiy, sodomite; liwáta, sodomy.

لوف - ليف loof (see leef).

لوق - لَوَّق (lóq) lawwaqa, he sowed seed and then smoothed and beat down the surface of the soil; sowing after the inundation, in soft soil.

لوكاندة locanda (Italian), hotel, restaurant.

لوم or ملام lóm, or malám, blame.

لام - يلوم láma, he blamed; yaloom, he blames.

ملام عليه molám 'aleih, fault, for which he is blamed.

ملاومة or تلاوم muláwama, or taláwum, mutual blame.

لون - الوان lón, pl. alwán, colour, tint, hue.

لَوَّن lawwana, he coloured.

تَلَوَّن talawwana, it became coloured; he was shifty, hypocritical.

ملوَّن molawwan, coloured, false, hypocrite.

لوى - يلوي lawa, he twisted, bent; yalwi, he twists.

التوى or تلوَّى iltawa, or talawwa, it became bent, twisted.

ملوي or ملتوي malwi, or multawi, bent, folded.

لواية liwáya, pad, or fold for the head as a rest for the water-jar.

الوية ـ لواء‎ *liwá*, pl. *alwiya*, flag, brigade flag; a small Turkish province under a brigadier, *sanjáq*. [ساجاق‎]

لواء باشا‎ *liwá báshá*, brigadier, a military officer of the third or lowest rank of pasha, equal to the civil *Meeri-meerán* pasha. [مير ميران‎]

ليت‎ *laita* (vulgarly *rait*), would that!

ليت شعري هذا الدنيا لمن‎ *laita shia'ri haza ed-dunyá li-men*. Would that I knew to whom this world belongs.

ليث‎ *laith*, lion. [اسد‎]

ليس ـ لست‎ *laisa*, he, it was not; *lasto*, I was not. [ايس‎]

ليس الا‎ *laisa illá* nothing but, mere; that is all.

ليس هو‎ *laisa hoa*, except him.

ليف‎ *leef*, date-palm fibre, of which the finer quality is used for sponges, and the coarser for ropes.

لوف‎ or لوفة‎ *loof*, or *loofa*, a plant like a cucumber, of which the fibre is used for sponges; serpentaria; *arisarum vulgare*.

ليق‎ *leeq*, cotton in Arab inkpots.

لياقة‎ *liyáqa*, fitness, propriety.

لائق‎ *láyiq*, fit, becoming, proper.

لاق ـ يليق ب‎ *láqa bi*, it befitted; *yaleeq*, it befits.

ليلة‎ *laila*, one night.

الف ليلة و ليلة‎ *alf laila wa laila*, 1001 nights, the Arabian Nights.

ليل ـ ليالي‎ *lail*, pl. *layáli*, night.

ليلاً و نهاراً‎ *lailán wa naharán*, by night and by day.

لئلا ـ لان لا‎ *lialla*, contraction for *li-an lá*, in order not to.

ليمون‎ *laimoon*, lemon, citron, lime.

ليمان‎ *leemán* (Greek *limeen*; Turkish), harbour; hence the hulks, or penal servitude in the Turkish code.

لينة‎ or لين‎ *leen*, or *leena*, softness.

لين‎ *layyin*, tender, soft; bowels open. [هين‎]

ليانة‎ *layána*, sofa, soft cushion.

لان ـ يلين‎ *lána*, it was soft; *yaleen*, it is soft.

لين‎ *layyana*, he softened, made supple.

تليين‎ *talyeen*, a making soft or supple; gymnastics or extension motions in drill.

ملين‎ *molayyin*, softener; a purge.

ليوان‎ or الايوان‎ *leewán*, raised dais in a room; hall. [ايوان‎]

لي‎ *lai*, pipe or long tube of the narghileh.

لية‎ *leyya*, fat tail of sheep; meat containing plenty of fat. [الية‎]

M.

م‎ *Meem*. Value = 40.

[N.B.—The following short list of participles, &c., is only given in order to assist the *beginner* in his search for the roots of derived forms.]

ماذا‎ or ما‎ *má*, or *mázá*, what?

لماذا‎ *li-mázá*, why?

ما *má*, that which; as long as; (as a suffix) -ever, -soever.

من اىّ سبب ما *min ai sabab má*, from any reason whatever.

ما بين *má bain*, between, that which is between.

ما دام *má dám*, while, as long as.

ما شآء الله *má shá 'llah*, what God has willed; how fine! bravo.

ما ـ ما اَعرِف *má*, not; *má a'rif*, I do not know. [؟]

ما ... شي *má ... sh* or *shi* (*má* before the verb and *sh* or *shi* after it, like *ne ... pas*), not.

ما اَعرِفش *má a'rifsh*, I do not know.

ما عدا *má 'adá*, except, not counting.

ما لم *má lam* (two negatives), unless.

و ما كان منهُ و اِنَّ ضربني *wa má kána minoh wa illá durabani*, and the next thing was that he (suddenly) beat me.

ما ـ مياه or امواه *má*, pl. *miyáh*, or *amwáh* (sometimes femin.), water.

ماوِي or مأوِيّ *máwiy*, or *máiy*, watery, aqueous.

مويَة *mwaya* (colloquial), water.

مآب ـ آب *maáb*, source, origin, focus (see *aába*).

مات ـ موت *máta*, he died (see *mōt*).

مآتم ـ اتم *máitam*, mourning, funeral (see *atem*).

مآدَّة ـ مدَّ *mádda*, matter, article (see *madda*).

مآذون ـ اذن *mázoon*, licensed (see *izn*).

ماري or مار *már*, or *mári* (Syriac), saint.

مار جرجس *már Jirjis*, St. George.

مارس *márs* (European), month of March.

مارستان *máristán* (Persian), asylum, hospital.

مارونيّ ـ موارنة *Márooniy*, pl. *Mawárna*, Maronite, Catholics of Mount Lebanon named after Bishop Marooni, 6th century A.D.

ماسورة ـ اسر *másoora*, tube, drain (see *asara*).

ماشة *másha* (Persian), tongs, pincers.

مأكولات ـ اكل *mákoolát*, eatables (see *akala*).

ماكنة *mákina* (European), machine, engine; *aála* is also used in this sense. [آلة]

مال ـ اموال ـ مول *mál*, pl. *amwál*, property, personal property as distinct from real property; goods, wealth (see *mōl*). [ملك]

مال ـ ميل *mála*, he leaned (see *mail*).

مآل ـ اول *maál*, signification (see *awl*).

مألوف ـ الف *máloof*, familiar (see *ilf*).

مأمور ـ امر *mámoor*, an official, prefect (see *amara*).

مأمول ـ امل *mámool*, hoped, desire (see *amal*).

مأمون ـ امن *mámoon*, trusted (see *amn*).

ماهِيَّة *máhiya* (from Persian *máh*, month), monthly pay.

ماهِيَّة *máhiya* (from *má*, that which, and *hía*, she is), actual, real.

مأوى ـ أوى *máwa*, place of shelter, abode (see *awa*).

مئة ـ or مائة *máya*, or *miya*, pl. *miyát*, hundred.

ميت *meet* (colloquial for *máya*), hundred.

مايو *máyo* (European), month of May.

مائدة *máyida*, table, large dinner tray.

مأيوس ـ ايس *máyoos*, despaired of (see *ayasa*).

مباح ـ بوح *mobáh*, lawful (see *bōh*).

مباشرة ـ بشر *mobásharatán*, direct (see *basharu*).

مباشر *mobáshir*, usher of a court. [بشر]

مباع ـ مبايعة ـ بيع *mobáa'*, sold; *mobáya'a*, sale (see *beea'*).

مباين ـ بيان or بين *mobáyin*, distinct (see *beyán* or *bain*).

مبتدئ ـ بداء *mobtadi*, beginner (see *budá*).

مبتلى ـ بلاء *mubtala*, afflicted (see *belá*).

مباحث ـ بحث *mabhas*, topic (see *bahs*).

مبرد ـ برد *mibrad*, file (see *barada*).

مبعوث ـ بعث *mab'aoos*, sent (see *ba'ta*).

مبلغ ـ بلغ *mablagh*, sum of money (see *balagha*).

مبلول ـ بل *mablool*, wetted, wet (see *balla*).

مبنيّ ـ بنى *mubniy*, founded, built (see *bana*).

مبيت ـ بيات *mabeet*, night's lodging (see *biyát*).

مبيع ـ بيع *mabeea'*, sale (see *beea'*).

مبيّن ـ بين or بيان *mobeen*, or *mobayyin*, showing (see *beyán*).

متأتّى ـ اتى *mataátti*, resulting (see *ata*).

متتابع ـ تبع *mutatábia'*, consecutive (see *tabu'a*).

متتالي ـ تلا *mutatáli*, consecutive (see *talá*).

متجر ـ تجر *matjar*, trade (see *tajara*).

متحد ـ احد *muttahid*, ally (see *ahad*).

مترجم ـ ترجم *mutarjim*, translator (see *tarjama*).

متراس ـ متاريس *mitras*, pl. *matáris*, rampart, trenches.

مترو ـ امتار *matro*, pl. *amtár* (French), mètre.

متزوّج ـ زوج *motazawwaj*, married (see *zōj*).

متزيّا ـ زي *mutazayyá*, dressed up (see *zee*).

متسبّب ـ سبب *motasabibb*, causer, seller (see *sabab*).

متّسع ـ وسع *mottasia'*, wide (see *wassa'a*).

متشرّد ـ شرد *matasharrid*, vagabond (a newly invented legal term) (see *sharada*).

متصرف (252) مثال

متصرّف ـ صرف *mutasarrif*, possessor, ruler (see *sarafa*).

متّصف ـ وصف *muttasif*, qualified (see *wasafa*).

متّصل ـ وصل *muttasil*, contiguous (see *wasala*).

متّضح ـ وضح *muttadih*, clear, evident (see *waddaha*).

متعة ـ متع *mota'a*, pl. *mota'*, profit, utility, the enjoyment of possession.

متاع ـ امتعة *matáa'*, pl. *amtia'a*, property, goods. [بضاعة]

تمتّع or استمتع ب *tamatta'a bi*, or *istamta'a bi*, he enjoyed, profited by.

بتاع ـ بتاعة ـ بتوع *batáa'*, (femin.) *batá'at*, pl. *botooa'* (colloquialism derived from *matáa'*, to supply the place of " *of* ").

الكتاب بتاعي *el-kitáb batáa'y*, my book, the book (which is) my property.

الحرمة بتاعته *el-horma batá'atoh*, his wife.

الكتب بتوعك *el-kotob botoo'ak*, thy books.

المفتاح بتاع الباب *el-miftáh batáa' el-báb*, the key belonging to the door.

متعاقدين ـ عقد *mota'áqideen*, the contracting parties (see *'aqada*).

متعصّب ـ عصب *mota'assib*, fanatic (see *'asab*).

متعلّق ـ علق *mota'alliq*, belonging to (see *a'liqa*).

متعهّد ـ عهد *mota'ahhid*, contractor (see *a'hda*).

متغيّب ـ غيب *motaghayyib*, absentee (see *ghaib*).

متفالس ـ فلس *motafális*, bankrupt (see *fallasa*).

متفرّق ـ فرق *motafarriq*, various (see *faraqa*).

متّفق ـ وفق *mottafiq*, agreed (see *wafy*).

متقن ـ تقن *motqan*, perfected (see *tiqn*).

متّقي ـ وقي *mottaqi*, pious (see *waqa*).

متلبّسًا بالجناية *motalabbisán biljináya*, caught in the act, *en flagrant délit*. [لبس]

متن or متنة *matn*, or *matána*, solidity, solid contents.

متن التقرير *matn et-taqreer*, the contents of a document; its text, substance.

متين *mateen*, solid.

متنوّع ـ نوع *mutanawwia'*, various (see *now'*).

متّهم or متهم ـ تهمة *muttaham*, or *mut-ham*, an accused man (see *tuhma*).

متى *mata*, whenever, at the time that.

أيّ متى *aiy mata (aimta)*, when?

مثبوت ـ ثبت *masboot*, proved (see *sabata*).

مثل ـ امثال *misl*, like, similar; *masal*, pl. *amsál*, simile, proverb, maxim.

مثال ـ امثلة *misál*, pl. *amsila*, example, sample; form of certain Arab verbs like وعد ـ يسر.

اِمْثُولَة *omsoola*, example, sample, lesson.

تِمْثَال *timsál*, statue, image.

مَثَّل *massala*, he compared, made similar.

تَمْثِيل *tamseel*, assimilation, analogy, portrait.

تَمَاثَل or مَاثَل *másala*, or *tamásala*, it resembled.

مُمَاثِل *momásil*, similar, analogous.

اِمْتَثَل *imtasala*, he obeyed, followed, complied.

مَثِيل *maseel*, similar.

مُثُول *mosool*, a standing humbly before a superior; *levée*, reception at Court.

مُثَلَّث ـ ثلّث *mutallat*, triangle, tripled (see *tult*).

مُثْمِر ـ ثمر *motmir*, fruitful (see *tamar*).

مَثَانَة *masána*, urinary bladder.

مُثَنَّى ـ ثُنَّى *motanna*, dual (see *sanna*).

مَجَاز ـ جواز *majáz*, metaphor (see *jawáz*).

مُجَاوِر ـ جوار *mojáwir*, student, adjacent (see *jiwár*).

مَجْد *majd*, glory, majesty, pomp.

مَجِيد *Majeed*, (God) the Glorious.

عبد المجيد *'Abd ul-Majeed*, slave of the Glorious One, name of a recent Sultan, d. 1861.

مَجِيدِيّ ـ مَجِيدِيَّة *majeediy*, (femin.) *majeediya*, Turkish gold coinage, and decoration named after Sultan 'Abdul-Majeed.

مَجْذُوب ـ جذب *majzool*, demented (see *jazaba*).

مَجَرّ ـ مَجْرُور ـ جرّ *majarr*, and *majroor* (see *jarra*).

المَجَرَّة *el-majarra*, the Milky Way. [جرّ]

مُجَرَّب ـ جرَّب *mojarrab*, tried, expert (see *jarraba*).

مُجَرَّد ـ جرد *mojarrad*, bare, simple, incorporeal (see *jarada*).

مُجْرِم ـ جرم *mojrim*, barefoot beggar, guilty (see *jarama*).

مَجْرَى ـ جرى *majra*, course, duct (see *jara*).

مُجَلِّد ـ جلد *mojallid*, bookbinder (see *jild*).

مَجْلِس ـ جلس *majlis*, council, assembly (see *julasa*).

مَجْمَع ـ جمع *majma'*, total (see *jam'aa*).

مَجْمَلَة ـ جملة *mojmal*, total (see *jomla*).

مَجْنُون ـ جنّ *majnoon*, mad (see *jonna*).

مَجَّانًا *majjánán*, gratis.

مَجْنَى ـ جنى *majna*, crime committed (see *jana*).

مِجْوَز ـ جوز *mijwiz*, double (see *jōz*).

مَجُوسِيّ *majoosiy*, magian, heathen, hindoo; magician.

مَجِيء ـ جاء *maji*, arrival (see *já*).

مُجِيب ـ جواب *mojeeb*, compliant. (see *jawáb*). [cf. موجب]

مَحَار *mahár*, oyster, shell-fish.

مُحَارَبَة ـ حرب *muhárabu*, war (see *harb*)

حسب ـ محاسبة‎ *mohásaba*, accounts (see *hasaba*).

محافظ ـ حفظ‎ *moháfiz*, governor (see *hafiza*).

محال ـ حول‎ *mohál*, absurd (see *hõl*).

محامى ـ حمى‎ *mohámi*, lawyer (see *hama*).

محبّ ـ محبوب ـ حبّ‎ *mohibb*, *mahboob*, lover (see *habba*).

محبوس ـ حبس‎ *mahboos*, imprisoned, prisoner (see *habasa*).

محتاج ـ حاجة‎ *muhtáj*, in need of (see *hája*).

محذور ـ حذر‎ *mahzoor*, danger (see *hizr*).

محراب ـ حرب‎ *mihráb*, part of a Mosque (see *harb*).

محراث ـ حرث‎ *mihrát*, plough (see *harasa*).

محروسة ـ حرس‎ *mahroosa*, Cairo, the guarded (see *harasa*).

محرّم ـ حرم‎ *Moharram*, first month of Moslem year (see *harama*).

محصول ـ حصل‎ *mahsool*, result, crop, revenue (see *hasala*).

محض‎ or محضا‎ *mahd*, or *mahdán*, sheer, mere, quite.

محضر ـ حضر‎ *mohdir*, usher; *mahdar*, report (see *hadara*).

محطّة ـ حطّ‎ *mahatta*, railway station (see *hatta*).

محفر ـ حفر‎ *mihfar*, spade (see *hafara*).

محقّق ـ حقّ‎ *mohaqqaq*, verified (see *haqq*).

محكمة ـ حكم‎ *mahkama*, tribunal (see *hakama*).

محلّ ـ حلّ‎ *mahall*, place, spot (see *halla*).

فى محلّه‎ *fi mahalloh*, quite right, in its right place.

محمّد ـ حمد‎ *Mohammad*, praiseworthy (see *hamida*).

محمل ـ حمل‎ *mahmal*, litter (see *hamala*).

امتحن‎ or محن‎ *mahana*, or commonly, *imtahana*, he put to the proof, examined a candidate.

امتحان‎ or محنة‎ *mihna*, or *imtihan*, trial, examination.

ممتحن‎ *mumtahan*, candidate, on probation.

محا ـ محو‎ *mahá*, he obliterated; *maho*, obliteration.

ممحوّ‎ or ممحىّ‎ *mamhee*, or *mamhoo*, obliterated.

محاط ـ محيط ـ حاط‎ *mohát*, *moheet* (see *háta*).

محور‎ *mihwar*, axis, cylinder.

محيى ـ حيى‎ *mohee*, God, the Maker Alive (see *haya*).

محيل ـ حول‎ *moheel*, transferor, endorser (see *hõl*).

مخّ ـ مخاخ‎ *mokhkh*, pl. *mikhákh*, brain, marrow.

مخا‎ *makhá*, Moka, or Mocca, in S. Arabia.

مخاط ـ مخطّى‎ *mokhát*, mucus; *mokhátiy*, mucous.

مخاطب ـ خطب‎ *mokhátab*, second person (in grammar) (see *khataba*).

مخالف ـ خالف *mokhálif*, contrary (see *khalafa*).

مخبر ـ خبر *mokhbir*, informant (see *khabar*).

مخبزة ـ خبز *makhbaza*, bakery (see *khobz*).

مختار ـ خيار *mokhtár*, chosen (see *khiyár*).

مختصّ ـ خصّ *mokhtass*, competent (see *khassa*).

مختصر ـ خاصرة *mokhtasar*, summarized (see *khásira*).

مختلّ ـ مخلّ ـ خلل *mokhtall*, and *mokhill* (see *khalel*).

مختلس ـ خلس *mokhtalis*, swindler (see *khalasa*).

مختلط ـ خلط *mokhtalit*, mixed (see *khalata*).

مخدّة ـ خدّ *mikhadda*, pillow (see *khadd*).

مخدوم ـ خدم *makhdoom*, master (see *khadama*).

مخزن ـ خزّن *makhzan*, magazine, insulator (see *khazzana*).

مخستك ـ خستكه *mokhastik*, sick (see *khastaka*).

مختشي ـ خشي *mikhtishi*, bashful (see *khashia*).

مخصوص ـ خصّ *makhsoos*, special (see *khassa*).

مخضت *makhidat*, she was in labour.

مخاض ـ ماخض *makhád*, parturition; *mákhid*, in labour.

مخفي ـ خفا *makhfi*, stealth, hidden (see *khafá*).

مخلى ـ خلى *mikhla*, scythe, sickle (see *khala*).

مخلاة ـ خلى *mikhlá*, nose-bag for horses (see *khala*).

مخلوقات ـ خلق *makhlooqát*, creatures (see *khalaqa*).

مخلول *makhlool*, cracked, insane.

[خلل]

مخيّر ـ خيار *mokhayyar*, he who has the option (see *khiyár*).

مخيف ـ خوف *mokheef*, terrific (see *kháf*).

مدّ *madda*, he extended, it reached, rose.

مدّد *maddada*, he made extend, prolonged.

امدّ *amadda*, he helped, aided.

امتدّ *imtadda*, it reached, was extended.

استمدّ *istamadda*, he asked help.

مدّ ـ مدود *madd*, pl. *modood*, reach, extension, flood-tide.

مدّ وجزر البحر *madd wa jazr el-bahr*, flow and ebb of the sea.

مدّة ـ آ ـ ٱ *madda*, (in grammar) prolongation of the voice, the mark ~ over the alif, instead of a double *a*.

مدّ *modd*, measure of grain; one litre.

مدّة ـ مدد *modda*, pl. *modad*, interval, space of time.

مديد *madeed*, long, extensive.

مدّة مديدة *modda madeeda*, a long period of time.

مضي مدّة طويلة *modiy modda taweela*, "*prescription*" or legal limitation, lapse of a long period.

امداد or مدد madad, or imdád, succour; invocation.

امدادیّ imdádiy, reinforcing (as troops in reserve).

مادّة – موادّ mádda, pl. mawádd, matter, article of a code, item in a list.

موادّ جزئيّة mawádd juziya, petty affairs, "justice sommaire."

مادّيّ or مادّوي máddiy, or máddawiy, material, real.

امتداد imtidád, a being extended, extensive.

ممدود or مُمَدَّد mamdood, or momaddad, stretched, extended.

مدار – دور madár, pivot (see dōr).

مداس – دوسة madás, shoes (see dōsa).

مدان – دون modán, guilty, accused (see doon).

مداولة – دول modáwala, deliberation (see dōl).

مدایین – دین modáyin, creditor (see dain).

مدبّر – دبر modabbir, manager (see dubr).

مدبغ – دبغ madbagh, tannery (see dubagha).

مدحرج – دحرج modahraj, rolled, circular (see dahraja).

مدخنة – دخن madkhana, chimney (see dakhana).

مدر madar, clay, building material.

مدرى or مذرى midra, bar, pitchfork. [cf. ذرى]

امتدح or مدح madaha, or imtadaha, he praised. [cf. حمد

مدح نفسه madaha nafsaho, he flattered himself.

مدرج – درج modraj, roll, scroll (see daraja).

مدرسة – درس madrasa, school (see darasa).

مدرك – درك modrik, intelligent (see darak).

مدعوّ – دعا mada'oo, named (see da'á).

مدّعي – دعا modda'y, plaintiff (see da'á).

مدفع – دفع madfa', cannon (see dafa'a).

مدمن – دمن modmin, persevering (see damana).

مدین – دون modeen, accuser (see doon).

مدین – دین madeen, debtor (see dain).

مدینة – مدن or مدائن madeena, pl. modon, or madáyin, town, city.

المدينة El-Madeena, Medina in Arabia, the city of Mahomet par excellence.

مدنيّ madaniy, civil, not criminal (law).

قانون مدنيّ qánoon madaniy, code civil, civil law.

حقوق مدنيّة hoqooq madaniya, civil rights; claim for damages in a criminal case.

مدّن maddana, he civilised.

تَمَدَّنَ *tamaddana*, he became civilised.

مُتَمَدِّن *motamaddin*, civilised.

مُدَوَّر *modawwar*, round (see *dōr*).

مُدَوَّن - دون *modawwan*, inscribed (see *doon*).

مَدًى or مَدِيَّة *mada*, or *modya*, limit, interval, reach, range; as far as.

مُدِير - دور *modeer*, mudir, administrator, governor of a province (see *dōr*).

مَدْيُون - دين *madyoon*, debtor (see *dain*).

مُذْ or مُنْذُ *muz*, or *munz*, since (of time).

مِذْرَى - ذرى *midra*, pitchfork (see *dara*).

مَذْكُور - ذكر *mazkoor*, above-mentioned (see *zakara*).

مَذْلُول - ذلّ *mazlool*, cringing (see *zill*).

مَذْهَب - ذهب *madhab*, religion (see *dahaba*).

مَذْوَد - ذود *madwid*, manger (see *dōd*).

مَرَّ *marra*, he passed, went by. [عَبَرَ - فَوْت]

مُرُور *moroor*, passage, lapse of time; a name for the market at Cairo.

مَارّ *márr*, a passer by, who passes; gone.

المَارّ ذِكْرُهُ *el-márr zikroh*, aforesaid.

مَرَّة - مَرَّات - مِرَار *marra*, pl. *marrát*, or *mirár*, once, a time. [نَوْبَة - دَفْعَة]

بِالمَرَّة *bil-marra*, quite, emphatically.

مِرَارًا *mirárán*, at times, sometimes.

جُمْلَة مِرَار *jomla mirár*, several times, often.

غَيْر مَرَّة *ghair marra*, more than once.

مَمَرّ *mamarr*, place of passage, vestibule.

اسْتَمَرّ *istamarra*, he continued, was constant.

اسْتَمِرّ *istamirr* (imperative), Proceed! continue!

اسْتِمْرَار *istimrár*, constancy, continuance.

مُسْتَمِرّ *mostamirr*, constant, continuous, permanent.

مُرّ - اَمْرَار *morr*, pl. *amrár*, bitter, myrrh.

مَرَارَة *marára*, bitterness; gallbladder.

مَرَار *marár*, centaurea calcitrapa,

اَمَرّ - مُرَّى *amarr*, (femin.) *morra*, more bitter.

اَمْرَأ or مَرْء *mara*, man, male (rarely used).

مُرُوءَة *morooa*, virility, humanity, courage.

اِمْرَأَة or مَرَة *mara* (*imrát*), woman, wife. [نِسَاء]

مَرِيء *maria*, œsophagus.

مُرَاءٍ *morá*, hypocrite (see *ráa*).

مِرْآة - رَأَى *miráat*, or *miráya*, mirror, (see *ráa*).

مُرَابِي - رِبَا *morábi*, usurer (see *ribá*).

مُرَاجَعَة - رجع *morája'a*, control, inspection (see *raja'a*).

مراد ـ راود *morád*, desire (see *ráwada*).

مراعاة ـ رعى *moráa'a*, respect, regard (see *ra'a*).

مرافعة ـ رفع *morúfa'a*, legal procedure, proceedings at a trial (see *rafa'a*).

مراقبة ـ رقب *moráqaba*, inspection, control (see *raqaba*).

مراكش *Marákesh*, Morocco. [مغربيّ

مراهق ـ رهاق *moráhiq*, young man (see *riháq*).

مربع ـ ربع *marba'*, pasture ground (see *roba'*).

مرتاب ـ ريب *mortáb*, doubtful (see *raib*).

مرتاح ـ روح *mortáh*, at ease, at rest (see *rawáh*).

مرتبة ـ رتب *martaba*, rank, high place, mattrass (see *rataba*).

مرتشي ـ رشا *murtashi*, taker of bribe (see *rashá*).

مرتفقات ـ رفق *mortafaqát*, latrines (see *rafaqa*).

مرتكب ـ ركب *murtakib*, criminal, guilty (see *rakiba*).

مرج ـ مروج *marj*, pl. *morooj*, meadow; a village in Cyrenaica, site of ancient Barca.

مرجان *marján*, coral; white coral stone from reefs.

مرجع ـ رجع *marja'*, turning point (see *raja'a*).

مرجوّ ـ رجا *marjoo*, requested (see *rajá*).

مرجيحة ـ رجح *marjaiha*, swing, see-saw (see *rajaha*).

مرح or مرخ *maraha*, he anointed, rubbed.

مرحاض ـ رحض *marhád*, latrine (see *rahada*).

مرحباً ـ رحب *marhabá*, welcome! (see *rahiba*).

مرحمة ـ مرحوم ـ رحم *marhama*, pity; *marhoom*, deceased (see *rahima*).

مرخ or مرح *marakha*, he anointed, rubbed.

مرخ *markh*, tinder, broom-plant; leptadenia pyrotechnica.

مرّيخ *mirreekh*, Planet Mars.

مرخّص ـ رخص *murakhkhas*, authorised (see *rukhs*).

مرد or مرودة *marad*, or *morooda*, beardlessness.

أمرد ـ مرد *amrad*, pl. *mord*, beardless youth.

مرّيد or مارد *marreed*, or *márid*, evil genie, rebel. [عفريت

تمرّد *tamarrada*, he revolted.

مرس or مارس *marasa* or *márasa*, he practised, tried, made a contract with; soaked, steeped.

ممارسة *momárasa*, facility from practice; a private arrangement or contract.

مرسة ـ مرسى ـ رسا *mirsá*, anchor; *marsa*, harbour (see *rasa*).

مريسى *mireesi* (Coptic), hot south wind.

مريسة *mareesa*, Soudanese wine of dates steeped in water. [برظان

مرسم *marsah*, theatre, ball.

مرسين *marseen*, myrtle. [آس]

مرشحة - رشح *mirshaha*, pack-saddle (see *rashaha*).

مرصد - رصد *marsad*, observatory (see *rasada*).

مرض - امراض *marad*, pl. *amrád*, illness, disease.

مريض - مرضى *mareed*, pl. *marda*, sick, ill. [عَيَّان]

تمارض *tamárada*, he shammed sick.

مرضعة - رضع *mordia'a*, wet-nurse (see *radia'*).

مرطبان *martabán*, jar, ewer.

مرعى *mara'*, pasturage. [رعى]

مرغ *maragha*, he hesitated, declined.

مرفأ *mirfá*, quay, port. [رفأ]

مرفق - رفق *mirfaq*, elbow (see *rafaqa*). [كوع]

مرقة *maraqa*, soup, broth.

ممرق *memraq*, skylight.

مركب - مركوب - ركب *markab*, ship; *markoob*, shoe (see *rakiba*).

مركز - ر-ك-ز *markaz*, centre (see *rakaza*).

مرمّة - رمّ *maramma*, repairs (see *ramma*).

مرمر *marmar*, marble. [رخام]

مرمش *marmasha* (colloquial), he winked, screwed up his eyes, guawed. [or قرنش]

مرمط *marmata* (colloquial), he injured, spoilt, knocked about.

مرملة - رمل *marmala*, sand-pot (see *raml*).

مرمي - رمى *marmiy*, thrown, projectile (see *rama*).

مرميس *mirmees*, rhinoceros.

مرن *marana*, it was supple, elastic.

مرن *marin*, supple, elastic.

مرانة *marána*, elasticity.

مرّن *marrana*, he made supple, he made practice, enured.

تمرين *tamreen*, exercise, practice, probation.

مروحة - رواح *mirwaha*, fan (see *rawáh*).

مرهم - مراهم *marham*, pl. *maráhim*, ointment.

مرهون - رهن *marhoon*, pledged, mortgaged (see *rahana*).

مريم *Mariam*, Miriam, Mary.

مريوح - رواح *maryooh*, bewitched (see *rawáh*).

مزّ *mazza*, he tasted, sipped.

مزّة *mazza*, a taste, relish, appetizer.

مزز *miziz*, acid taste of lemon, unripe fruit, &c.

مزاد - مزايدة - زيد *mazád*, or *mozáyada*, auction (see *zaid*).

مزار - زيارة *mazár*, place visited, shrine (see *ziyára*).

مزارع - زرع *mozária'*, farmer (see *zara'a*).

مزج *mazaja*, he mixed.

مزاج *mizáj*, mixture, humour, temperament.

مزاجي *mizájiy*, kerchief.

امتزج *imtazaja*, it became mixed, mingled.

مزح or مازح *mazaha*, or *mázaha*, he joked, chaffed.

مزاح - مازح *mozáh*, joke, joking; *mázih*, joker.

مزد *mezd*, or *mezz* (Persian), yellow leather slippers.

مزراب *mizráb*, gutter, drain. [زرب]

مزراق - زرّق *mizráq*, spear (see *zarraqa*).

مزركش - زركش *mozarkash*, brocade (see *zarkasha*).

مزرود - زرد *mazrood*, flushed, red in face (see *zard*).

مزري - زري *mozri*, injurious (see *zara*).

مزعم - زعم *maza'm*, doubtful (see *za'm*).

مزّق *mazzaqa*, he tore to pieces. [شرط]

تمزيق *tamzeeq*, a tearing up.

ممزّق *momazzaq*, torn up.

مزلقان - زلق *mazlaqán*, slope, slippery place (see *zalaqa*).

مزمار - مزمور - زمر *mizmár*, glottis; *mazmoor*, psalm (see *zamr*).

مزمن - زمن *mozmin*, chronic (disease) (see *zaman*).

مزنقة - زنق *maznaqa*, necklace (see *zanaqa*).

مزور - زور *mazwar*, oblique (see *zōr*).

مزوّر - زور *mozawwir*, forgerer, perjurer (see *zoor*).

مزيد - زيد *mazeed*, growth; complex (see *zaid*).

مزيّن - زين *mozayyin*, barber (see *zain*).

مزايا *mazáyá*, advantages, merits, privileges.

مسّ *massa*, he touched, handled. [لمس - جسّ]

مسّ or مسيس *mass*, or *masees*, touch, contact; insanity.

ماسّ *máss*, he who touches.

تماسّ *tamássa*, he touched mutually, fondled.

مماسّة or مساس *misás*, or *momássa*, contact.

ممسوس *mamsoos*, touched, maniac.

مساء *masá*, evening.

امس *ams*, yesterday, eve of to-day.

امسى *amsa*, he passed the evening at.

مساعدة - سعد *mosáa'da*, help, favour (see *sa'd*).

مساعي - سعى *masáa'y*, efforts (see *sa'a*).

مسافر - سفر *mosáfir*, traveller, guest (see *safar*).

مسافة - سوف *masáfa*, distance (see *sōf*).

مسامّ - سمّ *masámm*, pore of skin (see *samma*).

مسئلة or مسألة - سأل *masála*, or *masala*, question, affair (see *sáála*).

مساوي - سوي *mosáwi*, equal (see *sawia*).

مساهمة - سهم *mosáhuma*, joint-stock (see *sahm*).

مستأجر ـ اجرة *mostájir*, tenant, hirer (see *ujra*).

مستاهل ـ اهل *mostáhil*, deserving (see *ahl*).

مستبدّ ـ بدّ *mostabidd*, tyrant (see *badda*).

مستثنى ـ ثني *mostasná*, excepted (see *thiny*).

مستحقّ ـ حقّ *mostahaqq*, deserved (see *haqq*).

مستحيل ـ حول *mustaheel*, absurd (see *hôl*).

مستخدم ـ خدم *mustakhdam*, employé (see *khadama*).

مستشار ـ شورى *mustashár*, councillor (see *shoora*).

مستطيل ـ طول *mostateel*, oblong (see *tool*).

مستعجل ـ عجل *mosta'jil*, in haste (see *'ajila*).

مستعدّ ـ عدّ *mosta'idd*, ready (see *a'dda*).

مستعمل ـ عمل *mosta'mal*, used (see *a'mila*).

مستقبل ـ قبل *mustaqbil*, the future (see *qabala*).

مستقلّ ـ قلّ *mustaqill*, independent (see *qalla*).

مستقيم ـ قوم *mostaqeem*, upright, straight (see *qôm*).

مستنقع ـ نقع *mostanqa'* tank (see *naqa'a*).

مستوجب ـ وجب *mostawjib*, causing, necessitating (see *wajaba*).

مستوفى ـ وفى *mostawfi*, sufficient, completing (see *wafa*).

مستوقد ـ وقد *mustawqad*, furnace (see *waqada*).

مستوي ـ سوي *mistiwi*, ripe, cooked (see *sawia*).

مستيقظ ـ يقظ *mustaiqaz*, awake (see *yaqiza*).

مسجد ـ سجد *masjid*, mosque (see *sajada*).

مسجّل ـ سجل *mosajjal*, registered (see *sijil*).

مسجون ـ سجن *masjoon*, imprisoned (see *sajana*).

مسح *masaha*, he measured surface, surveyed land.

مساحة *masáha*, area, surveying of land, surface, dimensions.

مسّاح *massáh*, land surveyor.

مسح *masaha*, he wiped, purified by laying on of hands, anointed.

المسيح *El-Maseeh*, the Anointed, Messiah.

مسيحي *maseehiy*, Christian.

مسخ *maskh*, metamorphosis into a viler shape; buffoon.

ماسخ *másikh*, insipid, stupid.

مسخّر ـ سخّر *mosakhkhar*, tyrannised over (see *sakhara*).

مسخرة *maskhara*, ridiculous, mockery.

تمسخر على *tamaskhara a'la*, he mocked at.

مسخوطة ـ سخط *maskhoota*, statue, idol (see *sakhata*).

مسرب ـ سرب *masrab*, path, course (see *sarab*).

سرع - مُسرِع *mosria'* hastening (see *sar'ou*).

مُسَرَّة - مَسرور - سَرّ *masarra*, joy; *masroor*, glad (see *sarra*).

مِسرى *Misra*, Coptic month of August, the first month of high Nile.

مِسطاح - سطح *mistáh*, area, surface (see *sataha*).

مسطي عليه - سطا *masti 'aleih*, victim of attack (see *satá*).

مسقط اليه - سقط *mosqat ileih*, "concessionaire" (see *saqata*).

مَسقَف or مَسقوف *mosqof*, Muscovy, Russia.

مِسقاة - مسقاوى - سقى *misqát*, small canal; *masqáwi*, lands irrigated by a *sáqiya* (see *saqa*).

مسك في *masaka* (colloquially *misik fi*), he seized, held.

امسك *amsaka*, he held back, restrained.

امساك *imsák*, restraint; fast.

تمسّك *tamassaka*, he clung to, relied upon; opposed.

تمسّك *tamassuk*, reliance, opposition, lien or obligation.

مسك *mask*, a grip, catch; a goatskin of water. [قِربة]

مسك *misk*, musk perfume.

مِسكة *miska*, dung-cake for fuel. [جِلّة]

ماسك *másik*, holder, tongs.

ممسك *momsik*, restraining; constipative.

مسكر - سكر *muskir*, intoxicating (see *sakr*).

مسكن - مسكين - سكن *maskan*, abode; *maskeen*, poor (see *sakana*).

مسكوكات - سكّ *maskookát*, coined money (see *sakka*).

مسلوب - سلب *masloob*, pillaged; weak in intellect (see *salaba*).

مُسلّح - سلاح *mosallah*, armed (see *siláh*).

مِسَلَّة - سلّ *misalla*, obelisk (see *salla*).

مسلول - سلّ *maslool*, unsheathed; consumptive (see *salla*).

مَسلي - سلاء *masli*, cooking-butter (see *silá*).

مسلم - سلم *muslim*, Moslem, Musulman (see *silm*).

مسمار - سمّر *mismár*, peg, nail (see *sammara*).

مسمّى - سمّى *mosamma*, named (see *samma*).

مِسَنّ - سنّ *misann*, grindstone; *mosinn*, aged (see *sanna, sinn*).

مسنون - سنّة *masnoon*, customary (see *sonna*).

مسهل - سهل *mos-hil*, purgative (see *sahula*).

مسوّدة - سواد *maswada* rough draft (see *sawád*).

مسؤول - سأل *masool*, asked, responsible (see *sáála*).

مسير - سير *maseer*, course (see *sair*).

مش *mishsh*, cheese, curds and whey.

مشاجرة - شجر *moshájara*, quarrel (see *shujar*).

مشارٌ (263) مشي

مشارٌ اليه - شورى mushároh ileih, aforesaid (see *shoora*).

مشال - شال mashál, porterage; removal (see *shála*).

مشايخ - شيخ masháyikh, pl. of *shaikh*.

مشتاق - شوق mushtáq, eager (see *shóq*).

مشترى - شرا mushtari, buyer; Planet Jupiter; *mushtara*, purchased, a purchase (see *shirá*).

مشحون - شحن mash-hoon, laden (see *shahana*).

مشربية - شربية mashrabiya (see *mushrifiya*).

مشرط - شرط mishrat, lancet (see *sharata*). [فصد]

مشرفية - شرف mushrifiya, a projecting window, generally called *mushrabiya* (see *sharaf*).

مشرق - شرق mashriq, east, place of sunrise (see *sharq*).

مشرك - شرك moshrik, accuser (see *shirk*).

مشرمط - شرمط mosharmat, torn (see *sharmata*).

مشروع - شرع mashrooa', begun; a written contract, project, draft of a law (see *shara'a*).

مشط mashata, he combed the hair.

مشط misht, comb; instep or forepart of the foot.

ماشطة máshita, she who combs, female barber.

مشعرانى - شعر masha'rániy, hairy (see *sha'r*).

مشعل - شعل misha'l, torch (see *sha'la*).

مشغول - شغل mashyhool, busy (see *shoghl*).

مشق mashaqa, he tore, pulled to pieces.

مشقة - شق mashaqqa, difficulty (see *shaqqa*).

مشكل - شكل mushkil, difficult (see *shekl*).

مشمّس - شمس moshammas, sunstruck (see *shams*).

مشمش mishmish, apricot.

مشمش mashmasha (vulgarism), he beat soft like an apricot, pummelled, thumped.

مشمّع - شمع moshamma', waterproof (see *shama'*).

مشملا mushmilá, "*nèfle*," medlar.

مشنة mishanna, rush basket.

مشنقة - شنق mashnaqa, gallows (see *shanaqa*).

مشهد - شهد mash-had, funeral (see *shahida*).

مشهور - شهر mash-hoor, famous (see *shahr*).

مشوار - مشورة - شورى mishwár, errand; *mashwara*, deliberation (see *shoora*).

مشوى - شوى mishwi, grilled (see *shawa*).

مشى masha, or *mishi*, he walked.

امشى imshi (imperative), off with you! get along!

مشى mashi, act of walking.

ماشي - مُشاة *máshi*, he who walks, moves; on foot; pl. *mushát*, infantry. [بيادة]

ماشية - مواشي *máshiya*, pl. *mawáshi* (femin.), she who walks; (in pl.) cattle. [بهائم]

مشّى *mashsha*, he made walk, exercised a horse.

تماشى or تماشا *tamásha*, a promenading together; show, public sight.

مشير - شورى *musheer*, Field-Marshal (see *shoora*).

مشيمة - شيم *masheema*, placenta (see *shaim*).

مشيئة - شاء *mashiya*, wish (see *sháá*).

مصّ *massa*, he sucked; *mass*, a suck. [cf. مسّ]

قصب المصّ *qasab el-mass*, sugar-cane for sucking.

مصّاص - مصيص *massás*, sucker; *masees*, cement.

امتصّ *imtassa*, it absorbed.

امتصاص *imtisás*, absorption.

مصاب - صوب *mosáb*, hit, wounded (see *sob*).

مصائب - صعب *masá'yib*, difficulties (see *sa'oba*).

مصاغ - صوغ *maságh*, jewellery (see *sogh*).

مصبّ - صبّ *masabb*, embouchure, mould (see *sabba*).

مصبغة - صبغ *masbagha*, dyer's yard (see *sabagha*).

مصبنة - صابون *masbana*, soap-works (see *sáboon*).

المصحف - صحف *El Mos-haf*, The Book, Koran (see *sahafa*).

مصدر - صدر *masdar*, infinitive, source (see *sahara*).

مصدَّق - صدق *mosaddaq*, believed; double guarantee (see *sidq*).

مصر - امصار *masr*, pl. *amsár*, town.

مصر *Masr*, ("Mizraim") Egypt; Cairo; in Turkish, *Misr*.

مصر المحروسة *Masr el-mahroosa*, Cairo the protected, the capital.

مصريّ - مصريّة *masriy*, (femin.) *masriya*, Egyptian.

مصريّة اقاليم or اقطار or ديار *diyár* (or *aqtár*, or *aqáleem*), *masriya*, provinces of Egypt.

مصريّة - مصاري *masriya*, pl. *masári*, (Syrian) pence, paras.

مصرّ - صرّة *mosirr*, persistent; *masroor*, folded up in a bundle (see *sorra*).

مصير - مصارّ - مصارين *maseer* (or *masárr*), pl. *masáreen*, bowels, intestines. [معي]

مصراع - مصروع - صرع *misráa'*, valve; *masrooa'*, epileptic (see *sara'a*).

مصرف - مصاريف - مصروف - صرف *masraf*, *masáreef*, *masroof*, outlay, expenses (see *sarafa*).

مصطبة - صطب *mastaba*, dais, bench (see *satab*).

مصطفى - صفو *mustafa*, chosen, pure (see *safw*).

مصطكى mastaki, gum-mastic, a liqueur flavoured with aniseed ; raki, arrack. [مرق

مصطنع ـ صنع mustana' artificial (see sana'a).

مصفاة ـ صفو misfát, filter (see safw).

مصلح ـ مصلحة ـ صلح moslih, salt ; maslaha, business, &c. (see saloha).

مصمت masmat, cookshop.

مصور ـ صورة mosawwir, artist (see soora).

مصوع Masowa', Massowah ; an Italian settlement on the Red Sea coast of Abyssinia.

مصون ـ صون masoon, chaste, guarded (see sön).

مصيدة ـ صيد misiada, trap, net (see said).

مصير ـ صار maseer, fact, matter-of-fact (see sára).

مضاربة ـ ضرب modáraba, conflict (see daraba).

مضارع ـ ضرع modária', Aorist Tense (see dara').

مضاعفة ـ ضعف modáa'fa, double (see di'f).

مضاف ـ ضيف modáf, added (see daif).

مضاهاة ـ ضهي modáhát, similarity (see dahiy).

مضبطة ـ ضبط mazbata, written report (see zabata).

مضحك ـ ضحك modhik, funny (see dahika).

مضرّ ب ـ ضرّ modirr bi, injurious (see darra).

مضطرب ـ ضرب modtarib, anxious (see daraba).

مضطهد ـ ضهد modtahid, tyrannical (see dahada).

مضغ madayha, he chewed ; madgh, mastication.

مضمون ـ ضمن madmoon, contents, guaranteed (see dimn).

مضمضة madmada, a gargling, rinsing the mouth.

مضي ـ ضو modi, brilliant (see dö).

مضى mada, it (time) passed. [مدى

مضي modiy, lapse of time.

مضي المدّة الطويلة modiy el-modda et-taweela, lapse of a long period ; "prescription" ; Statute of Limitations.

ماضي mádi, passing; passed, past, past tense.

امضى amda, he signed his name.

امضاء imdá, signature.

امضاته ـ امضاه imdátoh (vulgarism for imdáh), his signature.

ممضى momdi, signer ; momda, signed.

مطاع ـ طوع motáa', obeyed (see taw').

مطالبة ـ طلب motálaba, claim for payment (see talaba).

مطالعة ـ طلع motála'a, study (see tala'a).

مطبخ ـ طبخ matbakh, kitchen (see tabkh).

مطبعة ـ طبع matba'a, printing-press (see taba'a).

مطر ـ امطار matar, pl. amtár, rain.

M M

مطر or امطر *matara*, or *amtara*, it rained.

مطارية *Matáriya*, Heliopolis; a suburb of Cairo.

مطران *matrán*, metropolitan, archbishop.

مطرب - طرب *motrib*, musician (see *tariba*).

مطرح - طرح *matrah*, place (see *taraha*).

مطرق - طرق *mitraq*, hammer (see *taraqa*).

مطل *matl*, delay, adjournment.

مطلّ على - طلّ *motill 'ala*, looking out upon (see *talla*).

مطلقاً - طلق *motlaqán*, absolutely (see *talaqa*).

مطمئنّ - طمن *motmayinn*, confident (see *tamn*).

مطوة - طوى *matwa*, penknife (see *tawa*).

مطيع - طوع *motcea'*, obedient (see *taw'*).

مطيّة *matiya*, horse, nag.

مظلوم - ظلم *mozlim*, dark; *mazloom*, victim (see *zolm*).

مع *ma'*, with; *ma'á*, together.

مع ذلك *ma' zalik*, nevertheless, with all that.

مع ان *ma' an*, although.

مع كون *ma' kōn*, with being, although.

معيّة *ma'iya*, "withness;" suite, privy department or household of a King, or of the Khedive.

معاذ الله - عزف *ma'áz Allahi*, God forbid! (see *'oz*).

معارضة - عرض *mo'-árada*, opposition (see *'arada*).

معاش - عيش *ma'ásh*, means of life, pension (see *'aish*).

معاف - عفو *mo'áf*, pardoned (see *'afw*).

معاقبة - عقب *mo'-áqaba*, punishment (see *a'qaba*).

معالجة - علج *mo'-álaja*, medical treatment (see *'alaja*).

معاملة - عمل *mo'-ámala*, treatment, conduct (see *a'milu*).

معاونة - عون *mo'-áwana*, assistance (see *'ōn*).

معاوية *Mo'-áwiya*, the first Caliph of Damascus, A.D. 661, founder of the Omaya dynasty (see أميّة).

معاينة - عين *mo'-áyana*, inspection (see *'ain*).

معبد - عبد *ma'bad*, place of worship (see *'abada*).

معبر - عبر *ma'bar*, place of passing (see *'abara*).

معتاد - عود *mo-a'tád*, usual (see *ō'd*).

معتبر - عبر *mo-a'tabar*, respectable (see *'abara*).

معترى - عرا *mo-a'tari*, afflicted (see *'ara*).

معتلّ - علة *mo'tall*, diseased (see *'illa*).

معتمد - عمد *mo-a'tamad*, trustworthy (see *a'mada*).

معتوق - عتق *ma'tooq*, freed (see *a'taqa*).

معتوه ـ عته ma'tooh, mad, demented (see a'tah).

معجب ـ عجب mo-a'jib, pleased, gratified (see a'jiba).

معجور ma'joor, basin, dough-pan.

معجزة ـ عجز mo'jiza, miracle (see 'ajaza).

معجون ـ عجن ma'joon, paste (see a'jana).

معدّ ـ عدّ mo-'add (mo-'idd), set apart for (see a'dda).

معدن ـ عدن ma'din, mine, metal (see a'dan).

معدة ـ معديّ mia'da, stomach; mia'diy, gastric.

معدي ـ عدا mo'di, infectious; ma'da, ferry (see a'da).

معذور ـ عذر ma'zoor, excused (see a'zara).

معراج ـ عرج mia'ráj, ladder, ascent (see a'raja).

معرض ـ عرض ma'rad, exhibition; ma'rood, petition (see a'rada).

معرفة ـ معروف ـ عرف ma'rifa, knowledge, means; ma'rafu, mane; ma'roof, favour (see a'rafa).

معرّى ـ عري mo-a'rra, stripped (see 'aria).

معز or معيز ـ ماعز ma'z, or ma'yeez, goats; may'iz, a goat.

معزز ـ عز mo-a'zzaz, corroborated (see a'zza).

معسر ـ عسر mo-a'sir, insolvent (see a'sara).

معسكر ـ عسكر mo-a'skar, camp (see a'skar).

معصم ـ معصومة mia'sam, wrist; ma'soom, infallible, above suspicion (see 'isma).

معطي ـ عطا mo'ti, (God) the Giver (see a'tá).

معظّمة ـ معظم ـ عظمة mo'azzama, magnifier; mo'zam, majority (see a'zama).

معفوّ ـ عفو ma'foo, pardoned (see a'fw).

معقول ـ عقل ma'qool, intelligible (see a'ql).

معك ma'aka, he rubbed.

معكوس ـ عكس ma'koos, upside down (see a'ks).

معلّم ـ معلوم ـ علم mo'allim, teacher; ma'loom, known (see a'lima).

معمار ـ عمر mia'már, architect (see o'mr).

معمل ـ عمل ma'amal, workshop (see a'mila).

معمّى ـ عمى mo-a'mma, enigma (see a'ma).

معن ـ ماعون (ma'n), máo'on, utensil, vessel.

معنون ـ عنوان ma'nwin, addressed (see o'nwán).

معنى ـ عنى ma'na, meaning (see a'na).

معهود ـ عهد ma'hood, contracted (see a'hida).

معيار ـ عيار mi'yár, legal standard (see i'yár).

معى - اعماء *ma'iy*, or *mi'a*, pl. *ama'á*, intestines.

معوىّ *ma'wiy*, intestinal.

معيشة - عيش *ma'yisha*, means of life (see *a'ish*).

معيّن - عين *moa'yyan*, appointed (see *a'in*).

مغارة or غار *maghára*, or *ghár*, cavern.

مغازن - خزن *magháza* (Turkish for *makhzan*), magazine.

مغاير - غيار *mogháyir*, contrary (see *ghiyár*).

مغرب - غرب *maghrib*, west, sunset (see *gharaba*).

مغرفة - غرف *mighrafa*, ladle (see *gharafa*).

مغشوش - غش *maghshoosh*, adulterated (see *ghushsha*).

مغص *maghas*, colic, gripes.

مغطس - غطس *mightas*, tank (see *ghatasa*).

مغطّى - غطا *moghatta*, covered (see *ghatá*).

مغلق - غلق *maghlaq*, timber-yard, enclosure (see *ghalaqa*).

مغنطيس *maghnátees* (Greek), magnet.

مغنّي - غذا *moghanni*, singer (see *ghiná*).

مغونة *maghōna*, lighter, barge.

مفاوضة - فوضى *mofáwada*, community of interests (see *fóda*).

مفتاح - فتح *miftáh*, key (see *fataha*).

مفترى - فرية *moftari*, slanderer (see *firiya*).

مفترس - فرس *moftaris*, fierce (animal) (see *farasa*).

مفتن - فتن *moftin*, plotter (see *fatana*).

مفتي - فتوى *mufti*, Moslem judge (see *fatwa*).

مفرد - فرد *mofrad*, alone, solitary (see *fard*).

مفرط - فرط *mofrit*, excessive (see *farata*).

مفرهد - فرهد *mofarhad*, confounded (see *farhada*).

مفسد - فساد *mofsid*, corrupter (see *fasád*).

مفصد - فصد *mifsad*, lancet (see *fasada*).

مفصل - فصل *mafsil*, joint (see *fasl*).

مفلس - فلس *muflis*, bankrupt (see *fals*).

مفلوج - فلج *maflooj*, paralytic, split (see *falaja*).

مفيد - فيد *mofeed*, informer, useful (see *faid*).

مقاتّ - قثّا *maqátt*, cucumber garden (see *quttá*).

مقاسات - قياس *maqását*, dimensions (see *qiyás*).

مقاصّة - قصّ *maqássa*, compensation (see *qassa*).

مقال - مقاولة - قول *maqál*, speech; *moqáwala*, bargain (see *qōl*).

مقام - مقاومة - قوم *maqám*, place; *moqáwama*, resistance (see *qōm*).

مقبرة ـ قبر *maqbara*, cemetery (see *qabara*).

مقبول ـ مقبل ـ قبل *moqbil*, coming; *maqbool*, accepted (see *qabala*).

مقيت ـ مقت *maqt*, hatred; *maqeet*, detestable.

مقتضى ـ قضى *moqtada*, necessary (see *qada*).

مقتدر ـ مقدار ـ قدر *miqdár*, quantity; *muqtadir*, able (see *qadara*).

مقدم ـ قدم *muqdim*, forepart (see *qadam*).

مقذاف ـ قذف *miqdáf*, oar (see *qazafa*).

مقرّر ـ مقرّ ـ قرّ *moqirr*, confessing; *maqarr*, fixed place; *moqarrar*, certain, direct (see *qarra*).

مقربة ـ قرب *maqriba*, vicinity (see *qariba*).

مقرف ـ قرفة *moqrif*, cross, bad tempered (see *qarafa*).

مقشة ـ قش *miqashsha*, broom (see *qashsh*).

مقص ـ قص *maqass*, scissors (see *qassa*).

مقصد ـ قصد *maqsad*, aim, object (see *qasada*).

مقصورة ـ قصر *maqsoora*, chamber (see *qasara*).

مقطف ـ قطف *maqtaf*, basket (see *qatafa*).

مقطم ـ قطم *moqattam*, cliffs near Cairo (see *qatama*).

مقطور ـ قطر *maqtoor*, towed (see *qatara*).

مقعد ـ قعد *maqa'd*, seat; *maqa'id*, cripple (see *qu'da*).

مقفى ـ قفا *moqaffa*, rhymed (see *qafá*).

مقل *moql*, fruit of dom. palm, *hyphaëne thebaica*.

مقلى ـ قلا *maqli*, fried; *miqla*, frying-pan (see *qalá*).

مقمر ـ قمر *moqmir*, moon-lit (see *qamar*).

مقنع ـ قنع *moqnia'*, convincing (see *qania'a*).

مقود ـ قود *miqwad*, halter (see *qöd*).

مقولة ـ قول *maqoola*, category (see *qöl*).

مقوّى ـ قوّة *moqawwa*, cardboard (see *qowwa*).

مقياس ـ قياس *miqyás*, instrument for measuring (see *qiyás*).

مقيّد ـ قيد *moqayyad*, registered, bound (see *qaid*).

مقيم ـ قوم *moqeem*, resident (see *qöm*).

مقىء ـ قاء *moqayya*, or *moqeey*, emetic (see *qá*).

مكة *Makka*, Mecca in Arabia.

مكي or مكاوي *Makkáwiy*, or *Makkiy*, Meccan.

مكوك *makkook*, weaver's beam.

مكابدة ـ كبد *mokábada*, perseverance, endurance (see *kibd*).

مكاراة ـ كرا *mokárát*, hire (see *kirá*).

مكافاة ـ كفاء *mokáfát*, reward (see *kafá*).

مكان ـ كون *makán*, place (see *kön*).

مكتب ـ كتب *maktab*, school, office (see *kataba*).

مكث *makasa*, he remained, passed time; *muks*, duration, stay.

محكلة ـ كحل *mik-hala*, kohl bottle (see *kohl*).

مكد ـ ماكد *makada*, he remained; *mákid*, firm, constant.

مكر *makara*, he deceived; *makr*, trickery, deceit.

مكار *makkár*, trickster, deceiver.

مكرر ـ كرّ *mokarrar*, repeated (see *karra*).

مكروه ـ كره *makrooh*, hated (see *karaha*).

مكس *maks*, octroi; Mex. [دخوانيّة]

مكّس *makkasa*, he levied octroi.

مكّاس *makkás*, octroi official.

مكسب ـ كسب *maksab*, gain (see *kasaba*).

مكسوف ـ كسف *maksoof*, sorry (see *kasafa*).

مكعّب ـ كعب *moka'a'b*, cubic (see *ka'b*).

مكلوب ـ كلب *makloob*, rabid (see *kelb*).

مكلّف ـ كلف *mokallaf*, responsible (see *kalifa*).

مكنة *mukna*, or *mikna*, power.

ماكن or مكين *mákin*, or *makeen*, strong.

مكان ـ اماكن *makán*, pl. *amákin*, place, spot. [كون]

امكن ـ يمكن *amkana*, it was possible; *yomkin*, it is possible.

يمكنني or يمكن لي ان *yomkin-ni*, or *yomkin li an*, I can, it is possible for me to ――. [قدر]

يمكنه or يمكن له ان *yomkin-oh*, or *yomkin laho an*, he can.

ممكن *momkin*, possible.

امكان *imkán*, possibility.

على قدر الامكان *'ala qadr el-imkán*, as much as possible.

مكّن *makkana*, he made possible, permitted.

تمكين ـ تماكين *tamkeen*, pl. *tamákeen*, licence, permit.

تمكّن من *tamakkana min*, he could, succeeded in.

مكنسة ـ كنس *miknasa*, broom (see *kanasa*).

مكوة ـ كيّ *mikwa*, flat-iron (see *kaiy*).

مكيدة or كيد *makeeda*, or *kaid*, intrigue.

مكيال ـ كيل *mikyál*, grain-measure (see *kiyála*).

ملل *malal*, weariness.

ملّ ـ مال *malla*, it wearied, annoyed; *máll*, wearisome.

ملّة ـ ملل *milla*, pl. *milal*, sect, nation, religion.

ملا ـ ملئ *malá*, he filled; *mulia*, it became full.

ملّا ـ تملئة *mallá*, he filled; *tamliya*, a making full.

امتلا *imtalá*, it became full.

ملا or ملأة *malá*, fullness.

ملوة *malwa*, measure of 3¾ quarts; nearly a gallon.

ملاية *miláya*, woman's plaid or check shawl.

ملايات الفرش *miláyát el-farsh*, bed-clothes.

ملآن ـ مملو *malán*, full; *mamloo*, filled.

ملابس ـ لبس *malábis*, clothes (see *labisa*).

ملازم ـ ملتزم ـ لزم *mulázim*, lieutenant; *multazim*, contractor (see *lazima*).

ملاقاة ـ لقاء *muláyát*, interview (see *liqá*).

ملام ـ لوم *malám*, blame (see *lom*).

ملبس ـ ملبوس ـ لبس *mulabbas*, sweetmeats; *malboos*, clothed (see *labisa*).

ملتبس ـ لبس *multabis*, ambiguous (see *labisa*).

ملتفت ـ لفت *multafit*, attentive (see *lafata*).

ملجأ ـ لجاء *maljá*, place of refuge (see *lajá*).

ملح *milh*, salt.

ملّاح *malláh*, sailor, mariner.

مالح *málih*, saline, sea-fish, &c.

ملاحة or ممـلحة *malláha*, or *mamlaha*, a saline, lagoon, salt-pan; *mimlaha*, salt-cellar.

ملاحة *maláha*, beauty, excellence.

مليح ـ ملاح *maleeh*, pl. *miláh*, good, excellent; salted.

املح *amlah*, better.

ملحق ـ لحق *mulhaq*, annexe (see *lahiqa*).

ملحوظ ـ لحظ *malhooz*, observed (see *lahaza*).

ملخ *malakha*, he plucked, spoilt.

ماوخية *malookhiya*, mallow, a favourite dish of vegetables in Egypt, *corchorus olitorius*.

ملزوم ـ لزم *malzoom*, responsible (see *lazima*).

ملس *malas*, chemise, thin blue smock, or veil.

ملاسة ـ املس *malása*, smoothness; *imlis*, smooth.

ملّس *mallasa*, he smoothed, stroked.

ملط *malt*, sheer, quite.

مالطة *Málta*, Malta.

ملعقة ـ لعق *mila'qa*, spoon (see *la'iqa*).

ملعون ـ لعن *mala'oon*, accursed (see *l'ana*).

ملغي ـ لغو *malghi*, annulled (see *laghw*).

ملف ـ ملفوف ـ لفّ *milaff*, envelope; *malfoof*, cabbage (see *laffa*).

ملفق ـ لفق *mulaffaq*, trumped up (see *laffaqa*).

ملق or تملق *maliqa*, or *tamallaqa*, he fawned upon.

ملق ـ ملقة *malaq*, open country; in Upper Egypt, undulating surface of lands covered by high Nile, called in Lower Egypt, *rátib* (راتب); *malqa*, or *malaqa*, distance, league.

ملقف ـ لقف *mulyaf*, air-shaft (see *laqifa*).

لقاء ‍ ـ ماقى‍ *mulyi*, thrown down (see *liqá*).

املاك ‍ ـ ملك‍ *mulk*, or *milk*, pl. *amlák*, right, property; real property, freehold; royalty.

املاك و اموال‍ *amlák wa amwál*, real and personal property.

املاك ميرية‍ *amlák meeriya*, government lands, "domaine public."

ملكية‍ *mulkiya (malakiya)*, right, property.

ملكي‍ *mulkiy*, belonging to government; civilian employé, civil, not military.

ملك ـ امتلك‍ *malaka*, or *imtalaka*, he possessed.

ملك‍ *mallaka*, he transferred property, gave a right.

تمليك‍ *tamleek*, transfer of property or right.

تملك‍ or امتلك‍ *imtalaka*, or *tamallaka*, he appropriated to himself, took possession.

استملك‍ *istamlaka*, he wished to possess, founded a colony.

ملاك ـ مالك‍ *málik*, pl. *mollák*, owner; king.

ملك ـ ملوك‍ *malik*, pl. *molook*, king.

ملكة‍ *malika*, queen; *malaka*, royalty.

جلالة الملكة‍ *jalálat el-malika*, H.M. The Queen.

ملاك ـ لاك‍ *malák*, angel (see *láka*).

مالك ـ مالكي‍ *Málik*, Abdullah Malik ibn Anas, founder of the *Málikiy*, one of the four great Sunni schools of orthodox Islam. Medina 715—795 A.D. (see شانعي ـ حنيفة ـ حنبل‍).

مملك‍ *momallik*, transferor of property.

مملكة ـ ممالك‍ *mamlaka*, pl. *mamálik*, kingdom.

مملوك ـ مماليك‍ *mamlook*, pl. *mamáleek*, thing or slave possessed; Mameluke.

مملوكات‍ *mamlookát*, possessions, property.

مستملك‍ *mustamlak*, colony.

ملوث ـ لوّث‍ *molawwas*, soiled, stained (see *lawwasa*).

ملوى ـ لوى‍ *malwi*, folded (see *lawa*).

ملى‍ or ملا‍ *mala*, he walked.

املى‍ *amla*, he made proceed, dictated writing.

املاء‍ *imlá*, dictation for writing.

ملي‍ *milli* (French), millimètre.

مليّن ـ لين‍ *molayyin*, softener, purge (see *leen*).

مليون‍ *milyon* (European), million.

ممات ـ موت‍ *mamát*, death (see *mōt*).

من‍ *man* (usually pronounced *meen*), who? he, she, or they who.

من‍ *min*, from, out of, than, since. [ن‍

من العال‍ *min el-a'ál*, of the best, first-rate.

من حيث‍ *min hais*, whereas.

اكثر من دلك *aktar min zalik*, more than that.

مِمَّا - من ما *mim-má*, for *min-má*, from that which.

مناورة *manáwara* (French), manœuvre, trick.

من *mann*, manna, gift, favour.

منَّة - منن *minna*, pl. *minan*, gift; reproach for ingratitude.

منّان *mannán*, benefactor, God.

ممنون *mamnoon*, favoured; glad, willing.

ممنونيّة *mamnooniya*, delight, willingness.

مناخ *manákh*, a place where a camel kneels. [نخ and نوخ]

منادي - ندا *monádi*, public crier (see *nadá*).

منارة - نور *manára*, minaret (see *noor*).

مناسب - نسب *monásib*, fit, suitable (see *nasab*).

مناقشة - نقش *monáqasha*, quarrel, débats (see *naqasha*).

منام - نوم *manám*, dream (see *nōm*).

مناوبة - نوبة *monáwaba*, alternation (see *nōba*).

مناوشة - نوش *monáwasha*, battle, quarrel (see *nōsh*).

منبت - نبات *monbit*, fertile (see *nabát*).

منبر - نبر *minbar*, pulpit (see *nabara*).

منبع - نبع *manba'*, source (see *naba'a*).

منتبه - نبه *montabih*, attentive (see *nubh*).

منتصف - نصف *muntasif*, about half (see *nusf*).

منتن - نتن *muntin*, stinking (see *natana*).

منثور - نثر *manthoor*, scattered, prose (see *nathara*).

منجل - نجل *minjal*, scythe (see *najala*).

منح *manaha*, he favoured, granted.

منحة - منح *minha*, pl. *minah*, favour.

منخار - نخير *minkhár*, nostril (see *nakheer*).

منخل - نخل *monkhol*, sieve (see *nakhala*).

مندوب - ندب *mandoob*, nominee, delegate (see *nadaba*).

مندرة - منادر *mandara*, pl. *manádir*, saloon, outer hall, rooms on the ground floor.

ضرب المندل *darb el-mandal*, practice of false magic; magic circle, square, mirror, &c. [سيمياء]

منديل - مناديل *mandeel*, pl. *manádeel*, handkerchief, bundle.

منذ or مذ *munz*, since (of time past).

منزل - نزل *manzil*, house (see *nizila*).

منزوي - زاوية *munzawi*, hermit (see *záwiya*).

منسك - نسك *mansak*, rite (see *nusk*).

منسيّ - نسي *mansiy*, forgotten (see *nasia*).

منشّة - نشّ *minashsha*, fly-flip (see *nashsha*).

منشور - منشار - نشر *manshoor*, ministerial order; *minshár*, saw (see *nashara*).

منشي - نشو *munshi*, tutor (see *nasho*).

منشية or منشأة *menshiya*, or *minshát* (Coptic), place, village, public square.

منصب ـ مَنْصِب *mansib*, office, post (see *nasb*).

منصر ـ مَنْصَر *mansar*, gang, clique (see *nasr*).

المنصورة ـ نصر *el-Mansoora*, the victorious (city) (see *nasr*).

منصف ـ نصف *munsif*, just (see *nusf*).

منطق ـ نطق *mintaq*, zone; *mantiq*, logic, speech (see *nataqa*).

منظر ـ نظر *manzar*, point of view (see *nazar*).

منظوم ـ نظم *manzoom*, arranged, verse (see *nazm*).

منع *mana'a*, he prevented, forbad.

منع *mana'*, prevention, prohibition.

مانع ـ موانع *mánia'*, pl. *mawánia'*, preventing, obstacle, objection.

ممنوع *mamnooa'*, forbidden.

امتنع عن *imtana'a a'n*, he abstained from, declined, refused.

منغال or منقال *manghál*, or *manqál*, brazier, pan for charcoal.

منف *Manf* (Coptic), Memphis.

منوفية *Manoofiya*, a province of the Delta near Cairo.

منفاخ ـ نفخ *minfákh*, bellows (see *nafakha*).

منفذ ـ نفذ *manfaz*, passage (see *nafaza*).

منفس ـ نفس *minfas*, air-hole (see *nafas*).

منفضة ـ نفض *manfada*, ash-tray (see *nafada*).

منفعة ـ نفع *manfa'a*, advantage (see *nafa'a*).

منفى ـ نفى *manfa*, place of exile; *manfi*, exiled (see *nafa*).

منقاد ـ نقد *minqád*, beak (see *naqada*).

منقاد . قود *monqád*, docile (see *qód*).

منقار ـ نقر *minqár*, chisel, pickaxe (see *naqara*).

منقول ـ نقل *manqool*, moveable, moved (see *naqala*).

منكب ـ نكبة *mankib*, shoulder (see *nakba*).

منور ـ نور *minwár*, skylight (see *noor*).

منوط ـ نوط *manoot*, dependent (see *nót*).

منوال ـ نول *minwál*, manner (see *nól*).

منهج ـ نهج *manhaj*, road, track (see *nahj*).

منى *Mina*, or *Moona*, a valley near Mecca, scene of the Korban sacrifice.

منية *munia*, wish; *mani*, semen.

امنية ـ امانى *umniya*, pl. *amáni*, wish. [cf. *amniya*, security, امن p. 10.]

تمنى *tamanna*, he wished, begged, saluted a superior.

منيا *Miniá* (Coptic), place, town; a town and province in Upper Egypt.

منيل *Minyal* (Coptic), a part of Old Cairo, the island of Roda.

مهابة ـ هيبة *mahába*, majesty (see *haiba*).

مهاجر ـ هجر *mohájir*, emigrant (see *hajara*).

مهاودة ـ هوادة *moháwida*, moderate (prices) (see *hawáda*).

مهبل *mahbil*, vagina. [هبل]

محجّ *mihajj*, socket of bolt of a door.

مهد *mahd*, cradle.

مهّد *mahhada*, he spread out, made smooth, facilitated, prepared the way.

تمهيديّ *tamheediy*, in *hokm tamheediy*, "jugement interlocutoire."

مهدي - هدى *Mahdi*, led (by God); "Mahdi" (see *hada*).

مهر - مهور *mahr*, pl. *mohoor*, dower settled on the wife by the husband at marriage; bride's wealth at time of marriage.

مهر معجّل - مؤجّل *mahr mo-a'jjal*, dower paid down *quickly* at marriage; *mahr mo-ajjal*, dower *deferred*, and payable at his death or on divorce. [عجل - اجل]

مهر - امهار *mohr*, pl. *amhár*, colt, foal.

مهر *muhr* (Persian), seal, signet.

مهارة *mahára*, skill. [شطارة]

ماهر - مهرة *máhir*, pl. *mahara*, expert.

مهرجان *mahrján* (Persian), fête, autumnal equinox.

مهران *mahrán* (Persian), military review.

مهل *mahala*, he went slow, was deliberate.

امهل *amhala*, he deferred, granted a delay.

مهل *mahl*, gentleness, slowness.

على مهلك *'ala mahlak*, slowly! Go slow!

مهلة *mohla*, delay, interval, respite.

مهمّ - همّ *mohimm*, important (see *hamm*).

مهما *mahmá*, whatever, whenever.

مهنة *mihna*, service, skill, profession.

مهندس - هندسة *mohandis*, engineer (see *handasa*).

مهول - هول *mahool*, terror (see *hōl*).

مهيّأ - هيّأ *mohayyá*, prepared (see *hayyá*).

مواّد - مدّ *mawádd*, matters (see *madda*).

مؤاخذة - اخذ *mo-ákhaza*, blame (see *akhaza*).

مؤبّدا - ابد *mo-abbadán*, for life (see *abad*).

موازاة - وازى *mowázát*, equality (see *wáza*).

موازنة - وزن *mowázana*, equilibrium (see *wazana*).

مواشي - مشى *mawáshi*, cattle (see *masha*).

موافق - وفق *mowáfiq*, ally, consenting (see *wafy*).

موت *mōt*, death.

مات - يموت *máta*, he died; *ya-moot*, he is dying.

موّت *muwwata*, he killed.

تماوت *tamáwata*, he shammed dead.

مائت *máyit*, dying.

ميّت - اموات or موتى *mayyit*, pl. *amwát*, or *mota*, dead.

موات *mawát*, dead, uncultivated lands without an owner.

ممات or ميتوتة *mamát*, or *maitoota*, death.

مؤتمر - امر *mo-atamar*, congress (see *amara*).

مؤتمن - امن *mo-ataman*, trustworthy (see *amn*).

موج - امواج *mōj*, pl. *amwáj*, wave, billow.

موجب - وجب *moojib*, causing (see *wajaba*).

موجز *moojiz*, brief, concise (see *wajaza*).

موجود - وجد *mowjood*, found, present (see *wajada*).

مودَّب - ودَّب *mowaddab*, fitted up (see *waddaba*).

مودع - ودع *moodia'*, depositor (see *wada'a*).

مودَّة - ودَّ *mawadda*, love (see *wadda*).

مؤذِّن - اذان *mo-addin*, crier to prayer (see *edán*).

مؤرِّخ - ارَّخ *mowarrakh*, dated (see *arrakha*).

مورِدة - ورد *mawrada*, landing-place (see *warada*).

مورة *Mora*, Morea, Peloponnesus.

موز - موزة *mōza*, pl. *mōz*, banana.

مؤسَّس - اسّ *mo-assas*, founded (see *uss*).

موسر - يسر *moosir*, solvent, rich (see *yasara*).

موسم - وسم *mōsim*, season, monsoon, fête (see *wasama*).

موسى or موس *moosa* (vulgarly, *moos*), razor; *Moosa*, Moses.

موسيقة *mooseeqa* (European), music.

موشَّحة - وشاح *mowashshaha*, lyric, ode, hymn (see *wisháh*).

موصل *Mosul*, a village near ancient Nineveh.

موصى - وصَّى *moosi*, testator (see *wassa*).

موضع - موضوع - وضع *mawda'*, place; *mawdooa'*, placed (see *wada'a*).

موظَّف - وظيفة *mowazzaf*, employé (see *wazeefa*).

موقَّت - موقت - وقت *mowaqqat*, temporary; *mōqit*, fixed time (see *waqt*).

موقع - وقع *mawqia'*, place (see *waqa'a*).

موقف - وقف *mōqif*, place; *mawqoof*, arrested (see *waqafa*).

موكب *mawkib*, procession. [وكب]

مؤكَّد - وكَّد *mo-akkad*, confirmed (see *wakkada*).

موكَّل - وكيل *mowakkil*, principal (see *wakeel*, agent).

مول *mōl*, a being rich.

مال - اموال *mál*, pl. *amwál*, wealth, riches; personal property, goods.

اموال الميري *amwál el-meeriy*, taxes, wealth of the state.

رأس المال *rás el-mál*, capital (in money).

بيت المال *bait el-mál*, Sacred Moslem treasury, under the Sheria't law. [see بيت]

مالية *máliya*, financial, finances.

نظارة المالية *nazáret el-máliya*, Ministry of Finance.

اموال منقولة و ثابتة *amwál manqoola*, moveables ; *amwál sábita*, real property, immoveables.

اموال مقررة *amwál moqarrara*, direct taxes.

اموال - املاك *amwál*, goods, personal property ; *amlák*, lands, houses, real property.

موّل - تمويل *mawwala*, he imposed a tax ; *tamweel*, taxation.

موّل *momawwil*, creditor, the State as the possessor of *amwál*, or imposer of taxes.

موّل *momawwal*, debtor, taxpayer.

مولد - مولود - ولد *mawlid*, birth ; *mowlood*, born (see *walada*).

مؤلف - الّف *mo-allif*, author (see *allafa*).

مؤلم - الم *moolim*, causing pain (see *alam*).

مولى - ولي *móla*, master (see *walia*).

موم *moom* (Persian), wax.

مؤمن - امن *moomin*, believer, Moslem ; insurer of property ; *mooman*, trusted in ; property assured (see *amn*).

مومیا *moomiyá*, mummy.

مؤنث - انثى *mo-annas*, feminine gender (see *unsa*).

مونة *moona*, provisions, rations ; cement made of lime, sand and powdered red stone.

موهوب - وهب *mawhoob*, given (see *wahaba*).

مؤيّد - ايد *mo-ayyad*, confirmed (see *aid*).

موية - ما *mwaya*, water (colloquial for *má*).

میت *meet* (Coptic), place, village.

میت - مائة *meet* (vulgarism for *maya*), hundred.

میدان - میادین *maidán*, pl. *mayádeen*, open space, a common ; public square.

میدان الای *maidán alái* (Turkish), review, march past.

مئذنة - اذان *maidna*, minaret (see *edán*).

میر - امیر *meer* (Persian for Arabic *ameer*), lord.

میر اخور *meer-i-akhor*, Master of the Horse.

میر الای *meer-i-alái*, colonel.

میر لواء *meer-i-liwá*, general of brigade.

میر میران *meer-i-meerán*, civilian Pasha of the third or lowest rank, equal to a *liwa*.

میری *meeriy* princely, relating to the government.

املاك المیری *amlák el-meeriy*, government lands, domains of the State.

خدمة میریة *khidma meeriya*, government service.

میراث - ورث *meerás*, inheritance (see *warasa*).

میّز *mayyaza*, he separated, distinguished ; was of years of discretion.

تمیّز *tamayyaza*, it became distinguished, selected.

امْتَاز *imtáza*, he was selected, privileged.

امْتِياز *imtiyáz*, selection, privilege, concession or grant for public works, &c.

مُمْتَاز *mumtáz*, select; *élite*, privileged.

تَمْييز *tamyeez*, selection; discretion, age of discretion; (in Turkey) Court of Cassation.

مُمَيِّز *mumayyiz*, arrived at years of discretion; he who separates, discerns.

مُتَمَيِّز *mutamayyiz*, selected, of select rank, senior rank of Bey.

مِيزَاب - مَاذَاب or ازب or وزب *meezáb*, gutter (see *azaba*, *wazaba*).

مِيزَان - وزن *meezán*, scales, Libra in Zodiac (see *wazana*).

مَيْسَرَة - يسر *maisara*, solvency wealth (see *yasara*).

مِيضَأَة - وضؤ *meedát*, mosque-tank for ablutions (see *wodoo*).

مَيْعَة *maya'a*, balm, perfume.

مِيعَاد - وعد *mee'yád*, fixed time (see *wa'da*).

مِيقَات - وقت *meeqát*, fixed time (see *waqt*).

مَيْل - اميال *mail*, pl. *amiál*, inclination, leaning, liking, partiality.

مَيَلَان *mayalán*, inclination, obliquity.

مَال - يَمِيل *mála*, he leaned; *yameel*, he leans.

مَائِل *máyil*, who leans, stoops; oblique; sympathetic, inclined to.

اَمْيَل *amial*, more leaning or oblique.

تَمَايَل *tamáyala*, he leaned towards, trembled.

مِيل - اَمْيَال *meel*, pl. *amyál* (European), mile.

مِيلَاد - ولد *meelád*, birth (see *walada*).

مِينَا - مِين or مَوَانِي - وني *meená*, pl. *miyán*, or *mawáni*, harbour, port (see *wana*).

مِينَا *meená* (Persian), enamel. [صدف

مِيَّة - مِئَة *meea*, or *meet* (for *máya*), hundred.

مَيْتَمَة - يتيم *maitama*, orphans (pl. of *yateem*).

مَيْمَنَة - يمن *maimana*, felicity (see *yamana*).

مَيْؤُوس or مَيُوس *mayoos*, despaired of. [يئس - ايس]

N.

ن *Noon*. Value = 50.

نَاب - نَوْبَة *nába*, it was instead of (see *nóba*).

نَاب - نِيب *náb*, canine tooth (see *neeb*).

نَاحِيَة - نحو *náhiya*, side, place, village (see *nahw*).

نَار - نور *nár*, fire (see *noor*).

نَاقَة - نَاقَات or نوق *náqa*, pl. *náqát*, or *nooq*, she-camel; star of Cassiopeia.

نَاقُوس *náqoos*, clapper, gong.

نَام - نوم *náma*, he slept (see *nóm*).

ناموس námoos (Greek *nomos*, used in Turkish), honour, reputation.

ناموس námoos, mosquitoes.

ناموسيّة námoosiya, mosquito-net.

ناي náy (Persian), flute, reed. [ارغول]

ناي or ني nai, or nee, raw (meat); unbaked (brick).

نبيّ ـ انبيا nabiy, pl. anbiyá, prophet, warner.

نبويّ nabawiy, prophetic, of the prophet Mahomet.

ست فاطمة نبويّة sitt Fátma nabawiya, the lady Fatima, daughter of the prophet.

نبوّة nubowa, status of prophet, prophecy.

انباء anba, he warned, pointed out.

انباء inbá, a warning, hint.

منبي munbi, pointing out, warning.

نبات ـ نباتات nabát, pl. nabátát, plant, vegetation.

انبت anbata, it sprouted, grew; the land was fertile.

منبت munbit, fertile.

نابت nábit, sprouting, growing.

نبوت ـ نبابيت naboot, pl. nabábeet, pole, long staff.

نبح nabaha, (the dog) barked; (the wound) throbbed. [عوى]

نباح nibáh, a dog's bark; throbbing pain.

نبيذ ـ انبذة nabeet, pl. anbida, wine; date-wine.

نبر nabara, he rose up, it grew.

نباري nabári, crops of grain (not cotton or sugar), a word in use in Upper Egypt.

انبار anbár (Persian), barn, pantry. [عنبر]

منبر minbar, pulpit.

نبش nabasha, he dug, scratched the ground.

نبضة nabda, pulse, pulsation.

نبط nabata, it resulted. [نتج]

استنبط istanbata, he deduced, inferred.

نبّط nabbata, he scoffed at, criticised.

نبع naba'a, it took its source.

منبع manba', source, fountain.

ينبوع Yanboa', Yembo, an Arabian port on the Red Sea.

نبق nabq, wild apple; *zizyphus spina Christi*, lotus. [سدر]

نبل nabl, arrow.

نبايل nabáyil, bracelets (of silver).

نبالة nabála, ability, capacity.

نبه nubh, sagacity, alertness.

نبّه nabbaha, he warned, ordered, aroused.

نبيه nabeeh, intelligent, alert, cautious.

تنبّه tanabbaha, he took care, was on his guard.

انتبه intabaha, he took care, was attentive.

انتباه intibáh, care, attention.

منتبه muntabih, careful, attentive.

تنبيه ـ تنبيهات tanbeeh, pl. tanbeehat, instructions, summons.

نتو notoo, swelling, tumour.

ذاتِي (280) نَجس

ذاتِي *náti*, protruding, swelling out.

نتج *nataja*, it resulted, was the result.

ينتج من ذلك *yantoj min zalik*, it results from that.

نَتَجَت *natajat*, (the animal) brought forth, foaled, calved, &c.

أنتج *antaja*, it produced, gave as result.

استنتج *istantaja*, he deduced, inferred.

نِتاج *nitáj*, parturition of animals; issue, calf, foal, whelp, young; increase of flocks and herds.

جاموسة ونتاجها *jámoosa wa nitáj-ha*, a she-buffalo and her calf.

ناتج *nátij*, resulting.

نَتيجة ‒ نَتائج *nateeja*, pl. *natáyij*, result, summary, précis; pocket almanac.

نتش *natasha*, he snatched. [هبر

نتف *natafa*, he plucked out hairs, depilated.

نَتف *natf*, depilation.

ناتِي *nátiy*, a fertile dam, she-animal.

استنتق *istantaqa*, he vomited.
[see also استنطق

نتن or أنتن *natana*, or *antana*, it stank. [عفن

نَتنة *natána*, stench.

مُنتِن *muntin*, stinking.

نثر *nathara*, he scattered, dispersed.

نثرِي *nathariy*, diverse, sundry, petty (expenses).

منثور *manthoor*, scattered; prose; gilly-flower.

نَجيب *najeeb*, noble, aristocrat, of good lineage.

نَجابة *najába*, nobility, purity of race.

نَجابتلو *najábetlu* (Turkish title for the Sultan's family), noble, of pure race.

نجح *najaha*, he prospered, succeeded in. [فلح

نَجاح *najáh*, success, prosperity.

ناجح *nájih*, successful, beneficial, useful.

نَجد ‒ نُجود *najd*, pl. *nojood*, bulwark, buttress; firm cushion or mattrass.

النَجد *El-Najd*, the high inner plateau of Arabia.

مُنَجِّد *monajjid*, maker or stuffer of cushions. [حلّج

أنجد *anjada*, he helped, rescued.
[أغاث

أنجِدني *injid-ni* (Imperative), help me! help!

استنجد به *istanjada boh*, he asked for help.

نجر *najara*, he planed wood, carpentered.

نَجّار *najjár*, carpenter, joiner.

أنجز or نجز *najaza*, or *anjaza*, he fulfilled, carried out.

نَجاز or إنجاز *najáz*, or *injáz*, completion, fulfilment, execution of duty.

نَجِس *nijisa*, it was impure, unclean.
[رجس

نَجاسة *najása*, impurity, defilement.

نَجِس *najis*, impure, defiled.

نجاشي *Najáshi*, Negus, Negoosa-Nagast, the title of the King of Abyssinia.

نجعة ـ نجع *naja'a*, pl. *nojoa'*, village or pasturage; a word in common use for Bedouin hamlets in Upper Egypt.

نجفة *najafa*, heap, cluster, group.

نجل *najala*, he begot, produced; cut open.

نجل ـ أنجال *najl*, pl. *anjál*, son, posterity. [نسل]

منجل *minjal*, scythe, sickle.

نجم ـ نجوم *najm*, pl. *nojoom*, star.

نجوم سيّارة *nojoom sayyára*, planets.

علم النجوم *'ilm en-nojoom*, astrology.

علم الفلك *'ilm el-falak*, astronomy.

منجّم *monajjim*, astrologer.

نجا *najá*, he escaped into safety.

أنجى *anja*, he saved, rescued.

نجاة *naját*, safety, salvation, deliverance.

ناجي *náji*, safe, saved (by God).

نحب *nahb*, time, lifetime; sob.

انقضى نحبه or قضى *qada*, or *inqada nahboh*, he died, his lifetime was over.

نحب *nahaba*, he sobbed.

نحت ـ دبش *naht*, hewn or dressed stone; *dabsh*, rough unhewn stone.

نحر ـ نحرير *nahr*, thorax; *nihreer*, skilful.

انتحر *intahara*, he committed suicide.

نحس *nahis*, of evil omen, unlucky, unwelcome.

نحاس *nuhás*, copper, a copper vessel, brass.

نحّاس *nahhás*, coppersmith.

نحيف *naheef*, thin, slender.

نحلة ـ نحل *nahla*, pl. *nahl*, bee.

خلاية النحل *khaláyat en-nahl*, beehive.

نحو *nahw*, syntax.

نحو ـ أنحاء *nahw*, pl. *anhá*, side; intention; place, vicinity, tendency.

نحو *nahw*, about, nearly, towards; like, as it were.

نحوه *nahwoh*, like it, near it, such like.

نحوي *nahwiy*, grammatical, syntactical; high-flown, too pedantic.

تنحّى *tanahha*, he withdrew himself to one side.

ناحية ـ نواحي *náhiya*, pl. *nawáhi*, district, village, place, direction, side.

الناحية دي *en-náhiyá dee* (colloquial), hither, to this side.

نخّ *nakhkha*, he grunted "*nakhkh*," as a sign to the camel to kneel; he crouched, knelt like a camel.

مناخ *manákhkh*, place of kneeling or halting of camels. [نوخ]

نخبة *nokhba*, the choice part, *élite*, pick.

انتخب *intakhaba*, he elected, chose.

انتخاب *intikháb*, choice, selection.

منتخب *muntakhab*, elected, chosen.

ناخوذة or ناخوذا *nákhoda* (Persian), captain of a sailing ship or dhow in the Eastern seas.

نخير *nakheer*, snore.

منخار *minkhár*, nostril.

مناخير *manákheer*, nostrils, the nose. [انف]

نخاع *nakháa'*, marrow, spinal marrow.

نخلة ـ نخيل *nakhla*, pl. *nakheel*, date-palm tree.

نخل *nakhala*, he sifted, winnowed.

نخالة *nokhála*, bran.

منخل or منخول *monkhool*, sieve, hair sieve.

ندّ (ندّد) *nadda*) *naddada*, he criticised, made remarks, pointed out.

تنديد *tandeed*, remark, criticism.

ندب *nadaba*, he lamented the dead, wept; *nabd*, alert.

ندّابة *naddába*, professional female mourner.

مندب *mandab*, tears, lamentation.

ندب *nadaba*, he invited, appointed an agent.

مندوب *mandoob*, nominee, agent, delegate.

انتدب *intadaba*, he deputed another.

انتدب *ontodiba* (passive voice), he was deputed to act for another.

نادر *nádir*, rare, seldom.

نوادر *nawádir*, pl., rare things, curiosities, witticisms.

ندل *nadala*, he handled, seized.

منديل ـ مناديل *mandeel*, pl. *manádeel*, handkerchief, napkin; bundle tied up in a cloth.

ندم *nadima*, he regretted, repented.

ندامة *nadáma*, regret, repentance.

نديم *nadeem*, boon-companion.

نداه *nadaha*, he called out to, cried out.

ندا *nadá*, he called out, cried out.

نادى *nádá*, he proclaimed.

نودي *noodia* (passive voice), it was cried out, or proclaimed.

ندو or نداء or مناداة *nado*, or *nidá*, or *munádát*, a calling to, invoking.

منادي *monádi*, public crier.

ندوة *nadwa*, club, place of meeting.

ندى *nadia*, it was damp. [رطب]

ندى *nada*, dampness, dew, mist.

نذر ـ نذور *nazr*, pl. *nozoor*, vow.

نذر or انتذر *nazara*, or *intazara*, he vowed.

نذير *nazeer*, vowed or devoted to; Nazarene.

انذر *anzara*, he warned, reprimanded.

انذار *inzár*, a warning, reprimand; a notice (to quit, &c.).

نرنج *narinj*, acid orange. [برتقان]

نزّ *názza*, it oozed.

نزح *nazaha*, he cleaned out (a well or cesspool); dredged; he lavished, wasted.

نزع *naza'a*, he pulled, plucked away, removed.

نزع (283) انتساب

نزع *naza'*, a pull, deprivation; *niza'a*, purely, entirely.

نزع الملكية *naza' el-malakiya*, deprivation of right, expropriation.

نازع *náza'a*, he quarrelled; went to law.

نزاع or منازعة *nizáa'*, or *munáza'a*, quarrel, litigation.

انزع *anza'a*, he evicted.

البيت المتنازع فيه *el-bait el-motanázia fih*, the house in dispute, which is the object of litigation.

نزف or نزيف *nazf*, or *nazeef*, loss of blood, bleeding from a wound, hæmorrhage.

نزل *nizila*, he descended, alighted, sank.

نزل *nozol*, store-house, commissariat store.

نزول *nozool*, descent, alighting.

نزلة *nazla*, halting-place; village; catarrh, influenza.

انزل *anzala*, he made descend; emitted.

نزّل *nazzala*, he made descend, deducted, subtracted.

تنزيل *tanzeel*, subtraction; to be deducted.

تنزّل *tanazzala*, he deigned, condescended.

تنازل عن *tanázala 'an*, he renounced, delivered up.

تنازل *tanázul*, renunciation; endorsing and transferring a bill.

استنزل *istanzala*, he wished to renounce, or withdraw from a claim, deducted.

منزل - منازل *manzil*, pl. *manázil*, place of alighting; house, abode, stage, station.

نزهة or نزاهة *nozha*, or *nazáha*, pleasure, recreation, purity.

انتزه or تنزّه *intazaha*, or *tanazzaha*, he took the air, strolled.

[تفسّح - تفرّج]

منتزهة *muntazaha*, promenade, park.

نسب - انساب *nasab*, pl. *ansáb*, lineage, descent from a common male ancestor.

نسيب *naseeb*, a relative, relation, cognate; son-in-law, father-in-law.

نسبة *nisba*, proportion, relation to; logarithm.

بالنسبة له *bin-nisba laho*, with regard to him.

نسبي *nisbiy*, proportionate, proportional.

نسب *nasaba*, he attributed, accused.

ما نسب اليه *má nosiba ileih* (passive), that which was laid to his charge.

منسوب *mansoob*, attributed, imputed; attribute.

نسّب *nassaba*, he applied, adapted.

تنسيب *tanseeb*, adaptation, application. [تطبيق]

انتسب *intasaba*, he attributed to himself, claimed.

انتساب *intisáb*, a claim to nationality or relationship, a connecting one's self.

ناسب (284) منشة

تناسب or ناسب *násaba*, or *tanásaba*, it was proportionate, fit, proper.

تناسب *tanásub*, arithmetical proportion, grace resulting from due proportions.

مناسب *munásib*, fit, proper, suitable.

مناسبة *munásaba*, proportion, fitness, aptitude.

نسج *nasaja*, he wove.

منسوجات *mansooját*, things woven, stuffs; tissues of the body (anatomy).

منسج *mansaj*, loom, embroidery-frame.

نسخ *nasakha*, he copied out; he abrogated, effaced.

نسخة ـ نسخ *nuskha*, pl. *nusakh*, copy.

نساخ *nassákh*, copying clerk.

نسخي *naskhiy*, ordinary current hand, usual style of calligraphy; *nusakhiy*, quack druggist.

استنسخ *istansakha*, he asked for a copy to be made, ordered or took a copy.

تناسخ or مناسخة *tanásukh*, or *munásakha*, succession or uninterrupted inheritance to an entire estate.

تناسخ or تناسخ *tanásukh*, or *tanassukh*, transmigration of souls, metempsychosis, metamorphosis.

نسر ـ نسور *nasr*, pl. *nosoor*, eagle.

ناسور *násoor*, fistula, wart, corn.

نسق *nasq*, order, arrangement, rhythm.

نسق ـ نسق *nasaqa*, or *nassaqa*, he set in order.

تنسيق *tanseeq*, ordinance, arrangement.

نسك *nusk*, rite, devotion.

منسك ـ مناسك *mansak*, pl. *manásik*, rite, ceremony.

نسل ـ انسال *nasl*, pl. *ansál*, progeny, generation, posterity.

نسل or تناسل *nasala*, or *tanásala*, he begot. [ولّد]

نسالة *nosála*, fluff, loose threads or fibres.

نسيم *naseem*, breeze, zephyr.

شم النسيم *shamm en-naseem*, "Sniff the breeze," the great spring holiday in Egypt, which is held on the Greek Easter Monday.

نسناس *nisnás*, ape. [قرد]

نسي *nasia*, he forgot.

نسيان *nisyán*, a forgetting, forgetfulness.

منسي *mansiy*, forgotten.

نسىء *nasi*, the 5 or 6 days intercalated at the end of the Coptic year, in September.

نساء ـ نسوان or نسوة *nisá*, or *niswán*, or *niswa*, women; the plural of *mara*. [انس ـ امرأة]

نسائي *Nasáiy*, 'Abdur-Rahman En-Nasáiy, a great Moslem jurist, died A.D. 900.

نشّ *nashsha*, he drove away flies; he absorbed.

منشة *minashsha*, fly-flip, fly-whisk.

نشا or نشاستة *nashá* (for Persian *nishásta*), starch.

نشّى *nashsha*, he starched (linen).

نشو *nasho*, growth.

نشأة *nashát*, growth, result.

ناشىء *náshi*, growing, resulting from.

نشأ *nashá*, he grew up, it sprang or resulted from.

انشأ or انشىء *anshá*, he created, caused to grow or result; he built; composed (writing).

انشا *inshá*, creation; building; model of style, delectus or book of exercises.

منشىء *munshi*, tutor, teacher of a language.

منشية *manshiya* (Coptic), place, village; a public square.

نشادر *nushádir*, sal ammoniac.

نشد or انشد *nashada*, or *anshada*, he recited prayers, or verses.

نشيد الانشاد or اناشيد *nasheed el-anshád*, or *nasheed el-anásheed*, the Song of Songs (of Solomon).

منشد ـ ذكر *munshid*, a reciter of prayers, or the *zikr*.

نشر *nashr*, publication, diffusion.

نشر *nashara*, he spread out, aired, published; sawed wood.

انتشر *intashara*, it became spread, dilated, diffused, or disseminated.

نشارة *noshára*, saw-dust.

نشور *noshoor*, the resurrection.

منشار *minshár*, carpenter's saw.

منشور *manshoor*, published; especially an official circular from a Ministry of State to a minor department; regulation; diploma; prism.

ناشزة *náshiza*, a rebellious wife.

نشاط *nashát*, liveliness, alertness, energy.

ناشط or نشيط *nasheet*, or *náshit*, loose and free of limb, energetic, alert, gay.

نشف *nashifa*, it absorbed water, became dry.

نشّف *nashshafa*, he dried, made dry.

نشافة *nasháfa*, dryness.

ناشف *náshif*, dry.

نشّاف *nashsháf*, a dryer; blotting-paper.

منشفة *minshafa*, towel.

نشق *nashiqa*, he sniffed at.

استنشق *istanshaqa*, he inhaled, respired.

نشوق *nashooq*, snuff (tobacco).

نشل *nashala*, he pilfered. [طرّ]

نشّال *nashshál*, pickpocket; an "Artful Dodger."

نشان ـ نياشين *nishán* (Persian), pl. *nayásheen*, aim, mark, butt; target; badge, medal, decoration; *nishán ál* (Turkish), present! take aim!

نشانجي *nishánji* (Turkish), marksman, sharpshooter.

نَشَّن nashshana, he took aim at a target.

نَشْوان nashawán (Persian), intoxicated. [سكران]

نَصَّ nassa, he defined, pointed out, designated.

نَصّ - نُصوص nass, pl. nosoos, an exact quotation, the exact text (e.g. of an article of a Code).

نَصّ القانون nass el-qánoon, authority of law.

نَصّ صَريح nass sareeh, a categorical or explicit statement, a distinct order on a definite point of law, &c.

مَنْصوص mansoos, the sense conveyed by the nass or text of an article of law.

نَصب - انصاب nasb, pl. ansáb, a setting up, a mark set up, sign, statue, idol; calamity; vegetation which grows; nasab, fatigue; nisb, share.

نَصبة nasba, fat-ha or "a" vowel-sound; cooking-niche.

نَصب nasb, fraud, embezzlement, swindling. [اختلاس]

نَصَّاب nassáb, swindler, rogue.

نَصب nasaba, he set upright, erected, swindled, planted.

نُصب nusb, idol, statue.

نَصيب naseeb, portion, share; fate; hence lottery or chance.

يانَصيب yánseeb, lottery.

نَصَّب nassaba, he appointed, erected.

مَنْصب - مَناصب mansab, pl. manásib, office, post, rank.

نَصَح nasaha, he gave advice.

نَصيحة - نَصائح naseeha, pl. nasáyih advice.

نَصر nasr, help, victory, from God. [غلبة]

نَصرٌ مِن الله و فتحٌ قريب nasrun min Ullah wa fat-hun qareebun, Help from God and a speedy victory!

نَصَر nasara, (God) gave the victory, helped.

ناصر or نَصير násir, or naseer, helper, auxiliary.

نَصْراني - نَصارى nasrániy, pl. nasára, Christian, Nazarene.

نَصْرانية nasrániya, Christianity.

نُصَيريّة Nosairiya, a pagan sect in Syria.

انتَصر intasara, he won, gained the victory.

انتِصار intisár, victory.

مُنْتَصر muntasir, victorious.

مَنْصور mansoor, rendered victorious (by God).

المَنْصورة - دَقَلية El-Mansoora, the victorious (city), site of the Moslem victory over the Crusaders in the 13th century; now the capital of the province Daq-haliya.

مَنْصر - مَناصر mansar, pl. manásir, clique or gang of thieves or rowdies. [عصبة]

تَنْصير tanseer, baptism, making (a child) a Christian or Nazarene.

نصف ‎ انصاف - ‎ *nusf* (vulg. pronounced *nuss*), pl. *ansáf*, half.

انصف ‎ *ansafa*, he bisected, was impartial.

انصاف ‎ *insáf*, equity, impartiality. [عدل]

منصف ‎ *munsif*, just, honest.

مناصفة ‎ *munásafa*, a going halves, sharing equally.

منتصف ‎ *muntasif*, in the course of, about half-way.

في منتصف الليل ‎ *fi muntasif el-lail*, about midnight.

نصل ‎ *nasl*, that which is detachable, fits in or takes out; head of arrow, haft of a knife.

تنصّل من ‎ *tanussala min*, he got out of, escaped from an embarrassment, detached himself from.

نطّ ‎ *natta*, he jumped, leaped.

نطّ ‎ *natt*, a jump, a jumping.

نطّاط ‎ *nattát*, a jumper, light of heel, pickpocket.

نطح ‎ *nataha*, it butted with its horns.

نطحة ‎ *nat-ha*, a butt with the horns.

نطرون ‎ *natrón*, natron, nitre.

نطع ‎ *nata'*, leather tray for meals or work.

نطفة ‎ *nutfa*, semen.

نطق ‎ *notq*, articulation of speech; the pronunciation of a word.

نطق ‎ *nataqa*, he articulated speech, pronounced.

ناطق ‎ *nátiq*, articulate, man as an articulating animal, with power of speech.

استنطق ‎ *istantaqa*, he elicited speech, interrogated a prisoner; (vulgarism) he vomited.

استنطاق - تحقيق ‎ *istintáq*, interrogatory of a prisoner, inquest, "instruction;" *istintáq* is used in Turkey, and *tahqeeq* in Egypt.

مستنطق ‎ or ‎ قاضي التحقيق ‎ *mustantiq* (legal term used in Turkey, for *qádi et-tahqeeq* in Egypt) "juge d'instruction," inquisitor.

نطاق ‎ *nitáq*, girdle.

منطقة ‎ or ‎ منطق ‎ *mintaq*, or *mintaqa*, girdle.

منطق البروج ‎ *mintaq el-borooj*, the Zodiac.

منطق ‎ *mantiq*, logic, the spoken word.

منطق نامه ‎ *mantiq-náma* (Persian *náma*, document), a legal term for a confession, especially a victim's dying confession.

منطوق ‎ *mantooq*, uttered; signification of a word.

نطل ‎ *natala*, he wetted.

نطّالة ‎ *nattála*, an instrument for wetting or irrigating the fields, a bag made of rushes used as a bucket, and swung by two men.

نظر - انظار ‎ *nazar*, pl. *anzár*, a look, glance; a look of favour, hence a gift, kindness.

نظراً ‎ *nazarán*, with regard to.

نظر ‎ *nazara*, he saw.

اِنْتَظَرَ or اِسْتَنْظَرَ *intazara*, or *istanzara*, he expected, looked for, waited for.

نَظَرِيَّات *nazariyát*, views; theory.

نَظِير *nazeer*, like to, regarding; *nadir* (astronomy).

بدون نَظِير *bidoon nazeer*, sanspareil, matchless.

نَاظِر ـ نُظَّار *názir*, pl. *nozzár*, he who sees; inspector; Minister of State.

مجلس النُظَّار *majlis en-nozzár*, Council of Ministers, the Cabinet.

نَظَارَة *nazára*, Ministry of State; office of inspector.

نَظَّارَة *naddára*, spectacles; telescope.

مَنْظَر *manzar*, point of view, view, appearance.

مَنْظُور *manzoor*, seen, provided for; foreseen; a schedule of Returns.

نَظَّف *naddafa*, he cleaned.

نَظَافَة *nadáfa*, cleanliness, cleanness.

نَظِيف *nadeef*, clean.

نَظْم *nazm*, order, arrangement; rhyme.

نِظَام *nizám*, rule, organization; regular army.

النِظَام العَام *en-nizám el-a'ám*, public order or security.

نِظَامِيّ *nizámiy*, organized, regular.

عَسَاكِر نِظَامِيَّة *'asákir nizámiya*, regular troops.

نَاظِم *názim*, ruler, organizer.

نَظَّم *nazzama*, he arranged, put in order.

تَنْظِيم ـ تَنْظِيمَات *tanzeem*, pl. *tanzeemát*, regulation, organization; rules; vestry of a town.

اِنْتَظَم *intazama*, it was in good order.

مُنْتَظِم *muntazam*, regular, organized.

مَنْظُوم *manzoom*, arranged; rhymed, rhyme.

نَعْت *na't*, description, explanation, guide.

نَعْجَة ـ نِعَاج *na'ja*, pl. *ni'áj*, ewe, sheep.

نَاعُورَة *ná'oora*, water-mill; water-power.

نُعَاس *no'ás*, sleepiness.

نَعْسَان *na'sán*, sleepy.

نَعْش *na'sh*, bier, coffin; the Great Bear (stars).

بَنَات نَعْش *banát na'sh*, the Great and Little Bear (stars).

نَعْل ـ نِعَال *na'l*, pl. *n'iál* (femin.), horse-shoe, coarse sandal; sole of foot.

نَعَم *na'm*, yes; (as an interrogative) please repeat, I did not understand.

نِعَم ـ أَنْعَام *na'm*, pl. *ana'ám*, gift, gift from God, cattle, flocks, herds.

نِعْمَة ـ نِعَم *ni'ama*, pl. *niy'am*, favour, bounty.

وَلِيّ النِعَم *wali en-niy'am*, Lord of Bounties; the King, Khedive.

أَنْعَم *an'ama*, he made happy, bestowed favour.

مُنْعِم *mona'im*, benefactor.

تَنَعَّم *tana'ama*, he was in luxury, luxuriated.

ناعم ná'yim, soft, tender, smooth, even; weak; powdery.

نعيم na'yeem, bliss, blissful; Paradise of bliss.

نعام na'ám, ostrich.

نعمان no'mán, anemone.

نعناع na'náa', herb mint.

نغص naghs, annoyance, trouble.

نغم naghama, he hummed, sang. [رنم]

نغمة naghma, tune, chant, song.

نفّ naffa, he blew his nose.

نفث الدم nafs ed-dam, a spitting of blood.

نفح nafaha, he diffused; (the wind) blew.

نفخ nafakha, he blew out, inflated.

انتفخ intafakha, it swelled.

انتفاخ intifákh, a swelling out.

منفاخ minfákh, bellows.

نفد or نفذ nafada, it disappeared, was consumed; he escaped, saved himself.

نفوذ or نفذ nafaz, or nofooz, influence, penetration, effectiveness; authority.

نفذ nafaza, it penetrated, was effectual.

نفذ or انفذ anfaza, or naffaza, he made penetrate, carried into execution.

تنفيذ tanfeez, execution of an order or law.

اوامر تنفيذيّة awámir tanfeeziya, executive orders.

تنفّذ tanaffaza, it was carried out, put into execution.

نافذ náfiz, influential; (a law) in force; a penetrating (wound).

منفذ manfaz, place of penetration or effect; passage; electrical insulator.

منفّذ monaffaz, put into execution, carried out.

نفر - انفار nafar, pl. anfár, individual, a person; private soldier.

نفر nafara, he was shy, afraid, hated, kept aloof.

نفور or نفرة or نفار or nafra, or nifár, or nofoor, a shunning, aversion, separation.

نفس - نفوس or انفس nafs, pl. nofoos, or anfos, soul, self; individuality; person; appetite.

نفسُه nafsoh, he himself.

نفسًا nafsán, personally. [ذاتًا]

من تلقاء نفسه min tilqá nafsihi, by his own right, spontaneously, d'office.

قتل نفسَه qatala nafsaho, he killed himself.

قتل نفسًا qatala nafsán, he killed a man.

تعداد النفوس ta'dád en-nofoos, census, a counting of souls.

نفس - انفاس nafas, pl. anfás, breath, respiration; style, manner, taste.

نفيس - انفس nafees (comparative anfas), precious, exquisite.

نفاس *nifás*, child-bed, parturition.

حمَّى النفاس *homma en-nifás*, puerperal fever.

نفسا *nafsá*, or *nafasa*, a woman in child-bed.

نفسانيّ *nafsániy*, sensual, selfish.

نفسانيّة *nafsániya*, spite, ill-will; selfish motive.

نافس *náfasa*, he quarrelled, was selfish.

منافسة *monáfasa*, quarrel, rivalry.

تنفّس *tanaffasa*, he drew or took breath; he cried out.

منفس - منافس *minfas*, pl. *manáfis*, air-hole.

نفض or نفض *naffada*, he shook out, dusted (carpets, &c.).

انتفض *intafada*, he shook himself.

منفضة *manfada*, ash-tray.

نفط *naft*, naphtha.

نفع *nafa'a*, it was useful, of advantage.

ينفع *yanfa'*, it is of use, serviceable.

نافع *náfia'*, useful, beneficial.

انتفع *intafa'a*, he profited by, took advantage of.

انتفاع *intifáa'*, profit, advantage.

حقّ الانتفاع *haqq el-intifá'a*, usufruct, right of use.

منفعة - منافع *manfa'a*, pl. *manáfia'*, advantage, benefit, profit.

منافقة or نفاق *nifáq*, or *monáfaqa*, hypocrisy.

منافق *monáfiq*, hypocrite.

نفقة *nafaqa*, alimony, maintenance of a wife.

نفق *nafaqa*, (the beast) perished.

نفل - انفال *nafl*, pl. *anfál*, superfluity, supererogation; booty, spoil; trefoil, clover.

نافل *náfil*, unnecessary, superfluous, of no avail.

تنفّل *tanaffala*, he did a work of supererogation.

نفى or نفا *nafa*, he drove off, repulsed, exiled, denied, repelled an accusation.

نفى *nafi*, negation, denial.

شهادة النفي *shahádat en-nafi*, evidence for the defence, rebutting evidence.

نفى *nafa*, or *nafi*, exilement.

منفيّ or نفيّ *nafiy*, or *manfiy*, an exiled man.

منفى *manfa*, place of exile.

نافى - ينافي *náfa*, he disproved, contradicted; *yonáfi*, he disproves.

نقب - انقاب *naqb*, pl. *anqáb*, a hole pierced.

نقب *naqaba*, he bored a hole.

نقب

نقب حائط المنزل *naqaba háyit el-manzil*, he made a hole in the wall of a house (legal term for a species of burglary).

نقّب عن *naqqaba 'an*, he examined carefully, pierced or penetrated a difficulty.

نقاب *niqáb*, veil, mask.

نقيب naqeeb, chief, leader.

نقّح naqqaha, he revised, elaborated a book; reformed.

تنقيح tanqeeh, revision (of a book, code, &c.); reform.

نقد naqada, he paid cash, tried good money.

نقد ـ نقود naqd, pl. noqood, cash, good coin.

كيس نقود kees noqood, purse of money.

نقداً naqdán, in cash, for ready money.

نقديّة naqdiya, cash, money.

نقاد niqád, a quarrel, breaking off, rupture.

انتقد intaqada, he tried, saw.

منقاد minqád, beak.

نقذ naqz, safety, rescue.

انقذ anqaza, he rescued, saved.

نقر naqara, he drummed; hollowed out, pecked at.

نقر or نقرة naqr, or noqra, a hollow, cavity.

ناقر náqara, he quarrelled.

نقار niqár, a quarrel.

نقّارة naqqára (pronounced naggára), drum, large drum for cavalry, or on camels.

نقر naqar (pronounced nuggur), a boat *hollowed out*; name for a Nile boat above the Cataracts.

منقار minqár, chisel, beak, pick-axe.

نقرس niqris, gout. [داء الملوك]

ناقوس náqoos, clapper, gong.

نقش naqasha, he painted, delineated, cut a seal, engraved.

ناقش náqasha, he disputed, litigated, argued a case in court.

نقش ـ نقوش naqsh, pl. noqoosh, design, engraving.

نقّاش naqqásh, engraver, sculptor.

مناقشة monáqasha, the arguing of a law-suit by both sides in court, *débats*. [مرافعة]

نقص naqasa, it became less, it lessened, was deficient.

نقّص naqqasa, he made less, subtracted.

ناقص náqasa, he called for tenders in order to obtain lowest prices.

نقصان noqsán, deficiency, deficit, shortcoming. [عجز]

ناقص náqis, deficient, imperfect, minus.

نقيصة ـ نقائص naqeesa, pl. naqáyis, defect; a large sack.

تنقيص tanqees, reduction, deduction, subtraction.

مناقصة monáqasa, a call for lowest tenders.

نقض naqada, he pulled to pieces, demolished, refuted a judgment of a lower court.

نقض naqd, demolition, refutation.

نقض و ابرام naqd wa ibrám, Cassation, the final Court of Appeal.

ناقض or تناقض náqada, or tanáqada, he contradicted, he differed emphatically.

نقض ‎ - ‎ انقاض ‎ *noqd*, pl. *anqád*, beam, rafter.

نقطة ‎ - ‎ نقط ‎ *noqta*, pl. *noqat*, point, vowel-point; spot; watchman's beat or station; drop.

نقوط ‎ *noqoot*, presents, *étrennes*.

نقع ‎ or ‎ استنقع ‎ *naqa'a*, or *istanqa'a*, it became stagnant.

انقع ‎ *anqoa'*, stagnant water; hollows where water collects.

مستنقع ‎ *mustanqa'*, tank, pond, aquarium.

نقل ‎ *naqala*, he conveyed, transported, narrated.

نقل ‎ - ‎ نقول ‎ *naql*, pl. *noqool*, transport, narrative; tradition, transfer; *noql*, dried fruit.

نقلي ‎ *naqliy*, traditional; *noqaliy*, seller of dried fruit.

نقلية ‎ *naqliya*, freight, means or cost of transport.

انتقل ‎ *intaqala*, he moved himself, went to another place; it came down by tradition or inheritance; he died, went to heaven.

منقول ‎ *manqool*, moved, narrated.

منقولات ‎ *manqoolát*, moveables, personal property.

منقولة و ثابتة ‎ *manqoola wa sábita*, personal and real (property).

نقم ‎ or ‎ انتقم ‎ *naqama* or (more commonly) *intaqama*, he revenged or avenged himself.

انتقام ‎ *intiqám*, vengeance, revenge.

نقمة ‎ *naqma*, vengeance, revenge, disgrace.

نقاء ‎ or ‎ نقو ‎ or ‎ نقاوة ‎ *naqá*, or *naqoo*, or *naqáwa*, purity; quintessence, pith, marrow, kernel.

نقي ‎ - ‎ انقياء ‎ *naqiy*, pl. *anqiyá*, pure, pious, choice.

تنقى ‎ *tanaqqa*, he pruned, sorted, picked out.

نكب ‎ - ‎ نكبة ‎ *nakba*, misfortune; *nakab*, deviation.

منكب ‎ - ‎ مناكب ‎ *mankib*, pl. *manákib*, shoulder.

نكتة ‎ *nukta*, wit, epigram, criticism; a witty fellow.

نكح ‎ *nakaha*, he married; consummated marriage.

نكاح ‎ - ‎ انكحة ‎ *nikáh*, pl. *ankiha*, marriage.

عقد النكاح ‎ *'aqada en-nikáh* (the priest) tied the marriage knot, solemnized the marriage.

منكوحة ‎ *mankooha*, married woman.

نكر ‎ *nakira*, he was ignorant of.

انكر ‎ *ankara*, he denied. [جحد]

انكار ‎ *inkár*, denial.

منكر ‎ or ‎ ناكر ‎ *munkir*, or *nákir*, he who denies.

نكر ‎ *nokr*, cunningness.

تنكر ‎ *tanakkara*, he denied.

نكس ‎ *nakasa*, he upset, turned upside down; he broke his word. [عكس]

نكس ‎ *nuks*, relapse, upset.

منكوس ‎ *mankoos*, upset, relapsed.

نكص ‎ *nakasa*, he turned aside, broke his word.

نكفة *nakfa*, tonsils; the mumps.

نكل *nakala*, he recoiled, drew back.

نكول *nokool*, withdrawal, retirement.

نكهة *nak-ha*, breath, odour of the breath.

نكاية *nikáya*, malice, injury done to spite another.

نمّ *namma*, he spoke ill of, was a backbiter.

نميمة *nameema*, a bit of slander, evil gossip.

نمر *nimr*, leopard, panther.

نمرة ـ نمر *nimra*, pl. *nimar* (European), numero, No.

نمّر *nammara*, he put numbers to, numbered.

منمّر *monammar*, numbered.

نمس *nims*, ichneumon.

نمسا ـ الالمانية *Nemsá*, Austria; *Alamánya*, Germany.

نمساوي *nemsáwiy*, Austrian.

ناموس *námoos*, mosquitoes.

ناموسية *námoosiya*, mosquito-net.

ناموس *námoos* (Greek *nomos*, used in Turkish), honour, reputation.

نمّق *nammaqa*, he wrote, copied out.

تنميق *tanmeeq*, a writing down, inditing.

نمل ـ نمال *naml*, pl. *nimál*, ant.

نمنم *namnama*, he muttered.

نموذج or انموذج *namoozaj*, or *onmoozaj* (Persian), sample, model, specimen. [عيّنة]

نمى ـ ينمي *nama*, it grew; *yanmi*, it grows.

نما *namá*, growth.

نهب *nahaba*, he plundered, pillaged. [سلب]

نهب *nahb*, pillage, act of pillage.

منهوبات *manhoobát*, things pillaged, spoils.

نهج *nahj*, road, track.

منهج or منهاج *manhaj*, road, track, course marked out.

نهد ـ نهود *nahd*, pl. *nohood*, rounded breast, a maiden's swelling bosom.

تنهّد *tanahhada*, he sighed, his bosom heaved.

ناهدة *náhida*, a maiden with swelling breasts.

نهاد *nuhád*, about, nearly.

نهر ـ انهر *nahr*, pl. *anhor*, river, stream. [جرى]

نهار *nahár*, daytime.

نهاراً وليلاً *nahárán wa lailán*, by day and by night.

في رابعة النهار *fi rábi'at en-nahár* (colloquial), in broad open day.

انتهار *intihár*, reprimand, repudiation.

نهز *nahaza*, it was near.

انتهز الفرصة *intahaza el-forsa*, he seized, or availed himself of, the opportunity.

نهض *nahada*, he arose, stood up.

نهوض *nohood*, a rising, getting up.

نهق *nahaqa*, (the ass) brayed.

نهيق *naheeq*, a bray.

نهك (294) نوط

انتهك or نهك *nahaka*, or *intahaka*, he injured, violated.

نهى - ينهى *naha*, he forbad; *yanha*, he forbids.

نهي *nahi*, prohibition.

نهي or انتهى *nohia*, or *intaha*, he arrived at, it came to an end.

انهى *anha*, he informed, hinted, warned.

نهو - نهاية - انتهأ *nahw*, or *niháya*, or *intihá*, the end.

منتهي or انتهائي or نهائي *niháiy*, or *intiháiy*, or *muntahi*, final.

نو *naw*, rain, storm; hot south wind.

نوبة *Nooba*, Nubia.

نوب - نوبي *Nob* or *Noob*, Nubians; *Noobiy*, Nubian.

نوب - نوبة *nōba*, pl. *nowab*, turn, alternation; a time, once, &c.; attack, fit, "*accès*."

نوبة *nōba* (military term), bugle-call.

نوبتجي *noobetji* (Turkish), sentry, orderly.

ناب عن *nába 'an*, he, it was instead of. [عوض]

تناوب or ناوب *náwaba*, or *tanáwaba*, he took his turn.

مناوبة *monáwaba*, alternation, in turns

نيابة *niyába*, substitution, proxy.

بالنيابة عنه *bin-niyába a'nho*, instead of him.

نيابة عمومية *niyába o'moomiya*, Parquet, *ministère public*; office of the Attorney-General or Public Prosecutor.

نائب - نواب *náyib*, pl. *nowwáb*, substitute; a member of the Parquet; a judge *suppléant* or vice-judge; "*nawab*."

نائب عمومي *náyib o'moomiy*, Attorney-General.

نوائب *nawáyib*, vicissitudes.

نوتي - نوتية *nōti*, pl. *nōtiya* (Latin *nauta*), sailor.

نوح *Nooh*, the "prophet" Noah.

نوحة or نياحة *nōha*, or *niyáha*, a lament, groan.

نوخ *nōkh* (see *nakhkha*).

نور - انوار *noor*, pl. *anwár*, a light.

نور *nawwara*, he lighted, informed.

تنوير *tanweer*, a lighting up, illumination, enlightenment.

تنور *tanawwara*, he was enlightened, informed; it was lighted up.

منور *manwár*, skylight, hole in wall.

منارة - منائر *manára*, pl. *manáyir*, minaret. [اذن]

نورة *noora*, a depilatory of arsenic and quicklime, &c.

نار - نيران *nár*, pl. *neerán* (fem.), fire.

نورج *nōraj*, threshing-sledge.

نوروز or نيروز سلطاني *naw-rōz*, or *neerōz Sultániy* (Persian), New Year; vernal equinox; in Persia, New Year's Day (March 21st); in Egypt, the autumnal equinox (Sept. 10th).

نوش - مناوشة (*nōsh*), *monáwasha*, battle, quarrel.

نوط *nōt*, suspension, dependency, appertaining.

ينوط ـ ناط *náta*, he hung up; *yanoot*, he hangs up.

نيط *neeta* (passive), it was hung up, depended, was attached.

يناطه بالخدمة *yonát-oh bil-khidma*, he is bound to serve, his service is obligatory.

منوط *manoot*, hung up, dependent, responsible.

انواع ـ نوع *no'w*, pl. *anwáa'*, species, sex, manner, style.

بنوع النصب *bi-now' en-nasb*, by fraud.

متنوّع *mutanawwia'*, of various kinds.

نوف *nöf*, summit, prominence.

نيف *naif*, surplus; *plus*, more than.

نيافة *niyáfa*, eminence, title of a bishop.

ناف *náfa*, it surpassed, was prominent.

ينوف or ينيف *yaneef*, or *yanoof*, it is prominent, surpasses, exceeds in amount.

نوفمبر *nofember* (European), November.

ناقة ـ نوق *nööq*, pl. of *náqa*, she-camel.

انوال ـ نول *nōl*, pl. *anwál*, gift, fashion, weaver's loom.

نولون *noloon*, freight, *nolis*.

ناول or نال *nála*, or *náwala*, he bestowed.

تناول *tanáwala*, he took (a gift), received, ate.

منوال *minwál*, manner, fashion, loom.

منيل *minyal* (Coptic), Island of Roda.

نيام or نوم *nōm*, or *niyám*, sleep.

ينام ـ نام *náma*, he slept; *yanám*, he sleeps.

نائم *náyim*, asleep, sleeping.

نوّم or نيّم *nawwama* (vulgarly *nayyama*), he put to sleep, made lie down.

تناوم *tanáwama*, he pretended to be asleep.

منام *manám*, dream.

منامة *manáma*, tomb.

ابو النوم *aboo n-nōm*, poppy. [خشخاش]

نون *noon*, the letter *n*.

نوّن ـ *nawwana*, he marked or pronounced the final *n* [namely, *on*, *an*, *in* or nominative, accusative and oblique case endings of nouns and adjectives].

تنوين *tanween*, marking the final *n*.

نوّه *nawwaha*, he called, mentioned.

منوّه *monawwah*, stated, mentioned.

نوى *nawa*, he intended, proposed.

ينوي *yinwi*, he intends.

نيّة ـ نيّات *niyya*, pl. *niyyát*, intention.

ناوي *náwi*, he who intends, intending.

نواة ـ نوى *nawát*, pl. *nawa*, date-stone.

ني *nee*, or *nay*, raw (meat); unbaked (brick).

نيب *naib*, being old, long in the tooth.

نيب or ناب *náb*, or *neeb*, canine tooth, fang.

نيروز - نوروز *neeröz* (see *nawröz*).

نيسان *Neesán*, Syrian month of April.

نيف - نوف *naif* (see *nöf*).

نيك *naik*, copulation. [جامع]

نيل - نائل - نول *nail*, success, attainment; *náyil*, gift; he who attains. [cf. *nöl*]

نيل or نيلة *neel*, or *neela*, indigo, indigo dye.

النيل or بحر النيل *En-Neel*, or *bahr en-Neel*; the Nile, the sea, or Great River Nile.

صيف النيل *saif en-neel*, summer of Nile; summer canal or irrigation.

H (a light aspirate).

ه - هـ *Hé*. Value = 5.

ه - ها *-ho*, or *-oh*, him, his; *-há*, her, hers.

هاء or هاهنا *há*, or *há-honá*, here! take!

هابيل و قابيل *Hábeel wa Qábeel*, Abel and Cain.

هات *hát*, bring! give! hand over! [هيت]

هاتور *Hátoor*, Coptic month of November.

هارون الرشيد *Hároon er-Rasheed*, Haroun al-Raschid, Aaron the Orthodox, the Great 'Abbási Caliph of Baghdad, A.D. 800.

هالة *hála*, halo, areola.

هامة *háma*, summit, crown of head.

هانم - خانم *hánum* (for Turkish *khánum*), lady, princess, Sultana.

هانم افندم *hánum efendim*, my lady!

هاون *háwan* (*háoon*), mortar (for pounding).

هاوية *háwiya*, hell, abyss. [هوى]

هب *habba*, the wind blew. [cf. حب]

هبوب *hoboob*, blast of wind.

هباب *habáb*, soot, smuts, smokiness.

هبب *habbaba*, he tore, ill-treated, injured.

هبد or هبت *habbada* (for *habbata*), he flung down.

هبر *habara*, he seized upon, tore to pieces.

هبش *habasha*, he scratched up into a heap.

هبط *habata*, it sank (in price, &c.).

هبوط *hoboot*, fall, decrease.

هابط *hábit*, falling, decreasing.

هبل - مهبل (*habala*), *mahbil*, vagina.

اهبل *ahbal*, stupid, idiot.

تهبيل *tahbeel*, vapour-bath, fomentation.

هبة - وهب *hiba*, gift (see *wahaba*).

هت *hatta*, he slandered, frightened.

هتر or هترس *hatara*, or *hatrasa*, he raved in delirium.

هتف على بالي *hatafa 'ala báli*, it occurred to my mind.

هتك *hataka*, he tore off a veil, violated.

هتك العرض *hatk el-'ird*, criminal assault, injury to (a woman's) honour.

هتم - اهتم *hatam*, toothlessness; *ahtam*, toothless.

هتان - هذان *hátain* (femin.), these two; (masc.) *házain*.

هجر *hajara*, he emigrated, abandoned.

هجرة *hijra*, flight of Mahomed from Mecca to Medina, A.D. 622.

سنة هجرية ١٣٠٨ *sana hijriya* 1308, year of the Hijra 1308, A.D. 1891.

هجران *hijrán*, desertion, abandonment.

مهاجر *mohájir*, emigrant, refugee.

مهجور *mahjoor*, absent, abroad, left the country.

هجار *hijár*, foot-rope, tether.

هجم على *hajama 'ala*, he rushed upon, attacked.

هجوم *hojoom*, onset, attack; charge!

هجين - هجن *hajeen*, pl. *hojon*, (colloquial meaning) dromedary, a camel for riding.

هجّان - هجّانة *hajján*, pl. *hajjána*, camel rider; troops mounted on camels, camel-corps.

كلام مستهجن *kalám mustahjin*, a silly, improper speech.

هجاء *hijá*, satire; spelling, syllable.

حروف الهجاء *horoof el-hijá*, letters of the alphabet.

ترتيب هجائي *tarteeb hijáiy*, alphabetical order.

هجّى or تهجّى *hajja*, or *tahajja*, he spelled.

اهجوّة *ohjowwa*, satire, lampoon.

هدّد - تهديد *haddada*, he threatened; *tahdeed*, threat.

هدو *hodoo*, repose, quiet.

هادىء *hádi*, gentle (wind); calm, tranquil.

هدب - اهداب *hodb*, pl. *ahdáb*, eyelash. [رمش]

هدر *hadr*, impunity, especially impunity in bloodshed.

هدف *hadaf*, butt, target.

هدّف *haddafa*, he aimed, threw at.

هدل *hadila*, it dangled.

هدم *hadama*, he demolished.

هدم *hadm*, demolition. [cf. هضم]

هدون *hodoon*, rest, repose.

هدانة or هدنة *hodna*, or *hodána*, truce, armistice.

هدهد *hudhud*, a cooing bird; lapwing.

هدى *hada*, he guided, showed the road.

هدى or هداية *hoda*, or *hidáya*, guidance (to salvation).

هديّة - هدايا *hadiya*, pl. *hadáyá*, gift, sacrifice.

اهدى *ahda*, he offered a present.

مهدي *Mahdi*, guided, led by God; a leader in Islam, the twelfth

Imam, forerunner of the Millenium; the Mahdi of Khartoum, 1882-85.

هذا ‎ـ ‎هذِي ‎ـ ‎هَوْلاء ‎*házá*, femin. *hazihi*, pl. *howlá*, this.

هذر ‎ـ ‎هذّر ‎*hazar*, nonsense; *hazzara*, he talked nonsense.

هذيان ‎*huzayán*, nonsense, jabber; delirium.

هرّ ‎ـ ‎عين ‎الهرّ ‎*hirr*, cat; *a'in el-hirr*, cat's eye. [قط]

هرب ‎*haraba*, he fled, escaped.

هروب ‎*horoob*, flight.

هارب ‎or ‎هربان ‎*hárib*, or *harbán*, fugitive, runaway.

فرّ ‎هاربًا ‎*farra háribán*, he fled as a fugitive, escaped (from justice).

هرّب ‎*harraba*, he put to flight; he allowed to escape; he smuggled.

تهريب ‎من ‎السجن ‎*tahreeb min es-sijn*, the allowing a prisoner to escape from prison.

تهريب ‎من ‎الكمرك ‎*tahreeb min el-gumruk*, smuggling through the custom house; contraband.

هرس ‎*hars*, a crushing, smashing.

هرش ‎*harsh*, itch, irritation, harshness.

هرّش ‎*harrasha*, he incited, set on.

هرع ‎*hara'a*, he hastened, ran.

هرولة ‎*harwala*, a kicking up of dust.

هرم ‎*harim*, very old, decrepit man.

هرم ‎ـ ‎هرام ‎or ‎اهرام ‎*haram*, pl. *hirám*, or *ahrám*, pyramid, pyramids of Ghizeh.

هري ‎*horee*, granary, magazine.

هزّ ‎or ‎هزّز ‎*hazza*, or *hazzaza*, he made shake, agitated.

اهتزّ ‎or ‎تهزّز ‎*ihtazza*, or *tahazzaza*, it shook, quaked.

هزّة ‎or ‎هزهزة ‎*hazza*, or *hazhaza*, agitation.

هزؤ ‎or ‎هزى ‎*hozoo*, or *hazá*, mockery.

استهزأ ‎*istahzá*, he ridiculed.

هزّر ‎*hazzara*, he joked, chaffed. [مزح]

هزار ‎*hizár*, a joking, "chaff."

هزل ‎*hazl*, satire, lampoon.

هزال ‎ـ ‎هزيل ‎*hozál*, feebleness; *hazeel*, feeble, slender.

هزّم ‎*huzzama*, he pressed, drove, put to flight.

انهزم ‎*inhazama*, he was routed.

هزيمة ‎or ‎انهزام ‎*hazeema*, or *inhizám*, rout, defeat.

هيس ‎*hus*, or *hoos*, hush! silence!

هشّ ‎*hashsha*, he brushed away (flies, &c.). [نشّ]

هشم ‎*hashama*, he wounded, slashed open.

هشم ‎ـ ‎هشام ‎*hashim*, generous; *hishám*, generosity.

هضم ‎*hadama*, he digested; *hadm*, digestion. [cf. هدم]

قوّة ‎هاضمة ‎*qowwa hádima*, digestive power.

هفت ‎ـ ‎تهافت ‎(*haft*), *taháfut*, annoyance, attack.

هفوة ‎*hafwa*, small mistake, slip. [شائبة]

هكذا ‎*hakazá*, thus. [ذا]

هل ‎*hel*, interrogative particle at the beginning of a sentence.

هل (299) همزة

هل تتذكّر *hel tatazakkar*, do you remember?

هلال ـ اهلیل *hilál*, pl. *aháleel*, new moon, crescent.

سنة هلالیّة *sana hiláliya*, lunar (Moslem) year of 354½ days.

اهلال or استهلال *ihlál*, or *istihlál*, beginning of a lunar month; new-born infant's first cry.

استهلّ *istohilla* (passive), the new moon began.

هلّل *hallala*, he praised God by saying the *tahleel*.

تهلیل ـ لا اله الا الله *tahleel*, the phrase, "There is no god but God;" *lá iláha illá Alláh*.

هلّل *hallala* (vulgar), he jeered at, shouted.

هلهولة *halhoola*, rag, thin cloth.

هلب *holb*, hair, bristle.

هالب *hallaba* (colloquial), he hopped on one leg.

هلج ـ اهلیلج (*halj*), *ihleelij*, ellipse.

هلس ـ هلّاس *hals*, nonsense, balderdash; *hallás*, braggart.

هلوسة *halwasa*, hallucination.

هلك *halaka*, it perished.

هلاك *halák*, ruin, destruction, loss.

اهلك *ahlaka*, he destroyed.

مهلك *mohlik*, destructive, dangerous.

تهلكة *tahlika*, danger.

استهلك *istahlaka*, he consumed, lessened a debt by a sinking fund.

استهلاك *istihlák*, consumption of produce; sinking fund, "*amortissement*."

هلوك *halook*, bean-blight; tares.

هلمّ *halomma*, come now! hullo!

هم ـ هنّ ـ هما *hom*, (femin.) *honna*, they, them, their; dual, *homá*, they or them two, their.

هلیون *halyoon*, asparagus.

هم ـ هموم *hamm*, pl. *homoom*, care, anxiety.

اهتمّ *ihtamma*, he was anxious for, careful for.

اهتمام *ihtimám*, anxiety, forethought.

همّة ـ همم *himma*, pl. *himam*, endeavour, intention.

اهمّ *ahamm*, more important.

اهمیّة *ahammiya*, importance.

مهمّ *mohimm*, important, urgent.

مهمّات *mohimmát*, important things, military stores, munitions.

مهامّ *mahámm*, serious, important duties.

هامّة ـ هوامّ *hámma*, pl. *hawámm*, reptile, insect.

همایون *humáyoon* (Persian), Imperial, of the government.

همایونی *humáyooniy* (from Persian), Imperial (as a law).

همز *hamaza*, he spurred, stung, pricked.

همزة *hamza*, the mark ء, placed over و or ى and over or under ا; a short *a* over a vowel when it begins a syllable.

مهموز mahmooz, marked with a hamza; spur.

مهماز mihmáz, spur, goad.

(همل) (اهمل) (hamel), ahmala, he neglected.

اهمال - مهمل ihmál, neglect; mohmil, negligent.

هنّ - هم honna (femin. of hom), they, them, their.

هناء haná, good health, congratulation.

هنّأ hanná, he congratulated.

تهنئة tahniya, congratulation.

هني hani, joyous, jovial, healthy.

هنيئا haneeyán, to your good health!

مهنّأ mohanná, congratulated.

هنا or هاهنا huná, or há huná, here.

هنا هو huná ho, here it is!

هناك or هنالك honák, or honálik, there.

هند - هنود hind, India; honood, Indians.

هندي hindiy, an Indian, Indian.

قيصر الهند Qaisar el-Hind, Empress (or Emperor) of India.

هندباء hindibá, chicory, endive.

هندسة اندازة handasa (from Persian endáza, ell), ell, measuring; geometry, engineering.

مهندس mohandis, engineer.

مهندس معماري mohandis mia'máriy, architect.

مهندس رياضي mohandis riyádiy, engineer, land-surveyor.

هنيهة honaiha, a moment; trifle.

هو - هي hoa, he, it; hia, she, it.

هود or يهود hood, or yahood, Jews.

هوادة hawáda, condescension, indulgence.

مهاود mohávid, moderate (price).

هوّد الليل hawwid el-lail, sinking of night, just before dawn.

هودج howdaj, camel-litter for women. [مخلوفة]

هورة hawra, danger, ruin.

هوّر - تهوّر hawwara, he injured, attacked; tahawwara, he annoyed.

هوس hawas, desire, passion of love; madness. [هوى]

هويس howais, dock for ships, canal-lock. [حوض]

هوشة hosha, confusion, tumult.

هول - هولة hōl, terror; hōla, cholera.

ابو الهول Aboo l-hōl, the sphinx.

هائل háyil, terrific; terror.

هوّل hawwala, he terrified.

مهيل - مهول maheel, terrible; mahool, terror.

هون hōn, rest, peace, seriousness; facility.

هان - يهون hána, it was easy; yahoon, it is easy.

هوّن hawwana, he made easy.

هينة heena, facility, repose.

تهاون taháwana, he took it easy, neglected.

هيّن - هاين hayyin, or hain, easy, light; ahwan, easier, lighter, cheaper.

اهان ahána, he treated with contempt, ill-treated.

اهانة ihána, ill-treatment, insult, contempt.

هوى or هاوى hawia, or háwa, he loved, desired.

هوى - اهواء hawa, pl. ahwá, desire, passion, love. [هوس]

على هوى نفسهِ 'ala hawa nafsihi, at his own (sweet) will.

اهوى ahwa, dearer, more desired.

هواء - اهوية hawá, pl. ahwiya, air, atmosphere, weather; tune.

هوائى hawáiy, atmospheric.

هاوية háwiya, hell, abyss.

هي - هنّ hia, pl. honna, she, it; they. [هو - هم]

هيئة - هيئات haiya, pl. haiyát, form, shape, body; astronomy.

هيئة المجلس haiyat el-majlis, a council or court regarded as a single body.

هيّأ hayyá, he prepared.

تهيئة tahyeea, preparation.

مهيّأ mohayyá, prepared.

هيبة or مهابة haiba, or mahába, fear, awe; modesty.

مهيوب or مهيب mahoob, or maheeb, feared, terrible.

هيت - هات (hait or heet), hát, bring, hand over!

هيجان hayján, commotion, stir, excitement.

هاج - يهيج hája, it was in commotion; yaheej, it is excited.

هيّج hayyaja, he stirred up, excited.

تهييج tahyeej, a stirring up, exciting.

مجنون هيجانى majnoon hayajániy, dangerous madman, raving mad.

هيش heesh, reeds, brushwood.

هيضة haida, cholera.

هيكل - هياكل haikal, pl. hayákil, temple, chancel, large edifice.

هيام hiyám, passion, love.

هيهات haihát (colloquial), Indeed! Is it so?

هيولى hayooli, atom, molecule, matter; atomic. [جوهر]

W, or Ō or Oo.

و Wáw. Value = 6.

و wa (often pronounced oo), and.

وايّا - مع wáyyá, with (a colloquialism for ma').

وايّاى - وايّاك wáyyái, with me; wáyyák, with thee.

والله Wallahi, By God!

و حياتك wa hayátak, By thy life I swear!

و لو wa law, and even if; although.

و لا for لا, و الّا for wa illá, unless, or, or else.

واى wáiy, alas!

وابور wáboor (European), "vapeur," "vapore;" steam-engine, steamer, train.

واح - واحات wáh, pl. wáhát, oasis.

واخرى - آخر wákhri, late (colloquial from aákhir).

وبا - اوبا wabá, pl. awbá, epidemic, pest.

وبّخ wabbakha, he reprimanded.

توبيخ tawbeekh, a reprimand.

وبر - اوبار wabar, pl. awbár, hair of goats or of camels, used for making tents, &c.

اهل الوبر ahl al-wabar, nomads, Bedouin Arabs, i.e. owners of camels and goats, or dwellers in tents made of hair.

وبريّ wabooriy, coarse native cloth.

وبال wabál, unhealthiness, danger.

وتد - اوتاد watad, pl. awtád, tent-peg, stake; slip of plant, shoot.

وتر watr, or witr, an odd number, single, a prayer; chord of arc.

وتر - اوتار watar, pl. awtár, chord, arc, tendon.

وترا watrán, one by one; odd and even.

تواتر tawátur, constant repetition, rumour.

وثب - يثب wathaba, he attacked, flew at; yathib, he attacks.

وثق - يثق wathiqa, or wasuqa, he relied upon, was firm; yathiq, he relies.

ثقة thiqa, or tiqa, confidence, worthy of confidence.

واثق or وثيق wáthiq, or watheeq, firm, constant; Vathek.

وثيقة - وثائق watheeqa, pl. watháyiq, valid title-deed.

وثيقة عقد الزواج watheeqa a'qd el-zawáj, marriage certificate.

وثاق witháq, bond of union; tether-rope.

اِستوثق istawsaqa, he assured himself, relied upon.

وثن - اوثان wasn, pl. awsán, idol. [صنم

وجب - يجب wajaba, it was a duty; yajib, it is a duty.

ما يجب له má yajib luho, his rights, due to him.

ما يجب عليه má yajib 'alaih, his duties, due from him.

وجوب wojoob, necessity.

واجب - واجبات wájib, pl. wájibát, duty.

من الواجب عليك min el-wájib a'laik, it is your duty.

اوجب awjaba, he caused, necessitated.

اِيجاب eejáb, causation, answer in the affirmative; proposal, offer.

اِيجاب و قبول eejáb wa qabool, offer and acceptance.

موجب moojib, causing, a cause.

بموجب bi-moojib, because.

اِستوجب istawjaba, it necessitated, called for, caused.

وجد - يجد wajada, he found; yajid, he finds.

وجد wojida, it was found, it existed.

يوجد yoojad, it exists, is found.

وجود wojood, existence; a finding; presence at.

موجود mowjood, found; present at; existing.

موجودات mowjoodát, pl., things found or extant.

وجدان or وجد‎ *wajd*, or *wijdán*, conscience, emotion, ecstasy.

اوجد‎ *awjada*, he created, invented.

ايجاد‎ *eejád*, creation, a bringing to light.

تواجدوا‎ *tawájadoo* (pl. 3rd person), they found themselves (mutually) present at a meeting.

وجز - يجز‎ *wajaza*, it was concise; *yajiz*, it is concise.

وجيز‎ *wajeez*, small, short, brief, trifling.

اوجز - ايجاز‎ *awjaza*, he abbreviated; *eejáz*, brevity.

موجز‎ *moojiz*, brief, concise.

وجع - يوجع‎ *waji'a*, it ached; *yōja'*, it aches.

وجع - وجاع‎ *waja'*, pl. *wijá'a*, ache, pain. [الم]

وجيع‎ *wajeea'*, painful.

وجاق - اوجاق‎ *wōjáq* (for Turkish *ojáq*), hearth, stove.

وجل‎ *wajal*, fear, emotion, anxiety.

وجنة‎ *wajna*, a plump cheek. [خد]

وجه or وجه - اوجه‎ *wajh*, pl. *wojooh*, or *awjoh*, face, surface, side, reason, manner; unit; paragraph or section; a harbour in Arabia on the Red Sea.

وجه قبلي - بحري‎ *wajh qibliy*, South (face); *wajh bahriy*, North, or Sea face.

على وجه العموم‎ *'ala wajh el-o'moom*, in a general way, in general.

لهذه الاوجه‎ *li-hazihi 'l-awjoh*, for these reasons.

وجوه و اعيان‎ *wojooh wa aa'yán*, grandees and notables.

وجهة‎ *wojha*, direction, destination.

جهة - جهات‎ *jeha*, pl. *jehát*, direction, place; reason.

وجاهة‎ *wajáha*, respectability, honour, good repute.

وجاه‎ *wijáh*, about (in number), in front of.

تجاه‎ *tojáh*, in front of, facing.

وجيه‎ *wajeeh*, seemly, proper, honourable.

اتجاه‎ *ittijáh*, a facing towards, direction.

وجّه‎ *wajjaha*, he faced, imputed, put a question, bestowed favour.

توجيهات‎ *tawjeehát*, promotions, honours.

توجّه‎ *tawajjaha*, he turned towards, went to.

واجه‎ *wájaha*, he came face to face, confronted.

مواجهة or وجاه‎ *wijáh*, or *mowájaha*, confrontation.

التهمة الموجّهة قبله‎ *et-tohma el-mowajjaha qibaloh*, the crime imputed to him.

واحد or حد‎ *wahad*, *wahid*, or *wáhid*, one, unit. [احد]

واحدة or حدة‎ *wahada*, *wahida*, or *wáhida* (femin.), one, unit.

احد - احدى‎ *ahad*, (femin.) *ihda*, one.

وحدى‎ *wahdi*, I alone, by myself.

حدة‎ *hida*, unity, unit.

وحيد‎ *waheed*, unique, incomparable.

وحد

وَحَّدَ *wahhada*, he unified, declared the unity of God.

توحيد *tawheed*, belief in God's unity; unification.

دين موحّد *dain mowahhad*, unified debt of Egypt.

وحّد *wahhid* (imperative), say God is One! the cry or challenge of night watchmen.

اتّحد *ittahada*, he united himself to, agreed.

اتّحاد *ittihád*, unity, unanimity, concord.

متّحد *muttahid*, ally, allied, accomplice.

وحشة *wahsha*, desert solitude, barbarism.

وحش - وحوش *wahsh*, pl. *wohoosh*, wild, savage (beast).

وحشيّ *wahshiy*, wild, savage; as a medical term, exterior surface.

توحّش *tawahhush*, savagery, barbarism.

أوحش *awhasha*, he made (us) sad; did not visit us, left us in barbarism.

أوحشتونا *awhashtooná* (colloquialism), you have made us sad by your absence; Welcome!

وحل *wahl*, clay, mire. [بط]

وحل *wahila*, it ran aground.

(وحم) وحّام *wahhám*, superstitious.

وحي *wahi*, divine inspiration. [الهام]

وخز *wakhaza*, he pierced, pricked, penetrated.

وخيم - وخامة *wakheem*, noxious; *wakhámá*, danger.

توديع

ودّ - يودّ *wadda*, he loved, desired; *yawadd*, he loves. [عشق - حبّ]

ودّ or مودّة *widd*, or *mawadda*, love.

وادّ *wádda*, he loved mutually.

وداد *widád*, mutual love.

ودود *wadood*, lover, friend.

مودود *mawdood*, beloved.

بودّي or بدّي *biwoddi*, or *biddi*, I wish to.

بدّي اكتب *biddi aktib*, I wish to, or will, or am going to write.

علاقات ودّيّة *'iláqát widdiya*, amorous bonds or relations.

ودّب *waddaba*, he fitted up, provided.

توديب *tawdeeb*, outfit, outfit-allowance.

مودّب *mowaddab*, fitted up, put right; (in a bad sense) trumped-up.

وداج *widáj*, jugular vein.

ودع - يدع *wada'a*, he put, deposited; *yada'*, he puts.

دعة *da'a*, tranquillity.

وداع *wadáa'*, Adieu!

وديعة - ودائع *wadeea'a*, pl. *wadáy'a*, money deposit, or thing pledged. [رهن]

ودّع or أودع *wada'a*, or *awda'a*, he deposited, delivered over; escorted, saw off.

توديع or ايداع *tawdeea'*, or *eedáa'*, delivery, deposit.

اســتودع istawda'a, he kept in reserve, entrusted, said farewell, retired from service.

استيداع isteedáa', a bidding farewell; retirement.

مســتودع mustawda', an official "en disponibilité," on the retired list.

مودع moodia', he who makes a deposit; moodu', the thing deposited.

مودع عنده mood'a a'ndoh, deposited with him; depositary.

ودع wada', cowrie, small shell.

ودّى wadda (colloquial), he gave, handed over. [اداء]

ودى wada, he paid the "diya," or price of blood.

دية diya, price of blood.

وادي - اودية wádi, pl. awdiya, valley, ravine, bed of river.

وادي حلفاء Wádi Halfá, Valley of Rushes; Southern frontier town and province of Egypt on the Nile.

الوادي الكبير el-Wádi el-Kabeer, the great river Guadalquivir of Spain.

وادي موسى Wádi Moosa, Valley of Moses, Petra.

وراء - وراني wará, behind, beyond; warániy, hinder-part.

ورّيني - رأى warreeni (colloquial, see ráa), show me!

ورب warb, obliquity, slanting.

ورث - يرث warisa, he inherited; yaris, he inherits.

ارث or وراثة irs, or wirása, heritage, succession.

حقّ الارث haqq el-irs, right of succession.

وارث - ورثة wáris, pl. warasa, heir, legatee.

ميراث - مواريث meerás, pl. mawárees, estate inherited.

آل له بالميراث aála laho bil-meerás, it came to him by inheritance.

ورّث warrasa, he named his heir. [وصّى]

توريث tawrees, appointing an heir.

حقوق توريثيّة hoqooq tawreesiya, rights of succession.

مورّث mowarris, testator, legator.

توارث tawárus, sharing an inheritance.

ورد - ورود ward, pl. worood, rose.

ورديّ wardiy, rosy.

مورّد mowarrad, reddened, rosy red.

ورد الطريقة wird et-tareeqa, watchword of a sect, password of initiation into a sect of Dervishes.

ورد - اوراد wird, pl. awrad, schedule showing receipts of instalments of taxes paid monthly. [مكلفة]

وردة warda (colloquial for Italian guarda), look out!

وريد - ورود wareed, pl. worood, vein, duct.

ورد - يرد warada, he arrived; yarid, he arrives.

ورود worood, arrival.

وارِد wárid, arriver, arrived; income; importation.

وارد و صادر wárid wa sádir, in-come and out-go.

واردات wáridát, income, revenue, imports.

ورّد warrada, he made come, paid in, entered in the accounts, supplied (see wird).

توريد tawreed, entry of payment in the accounts, supply.

تورّد tawarrada, it was entered in the accounts.

اورد awrada, he made come, paid in.

ايراد ـ ايرادات eerád, pl. eerádát, revenue.

ايراد و مصروف eerád wa masroof, income and expenditure.

المصلحة ذات الإيراد el-maslaha zát el-eerád, Department of Receipts of Revenue.

مورِدة mawrada, landing-place, quay; arrival.

ورشة ـ ورش warasha, pl. warash (European), factory, workshop. [معمل]

ورّط warrata, he flattered (another) into committing a crime.

ورطة warta, abyss, precipice.

توريط tawreet, flattery for a criminal purpose.

ورع wara', piety, abstinence, monasticism.

ورقة waraqa, leaf of tree, sheet of paper, layer.

ورق ـ اوراق waraq, pl. awráq, leaves, sheets of paper, paper, documents.

اوراق و سندات awráq wa sanadát, papers and documents.

وارق or وريق wáriq, or wareeq, a tree in leaf, in foliage.

تورّق tawarraqa, it became leafy.

ورك ـ اوراك wirk, pl. awrák (femin.), ischium, hip-bone, haunch.

ورم ـ يرم warima, it tumefied; yarim, it swells.

ورم ـ اورام waram, pl. awrám, tumour, tuberculosis. [سلّ]

مورّم mowarram, swollen.

ورن or ورنة waran, or warna, chameleon. [حرباء]

وزّ or اوزّ wizz, or awizz, goose. [بطّة] duck.

وزّ wazza, he incited, urged.

وزب wazaba, it flowed. [ازب]

ميزاب meezáb, gutter, drain.

وزر ـ يزر wazara, he bore a burden; yazir, he bears.

وزر wizr, burden.

وزارة wizára, responsibility of a Prime Minister, hence Vizierate, rank of Vizier.

وزير ـ وزراء wazeer, pl. wozará, Minister of State, Vizier, a civilian Pasha of the highest rank, equal to a Military Musheer or Marshal; a rank like that of Privy Councillor.

صدر اعظم sadr a'azam, Grand Vizier.

وزر ‎وزر - موزور‎ wizr, sin, crime; mawzoor, guilty, sinner.

‎وزّع‎ wazza'a, he distributed, apportioned.

‎توزيع‎ tawzeea', distribution, apportionment.

‎وزن - يزن‎ wazana, he weighed an object; yazin, he weighs.

‎وزن‎ or ‎زن‎ zina, or wazn, act of weighing.

‎وزن - اوزان‎ wazn, pl. awzán, a weight for weighing; metre of verse, grammatical form of word, paradigm of verb.

‎ميزان - موازين‎ meezán, pl. mawázeen, scales, balance; Libra in the Zodiac.

‎ميزانيّة ماليّة‎ meezániya máliya, Financial Budget.

‎موازنة‎ mowázana, equilibrium, a balancing.

‎وازى‎ or ‎آزى‎ wáza, or áza, it was opposite, parallel.

‎توازى‎ tawáza, it was (mutually) parallel.

‎موازاة‎ mowázát, parellelism, equality.

‎موازي‎ or ‎متوازي‎ mowázi, or motawázi, parallel.

‎وسخ‎ wasikh, dirty; wasakh, dirtiness, dirt.

‎وساخة‎ wasákha, dirtiness, dirt.

‎وسادة‎ wosáda, cushion. [‎خدّة‎]

‎وسط - اوساط‎ wast, or wasat, pl. awsát, middle, centre, waist, mean, medium, average; among, midst.

‎وسطي‎ or ‎وسطاني‎ wasatiy, or wastániy, central, middling.

‎واسطة - وسائط‎ wásita, pl. wasáyit, means, instrument or expedient, an intermediary, go-between.

‎بواسطة البوليس‎ bi-wásita el-bolees, by means of the police.

‎وساطة‎ wasáta, intervention.

‎وسيط‎ waseet, mediator, intermediary; go-between.

‎وسّط‎ wassata, he put in the middle, was the means of.

‎توسّط‎ tawassata, he intervened; became the average.

‎متوسّط‎ mutawassit, medial, average, indirect.

‎اوسط‎ awsat, most central.

‎وسع‎ or ‎وسّع‎ wassa'a, or awsa'a, be widened, made spacious.

‎وسع‎ or ‎وسعة‎ sa'a, or wosa'a, width, amplitude, capacity.

‎وسعة‎ wasa'a, an open space; a common.

‎واسع‎ or ‎وسيع‎ wásia', or waseea', wide, ample.

‎اتّسع‎ ittasa'a, it became wide, ample.

‎اتّساع‎ ittisá'a, width, amplitude, extensiveness.

‎متّسع‎ mottasia', wide, extensive.

‎اوسع‎ awsa', wider, ampler.

‎وسيلة - وسائل‎ waseela, pl. wasáyil, pretext, device, means, affinity.

‎وسم‎ wasama, he stamped, branded.

موسم - مواسم *mōsim*, pl. *mawásim*, season; local fair or fête; hence *monsoon*, rainy season.

وسوس *waswasa*, (the devil) prompted to evil.

توسوس *tawaswasa*, he doubted, felt scruples.

الوسواس *El-Waswás*, the Devil as Prompter of Evil.

وسوسة *waswasa*, scruple, malice.

وساية *wisáya*, back-biting, sneakishness.

وشاح *wisháh*, belt, girdle of honour.

موشّحة *mowashshaha*, lyric, ode, hymn.

وشع *washa'*, willow.

وشم *washm*, tattoo mark. [زينة]

وشم *washshama*, he tattooed.

وشوش *washwasha*, he whispered.

وشى *washa*, he embroidered, coloured cloth.

وصف - يصف *wasafa*, he attributed, described; *yasif*, he describes.

وصف - اوصاف *wasf*, pl. *awsáf*, description; quality, epithet; adjective, attribute.

صفة - صفات *sifa*, pl. *sifát*, qualification, quality.

صفة رسميّة *sifa rasmiya*, official capacity.

اتّصف *ittasafa*, he assumed a quality, personated or presumed, took upon himself.

اتّصاف *ittisáf*, assumption of a quality.

اتّصف بصفة رسميّة *ittasafa bi-sifa rasmiya*, he assumed an official capacity; pretended to be an official.

موصوف *mawsoof*, qualified, described, possessing attributes.

متّصف *muttasif*, qualified, assumed.

وصل - يصل *wasala*, he arrived, joined; *yasil*, he arrives. [ورد]

وصول *wosool*, arrival.

وصل or وصلة *wasl*, or *wasla*, union; conjunction, receipt.

وصّل or اوصل *wassala*, or *awsala*, he sent, made arrive.

توصيل or ايصال *tawseel*, or *ersál*, a sending.

اتّصل - اتّصال *ittasala*, he reached, was in contact; *ittisál*, contact.

توصّل على *tawassala 'ala*, he attained, succeeded in.

واصل *wásala*, it was contiguous.

وصال or مواصلة *wisál*, or *mowásala*, continuity, meeting.

موصل *Mōsul*, Mosul, a town near the ruins of Nineveh.

موصول *mōsool*, united, conjunctive.

متّصل *muttasil*, contiguous.

وصم *wasm*, defect, disease, vice.

اوصى or وصّى *wassa*, or *awsa*, he bequeathed, recommended.

توصية *tawsiya*, recommendation.

شركة التّوصية *shirka et-tawsiya*, "société en commandite."

وصاية *wasáya*, guardianship, *tutelle*. [ولاية]

وصية - وصايا *waseeya*, pl. *wasáyá*, will, testament.

وصيّ - اوصياً *wasiy*, pl. *awsiya*, (1) testator; but (2) more commonly the executor or guardian under the will.

موصي or موصّي *moosi*, or *mowassi*, testator.

موصى به *moosa boh*, legacy, thing bequeathed.

موصى له *moosa laho*, bequeathed to him, *i.e.* the legatee or inheritor by will.

وضوء *wodoo*, ablution before prayer; water of ablution.

وضيّ *wadi*, clean, pure.

توضّأ *tawaddá*, he performed his religious ablutions.

ميضأة *meedát*, tank (in Mosque) for ablutions.

وضّح or اوضح *waddaha*, or *awdaha*, he made clear, explained.

وضوح *wodooh*, obviousness, clearness.

واضح *wádih*, clear, evident.

توضيح or ايضاح *tawdeeh*, or *eedáh*, explanation.

ايضاحات *eedáhát*, explanations, remarks.

اتضح *ittadaha*, it was, or became clear, evident.

متّضح *muttadih*, clear, evident, showing itself.

وضع - يضع *wada'a*, he put, placed; *yada',* he places.

وضع - اوضاع *wada'*, pl. *awdá'a*, a placing, form, manner. [شخص]

اوضاع و قواعد *awdá'a wa qawá'yid*, forms and rules.

ضعة *da'a*, abasement.

ضع *da'i* (imperative), put thou!

وضيعة *wadeea'a*, tax, deposit; baggage.

موضع - مواضع *mawda'*, pl. *mawádia'*, spot, place.

موضوع *mawdooa'*, placed; subject of a discussion; the fact or merits of a case.

موضوعاً و شكلاً *mawdoo'án wa sheklán*, "au fond, et en la forme," on its merits, and technically, (legal terms).

وضيع *wadeea'*, humble.

وضاعة or تواضع *wadáa'a*, or *tawádua'*, humility.

وضع اليد على العقار *wada' el-yad 'ala el-'aqár*, he appropriated the landed estate. [اغتصب]

وطئ - يطأ *watia*, he trod, copulated; *yatá*, he treads.

وطء or وطأ *watá*, act of treading, copulation.

وطيّ *wati*, low, depressed, under.

فيضان وطيّ *fayadán wati*, a low flood (of Nile).

واطأ or تواطأ *wátá*, or *tawáta*, he connived at, deigned, favoured.

مواطَأة or تواطؤ mawátát, or tawátu, connivance, accord.

مَوطِىٌّ mawtee, trodden upon.

موطأ - مواطئ mawtá, pl. mawáti, low land.

طأة or وطأة táa, or watáa, a treading smooth or even.

وطد watada, he consolidated.

وطيد wateed, firm, solid.

وطن - اوطان watan, pl. awtán, native land, *patria*.

وطنيّ wataniy, native, national, *indigène*. [اهليّ]

حقوق وطنيّة hoqooq wataniya, civic rights.

توطّن tawattana, he domiciled himself.

موطّن mowattan, domiciled, naturalised.

وطواط watwát, the flying bat.

مواظبة or وظوب wozoob, or mowázaba, perseverance.

وظيفة - وظائف wazeefa, pl. wazáyif, duty, function.

تأدية وظيفته tá-diya wazeeftoh, the doing of his duty.

وظّف wazzafa, he employed, took into service. [إستخدم]

توظّف tawazzafa, he served, was employed.

موظّف mowazzaf, an official, "*employé*."

وعد - يعد wa'da, he promised; ya'id, he promises.

توعّد or اوعد tawa'a'da, or awa'da, he threatened.

وعدة or عدة i'da, or wa'da, a promising, term of delay.

وعد - وعود wa'd, pl. wo'-ood, promise.

وعيد wa'eed, threats.

ميعاد - مواعيد mee'yád, pl. mawáy'eed, a promised time, fixed time, season or delay.

موعود maw'ood, promised.

وعظ - يعظ wa'za, he preached; ya'iz, he preaches.

عظة or وعظ or عظة 'iza, or w'az, or w'aza, a preaching, sermon.

واعظ wáy'iz, preacher.

وعل wa'l, antelope.

وعاء - اوعية wi'yá, pl. awy'eea, vase, utensil; heart.

وعى - يعى waia, he was on the alert; ya'a, he is alert.

وعى - wa'a, cry, uproar.

اوعى ooú'a (imperative), look out!

واعي wá'iy, guardian, watchful.

وعكة wa'ka, illness, disease.

توغّل - وغل (waghala), tawaghghala, he entered, hastened in.

وفد - يفد wafada, he attended a levée or reception at Court; yafid, he attends, &c.; wafd, attendance or crowd of courtiers.

وافد - وفود wáfid, pl. wofood, courtier at a levée.

وفر (311) وقت

وَفْرَة or وُفُور or وَفْر wafr, or wofoor, or fíra, abundance.

تَوَفَّرَ tawaffara, it was abundant.

وَفَّرَ waffara, he economised, made abundant.

تَوْفِير tawfeer, economy; good management so as to have abundance.

وَافِر - أَوْفَر wáfir, abundant; awfar, more abundant.

وَفْق wafq, suitableness, success.

وَفَّقَ waffaqa, he made suitable; (God) made prosper.

تَوْفِيق tawfeeq, success, prosperity (from God), Tawfeeq.

تَوَفَّقَ tawaffaqa, he prospered, was successful.

تَوَافَقَ or وَافَقَ wáfaqa, or tawáfaqa, he agreed, contracted with.

مُوَافَقَة or وِفَاق wifáq, or mowáfaqa, unison, concord.

مُوَافِق mowáfiq, ally, consenting.

مُوَفَّق mowaffaq, successful, blessed by God.

اِتَّفَقَ ittafaqa, he agreed; it happened.

اِتِّفَاق ittifáq, union, concord, coincidence.

اِتِّفَاقًا ittifáqán, by agreement, by accident.

اِتِّفَاقِيّ ittifáqiy, accidental.

وَفَى - يَفِي wafa, he accomplished; yafi, he accomplishes.

لَمْ يَفِ lam yaf, he did not accomplish.

أَوْفَى or وَفَّى waffa, or awfa, he fulfilled, paid.

لَمْ يُوَفِّ lam yowwaf, he did not fulfil.

تَوْفِيَة or إِيفَاء or وَفَاء wafá, or eefá, or tawfiya, fulfilment, execution, payment, sincerity.

بَيْعُ الْوَفَاء beea' el-wafá, "vente à réméré;" "pacte de rachat;" a sale with option of repurchase within five years.

وَفَيَات - وَفَاة wafát, pl. wafayát, death.

أَوْفِيَاء - وَفِيّ wafiy, pl. awfiyá, complete, faithful.

اِسْتَوْفَى istawfa, he completed, fulfilled.

اِسْتِيفَاء isteefá, completion, fulfilment.

اِسْتِيفَائِيّ isteefáiy, complementary, supplementary.

مُسْتَوْفِي mustawfi, complementary, sufficient.

تُوُفِّيَ towuffia (also tawaffa), he died.

مُتَوَفَّى mutuwuffi, dead, deceased.

وَافِي wáfi, fulfilling, abundant.

وَقْب waqb, cavity, vessel, utensil.

أَوْقَات - وَقْت waqt, pl. awqát, time. [زَمَن

دِلْوَقْتِي or هٰذَا الْوَقْت or دِلْوَقْت del-waqt, or del-waqti, colloquial unwritten corruption of hazá l-waqt, this time, now.

وَقْتَئِذٍ *waqti-izin*, at that time, the time when.

وَقْتِيّ *waqtiy*, temporal, transitory.

مُوَقَّت *mowaqqat*, temporary, provisory.

مُوَقَّتًا *mowaqqatán*, provisionally, temporarily, for a term of years, not for life.

مِيقَات - مَوَاقِيت or مُوَقِّت *meeqát*, or *mūqit*, pl. *mawáqeet*, a fixed time; time-table for trains or the post.

وَقِح *waqih*, impudent.

قِحَة or وَقَاحَة *waqáha*, or *qiha*, impudence.

وَقَد - اِسْتَوْقَد or وَقَد *waqada*, or *istawqada*, it was on fire. [حرق]

وَقْدَة or وُقُود *woqood*, or *qida*, a being on fire; combustion.

وَقَد *waqad*, fire, combustion.

وَقِيد *waqeed*, fuel.

أَوْقَد *awqada*, he lighted a fire or lamp.

مُسْتَوْقَد *mustawqad*, furnace of Turkish bath.

وَقَار *waqár*, seriousness of demeanour, gravity.

وَقُور *waqoor*, dignified, serious, grave.

تَوَقَّر *tawaqqara*, he was serious, dignified, patient.

وَقَذ or وَقَز *waqaza*, he thrust at, poked. [وخز]

وَقَع - يَقَع *waqa'a*, he fell, it happened; *yaqa'*, he falls.

وُقُوع *woqoo'a*, fall, event, occurrence.

وَاقِع *wáqia'*, falling, happening.

وَاقِعَة *wáqia'a*, event, accident.

وَقِيعَة - وَقَائِع *waqee'ya*, pl. *waqáyá*, event, news.

وَقَّع *waqqa'a*, he made fall; imposed (a tax); registered, fixed his seal or signature.

تَوْقِيع *tawqeea'*, imposition or levying of a tax; signature, place of signature (L. S.).

تَوَقَّع *tawaqqa'a*, it happened, came to pass.

وَاقَع *wáqa'a*, he fell out with, fought.

وِقَاع or مُوَاقَعَة *wiqá'a*, or *mowáqa'a*, battle, conflict.

مَوْقِع - مَوَاقِع *mawqia'*, pl. *mawáqia'*, place, spot.

مُتَوَقِّع *mutawaqqia'*, happened, taken place.

وَقَفَ - يَقِف *waqafa*, he halted, stood up; *yaqif*, he stands.

اِقِف *oqof* (imperative), stand up!

وُقُوف *woqoof*, standing posture; a halt; knowledge, experience.

أَرْبَاب الوُقُوف *arbáb el-woqoof*, experts, men who know. [خبرة]

وَاقِف *wáqif*, standing, in suspense.

وَقْف or أَوْقَاف *waqf*, pause, halt, mortmain; in pl. *awqáf*, or *woqoof*, pious donations, estates in mortmain.

نَظَارَة الأَوْقَاف *nazáret el-awqáf*, Ministry of Mortmain or Religious Donations.

وقّاف *waqqáf*, he who constantly stands; overseer.

اوقف or وقّف *waqqafa*, or *awqafa*, he detained, arrested, made stand, stopped a performance, &c., gave as a *waqf*.

ايقاف or توقيف *tawqeef*, or *eeqáf*, detention, arrest; a giving to mortmain, or *waqf*; suspension, abeyance, deferment.

توقّف *tawaqqafa*, he stood, hesitated; it depended upon, consisted in.

مواقف - موقف *móqif*, pl. *mawáqif*, place of halt.

موقوف *mawqoof*, halted; property in mortmain.

يقي - وقى *waqa*, he guarded; *yaqi*, he guards.

قِ *qi* (imperative), guard thou!

وقاية *wiqáya*, guard, restraint.

اتّقى *ittaqa*, he feared God, was pious.

متّقي *muttaqi*, pious.

انقياء - تقيّ *taqiy*, pl. *atqiyá*, pious.

تقوى or تقى *toqa*, or *taqwa*, piety.

توقّى *tawaqqa*, he was on his guard.

اقّة or اوقّة or وقّة *oqqa*, a weight of 2¾ lbs.; 1.25 kilog.; 400 dirhems.

اوقيّة or اوقيّة or وقيّة *oqqiya*, ounce; 1½ oz. avdp.; 37½ grammes; 12 dirhems.

وكا - اتّكا على (*waki*), *ittaká a'la*, he leaned upon, reclined.

متّكى *muttaki*, reclining; on one's elbow.

موكب - وكب (*wakaba*), *mawkib*, procession, cortège.

اكّد or وكّد *wakkada*, or *akkada*, he strengthened, assured.

تأكيد or توكيد *tawkeed*, or *tá-keed*, a strengthening, assuring.

اكيد or وكيد *akeed*, or *wakeed*, certain, positive, firm.

مؤكّد *mo-akkad*, confirmed, certain.

وكس *waks*, loss, damage; eclipse.

وكلاء - وكيل *wakeel*, pl. *wokalá*, agent, attorney; station-master.

وكيل عنه *wakeel a'nho*, agent for him; his attorney.

باش وكيل *básh Vakeel*, head agent; title of the Turkish prime minister when the higher dignity of Grand Vizier is in abeyance.

وكالة *wakála*, agency, procuration; hence a block of buildings, "*okelle*," in charge of an agent.

وكّل *wakkala*, he appointed an agent, gave a power of attorney.

توكيل *tawkeel*, a giving a procuration, or appointment of attorney; act of procuration, power of attorney; direction; agent's office; station-master's office.

موكّل *mowakkil*, the principal who appoints the agent.

موكّل عنه *mowakkal u'nho*, the agent who is appointed.

توكّل على *tawakkala a'la*, he relied upon, entrusted his affairs to an agent.

توكّلتُ على الله *tawakkalto a'la 'llâh*, God is my trust!

وكّل ـ اكّل *wakkala* (vulgarism for *akkala*), he fed another, made eat.

ولج ـ يلج *walaja*, he penetrated, entered; *yalij*, he enters.

ولوج *wolooj*, penetration, entry, attack.

اولج *awlaja*, he thrust in, made penetrate.

ايلاج *eelâj*, a thrusting in; penetration, forcible entry.

ولد ـ يلد *walada*, he begot; *yalid*, he begets.

ولدت ـ تلد *waladet*, she bore; *talid*, she bears.

الله لم يلد و لم يولد *Allah lam yalid wa lam yoolad*, Allah did not beget and was not begotten.

اولدها *awladahâ*, he made her a mother.

توّلد *tawallada*, he was born; it sprang from.

استولد *istawlada*, he acknowledged his paternity.

ولادة or لدة *lida*, more commonly *wilâda*, birth, parturition. [نفاس

والدان ـ والدة ـ والد *wâlid* (femin.), *wâlida*, (dual) *wâlidân*, father, mother; both parents.

اولاد ـ ولد *walad*, pl. *awlâd*, child, son, boy.

ام الولد *umm el-walad*, the child's mother, a female slave who bears a child to her master.

ولدان ـ وليد *waleed*, pl. *wildân*, born, child.

موالد ـ مولد *mawlid*, pl. *mawâlid*, birthday.

مواليد ـ مولود *mawlood*, pl. *mawâleed*, born; births.

مولود له *mawlood laho*, born to him; father.

موّلد *mowallad*, born-slave.

مواليد ـ ميلاد *meelâd*, pl. *mawâleed*, birthday.

عيد الميلاد *'eed el-meelâd*, Christmas.

في السنة الميلاديّة *fis-sana l-meelâdiya*, Anno Domini.

مستولدة *mustawlida*, mother, especially slave-mother.

ولس *wils*, fraud, humbug.

ولع *wala'*, burning passion; piece of live coal.

ولوع *wolooa'*, a being on fire; love, passion.

اولع or ولّع *walla'a*, or *awla'a*, he set on fire, lighted.

مولع *moola'*, passionate; consumed with love; amateur, aspirant.

ولايم ـ وليمة *waleema*, pl. *walâyim*, banquet, feast.

وليان ـ وله *walah*, sadness; *walhân*, wild with grief.

ولول *walwala*, he screamed, lamented, wailed.

ولولة *walwala*, wail, lament.

ولى - يلى *walia*, he ruled over; was near, friendly; *yali*, he rules, &c.

ولا *walá*, nearness; *wilá*, sequence, friendship.

ولاية *wiláya*, government; a large Turkish province ruled by a *Wáli* or *Váli*; guardianship.

والى - ولاة *wáli*, pl. *wolát*, ruler, a *Váli* or Turkish governor-general of a province.

ولى - اولياء *waliy*, pl. *awliyá*, friend, master, saint, possessor.

ولية *waliya*, a polite term used in addressing a Moslem woman.

يا ولية *Yá waliya* (*Yowliya*), Oh woman!

ولى العهد *waliy el-a'hd*, heir apparent.

ولى النعم *waliy en-ni'am*, benefactor, King or Khedive as the source of favours.

اولياء الدم *awliyá ed-dam*, blood relations; relations claiming vengeance for blood. [ولا]

اولياء انشان *awliyá esh-shán*, the interested parties in a case.

ولّى *wallu*, he appointed as ruler.

تولية *tawliya*, appointment as ruler; accession to the throne.

ولّى الفرار *walla el-firár*, he took to flight.

اولى *awla*, he approached, favoured.

ايلاء *eelá*, favour. [cf. آلى]

والى *wála*, he was friendly, assisted.

موالاة *mowálát*, friendship.

توالى *tawála*, it followed consecutively.

متوالى *mutawáli*, consecutive. [

متوالى - متاولة *mutawáli*, pl. *matáwila*, "Metuali," a fanatic sect in Syria.

تولّى *tawalla*, he ruled over.

متولّى *mutawalli*, ruler.

استولى على *istawla 'ala*, he seized the power over, seized, embezzled, influenced.

استيلاء *isteelá*, aggression, seizure

مولى - موالى *mōla*, pl. *mawáli*, master, king; friend; Moslem priest [منلا *manlá*, doctor of law

مولوى - مولوية *mōlawiy*, femin *mōlawiya*, a Dervish sect, kingly

مولوية *mōlawiya*, sovereignty.

مولّى الفرار *mowalli el-firár*, fugitive

وما - ايما - مومأ اليه (*wamá, eemá, moomá ileih*, aforesaid.

ومس *wamasa*, he rubbed, handled

مومسة *moomisa*, prostitute.

ومق *wamiqa*, he loved, doated on

وناء *waná*, fatigue.

وانى *wáni*; fatigued, feeble.

توانى *tawáni*, delay, slowness.

مينا or موانى *meená*, p *mawáni*, or *meyan* (femin. harbour of rest.

وهب - يهب *wahaba*, he gave *yahab*, he gives.

وهَّاب, *wahháb*, God the constant Giver.

وهَّابيّ, *Wahhábiy*, a fanatical sect, followers of Abdul-Wahháb in Arabia, 1691—1818, crushed out by Mahomed Ali of Egypt in 1818.

هبوا *haboo* (imperative), give ye, grant, suppose that!

هبة *hiba*, gift.

تأهَّب *taahhaba*, he prepared.

موهب *mōhib*, donation, gift.

موهوب له *mawhoob laho*, given to him, donee.

وهران *Wahrán*, Oran in Algeria.

وهلة *wahla*, fear, anxiety.

أوَّل وهلة *awwal wahla*, at the first sight, or thought.

وهم - يوهم *wahama*, he imagined, had a notion, suspected; *ya-him*, he suspects.

أوهم *awhama*, he deceived, alarmed.

إيهام *eehám*, ambiguity, deception.

توهَّم *tawahhama*, he imagined, suspected.

وهم - أوهام *wahm*, pl. *awhám*, idea, notion, instinct; prejudice, alarm.

وهميّ *wahmiy*, imaginary, false.

تهمة - تهمات *tuhma*, pl. *tuhmát*, accusation, charge against a prisoner.

أتهم or اتَّهم *at-hama*, or *ittahama*, he accused, prosecuted a charge in a criminal court.

اتّهام *ittihám*, accusation, indictment.

ورقة الاتّهام *waraqat el-ittihám*, bill of indictment, charge-sheet against a prisoner.

متَّهم or متهم *muttaham*, or *mut-ham*, the accused man.

وهن *wahhana*, he weakened, tampered with.

وهنة *wahna*, feebleness.

وهي *wahi*, feebleness, unimportance.

واهي *wáhi*, trifling, unimportant.

وئام *wiám*, cordiality, concord.

ويبة *waiba*, a measure of capacity, about 7 gallons; 33 litres; ⅙th of *ardab*.

ويب or ويل *waib*, or *wail*, Alas! Fie! Shame!

ويكة *waika*, bamia cooked in a peculiar manner.

ويركو *wirkoo* (Turkish *verghi*), professional tax.

ويرك *wirk* (corrupted from *wirkoo*), fee, perquisite, commission paid for work done.

ويح or ويل *wail*, or *waih*, Alas! for shame! [ويب

Y, or ee.

ي *Ye*. Value = 10.

ي - ي *i* (final suffix), my; *kitábi*, my Look.

ي - اكتبي *i* (feminine suffix of imperative); *iktibi*, Write! (oh woman!).

ةّ - ّي - *iy* (femin.), *iya*, adjectival suffix.

مصري - مصر، *masr*, Egypt; *masriy*, Egyptian.

يلا - يا، *yá*, oh! *yálá*, get along!

ياترى *yátara* (colloquial) Query? Is it that?

يادوب *yá dōb*, almost.

ياهو *yá hoa*, or *yá hoo*, Oh He! *i.e.* Oh God!

يأس *yás*, despair.

يئس - ييئس *ya-isa*, he despaired; *yayás*, he despairs.

مأيوس - مأيس *máyis*, despairing; *máyoos*, despaired of.

ياسمين *yásmeen*, jasmine.

ياشا *yáshá* (Turkish), live thou! *vive!*

ياشا چوق افندیمز *Efendimiz choq yáshá!* (Turkish), Oh, our lord (Sultan, or Khedive) live long! God save the King!

ياشمق *yáshmaq* (Turkish), lady's gauze veil covering the lower half of the face.

يفطة or يافتة *yáfta* (Persian), placard, sign-board, label.

يقا or ياقة *yáqa* (Turkish), collar of coat or shirt.

ياقوت *yáqoot*, ruby, sapphire, topaz, jacinth.

يانسون *yánsoon*, aniseed.

ياور *yáwer* (Persian), assistant.

ياور الحرب *yáwer el-harb*, aide-de-camp.

يايات - يايّ *yáy*, pl. *yáyát* (Turkish) metal spring, springs of a carriage

يبس - ييبس *yabisa*, it became dry *yaibas*, it is drying [جفّ]

يابس or يبس *yabis*, dry.

يبوسة *yoboosa*, dryness.

تيبّس *tayabbasa*, it became dry stiff.

يتأتى - اتى *yatá-atta*, it is possible it results (see *ata*).

يتيم - ايتام or يتامى *yateem*, pl *aitám*, or *yatúma*, orphan.

ميتمة - يتم *maitama*, orphans *yotm*, orphanhood.

موتم *mootim*, widow with fatherless children.

يحيى or يحياء *Yahiá*, John the Baptist. [حيى]

يخت *yakht* (English), yacht.

يخني *yakhni* (Turkish), stew, ragout

يد - ايدي - ايادي *yed* (vulgarly *yeed* or *eed*), pl. *aidi*, or *ayád* (femin.), hand, handle, power.

اليدين or اليدان *el-yedán*, or *el-yedain*, the two hands.

بين يديه *bain yedaihi*, between his two hands, in his presence *i.e.* in the presence of a superior

اقرّ بين يدى المدير *aqarra bain yedai l-modeer*, he confessed in the presence of the Mudir.

على يد شهود *a'la yed shohood*, in the presence of witnesses.

يدهُ طويلة *yedoh taweela*, his hand is long; he is a thief.

يد متمرّنة *yed mutamarrina*, a practised hand.

يربوع *yarboa'*, jerboa, desert rat. [يرع

يراعة *yaráa'a*, glow-worm.

يرقان - مأروق *yaraqán*, jaundice; *márooq*, jaundiced.

ياسين *yá-seen*, the two letters Y and S, the title of chap. xxxvi. of the Koran, used as a man's name, like Taha. [يط

يسر - يبسر *yasara*, it was pleasant, easy; *yaisir*, it is easy.

يسر or يسرى or يسارة *yosr*, or *yasára*, facility, ease, comfort, wealth; black coral.

يسير *yaseer*, easy, slight, trifling.

يسرى or يسار or ايسر *aisar*, or *yasár*, or *yosra*, left-hand side.

برهة يسيرة *borha yaseera*, a short moment, brief interval.

ايسر *aisar*, easier.

ايسر *aisara*, he was solvent, rich.

ميسرة or يسار *yasár*, or *maisara*, solvency, wealth.

موسر *moosir*, solvent, wealthy.

موسر و معسر *moosir wa moa'sir*, solvent and insolvent.

تيسّر *tayassara*, it became easy, was possible; he was successful.

يسوعي *yasooa'iy*, Jesuit. [cf. عيسى

يساق *yasáq* (Turkish), forbidden.

يساقجي *yasáqji* (Turkish), consular constable.

يشب or يشب *yashb*, or *yasb*, jasper.

يشم *yashm*, agate, jade. [عقيب

يعقوب - عقب *ya'qoob*, he follows as a younger twin, Jacob (see *a'qaba*).

يعني - عنى *ya'ni*, that is to say (see *a'na*).

يافة *Yáfa*, Jaffa or Joppa.

يقوت *yaqoot*, ruby, sapphire, topaz, jacinth.

يقة or يقا or ياقة *yaqa* (Turkish), collar of coat or shirt.

استيقظ or تيقظ or يقظ *yaqiza*, or *tayaqqaza*, or more commonly *istaiqaza*, he was awake, became awake or woke up.

ايقظ *aiqaza*, he awoke (another person).

يقظة *yaqaza*, vigil, watchfulness.

يقظان *yaqzán*, awake, on the alert.

مستيقظ *mustaiqaz*, awake.

تيقن or يقن *yaqina*, or *tayaqqana*, he knew for certain.

يقيناً - يقين *yaqeen*, certainty; *yaqeenán*, for certain.

موقن *mooqin*, being certain of, easy in mind.

يكن *yegen* (Turkish), nephew.

ينكجري or يكيشري *yeni-jeri* (Turkish, *yeni-cheri*), new troops, janissary; consular constable.

يلك *yelek* (Turkish), waistcoat, vest.

يم - يموم *yamm*, pl. *yomoom*, sea.

تيمم *tayammama*, he rubbed his hands (for ablution) with sand or dust for want of water. [يمّ

تيمّم *tayammum*, " ablution " with sand.

يمام *yamám*, wild pigeon. [حمام]

يمن - يَيْمن *yamana*, he or it was lucky, it came from the right hand side ; *yaiman*, it is lucky.

يمن *yomn*, luck, felicity.

يمين *yameen* (femin.), right hand side ; oath.

يمين - ايمان *yameen*, pl. *aimán*, (femin.), oath, a lifting of the right hand to swear.

حلف يميناً *halafa yameenán*, he took the oath.

يمين حاسمة *yameen hásima*, decisive oath, *serment décisoire*.

يمنى or ايمن *yomna*, or *aiman*, right-hand side.

اليمن *El-Yemen*, Arabia Felix.

ميمنة *maimana*, felicity, prosperity.

ميمون *maimoon*, lucky ; monkey.

ينبوع - نبع *Yanboa'*, fountain, Yembo, an Arabian port on the Red Sea (see *naba'a*).

ينبغي - بغى *yanbaghi*, it is necessary (see *baghá*).

يهودي - يهود *yahoodiy*, a Jew, Jewish ; *yahood*, the Jews. [دون]

يوز - يوزباشي *yooz* (Turkish), a hundred ; *yooz-báshi*, captain in the army.

يوسف *Yoosuf*, Joseph.

يوسف افندي *yoosuf efendi*, small mandarin orange.

يوليّة or يوليو *yoolio*, or *yoolia* (European), July.

يوم - ايّام *yōm*, pl. *ayyám*, day.

نهار *nahár*, daylight, day-time.

اليوم *el-yōm*, to-day. [النهاردي]

يوماً فيوماً *yōmán fa-yōmán*, day by day.

يومي *yomiy*, daily.

يوميّة *yōmiya*, day's pay ; day book, journal.

يوم الاحد *yōm el-ahad* (*el-had*), Sunday.

يوم الاثنين *yōm el-etnain*, Monday.

يوم الثلاثاء *yōm et-talátá*, Tuesday.

يوم الاربعاء *yōm el-arba'á*, Wednesday.

يوم الخميس *yōm el-khamees*, Thursday.

يوم الجمعة *yōm el-joma'a*, Friday.

يوم السبت *yōm es-sabt*, Saturday.

يوم تاريخه *yōm táreekhoh*, this day's date, the same day mentioned.

يوم الدين *yōm ed-deen*, the day of Judgment.

ايّام *ayyám*, days, Chronicles of the Bible.

يونان *Yonán*, (Greek, Ionia), Greece, the Greeks.

يوناني *yonániy*, a Greek, Grecian.

يونس *Yoonis*, Jonas.

يونية or يونيو *yoonio*, or *yoonia*, (European) June.

ADDENDA.

Page 40, col. 1, جبه خانة jebá-khána (Persian), ammunition.
,, 54, ,, 2, حدوثة hadoota, anecdote, story.
,, 55, ,, 1, حداية hidáya, hawk, kite.
,, 60, ,, 2, استحصل istahsala, he acquired, obtained.
,, 61, ,, 1, حضور ‒ حضوريّاً hodoor, presence; hodooriyán (legal term), "*contradictoirement*," a case heard in the presence of both parties. [cf. غيابياً
,, 63, ,, 1, احقّيّة ahaqqiya (legal term), a better right, i. e., success in a civil suit.
,, 64, ,, 1, حكمدار hokmdár (Persian), governor-general, chief of police.
,, 69, ,, 1, حور hōr, coarse leather.
,, 73, ,, 2, خدم khadam (pl. of خادم kháḋim), servants.
,, 74, ,, 1, خراج khuráj, abscess.
,, 79, ,, 2, خلع khala'a, he wrenched off.
,, 80, ,, 1, تخلّف عن takhallafa 'an, he absented himself.
,, 92, ,, 2, ديده بان deeda-bán (Persian), sentry.
,, 104, ,, 2, ارتفاق irtifáq, servitude. [see حقّ
,, 108, ,, 2, ريّاح rayyáh, canal, relief canal [see ريّ
,, 109, ,, 2, روم ايلي بكلربكي Room-eeli Beylerbeyi (Turkish), a civilian pasha of the second rank, equal to a military *farreq*. [فريق
,, 109, ,, 2, رومس roomis, trellis, raft.

ADDENDA.

Page 110, col. 1, ريع *ree'a*, growth, increase; (legal term) income or revenue from land.

,, 123, ,, 1, بدل سفريّة *badal safariya*, travelling expenses.

,, 147, ,, 1, شهيّة *shahiya*, appetite for food.

,, 150, ,, 1, صبر *sabara*, he was patient.

,, 150, ,, 1, صابورة *sáboora* (Italian), ballast of a ship.

,, 156, ,, 1, صانع *sáni'a*, artisan.

,, 158, ,, 2, بضبط *biz-zabt*, precisely, with accuracy.

,, 184, ,, 2, عمّد ـ تعميد *'ammada*, he baptised; *ta'meed*, baptism.

,, 213, ,, 2, قتل *qatl*, a killing, putting to death.

,, 244, ,, 1, لازم *lázim* (intransitive verb).

,, 279, ,, 1, نبّ ـ انبوب (*nabba*) - *onbook*, reed, tube.

,, 281, ,, 2, نحنُ *nahno*, (vulgarly *ahna*) we.

ERRATA.

Page.	Column.	Arabic word.	
1	1	11	ابّد *abbada*, For *be* read *he* perpetuated.
6	1	11	اسر *asara*, for *be* read *he* bound captive.
10	1	7	For امير البحر read امير البحر *ameer el-bahr*, admiral.
15	2	3	For بنك باشي read بيك باشي *bing-báshi*, major.
27	2	6, 7	For بنك read بيك *bing*, or *bin* (Turkish), thousand, and بيكباشي *bing-báshi*, major.
37	1	10	For اثداء *asdá* read اثدي *asdi*, pl. breasts.
38	2	12	For ثانو مشي *tánoo masha*, &c. read ثنّ ماشي *tunno máshi*, he went on, continued his course.
47	2	11	For جنوب *jonoob*, read *janoob*, south.
82	1	11	For *or* read *pl. khiyyaf*, afraid.
104	2	12	For ارفق read رافق *ráfaqa*, he accompanied.
108	2	10	For *was* read *has* an evil spirit.
113	2	7	For زهو read زهر *zahr*, flower.
117	1	7	For *eulogies and titles of God*, read *couplets of praise and prayer*, &c.
118	1	19	For تجيع or سجع read تسجيع or سجع *saja'*, or *tasjeea*, rhythm, &c.
150	1	7	For هبوح read صبوح *sabooh*, morning drink.
152	1	16	For مرع read صرع *sar'a*, epilepsy.
153	1	1	For *roof* read *masroof*, &c., spent, &c.
168	1	9	For طوسة read طوشة *tōsha*, fuss, trifle.
178	1	7	For عشاش *ishásh* read *ishésh*, pl. of *'eshsha*.
192	2	9	After استغرق insert *istaghraqa*, he was overwhelmed, &c.
220	2	7	For *masqad* read *maqsad*.
235	2	9	For ثانتة read ثابتة *sábita*.

www.ingramcontent.com/pod-product-compliance
Lightning Source LLC
Chambersburg PA
CBHW022335230426
43664CB00040B/934